The Making of the 20th Century

This series of specially commissioned titles focuses attention on significant and often controversial events and themes of world history in the present century. Each book provides sufficient narrative and explanation for the newcomer to the subject while offering, for more advanced study, detailed source-references and bibliographies, together with interpretation and reassessment in the light of recent scholarship.

In the choice of subjects there is a balance between breadth in some spheres and detail in others; between the essentially political and matters economic or social. The series cannot be a comprehensive account of everything that has happened in the twentieth century, but it provides a guide to recent research and explains something of the times of extraordinary change and complexity in which we live. It is directed in the main to students of contemporary history and international relations, but includes titles which are of direct relevance to courses in economics, sociology, politics and geography.

The Making of the 20th Century

Series Editor: GEOFFREY WARNER

Already published

France and the Origins of the First World War

John F. V. Keiger

First published 1983 by
THE MACMILLAN PRESS LTD
London and Basingstoke
Companies and representatives
throughout the world

ISBN 0 333 28551 4 (hc)
ISBN 0 333 28552 2 (pbk)

Typeset by
WESSEX TYPESETTERS LTD
Frome, Somerset

Printed in Hong Kong

Contents

TO MY PARENTS

Acknowledgements

I should like to express my gratitude to those friends and colleagues who by their help and encouragement have made this study possible. First and foremost I owe an especial debt of gratitude to Dr Christopher Andrew of Corpus Christi College, Cambridge, for having first focused my attention on the French diplomatic history of this period and for then having guided and encouraged me along the academic road. I am very grateful to the late Jacques Millerand for his warm hospitality during my year-long stay in Paris and for having given me the benefit of his personal experience and knowledge of the personalities and the period I have chosen to study, and for having brought me a little closer to an understanding of their aims and objectives. Professor Jean-Claude Allain, now of the Université du Maine, was also very helpful during that year in Paris, while M. Louis Cambon very kindly allowed me to consult the family private papers in his possession.

Dr Robert Tombs of St John's College, Cambridge, deserves warm thanks for his enlightening comments and corrections to the manuscript and generally for his friendship and kindness which have stimulated my work and added to its being an enjoyable task. I am conscious too of the debt I owe my old friends from the Institut d'Etudes Politiques d'Aix-en-Provence, who first aroused my enthusiasm for France and her institutions.

Salford University and the Sir Ernest Cassel Educational Trust have provided financial support during the writing of this book. Dr Ralph White and Dr Chris Lyons and Mr Chris Ryder either suggested valuable alterations to the manuscript or helped with proof-reading, while Professor Geoffrey Warner, the editor of this series, suggested many useful improvements. Miss Jill Littlewood deserves special mention for painstakingly and patiently typing the manuscript, for suggesting many stylistic improvements and generally for cheerful and witty support. The staff of the many archives and libraries in which I have worked, in particular at the Ministère des Affaires Etrangères, the Bibliothèque de l'Institut de France and in the Archives Nationales in Paris, have been generous with their time and assistance and I gratefully acknowledge their help. My greatest debt of thanks, finally, is to my parents, who, I hope, understand what I owe them.

To everyone mentioned, and many others including Peter and little Ben, who at five already seems to be asking the questions that historians of my age should have been asking long ago, I express my sincerest thanks while accepting all responsibility for the errors and imperfections that remain.

Manchester   J.F.V.K.

Introduction

On 3 August 1914 France entered a world war from which she emerged victorious and yet the greatest casualty of all the nations involved. In just over four years, of the eight million Frenchmen who fought, nearly one-and-a-half million had been killed, and the country had sacrificed half of its national wealth. To a large extent the effects of that war were responsible for the crushing defeat and ignominious collaboration which France experienced some twenty years later in a second world war.

What then was France's share in the origins of the conflict? Not surprisingly much controversy has centred on this question, almost as much as on that surrounding Germany's role. Indeed the question of either country's responsibility is inextricably linked: the degree to which France could attribute blame to Germany conditioned the amount of blame France would herself have to shoulder, and vice versa. This is true of the states involved in the origins of any war; it was particularly true of the First World War. The Versailles Peace Treaty of 1919 took an unprecedented step: it included an article, number 231, which saddled Germany with the sole guilt for the outbreak of the First World War. And this article was made the justification for the massive war reparations Germany would have to pay, principally to France as the worst hit of all the nations. Consequently, if Germany could show that she was not solely responsible for the war, she could challenge the validity of article 231 and hence the payment of the reparations.[1]

France was an excellent scapegoat on to whom the blame could be shifted. Because in a war with Germany in 1870 she had lost the two provinces of Alsace–Lorraine, it was suggested that for virtually the next half-century she had prepared for a war of *revanche* against Germany to regain the lost territories. Because from 1912 France's new leader, Raymond Poincaré, who was a Lorrainer into the bargain, was determined to apply resolute policies and to strengthen the links with France's allies, particularly with Russia, it was suggested that he plotted a war of *revanche* against Germany. Germany began a campaign to promote such views, supported by reputable historians searching the available evidence to endorse them. A massive polemic developed during the 1920s. The criticism levelled against France struck out at the Franco-Russian Alliance for having caused the war. Poincaré was charged with having encouraged Russia to begin the conflict. The idea of 'Poincaré-la-guerre' gained currency. It was picked up and used for all ends. In France it was put to political use when Poincaré's political opponents wished to stop him returning to power in 1926. In the end when the argument subsided,

1

because facts had been manipulated and evidence distorted, inevitably confusion had resulted and some of the mud had stuck. The possibility of a fair re-trial was ruled out in the short term.

The debate on responsibility for the origins of the First World War is still very much alive today.[2] Recent research, using new lines of inquiry and new sources, has clarified the roles of Britain and Germany in the origins of the First World War. Such a study has not been undertaken for France. Recently, extensive studies have been made of specific issues affecting French foreign policy during the pre-war period, but useful as they are they do not tackle the fundamental issue of French involvement in the outbreak of the war. The wealth and value of new material made available to historians in recent years (in the form of private papers belonging to diplomats and politicians of the time) call for a reassessment of France's role. The relevance of this material is demonstrated by the state of French diplomacy in the pre-war years, which was such that diplomats carried on a secret parallel correspondence with Ministers in order to broach subjects which they would not have dared discuss in official communications. Indeed official communications were often subordinated to private correspondence; the latter was the key to the former. These new sources provide, therefore, the essential information needed to give a more complete picture of French diplomacy before the First World War by throwing light on the organisational and personal ingredients of policy-making. It is a platitude worth stating that decisions are made by men, and are affected by their education, upbringing, beliefs and even health as well as by purely political factors. This book will try to show how decisions were reached and the constraints and pressures that had to be reckoned with before a decision could be executed; the roles and motivations of the Ambassadors and so-called 'faceless' bureaucrats; the internecine squabbles and departmental politicking: in short the personalities and diplomatic institutions which were regularly blamed for the gap which so often existed between policy formulation and execution.

I begin with a look at France's new diplomatic position following defeat by Germany in 1870. The defensive posture she assumed was characterised by a search through a system of alliances for guarantees for her security which her own strength could no longer ensure. I try to show how, having achieved a measure of diplomatic security by the beginning of the century, the absence of strong leadership at the French Foreign Office brought incoherence to French foreign policy and the country to the brink of war. This was followed by a period in which the style of French foreign policy was a good deal more vigorous. The central figure in diplomacy and policy-making during these two-and-a-half years leading up to the war was, of course, Raymond Poincaré. Any study of France and the origins of the First World War must therefore focus on the person of Poincaré: how he conceived his policy, how he strove to sustain it and what the result was. This book aims to do that by concentrating on the years before the war and by explaining the general motive behind Poincaré's diplomacy, his view of how the system of international states should be organised and how French foreign policy towards individual countries had to conform to that way of thinking. I have tried to shed some new light on the old myths concerning his attitude towards countries such as Russia and Germany. I have attempted to do the same with such old chestnuts as the Alsace–Lorraine question, *revanche* and the nationalist revival. Much controversy surrounds the question of Poincaré's policies and the outbreak of the First World War. In attempting to throw new light on some of them, I hope I have contributed to reducing the controversy surrounding France and the origins of the First World War.

1 The Search for Security: French Foreign Policy, 1871–1907

In 1815 the might of France in Europe was still considerable. Although Napoleon's bid for mastery of Europe had been thwarted, it was still believed that France could and would renew the attempt. Compared to Prussia, who would progressively become her principal enemy, France was far superior demographically, economically and militarily. The year 1871 was almost the point of intersection of the might and fortunes of the two countries. The population of the newly formed German Empire was 41 millions, whereas that of France was 36 millions. Iron and steel production was equal. Although Germany's coal production was two-and-a-half times France's, the latter's manufacturing production was twice that of the former. As A. J. P. Taylor has stated, the Franco-Prussian War was from the economic point of view a war between equals.[1] France lost and the French bid for the mastery of Europe ended. Henceforth the power of Germany would increasingly overshadow that of her neighbour. By 1910 the strength and fortunes of the two countries' 1815 positions were completely reversed. Germany was now the most powerful nation on the continent, dominating France in nearly every domain. The German population was 65 millions compared with France's 39 millions; the former's iron production was three times the latter's, steel production was four times as great, coal production seven times as great, and Germany's defence estimates were twice the size of France's. Thus from 1871 onwards France would have to seek, through a system of alliances, guarantees for her security which her own strength could no longer ensure.

The Franco-Prussian War was started by Napoleon III, but welcomed by Bismarck. France entered the war in 1870 only to emerge militarily destroyed, territorially mutilated, politically in a state of anarchy and occupied. The devastating defeat of the French army at Sedan on 2 September 1870 had also toppled the régime which was responsible for it – the Second Empire. The Third Republic, declared on 4 September 1870, was born of a humiliating defeat just as it would die by one seventy years later. Ironically, in the short term success in establishing the Republic made the Republicans' task harder by lessening the chances of finding allies in monarchical Europe. The provisional government could do nothing but accept defeat in January 1871, which in turn gave rise to the revolutionary Commune of Paris further adding

4

to the turmoil and misery of France's plight.

To say that France's loss was Prussia's gain is a gross understatement. The balance of power in Europe had been destroyed completely. 'Europe had lost a mistress and gained a master'[2] was how one diplomat viewed things. And Bismarck did all he could to impose a victor's peace according to the Napoleonic model. On the back of French defeat he completed the re-organisation of Germany by uniting the four south German states with the Confederation of 1867 to form the German Empire, of which the King of Prussia became Emperor. He rubbed salt in France's wounds by proclaiming the new German state in the Hall of Mirrors in the Palace of Versailles, which for two centuries had been a great symbol of French power.[3] But it was the annexation of the French provinces of Alsace and Lorraine, demanded by both the northern and southern German states, which sealed the Empire and was the most serious blow to France. This, together with the payment of a huge indemnity (exactly proportionate with the one imposed by Napoleon I on Prussia in 1807) and a temporary German army of occupation, was enshrined in the formal Peace Treaty of Frankfurt on 10 May 1871. Bismarck knew that annexation of the two provinces would delay any reconciliation with France for a long time. Nevertheless he was determined to secure the territories for strategic reasons. Following Sedan he had declared: 'After this war we must expect another aggression, not a durable peace, whatever the conditions we impose. France will consider any peace a truce, and will try to avenge her defeat directly she feels strong enough, alone or with allies.'[4] Alsace and Lorraine would, as in the past, be launching platforms for a French attack and therefore had to be annexed. The possibility of France seeking revenge with allies had also to be destroyed. In 1815 the anti-French alliance was already in existence before the peace settlement of the Napoleonic wars was reached. In 1871 Bismarck was alone and had to create an anti-French network of alliances to block such a possibility.[5] He was to prove successful in keeping France in quarantine for twenty years.

FROM ISOLATION TO ALLIANCE, 1871-94

The Treaty of Frankfurt possessed no more moral authority for Frenchmen than would the Treaty of Versailles for Germans. It gave birth to what became the *leitmotiv* in any discussion of French foreign policy – *la revanche*, the reconquest of the lost provinces. It was the source of the quarrel between Paris and Berlin which dominated and poisoned the life of the continent after 1870. Yet the myth of the *revanche* was greater than the reality. As it is argued below, France was overall a good deal more philosophical about the return of the lost provinces than Germany gave her credit for. However, Berlin shaped an intimidatory foreign policy to fit the distorted picture she had of what Paris was 'really' working for. In doing so she kept the myth alive.

Bismarck's web of alliances and understandings with other powers was mainly responsible for keeping France isolated until 1892. Russia seemed the most likely ally for France, therefore in 1873 the Iron Chancellor brought Austria–Hungary and Russia together in the League of the Three Emperors. The *Dreikaiserbund* killed two birds with one stone; it ensured common abstention from a French alliance while consolidating the present state of peace in Europe – 'la paix allemande' as the French saw it. But differences between Vienna and St Petersburg broke out over the Eastern question from 1875 to 1878. At the Congress of Berlin in 1878 Bismarck sided with Austria–Hungary, leaving the Tsar to declare the Three Emperors' League dead. So Bismarck immediately set about replacing it with something more solid. In 1879 Germany and Austria–Hungary made another alliance. But Bismarck needed to keep Russia firmly in the German orbit, and by dint of his diplomatic skill was able to resurrect the *Dreikaiserbund* in 1881. It provided for Russian neutrality in the event of a war with France. The new league did not alter the Dual Alliance between Vienna and Berlin. Indeed the following year that alliance was reinforced. Italy opted to join to break her isolation and participate more fully in international relations, and the Triple Alliance was born on 20 May 1882. That Alliance would be continually renewed for over thirty years, becoming one of the major axes of the European diplomatic system. Germany now had a pledge of Italian military support against any unprovoked attack by France, while France was faced with the prospect of fighting on a second front along her Alpine frontier in a war with Germany. It was another bar in her diplomatic prison. But the *Dreikaiserbund* was due to expire in June 1887 and the Tsar appeared unlikely to want to renew it. Bismarck would not be satisfied until all risk of a Franco-Russian alliance was destroyed. That satisfaction was gained in June 1887 when, after a change of Foreign Minister, Russia signed the secret Reinsurance Treaty with Germany for three years. It assured Germany of Russian neutrality in the event of a defensive war against France. This was the apogee of the Bismarckian system of alliances. At no point was France more isolated.

France adapted very well to her isolation. In the short term, at least, domestic tasks occupied her fully. She had to pay off her indemnity, terminate the German occupation, frame a new constitution, restore the nation's finances and reform her devastated army. This was achieved with remarkable speed. By mobilising national spirit at home and international credit abroad, in which fourteen German banks participated, France was able to pay off the indemnity in full by the autumn of 1873, six months before the date stipulated in the treaty. With that the army of occupation departed. It was Adolphe Thiers, the first President of the new Republic, who ensured that despite a monarchist majority in the Chamber the Republic would remain, albeit in a conservative form. But the struggles between conservatives and republicans would continue to sap France's strength, despite the passing of the organic laws of the Third Republic in 1875. Things came to a head on 16 May 1877 when the conservative President MacMahon dissolved the republican Chamber before the expiration of its term in the hope of a conservative one being returned after new elections. A republican Chamber was again returned and MacMahon submitted. His constitutional *coup d'état* had failed. The presidential power to dissolve the Chamber fell into disrepute and disuse. The Republic of the republicans had triumphed. But that was no substantial advantage in itself for it increased France's isolation among potential monarchical allies. And though it brought stability to the regime it did not in any way bring stability to the governments. The French Chamber was to be hag-ridden with ministerial crises bringing to power thirteen different foreign ministers from 1871 to 1890 and even more governments, with all the obvious drawbacks for a consistent and stable foreign policy.

Bismarck had hoped that an early payment of the indemnity would cripple France's finances and ruin her chances of rebuilding her military strength. He was wrong on both counts. One of the two major loans raised to meet the indemnity had been covered thirteen times over. The ability to pay Germany so quickly demonstrated the size of the French capitalists' purse, and foreshadowed its use as a financial weapon and France's role as 'Europe's Banker'. France's financial position improved so rapidly that it was possible to devote large sums to military reconstruction. As early as 1872 republicans and royalists had voted the necessary credits to allow five-year military service to be made compulsory for all men aged between twenty and forty. A vast programme for the improvement of national defence was embarked upon, so that in arms and men the French and German armies were almost equal in strength by 1875. This combined with Thiers's fall from power in 1873 and replacement by men with royalist and catholic tendencies seriously worried Bismarck. He saw the possibility of a strong France uniting with Austria–Hungary in a Catholic league against Germany. In April 1875 Bismarck unleashed a violent German press campaign against French army reforms. An article in the Berlin *Post* entitled 'Is War in Sight?' was the highlight of what became known as the 'war scare' of 1875. The French were extremely alarmed at the possibility of a preventive war by Germany. In fact all Bismarck really wanted was to intimidate her into abandoning her military reforms. However, the fear of a possible danger to peace led Britain and Russia to make representations to Berlin on France's behalf and calm was restored. The scare was important in demonstrating the limits to which the other great powers would allow German intimidation of France to go. Most of all it pointed to Russia as a possible future ally.

The victory of the Republicans in the elections of December 1877 removed the fear of a monarchist restoration and opened a new era in Franco-German relations – a period of *détente* from 1878 to 1885. By always remaining one jump ahead in neutralising any possibility France had of forming an alliance in Europe, Bismarck was able to isolate her and manage her on his own terms. During this period, which opened with the triumph of the 'peaceful' Republicans, a number of factors mitigated in favour of improved Franco-

German relations. French intellectuals professed a clear admiration of German thinking, art and education. The great French thinkers and historians, Renan, Taine, Lavisse and Gabriel Monod, were seduced by the German model, as was the father of sociology, Emile Durckheim. The same was true of French philosophers, and particularly poets and writers, whose enthusiasm for the music of Wagner during the 1880s was remarkable. The portrayal of German culture in such a favourable light softened her brutal militarist image and helped to pave the way towards *détente*.[6]

The rise of an international socialist movement during the 1880s helped in a similar way by fostering contacts between the French and German movements, especially as the latter had publicly condemned the annexation of Alsace–Lorraine.[7]

The balance in the military forces of Germany and France during the period also encouraged more peaceful relations by discouraging either a preventive war or a war of *revanche*. It was only after 1887, with the increase in the number of German troops to 461,000 (France had 435,000), that her superiority was regained.

Finally, renewed and increasing links between the two countries in the realm of finance, trade and commerce also encouraged a *rapprochement*. In collaboration French and German banks came to dominate Europe and Turkey financially and to play substantial roles in the Balkans, Sweden and South America. Ironically, the annexed provinces of Alsace and Lorraine often provided the intermediary link between French and German banks and industry. It was also ironical that one of the few articles in the Treaty of Frankfurt with which France had been pleased, article XI, which established the principle of reciprocal commercial treatment on the basis of a most-favoured nation clause, became an obstacle to improved Franco-German relations because of the international recession and the adoption of protectionist policies. But even this gave rise to serious discussions on the possibility of a customs union between the two countries after 1879. It was ironical again, or perhaps straightforwardly understandable, that one of the main proponents of such an idea was a former Alsatian and ex-member of the French Parliament, Count Paul de Leusse. His pamphlet, published in 1888 and entitled *Peace by a Franco-German Customs Union*, encouraged collaboration in the hope that it would also lead to a settlement of other questions dividing the two countries. Though Bismarck was in favour, the German press opposed it. Nevertheless during this period Franco-German trade expanded spectacularly, albeit with Germany taking the lion's share to French cries of 'economic Sedan'. But by 1887 Germany was France's third biggest supplier, and Germany was France's fourth biggest client.[8]

Bismarck intended to turn this prevailing wind of *détente* to Germany's advantage. He decided to encourage French colonial expansion in order to distract her from the vexed question of the 'lost provinces', and to lead her into conflict with Great Britain and Italy thereby lessening the likelihood of her waging a war of *revanche* against Germany. France did not really need much encouraging. As Bismarck had virtually neutralised France's role in Europe her energies had to find an outlet elsewhere. Unlike that of other colonial powers, French imperial expansion was not motivated by economic factors. Since the Second Empire, France had had a relatively self-sufficient economy with little need for a large overseas trade. Though already a leading exporter of capital she had sufficient outlets not to need colonies. And although leading colonialist politicians might outwardly defend their policies of overseas expansion in economic terms, such as the growth of protectionism in Europe requiring the discovery of new markets abroad, inwardly they knew otherwise. From a scattering of islands and trading settlements in West Africa and Indo-China in 1870, France had acquired by 1900 an immense colonial empire second only to that of Britain. Yet unlike those of her rival, in 1914 French colonies accounted for a mere 11 per cent of French exports, 9 per cent of French imports and 9 per cent of her foreign investment.[9] France's overseas 'expansive urge' during the 1880s was motivated by a nationalist reaction to the defeat of 1870, as a means to material and psychological compensation for Alsace–Lorraine, though even the most fervent colonialist probably never believed it could completely bridge that gap. To some extent the whole French Empire became for certain politicians, explorers and particularly the military 'a gigantic system of outdoor relief'[10] and an opportunity to show that France was still capable of playing a role in the world.

Thus French colonial expansion was of mutual interest to Paris and Berlin and became the key-stone of Franco-German *détente*. The private remark by the President of the French National Assembly, Jules Grévy, in the early 1870s that 'France must not think of war. She must accept the *fait accompli*, she must renounce Alsace', was by the end of the decade being uttered more generally. Certainly the inhabitants of Alsace were beginning to think in similar terms when in 1877 they elected five autonomist deputies out of a total of fifteen to the Reichstag. Even the fiery Gambetta, hitherto 'homme de la revanche', was speaking of a peaceful foreign policy and a peaceful settlement of the Alsace–Lorraine question at the beginning of the 1880s. In France Alsace–Lorraine was not very often mentioned in the press, almost never in Parliament. According to an observer in 1881, 'One would say that a century has elapsed since 1871!'[11] Even Bismarck saw the possibility of reconciling French public opinion to the loss of Alsace–Lorraine by encouraging her overseas expansion, as he later informed Jules Ferry: 'I hope to reach the point when you will forgive Sedan as you have forgiven Waterloo. Renounce the Rhine, and I will help you to secure everywhere else the satisfactions you desire.'[12]

Bismarck backed French intervention in Tunisia in 1881, encouraged and supported her in Morocco during the 1880s, on the West African coast in 1884, in Egypt, Madagascar and Tonkin in the same year. At the same time he worked to change this *détente* into a *rapprochement*, particularly from 1883 to

1885. The Lorrainer and leading colonialist politician, Jules Ferry, whose governments dominated this period welcomed these overtures. There was serious talk of an *entente*, even of an alliance in 1884. The French Minister of War, General Campenon, informed the head of a German mission of officers that he was always telling his colleagues to recognise the Treaty of Frankfurt and to make an alliance with Germany: 'With such an alliance France would at one blow regain her standing. France and Germany united would rule the world.'[13] But Ferry never followed this policy through because he sensed that Bismarck was trying to manoeuvre France. He felt, anyway, that public opinion would not have allowed him to go any further than his 'occasional collaboration' with Germany. Bigoted patriotic extremists, such as Déroulède, who in 1882 founded his *Ligue des Patriotes*, though in a minority, still clamoured for immediate *revanche* and denounced all colonial expansion as a distraction from the 'blue-line of the Vosges'. Though Ferry was able to reply to this: 'You will end by making me think you prefer Alsace–Lorraine to France,' and to ask why France should not take compensations elsewhere, back had come Déroulède's famous line: 'I have lost two sisters and you offer me twenty chambermaids!'[14] But what really ended this period of *détente* was the defeat of Ferry and his colonial policy in the French Parliament in March 1885 after the military collapse of Tonkin. The Radicals, and in particular Clemenceau, who accused Ferry of 'high treason', played on the memories of 1871 to defeat their opportunist political opponents. There followed a wave of public revulsion against colonial expansion and a return to continental preoccupations. Over the next decade French policy switched to strengthening the army and seeking allies. Fearing a renewal of revanchist policies, Bismarck abandoned his efforts to conciliate France and returned to a policy of intimidation.

Bismarck had reason to be anxious. There was nothing at all aggressive in the new direction of French foreign policy, the tone of which was set by the Brisson Cabinet: 'The Republic desires nothing but peace, peace accompanied by the dignity which a nation like ours demands, peace assured by a solid army of defence.'[15] But the leader of a new government in 1886, Freycinet, though desirous of continuing friendly relations with Berlin, made the grave error of appointing a Minister of War whose activities nearly brought France and Germany to war. General Boulanger quickly became popular through his reforms in the organisation and munitioning of the army, as well as through the importance he placed on reinforcing the country's national defences, on which France's mind was concentrated at the time. It was chiefly the support given to him by Déroulède's *Ligue des Patriotes* and the tone of nationalist journals calling for *revanche* which seriously worried Berlin. The German Chancellor feared 'the stirring of the flames by an active minority'[16] and the promotion of 'général revanche' to the premiership, despite French government attempts to quell his fears. Bismarck preferred more tangible guarantees. In January 1887 he dissolved the Reichstag, which had refused an increase in army numbers, had a new military law voted, called up reservists and took more rigorous measures against those who in Alsace–Lorraine were rejecting Germanisation, and began to talk of war.

Franco-German relations reached their nadir in April 1887 during the Schnaebelé affair. Schnaebelé, a senior French customs official on the German border was invited to a discussion of administrative business by his German counterpart. On crossing the frontier he was immediately seized by German police. The French government demanded his release. While Boulanger pandered to nationalist opinion and called for a military demonstration, other members of the government were able to secure his release through peaceful negotiations. The peaceful President of the Republic, Jules Grévy, saw to it that Boulanger was not included in the next ministry. However, that was not the end of the darling of the nationalists, who, after a series of by-election victories in 1889, was called upon by his supporters to march on the Elysée. He lost his nerve and instead fled to Brussels. Condemned *in absentia* for treason in September 1891, he committed suicide on his mistress's grave. A new war scare had ended. But it was followed on both sides of the Rhine by further efforts to reinforce the two countries' military positions. France was left with the impression that Bismarck had not finished with his intimidatory methods. However, with the Iron Chancellor's fall from power in 1890, France broke out of the diplomatic strait-jacket in which he had tied her.

During the 1880s the Russian economy, though predominantly rural, had reached the 'take-off' phase. Industrialisation was under way with the development of the textile and heavy industries. But Russia already had an enormous public debt which could not be reduced by further taxation. Traditionally, Germany had been Russia's banker, but those funds were in increasingly short supply and economic relations between the two countries continued to deteriorate as a result of a series of tariff wars. The problem Russia faced was where to find the funds to build new railways, increase her armaments and service her debt. The Russian autocracy's traditional scruples about republican governments began to waver with the prospect of republican gold. The idea of providing Russia with loans also appealed to French bankers, who knew that they provided a better return than French loans and that Russia was a good creditor. The first contract between French banks and the Russian government was signed in November 1888.

As yet there was no hurry on either side to begin political relations, with France fearing reprisals from her enemies and Russia still suspicious of the Republic, its internal stability and the outcome of the Boulanger affair. But with the intensification of economic and financial relations in January 1889 and May 1891 increasing the Russian stock held by France and making her an ever more indispensible ally, with a return to moderation in French domestic politics after the eclipsing of Boulanger, and with worsening Russo-German relations, especially after Bismarck's fall in March 1890, the appeal of France as an ally increased. In 1889 Tsar Alexander III had even allowed Russian industrialists and traders to participate in the International Paris Exhibition to celebrate the centenary of the French Revolution. The attraction was mutual. Within two years France had lent Russia two billion francs. French investors were becoming avid for Russian stock because of its high interest yield and security. This was particularly important as they had recently been hit by the collapse of copper prices, which had bankrupted a major French bank, the Comptoir d'Escompte, in March 1889, by the collapse of Brazilian and Argentinian share prices in the autumn of 1890, and by growing difficulties over the Panama Canal. French opinion was further prepared for an alliance with Russia by a growth of French cultural interest in the Empire, sparked off by Jules Verne's book, *Michel Strogoff*, first published in 1877. Russian novels, particularly by Tolstoy and Dostoyevsky, became so fashionable that the number of translations of Russian books increased from three or four per year from 1880 to 1885, to twenty five in 1888. As the French public got to know the Tsarist Empire, the right-wing press began to stress her qualities such as order and military power, while the centre-left evoked her usefulness as a potential counter-weight to German threats.[17] The ground was prepared.

In August 1890 at the manoeuvres of the Russian army, Russian generals hinted to the Deputy Chief of the French General Staff that a military convention between the two countries was possible. In March 1891, a year after Bismarck's forced resignation, the new German administration abandoned the Iron Chancellor's policy of friendship with Russia and refused to prolong the Reinsurance Treaty with her on the grounds that it undermined the Austro-German alliance. That very month the Tsar conferred Russia's highest decoration on the French President of the Republic. With the worsening of Russo-German economic relations, closer links between London, Rome and Berlin and the pre-term renewal of the Triple Alliance on 6 May 1891, Russia was as isolated as France. Though St Petersburg would have preferred only an *entente* with France she was increasingly pushed towards an alliance. More and more decorations were conferred. In July the French fleet was enthusiastically welcomed in Kronstadt and the Tsar stood bare-headed while the revolutionary 'Marseillaise' was played. On 27 August 1891 France pressed Russia into an exchange of letters in which it was agreed that the two states would concert 'on all questions likely to upset the general peace'. Though not a formal alliance it was a start. As the French Foreign Minister, Alexandre Ribot, remarked: 'The tree is planted.'[18] And after a good deal of pressure from the French, the Tsar agreed in July 1892 to open discussions on a military convention.

General de Boisdeffre was despatched to Russia to negotiate with the Chief of the Russian General Staff, General Obruchev. But there were a number of difficulties. In the event of a war with the Triple Alliance, France wanted Russia to direct her forces principally against Germany. However, Russia viewed Austria–Hungary as her main adversary. A compromise was reached and on 17 August 1892 the secret Franco-Russian military convention was signed. It was to have the same duration as the Triple Alliance and its main clauses were:

> France and Russia, being animated by an equal desire to preserve peace, and having no other object than to meet the necessities of a defensive war, provoked by an attack of the forces of the Triple Alliance against the one or the other of them, have agreed upon the following provisions:
>
> 1) If France is attacked by Germany, or by Italy supported by Germany, Russia shall employ all her available forces to attack Germany. If Russia is attacked by Germany, or by Austria supported by Germany, France shall employ all her available forces to fight Germany.
>
> 2) In case the forces of the Triple Alliance, or one of the powers comprising it, should mobilise, France and Russia, at the first news of the event and without the necessity of any previous concert, shall mobilise immediately and simultaneously the whole of their forces and shall move them as close as possible to their frontiers.
>
> 3) The available forces to be employed against Germany shall be, on the part of France, 1,300,000 men, on the part of Russia, 700,000 or 800,000 men.

There was no doubt about the defensive nature of the convention. However another eighteen months elapsed before ratification took place. France was worried about having to mobilise if Austria–Hungary did so against Russia without Germany, even though she was not obliged to go to war. She tried to get certain changes made and failed. But it was Russia who dragged her feet – the Tsar was beginning to have second thoughts about an alliance with the Republic as the Panama scandal, in which leading politicians and even his Ambassador were implicated, reached its climax. However, increased military spending by Germany and a renewed tariff war with her, convinced Russia of the need to ratify, which Alexander III did on 27 December 1893. The French government reciprocated on 4 January 1894.

The Franco-Russian Alliance, the existence of which was not made public until 1897 and the clauses of which remained so secret that few French Ministers even knew of their details until the First World War, ended the Bismarckian system of alliances on which German hegemony of Europe had depended. Above all, the Alliance put over twenty years of isolation behind France. It was to be the cornerstone of French security up to the First World War. The immediate effect of this new-found security was to encourage French colonial expansion once more.

FROM THE FASHODA STRATEGY TO THE ENTENTE CORDIALE, 1894–1904

From May 1894 to June 1898, except for six months, France's Foreign Minister was Gabriel Hanotaux. His policy was twofold: to encourage French imperial expansion and to link this with a conciliatory strategy in Europe which would reinforce France's rearguard while she operated overseas. Its effect was to bring France closer to Germany in Europe, but to the brink of war with Britain in Africa. The Fashoda crisis demonstrated the limits of the Franco-Russian Alliance and the need to remove the sources of dispute with Britain, which finally emerged as the Entente Cordiale.

Until the last decade of the nineteenth century French public interest in colonial expansion was best summed up by Jules Ferry: 'All that interests the French public about the Empire is the belly dance.'[19] From about 1890 French imperialism shifted from being the preoccupation of a few enthusiasts to becoming an issue which raised popular passions. But that passion did not develop through any intrinsic love of Empire; it owed much more to the European powers' scramble for Africa and above all the rivalry which that fostered. Two overlapping groups in French society used European colonial rivalries to strike the nationalist chord and increase popular support for French imperialism, thereby making local problems into European ones and adding to existing tensions. They were, not surprisingly, a small number of politicians and civil servants responsible for colonial affairs and militants of the colonial movement. Profiting from the notorious weakness of Third Republican governments and their indifference to foreign affairs, they became the inspirers and initiators of the series of grand designs which dominated French expansion during the quarter-century before the First World War,[20] not least of which was the Fashoda strategy.

France's great enemy in Europe may have been Germany, but her great rival abroad was Britain. At the beginning of the 1890s the likely flashpoint for Franco-British rivalry was Africa, along the Nile valley. Paris had never accepted the British occupation of Egypt, where France had had longstanding interests dating from the Napoleonic conquests. Tension increased between the two powers in the area over the Sudan question after 1895. The Nile valley of the Sudan particularly interested the British for two reasons. Firstly, it controlled the upper waters of the Nile and therefore Egypt, which depended on them for its agricultural prosperity. Secondly, it provided Britain with a band of territory which would enable her to realise Cecil Rhodes's dream of a north–south link between the South African Cape and Cairo, possibly by rail. Since the disaster at Khartoum in 1885, Britain had painstakingly prepared a reconquest of the country by diplomatic trade-offs with other colonial powers. The one exception was France. She too had a great interest in the Sudan, which formed an integral part of her plans for joining up her North African Empire in the west with her possessions on the African coast in the east – a Dakar to Djibouti link. The two imperial powers' plans were bound to clash; they would do so at the point of intersection of the two axes of colonisation along the Upper Nile.

A forward policy by France overseas necessarily demanded improved relations with Germany in Europe to avoid action on two 'fronts'. At the beginning of the 1890s there was already a basis for better relations between Paris and Berlin on the most sensitive issue dividing the two countries. From 1893 onwards protest against Germany in Alsace–Lorraine declined, aided by the provinces' participation in the Empire's increasing prosperity and a successful Germanisation policy. A new generation of Alsace–Lorrainers had emerged, educated by German schoolmasters, having done military service in old Germany and with no first-hand experience of France. This was helped by daily contact with Germans living in the two provinces, whose numbers increased from 70,000 in 1875 to 300,000 in 1910 (15·7 per cent of the total population). From 1890 Germans constituted 40 per cent of the population of Strasbourg, the administrative capital, and over 50 per cent of that of Metz. Inevitably mixed marriages resulted, especially after 1895, so that by 1909 16·4 per cent of marriages were between couples in which one partner was German and the other from Alsace–Lorraine.[21]

Alsace–Lorrainers, both old and young, were increasingly disappointed by France's attitude. The idea of *revanche* had virtually disappeared, French protectionist policies operated against the 'lost provinces' and French anti-clericalism especially irritated the clergy, who had been the backbone of the protest. Those anti-clericalist policies, leading to a separation of church and state in France in 1905, seriously offended the pious Alsace–Lorrainers, and together with the progress of the French socialists encouraged autonomist feeling in the provinces. This was reflected in the 1898 elections to the Reichstag when twelve of the fifteen deputies from the Reichsland of Alsace–Lorraine declared their loyalty to the Empire, with some demanding a confederate status and even autonomy for the provinces. The weakening of ties with France was also shown in the move towards cultural autonomy and a revival of the Alsatian dialect.[22]

In France too the 'lost provinces' continued to lose their sentimental effect as a feeling of resignation set in, encouraged by the development of the French socialist movement, pacifist and anti-militarist in sentiment and in favour of Franco-German *détente*. Closer economic and financial ties had a similar effect. In this last decade of the nineteenth century it was clear that the Alsace–Lorraine myth was in sharp decline and that virtually nobody in France recommended war to return the provinces to France.[23] Some still wished for their peaceful return sometime in the future, but true *revanche* was dead. And this did not go unnoticed by Germany, whose Ambassador in Paris claimed in 1898 that most Frenchmen were beginning 'to forget Alsace–Lorraine'.[24]

In ruling circles in France attitudes had changed. Hanotaux, who had worked with Jules Ferry, belonged to the school which recognised the necessity for collaboration with Germany, either to ensure peace or to give French foreign policy greater room for manoeuvre (a policy later espoused by the French Ambassador in Berlin, Jules Cambon). This even meant, in the words attributed to Hanotaux, leaving the Alsace–Lorraine question 'out of practical politics'. Though no French politician would dare to recognise officially the clauses of the Frankfurt Treaty, some form of compromise now seemed possible, perhaps in conjunction with colonial compensations. Furthermore, that school believed, as Jules Cambon would maintain, that by improved relations with Germany, and by encouraging her to find her 'place in the sun', her expansionary drive would be diverted from Europe, thereby further increasing French room for manoeuvre.[25]

Manifestations of the *détente* were Kaiser William II's invitation to France to participate with warships in the ceremony for the opening of the Kiel Canal in 1895, and Germany's agreement to participate in the 1900 Exposition Universelle de Paris, attended for the first time since 1867 by thousands of Germans who turned out to be the most numerous visitors. From the spring of 1894 there was a move towards colonial agreements between Paris and Berlin in Africa.[26] The Fashoda crisis would give considerable stimulus to the idea of a *rapprochement*.

Under considerable influence from the Colonial Party Hanotaux accepted the Fashoda strategy in the autumn of 1895. The idea was to despatch from France, in June 1896, a small military force under Colonel Marchand which would make its way to the Belgian Congo, and from there proceed to the upper Nile in the Sudan to make a military demonstration. Hanotaux believed, very optimistically, that the expedition could be used to increase pressure on Britain for a negotiated settlement on Egypt or, failing that, force her to an international conference. However, when Marchand with his 150 men eventually arrived at Fashoda, the site of an old Egyptian fort, in July 1898 this intended show of force was more than cancelled out by the simultaneous arrival in the Sudan of General Kitchener's army fresh from its great victory at Omdurman. The crisis was grave with war threatened between Britain and France. But the French government recognised that they were in no position to wage war, accepted the inevitable and ordered Marchand's unconditional withdrawal from the area.

The Fashoda strategy was a gamble that proved humiliating. Its initiation and subsequent failure reveal two things about French diplomacy of the time: the first, apparent with hindsight, was a fundamental flaw in foreign policy-making; the second was the contradiction inherent in France's international position.

The initiative for the Fashoda strategy lay principally with the Colonial Party. The ease with which they secured acceptance of their ideas demonstrates that fundamental flaw in French policy-making during the first half of the Third Republic which was to have further serious consequences later on. That flaw was the virtual absence of cabinet control over foreign and colonial policy. This was largely due to ministers having not the slightest interest in foreign affairs, nor, had they so wanted to do, the time to acquaint themselves with the subject when governments of the Third Republic lasted on average only a year. This inevitably placed excessive power in the hands of the Foreign and Colonial Ministers. But even they were not immune to the short life-span of a ministry which often made them as ignorant as their colleagues about foreign affairs. The Colonial Minister, Chautemps, was reputed to have confused 'Madagascar with Gibraltar [and] Gabon with the Sudan'.[27] This left the way open for permanent officials and diplomats to exert considerable influence over their ministers. The important role played in the formulation and execution of the Fashoda strategy by the permanent officials of the foreign and colonial ministries, supporters themselves of the colonial movement, demonstrated this. As the power of permanent officials and diplomats abroad committed to colonial or other causes increased proportionally to the weakness of governments, after the departure of Delcassé in 1905 French foreign policy-making would enter one of its least coherent phases. Not surprisingly the second most fateful expedition in the history of French African expansion occurred during that period. Fashoda had taken France to the brink of war with Britain, the Fez expedition in 1911 took her to the brink of war with Germany.[28]

The contradiction in the international position of the Third Republic resulted from France being both a great continental and a great colonial power. Though France might have Germany as an enemy on the continent and Britain as a rival in the colonies, as a continental power she needed British support against Germany, and as a colonial power German support against Britain.[29] That German support had not been forthcoming over Egypt (nor more importantly had Russia's) mainly because the diplomatic ground had not been properly prepared. Those who first realised this were the members of the French colonial movement and in particular the Comité de l'Afrique Française. They clearly stated the need for a colonial *entente* with Germany. But they insisted at the same time that this was in no way incompatible with the more revolutionary idea of an arrangement with Britain to solve the major disagreements between the two countries. And they made it clear as early as February 1899 that this should be based on a colonial barter of English influence in Egypt for French influence in Morocco. In the five years following the Fashoda crisis the *Comité de l'Afrique Française* made persistent efforts to convince Théophile Delcassé, who had become Foreign Minister in June 1898 as the candidate of the Colonial Party, to seek such an agreement with Britain.[30] The result was the Entente Cordiale of 1904.

Fashoda was arguably the worst crisis in Franco-British relations since Waterloo. France had hoped for diplomatic support from Germany and Russia but had received none – the latter on the grounds that France was unwilling to support her in the Balkans. Delcassé set about improving that position. The Fashoda crisis encouraged a Franco-German *rapprochement*. Hatred of Great Britain pushed *revanche* even further from the minds of Frenchmen and enhanced the idea of Franco-German collaboration. Delcassé, despite his later Germanophobic label, agreed with this. On coming to the Foreign Ministry he was hoping for a peaceful settlement of the Alsace–Lorraine question. From the beginning of December 1898 France took the initiative in seeking a *rapprochement* with Germany. When the German envoy, von Huhn, came to Paris for talks, the French were talking of 'forgetting the past' and of 'substituting for the policy of sentiment a new policy which responds to real interests'. And Delcassé insisted to von Huhn that France was ready 'to support German colonial aspirations everywhere, particularly in China'. Though the French press firmly backed such a policy, the Germans did not respond to French overtures. But Delcassé did not give up. With Britain weakened after 1899 by the Boer War, he made further efforts to secure German and Russian support for intervention in the conflict but to no avail. Germany's reticence and apparent double-dealing with Britain began to increase his suspicions about her.[31]

Of course these suspicions were always at the back of his mind and had been an important factor in his desire to reinforce the Franco-Russian Alliance. The reshaping of the Dual Alliance in August 1899 extended the scope of the Alliance to cover the contingency of war with Britain and also the preservation of the European balance of power. This last idea was motivated by the desire to check eventual German claims to the lion's share of the declining Austro-Hungarian Empire when, as everyone expected, it broke up. Delcassé believed this would allow Germany not only to dominate the continent from the North Sea and the Baltic to the Alps and the Adriatic, but also provide her with an outlet to the Mediterranean. As Delcassé believed that France's future role should be that of a Mediterranean power with an African empire stretching from Algeria to Tunisia in the north to the French Congo in the south, the modification of the Alliance was vital. What followed naturally from this grand Mediterranean design was that France should bring Morocco under French rule.[32]

Though his recent overtures to Berlin had proved fruitless and his suspicions about Germany were growing, he still hoped to enlist her support together with that of Italy and Spain in gaining recognition of French control of Morocco despite British reticence. Envoys were sent to Berlin in the summer of 1901 to offer French colonial compensation in Africa for German acquiescence. This time Berlin's reluctance to commit herself to France and lose the possibility of an alliance with Britain, led Delcassé to realise that he must seek a favourable settlement of the Moroccan question by other means. The fact that some six months later Britain also failed to reach an agreement with Germany on the Far East helped to drive the two countries into each other's arms.

At the end of 1902 Delcassé had obtained a guarantee of Italian support on the Moroccan question[33] and was negotiating with Spain. By the spring of 1903 he had been converted, with a good deal of pressure from Eugène Etienne, the leader of the Colonial Party, to the idea of an agreement with Britain on Morocco. Unofficial attempts to open negotiations along these lines had already been started in London in 1901 by the French Ambassador, Paul Cambon, acting on his own initiative. By 1903 the British and French press, after the period of great antagonism during the Boer War, were clearly coming round to the idea of a diplomatic understanding between the two countries.[34]

The traumatic experience of the Boer War was a major cause of Britain's changed attitude towards France. It showed up a number of British military weaknesses, and it underlined her diplomatic isolation. To improve the military position the Committee of Imperial Defence was created in 1902. On the diplomatic front the popularity of 'Splendid Isolation' was on the wane and Britain began to look towards the continent for support. British public opinion was growing increasingly hostile to an arrangement with Germany, whose *Weltpolitik* was beginning to threaten Britain in the colonies and, by the expansion of the German navy, at sea. In the Foreign Office the idea of an *entente* with France on the basis of a colonial agreement became more and more appealing.

The growth of British hostility towards Germany also encouraged French opinion to believe that an understanding with Britain would be of mutual benefit. It was Paul Cambon who set about arousing the interest of the British government and British public opinion in the idea of an Egyptian-Moroccan barter by having *The Times* publish a report on the subject in February 1903. The state visit to Paris in May by Edward VII, and to London in July by President Loubet, mustered further public support for an *entente*. When Delcassé arrived in London with Loubet he was of the firm opinion that an agreement on Morocco with Britain was urgently necessary. From the beginning of 1903 there was evidence that Germany was being encouraged by the Pan-German League to gain a foothold in Morocco. The first steps in the talks which led to the Entente Cordiale nine months later were taken by Delcassé during his stay in London. Whereas the British Foreign Secretary, Lord Lansdowne, sounded out other government authorities on the proposed agreement before negotiations began in earnest on 1 October 1903, Delcassé did not consult his cabinet colleagues until early the following year. In France the Entente Cordiale was the result of a personal decision by Delcassé influenced to a far greater extent by someone who was not even a member of the government, Eugène Etienne, than by the Prime Minister.[35]

The Franco-British Agreement was signed on 8 April 1904. It settled the colonial differences between the two countries in three main areas. Firstly, France exchanged her exclusive fishing rights around Newfoundland for territorial compensation in Black Africa (a small portion of the Gambia, a larger slice of northern Nigeria and the Iles de Los, off the coast of French Guinea). Secondly, Siam was divided into two zones of influence, and a condominium was established in the New Hebrides. Thirdly, and most important of all, France agreed not to obstruct British action in Egypt, while Britain recognised France's right to maintain the peace in Morocco, and secret clauses provided for a future protectorate by France over Morocco and by Britain over Egypt. The agreement contained no statement of general policy, nor, more importantly, did it commit either of the two parties to anything more that the execution of the above-mentioned clauses. It was in no way comparable to the Franco-Russian Alliance, for both partners retained complete freedom of action. But what was most important was the spirit of the Entente Cordiale. As it replaced the main sources of friction between the two powers with a new cordiality it presaged an even closer union. Certainly Germany had no doubt about the agreement marking the beginning of a new alignment of the powers in Europe. And she was sufficiently worried to take steps to break it up. By the *entente* with Britain, France had come another step closer to her goal of achieving security in Europe. Germany's particularly ham-fisted attempts to disrupt this process merely confirmed France's worst suspicions about her neighbour and in turn encouraged Paris to strengthen still further her diplomatic ties.

FROM THE FIRST MOROCCAN CRISIS TO THE TRIPLE ENTENTE, 1905-7

The idea of establishing a Triple Entente between France, Britain and Russia had attracted Delcassé for at least ten years before he became Foreign Minister. He lost hope for a few years following the Fashoda crisis. But by 1903 he was again optimistic after receiving evidence that Edward VII and Joseph Chamberlain, whom he regarded as the most influential figures in British diplomacy, favoured an agreement with the Franco-Russian Alliance. With hindsight the Entente Cordiale seems a major step in the right direction. But at the time the Germans, for instance, viewed any *rapprochement* between France and Britain as likely to weaken the Franco-Russian Alliance. Britain and Russia were generally considered to be irreconcilable enemies because of their differences in central Asia and the Far East. The outbreak of the Russo-Japanese war on 8 February 1904, following an unprovoked Japanese attack on Russia, seemed likely therefore to ruin Delcassé's plans. Russian suspicion of Britain, as Japan's ally, was bound to reach new heights, and that suspicion was likely to reflect on France as the friend of Britain. But Delcassé was able to maintain Russian confidence by violating French status as a neutral power and allowing the Russian Baltic fleet to stop off at French colonial ports on its way to the Far East. He also pleased Russia through his mediation in the Dogger Bank crisis, which brought Russia and Britain to the verge of war in autumn 1904, after the Russian squadron, which was on its way to the Far East, opened fire on 21 October on English trawlers on the Dogger Bank, having mistaken them for Japanese torpedo boats.[36] Delcassé's skilful diplomacy was proving successful in maintaining both the *entente* with Britain and the alliance with Russia, much to Germany's consternation. As disintegration of France's new diplomatic links was not going to happen on its own, Germany decided to take an active hand in promoting it.

As soon as the Dogger Bank crisis occurred, the *eminence grise* of the

German Foreign Office, von Holstein, seized on it to destroy the Dual Alliance by suggesting a Russo-German alliance to the Russian Ambassador, which was backed up by a similar suggestion from the Kaiser to the Tsar. As these overtures to Russia in October 1904 were favourably received, Holstein went ahead with the second part of his plan, which was to try and persuade France to abandon the Entente Cordiale and accept a place as junior partner in the Russo-German alliance. Delcassé immediately took steps to counter this by informing London and by protesting to the Russian Ambassador. Fortunately the Tsar had already told the Kaiser that France must be informed before the alliance was signed. Because Germany insisted on the reverse, the affair fell through. The Kaiser was extremely disappointed and held Delcassé responsible.[37] This was not the end of the matter, the Kaiser was to propose the same idea again in July 1905 at Björkö. For Delcassé the whole affair heightened his suspicions of Germany, whom he now regarded as fully intent on disrupting France's diplomatic ties. The First Moroccan Crisis confirmed that impression.

Delcassé had first sought to gain control of Morocco with German support against Britain; he now tried with British support against Germany. Having secured Italian, British and Spanish consent for French ambitions in Morocco, he believed that Germany could be confronted with a *fait accompli*. At the close of 1904 the French Minister in Morocco, Saint-René Taillandier, put substantial pressure on the Sultan of Morocco to accept a series of reforms proposed by France. The Sultan gave way and in January 1905 a French mission arrived in Fez to begin discussions on the reforms. As a signatory and guardian of the Madrid Convention of 1880, which guaranteed the independence of Morocco, Germany had every right to feel aggrieved at such action. She was thus presented with a perfect opportunity for continuing her objective of disrupting France's diplomatic links, and at a time when France was at her weakest since the signing of the Dual Alliance.

At the beginning of 1905 Russia was on the brink of a devastating defeat in the Far East that would considerably reduce her effectiveness as an ally in Europe. In France the Minister of War had embarked on a republican crusade to rid the High Command of its monarchical and clerical elements, which had the effect of demoralising and disorganising the army. The naval building programme authorised in 1900 was nowhere near realisation. France was unprepared for war and Germany knew it. Chancellor von Bülow and Holstein hoped to force France into a confrontation with Germany over Morocco in the belief that Britain would refuse, and Russia be unable, to support France. In one fell swoop, Germany calculated, the Entente Cordiale would be destroyed, the Dual Alliance would be shown to be useless and France could be drawn into the German orbit.[38]

Delcassé's stubbornness in refusing to heed a German warning issued in February 1905 about French action in Morocco merely played into Berlin's hands. Under pressure from von Bülow the Kaiser reluctantly agreed to call at

Tangier during his annual Mediterranean cruise at the end of March. There the Kaiser asserted Germany's demand for free trade and equal rights in Morocco and confirmed the Sultan's status as ruler of an independent country. An international dispute had developed. By April Delcassé was making some half-hearted attempts to appease the Germans. But by May he had both unofficial and official indications of support from Britain which led him to believe that Germany would give way. Prime Minister Rouvier was a good deal more pessimistic, fearing a surprise German attack would lead France 'to defeat and to the Commune'. After private contacts with Germany he agreed to force Delcassé to resign. When the Germans learnt that Delcassé's attempts to mediate in the Russo-Japanese War were likely to be successful and increase the possibility of a Triple Alliance between France, Russia and Britain, they issued Rouvier with an ultimatum for Delcassé's dismissal at the end of May. At a Cabinet meeting on 6 June 1905 Rouvier won the support of his Ministers on the question of the credibility of a German invasion and Delcassé duly resigned. Rouvier assumed control of the Foreign Ministry until October 1906 when Stephen Pichon became Foreign Minister. Ironically, Delcassé knew enough of Rouvier's secret negotiations with Germany to unseat him through German telegrams intercepted at the Quai d'Orsay, but refused to use them in his defence for fear the Germans should learn of the French cryptographic breakthrough.[39] He could perhaps take solace from the fact that in the short term Rouvier's diplomacy did not pay off, whereas within two years his own diplomacy was rewarded by the signing of a Russo-British agreement which effectively established the Triple Entente.

To mark what appeared to be a massive German triumph, on the day of Delcassé's resignation von Bülow was made a prince. Rouvier's belief that sacrificing Delcassé would appease Germany was wrong. Germany continued to insist on, and got, an international conference to settle the Moroccan question. But in the end, instead of destroying the Entente Cordiale and pulling France into dependence on Germany, Germany's bluff diplomacy merely strengthened the Entente and turned French opinion against closer ties with her.[40] The emotional meeting between the Kaiser and the weak Tsar at Björkö in the Gulf of Finland in July 1905 produced an agreement for a Russo-German alliance, which the Russian Foreign Office, however, loyal to the Franco-Russian Alliance, rejected in November. Germany placed all her hopes on a victory at the forthcoming international conference.

Against all German expectations the Algeciras conference, attended by thirteen nations from 16 January to 7 April 1906, was a resounding diplomatic defeat for Germany. France was firmly supported by Russia, the new Liberal British Foreign Secretary, Sir Edward Grey, and a majority of the other delegates, while Germany, deserted by Italy, only received the backing of Austria–Hungary and Morocco. Though the final act proclaimed the independence and integrity of Morocco, the vital issue of policing was handed over to France and Spain, and France was given the major stake in the *Banque d'Etat*, which effectively gave her control of the economic development of the country. Germany's diplomacy had backfired. To a large extent she had conspired towards her own isolation.

Germany's tactics during the First Moroccan Crisis had seriously worried Britain. Her attempts to form a continental alliance at Björko increased those fears. Britain was beginning to consider that the Entente Cordiale was as much a guarantee of France's security as her own. In February 1906 Grey had written: 'An entente between Russia, France and ourselves would be absolutely secure. If it is necessary to check Germany it could then be done.'[41] In April 1906 negotiations began between Russia and Britain, leading to an agreement which was signed on 31 August 1907.

Grey's desire for an agreement with Russia to settle the two countries' differences in Asia was motivated by a number of factors: the cost of defending the Indian Empire, principally against Russian expansion, was becoming too great; Russia's crushing defeat in the Far East together with revolution at home could only encourage Germany to take advantage of her weakness to increase her own power, which after discovery of the new German naval programme in May 1906 Britain seriously feared; finally, an agreement with St Petersburg would head off any Russo-German alliance and establish real security in Europe. Grey's ideas dovetailed with those of the new Russian Foreign Minister, Alexander Isvolsky, who had come to power in May 1906. Isvolsky knew from former negotiations that a political agreement with Britain would open up the London money market to Russian loans. He also believed that in the light of her recent disasters, Russia should switch her attention from the Far East to the Balkans, and to gaining control of the Dardanelles Straits, which would give her Black Sea fleet access to the Mediterranean. He was aware, however, that diplomatic support for such a policy would be needed in the face of obvious opposition from Austria–Hungary. He also knew that the prerequisite for an agreement with Britain would entail Russia renouncing all action in Asia which threatened the security of India. But as this involved little more than acknowledging what was a reality – Russia no longer had the military capability to stand up to a threat of war from Britain – it was better therefore to negotiate the sacrifice and get what one could for it. Finally, improved Russo-British relations were the best means of strengthening still further the Franco-Russian Alliance.[42]

Like the Entente Cordiale the Russo-British agreement dealt only with extra-European issues, though during negotiations Grey did hint that Britain might in future agree to an alteration of the rule of the Straits in Russia's favour. In exchange for the renunciation of Russian claims to Afghanistan and the recognition of British interests in Tibet, Persia was divided into zones of influence, Britain's being in the south, Russia's in the north and a neutral zone in between. There was no statement or commitment to anything other than the colonial settlement. But as with the Entente Cordiale, what was important was the spirit of the agreement, which paved the way to closer links between the two countries. Though the German press protested at this 'encirclement', the series of agreements that formed the Triple Entente were purely defensive in nature. They were a reaction to the activities of the Triple Alliance and the increasingly threatening attitude of Germany, made so clear in the Moroccan crisis. In general terms what was more significant about the agreement was that it marked the shift in the centre of gravity of great-power rivalry from empire to continental Europe. More sinister was the fact that henceforth international relations would be dominated by the rivalry of Triple Alliance and Triple Entente. In Europe the growing differences between the great powers led governments to seek to reinforce their security by further diplomatic and military agreements, thereby tightening the two blocs and sending them spiralling towards conflict. This was not clear in 1907. At that time Germany claimed that she was being imprisoned by the Triple Entente. This was not true. The agreement was defensive and had been brought about by a general feeling of insecurity which German policies and attitudes had fathered. No one understood that insecurity better than France, having herself spent thirty-six years trying to break free from German imprisonment.

Delcassé's seven-year term as Foreign Minister was the longest in the history of the Third Republic. That period was remarkable for the Foreign Minister's mastery of foreign policy aided to a large extent by the loyalty he inspired among members of his foreign service. He was replaced by foreign ministers who had neither the personality nor the skill to give firm direction to French foreign policy. Though motivated by the desire for more conciliatory action towards Germany, they were not able to sustain such a policy in the absence of firm control over the foreign service. From having a reputation as high as at any time in the history of republican France in 1905,[43] by 1911 the standing of French diplomacy had slumped to the bottom end of that scale. The intervening period was one of incoherence, in which the independent policies of bureaucrats in Paris and diplomats abroad vied for supremacy, finally taking France to the brink of war with Germany.

2 Bureaucrats and Diplomats: A Period of Independence 1905–11

By the end of the nineteenth century the foreign ministries of the major European powers were in need of reform. The rapid expansion of trade, finance and colonial acquisition had put new strains on the old machinery of diplomacy. Apart from the sheer increase in work-load the nature of diplomacy was changing. The monitoring and collation of political, economic and social data pointed to the end of amateur policy-making. Professionalism demanded team-work, team-work demanded organisation and training, and this in turn demanded reform. But reform was not likely to be welcomed by diplomats and officials who instinctively drew back at the thought of any encroachment on their privileges and traditions. There was a popular image of the functionary at the Quai d'Orsay weaving devious policies in the elegant building along the Seine and jealously protecting his prized isolation. This was not far from the truth. The lack of parliamentary interest in foreign affairs could take some of the blame, as could the Quai d'Orsay's contempt for the parliamentary institutions themselves. This was partly a legacy from the old nobility, who were still an important influence in the Ministry despite the republican purges of Prime Minister Freycinet in the 1890s, partly the ancestral idea of diplomacy as purely the prerogative of diplomats, and partly the proverbial instability of French Cabinets which undermined the position and authority of the Foreign Minister. Count Beaupoil de Saint Aulaire described how the legacy of contempt was passed on to each new *attaché* by his mentor, whom he quotes as saying:

I suppose that the great genius of France placed the Foreign Ministry between Napoleon's tomb and the cradle of another scourge, our parliamentarianism, to advise it to keep equal distances from imperialism, which causes the fall of empires, and pacifism which is the strong point of the Chambers and the weakness of states; at the moment it is from the Palais Bourbon that the most pernicious air blows. It is subject to swift upturns, which on average bring us a new Minister every year, whose programme consists in doing the opposite of that of his predecessor. In this at least we have a tradition, that of incoherence in tumult, instead of continuity in silence, the principle of all national grandeur.

And de Saint Aulaire describes him as pointing angrily first at the Palais

Bourbon and then at the Quai d'Orsay, and concluding: 'No diplomacy possible as long as this dominates that.'[1] It must be said that such contempt was often well-founded, as in the case of the parliamentary commissions, called to investigate foreign affairs, whose members were known to 'gossip a lot; they explain confidential information to their wives, to their mistresses, to their intimate friends, who, themselves, also gossip'.[2]

Thus because diplomacy was regarded as arcane and evoked little public interest before the turn of the century, the Quai d'Orsay was able to resist any stringent review of its organisation. 1905 was the watershed. The Russian defeat in the Far East and the First Moroccan Crisis produced a new tension in Europe and brought problems nearer home. Subsequent incidents recorded in the rapidly rising popular press heralded a new interest in foreign affairs. As Louis Marin, the Chamber of Deputies' *rapporteur* for the foreign affairs budget in 1914, was to remark: 'In the course of the international crises which have taken place since the Russo-Japanese war all the great states have concerned themselves with deep reforms of their diplomatic services.'[3] France began in 1906.[4] But the reform did not have the desired effect, instituted as it was by a weak and inexperienced Foreign Minister unable to grasp the implications for the administration of foreign affairs. The even greater weakness of his successors merely exacerbated the effects of the reform. The power of the permanent officials in the Paris offices, known generally as the 'bureaux', increased substantially, with the concomitant effect of increasing the independence of the self-appointed custodians of France's 'true' interests – the ten Ambassadors. Thus the insubordinate 'bureaux' took their place in that triangular struggle with weak Foreign Ministers and independent diplomatic corps which characterised French foreign policy after 1905. The upshot of this uneven struggle was fateful: for it was above all the hostility of the 'bureaux' to Germany which brought France to the brink of war in 1911. Indeed, the characteristic incoherence of French foreign policy in this period mirrored the contradictions of its organisation.

THE 1907 REORGANISATION OF THE QUAI D'ORSAY

The French Parliament had few means of scrutinising foreign policy – commissions for foreign affairs existed merely on an *ad hoc* basis. Only the budget commissions of the Chamber of Deputies, wielding the power of the purse, exercised some influence before the First World War. Thus it was Paul Deschanel's 1906 budget commission report which brought to light anomalies and abuses prevalent in the Foreign Ministry. The fact that it coincided with a left-wing victory at the elections, and the formation of Clemenceau's Radical ministry in October 1906, meant that the Quai would have to undergo some changes. On 6 November 1906 Stephen Pichon, the new Foreign Minister, appointed the Foreign Ministry official, Philippe Berthelot, as *rapporteur* of the

'Commission for the reorganisation of the interior and exterior services of the Ministry of Foreign Affairs'. His report led to the decree of 29 April 1907 reorganising the Ministry.

The purpose of the 1907 reform was to carry out a structural and managerial overhaul of the Ministry and prepare it for the new exigencies of policy-making. The reorganisation centred on three points. Firstly, with a view to achieving a greater unity of policy, it fused the hitherto independent political and commercial departments, which became the Political and Commercial Division. The division of responsibilities would now be geographical, with specialised technicians and counsellors in each section. Secondly, a Political and Commercial Director would take charge of this department seconded by an Assistant Director, who was also head of the European sub-division. A separate department with its own Director would deal solely with administrative and technical affairs. The third, and most controversial, aspect of the reform centred on the *cabinet du ministre*, which remained independent and retained control of the Personnel Division. Criticism of the *cabinet*'s excessive power was thus ignored. The Foreign Minister would still be able to choose his own staff for the *cabinet*, though it was hoped that appointments would be made according to merit as well as politics. This last clause went unheeded. Thus, the main sections of the new administration were the *cabinet du ministre*, the Political and Commercial Division, the Administrative and Technical Division and the Funds and Accounting Division.

This organisation remained in place until Poincaré arrived. The effects of the reform were disappointing. Indeed, it can be held partly responsible for the two major problems which would affect French foreign policy from 1907 to 1912: the independence and insubordination of both the 'bureaux' and the Ambassadors. During this period the Quai d'Orsay fell prey to a number of young, ambitious and unscrupulous officials who were characterised by a hostility towards certain Ambassadors. This culminated in the confused negotiations of the Agadir crisis which finally brought to light the disorganisation and intrigue in the Ministry.

It was symptomatic of the state of the Quai that the reform was prepared, drafted and administered by Berthelot, a highly ambitious official who had spent virtually all his life in the Paris offices. That he should have been commissioned by an inexperienced and ineffectual Minister merely underlined the problem. Thus the *cabinet du ministre* gained most from the reorganisation, emerging as the all-powerful organ of the Ministry. This was contrary to the suggestions of the reform commission, which had criticised the hegemony of the Personnel Office, which formed part of the *cabinet du ministre*. Ignoring these recommendations left the way open for the *cabinet du ministre*, as another commissioner later explained in 1914, 'to encroach on the functions and prerogatives of the Directors and substitute itself for them, thereby creating the confusion which we witnessed at the time of the incidents which took place in 1911'.[5] The personnel department of any large, labour-intensive organisation is of strategic importance, with its powers over nomination, promotion and transfer. It is not hard to imagine the possibilities for corrupt or politically motivated chiefs to staff key administrative sections with political affiliates or threaten others with dismissal for refusing to execute certain policies. These were precisely the criticisms made in Paul Deschanel's foreign affairs budget report in 1912. For several years the Chamber of Deputies, he explained, had attempted to check the system of 'string-pulling', 'arbitrariness', and co-opting of outsiders, but to no avail.[6] This resulted in errors, delays and unsolved problems.

It was a sign of the times that a journalist could be better documented and produce a far more revealing report on the Quai d'Orsay than a parliamentary commission. Lindenlaub (pseudonym for Emile Lautier), diplomatic correspondent of Le Temps, and personal friend and colleague of the notorious journalist André Tardieu, made a study of the workings of the Foreign Ministry. His findings were included in a long personal letter written in 1911 to Ambassador Auguste Gérard, member of a five-man commission ordered to inquire into the activities of the recently suspended Political Director of the Ministry, Edmond Bapst. The Bapst case was a prime example of the hold the 'bureaux' had gained over foreign affairs. The circumstances in which orders had been given for the French occupation of the key Moroccan town of Fez in May 1911, which subsequently led to the Agadir crisis, were, to say the least, suspicious. When called before the Foreign Affairs Commission of the Chamber, Bapst refused to answer the questions. He was suspended pending an inquiry. Lindenlaub's letter of 14 November 1911 pressed Gérard to make full use of this opportunity to denounce the disorganisation and intrigue rife in the Ministry. 'It is known that in Talleyrand's "old firm" no direction exists any longer, that initiatives are taken by functionaries who are conveniently without responsibility. It must be stopped.' However, Lindenlaub's study was not solely composed of generalisations, it made detailed criticisms: once again the cabinet du ministre received particular attention. Its recent chief, Maurice Herbette, was cited as an example of how a secondary functionary could come to dominate the Ministry. Combining the functions of chef de cabinet and chef du personnel, as proscribed by the 1907 reform, he controlled, 'the future of whomsoever he likes or dislikes' and was 'the unsupervised master of diplomacy, men and offices'. A mere First Secretary like Herbette, with an 'appetite for power' and a 'taste for intrigue', could both usurp the powers of a weak Minister and be the judge of Ambassadors and Ministers Plenipotentiary, which Lindenlaub described as 'a monstrous anomaly', 'an intolerable abuse'.[7]

His report, however, was not confined to fault-finding; it set out proposals for reform. Deschanel's 1912 budget report reached the same conclusions on the need to revise the 1907 reform. The only clauses which met with his approval concerned the unification of the political and commercial departments and the geographical reorganisation of sub-departments. But Ambassadors such as Jules Cambon were not even satisfied with this and held the whole reform in contempt. As early as 1908 Cambon had written to his brother that as a result of the reorganisation the Political Director 'is submerged, and these young wolves who have carved for themselves personal domains in the Ministry are destroying all unity of service'.[8] The belief that the 1907 reform encouraged the development of factions was echoed more strongly later. A prematurely retired Consul General, Pognon, a victim of internecine quarrels of various clans, was sufficiently embittered to publish an attack on this state of affairs in a pamphlet addressed to the Foreign Minister, Gaston Doumergue, in 1913.[9] The 1907 reform had also knowingly ignored other abuses. Weak Foreign Ministers, from Pichon (holder of the office for nearly five years) to de Selves, had shied away from correcting them and they had worsened. The greatest of these was the antagonism between the central administration in Paris and the diplomatic corps abroad. Vendettas were waged, particularly against the Rome and Berlin embassies, by the Young Turks of the 'bureaux', who opposed the old Ambassadors' policies of *détente*. The vendettas could take a personal form, such as questioning Jules Cambon's expenses. More seriously, they culminated in blatant sabotage of proposals and policies. Consequently, Ambassadors were forced to intrigue to place their own men in key posts at the Quai. This contributed to the development of independent personal policies by frustrated Ambassadors and provided them with a convenient pretext for disclaiming all criticism from Paris, no matter how justified. This was to be the other aspect of the administrative problem which would surface in 1912: insubordination of Ambassadors jealous of their independence and privileges.

The 1907 reorganisation was quite obviously a failure, the effects of which were worsened by the increasing weakness of foreign ministers. Pichon was weak, but at least he represented a certain continuity from 1906 to 1911; his successors, Jean Cruppi and Justin de Selves, could not even claim that. It is significant that in the case of the latter even the Prime Minister, Joseph Caillaux, joined in negotiating behind his back during the Agadir crisis. This was the incoherent setting of French policy-making before 1912, but whom did it profit, what were their motives, and what did they hope to achieve?

THE 'BUREAUX'

Officially the 'bureaux' were the offices and departments of the central administration of the Quai d'Orsay. In diplomatic circles 'bureaux' came to be used as a pejorative term referring to the individuals and factions jockeying for position at the Foreign Ministry. Between 1905 and 1912 they exercised an important influence on the formulation and execution of French foreign policy. Some groups had no definite organisation but a common social and educational background and shared the same ideas and aspirations; others knew each other and met regularly. Some were united in one cause and opposed in others; some were ill-defined; some overlapped. One would not speak of an anti-German group, because in reality nearly everyone in the 'bureaux' belonged to it. The group in favour of Balkan nationalism might support Russia on occasions while remaining opposed to her autocratic régime; another might value the Entente Cordiale in Europe but oppose Britain in the colonies. The permutations were numerous but had one thing in common: the 'bureaux' often worked secretly, and sometimes subversively for their own ends. A favourite means of sabotaging policies with which they disagreed was by press leaks, and their success rate was impressive.

Their reputation for indiscretions was so widely known that it contributed to the rejection of Paris as the meeting place for the 1912 ambassadorial conference, thereby removing Poincaré's anticipated presidential election platform. However ill-defined, two groupings stand out within the 'bureaux' – the broad *Sciences Politiques* element and, overlapping it the more homogeneous and distinct 'Colonial' group.[10]

It is a commonplace, though insufficiently stressed in diplomatic history, that social and educational background play an important role in determining future political motives and actions. At the end of the nineteenth century a certain type of higher education created a caste among the permanent officials of the French Foreign Ministry. It was composed of the 'past pupils' of the Ecole Libre des Sciences Politiques. Its influence increased to such a point that between 1905 and 1927 of 192 men appointed to the diplomatic and consular services 153 were elected from among its graduates.[11] The *Annuaire Diplomatique et Consulaire* for 1914 lists some 18 per cent (approximately 135) of its members as graduates of Sciences Politiques, but this list includes retired diplomats who retained only tenuous links with the Ministry by their membership of unimportant committees. If only the key departments of the central administration are counted, approximately 45 per cent were from the School and only 13 per cent were born before 1871. (In the Personnel Division everyone was from Sciences Politiques and no one was born before 1871.) Although the British Foreign Office was, as Zara Steiner has shown, stocked with an élite principally from Eton, Winchester, Harrow, Rugby and Oxbridge,[12] it was the affiliation to a certain social order not the content of the education itself which produced its cohesion and determined its modes of thinking. With Sciences Po, the nature and aims of the education formed the new caste.

It was only after the Boer War that a demand for expertise and a general raising of administrative standards in British government took place. Even so, the 'emphasis continued to be on the gentleman trained in the classics or one of the humane subjects'.[13] In France the desire to improve the calibre of government had manifested itself considerably earlier and had different results. Whereas the amateurism and inefficiencies of the British system had been shown up by the Boer War, across the Channel the Franco-Prussian War had had the same effect over a quarter of a century before.[14] The French Civil Service already had a tradition of specialised education dating from Napoleon and before in the form of the *grandes écoles*, but it could only be applied in practical tasks such as engineering or soldiering – public administration and diplomacy usually came under the umbrella training of law. Typifying the growing interest of the age in the social sciences and the power of education, Emile Boutmy decided that the art of government needed its own specialised preparation and founded the Ecole Libre des Sciences Politiques in the rue St Guillaume in Paris in 1872.[15] His ideal, which became the school's, was an education based on the practical rather than the theoretical workings of the state, which at the same time would develop personal initiative, independence of mind and a spirit of leadership.

The School was an immediate success, aided by its position outside the state educational network. As a private foundation charging expensive fees it attracted French conservative society alienated from university circles by the spread of republicanism and anti-clericalism, especially after Dreyfus. Men aspiring to a career in the Civil Service enrolled in the section which prepared for the appropriate entrance examination: diplomacy, administration, public finance, private finance or general. 'A Sciences Po snobbery' developed which further encouraged the bright, ambitious, aristocratic and upper-middle-class youth to seek the 'diplome', which was soon a virtual condition of entry to the Quai d'Orsay. The diplomatic section prepared so thoroughly for the entrance examination that graduates were said to be certain of success.

It is not surprising that the *esprit de corps* of the school should continue into the Ministry. Diplomats willingly acknowledged their debt to the School.[16] What might be defined as a 'Sciences Po clique' appears to have grown up. Ambassadors like the Cambon brothers and Barrère, too old to have graduated from the rue St Guillaume, complained increasingly of the ambition, complacency and hostility of the younger elements in the 'bureaux'. Jules Cambon spoke of 'presumptuous and ambitious youngsters'. This was during a period when the graduates were a rapidly increasing majority of the new recruits to the Quai and it is not unreasonable to assume that they were largely to blame. They were certainly proud of their specialised training and eager to exploit it. It is not surprising therefore that the old Ambassadors, whom they regarded as being as entrenched in their posts as in their views, and whose absence of vocational training they were likely to deprecate, should come under attack. The ageing ambassadors even had to be careful in their choice of diplomatic illnesses. In December 1912, the French ambassador in Berlin, Jules Cambon, casting around for an excuse to turn down the tiresome task of representing the President of the Republic at a royal funeral in Munich could think of none other than health, and commented: 'But at our age one should no longer claim to be ill. They think you are senile.'[17]

Most graduates of Sciences Politiques adhered to the liberal political philosophy of Alexis de Tocqueville. But their nationalist spirit had been heightened. The diplomat, de Saint Aulaire, acknowledged his debt and that of the 'bureaux' to his former professors for the exclusively national character of their teaching. From the First Moroccan Crisis of 1905 nationalist sentiment developed among French upper-middle-class educated youth, with the Ecole des Sciences Politiques in the vanguard. A best-selling study of French contemporary youth entitled *Les jeunes gens d'aujourd'hui*, written by two nationalist writers under the pseudonym of Agathon, explained that: 'It is no longer . . . possible to find in the "grandes écoles" students who profess anti-patriotism . . . At the Faculty of Law, at the Ecole des Sciences Politiques, national feeling is extremely keen, almost irascible.'[18]

The graduates' nationalism was carried forward into the 'bureaux'. Jules Cambon's policy of *détente* with Germany was dogged to such an extent by this young element that he was forced to send most of his important despatches under the cover of personal correspondence direct to the Minister. On 21 November 1909, wishing to relate certain sensitive issues taking place in Alsace–Lorraine, he wrote to Foreign Minister Pichon: 'I am sending you this despatch in a personal letter because the squall which is building up in Alsace–Lorraine should, to my mind, be covered up with greater care than would be likely from the young men in the corridors of the Ministry if this despatch circulated too freely in the "bureaux".'[19] Before and during the Agadir negotiations Cambon was constantly obstructed by these young anti-Germans. Indeed, he laid a good deal of the blame for Agadir at their feet and at those of the Colonials. By July his 'heart full of bitterness' he was seriously contemplating resignation: 'We can no longer serve with the young rascals who direct us.'[20]

The Berlin embassy was not the only target; Camille Barrère's pro-Italian policy was constantly under fire from the 'bureaux', who saw any flirtation with Triple Alliance members as an anti-patriotic act.[21] Throughout his pamphlet Pognon referred to this phenomenon as 'the irresistable upsurge of the young'.[22] They also had policies of their own towards Austria–Hungary and the Ottoman Empire, based on national self-determination, where the influence of Sciences Politiques can clearly be seen once again. The diplomat, Robert de Billy, confessed:

> I believed like many students of Sciences Po, in the future of the Slav world . . . Already we considered Francis Joseph's demise imminent, and were constructing systems based on the finally autonomous Czecks and Yugoslavs. And then the division of the Ottoman Empire would make it possible to satisfy all Christendom.[23]

The effects of these beliefs, which became subversive policies when carried into the 'bureaux', were felt by ministers and Ambassadors alike. They blatantly conflicted with the tenets of traditional French foreign policy. At the beginning of the twentieth century France was opposed to any modification of the *status quo* in the Near East which might upset the Ottoman Empire and bring to an end France's privileged position in Syria and the Lebanon. From 1912 to 1914 Poincaré constantly worked to maintain the integrity of the Ottoman Empire in the face of substantial opposition from the 'bureaux'. Doubtless it was the Sciences Po grouping which systematically obstructed Ambassador Philippe Crozier's pro-Habsburg policy before 1912. It is perhaps significant that the diplomat chosen by Pichon to act as Plenipotentiary Minister at the Vienna embassy with strict instructions to tame Crozier's austrophile diplomacy, was de Saint Aulaire, a brilliant graduate of Sciences Po, who was to oppose his chief constantly and work to bring about his downfall. Maurice Bompard, Ambassador in Constantinople, and strongly in favour of maintaining the integrity of the Ottoman Empire, was almost used to attacks from the 'bureaux', but in April 1911 during negotiations over the construction of railways in Turkey he was forced to complain bitterly to Paul Cambon and ask for help in stopping their increase. He had already tried writing to Foreign Minister Cruppi, but there was not much the ineffectual Cruppi could do to discipline them at a time when they were at their most powerful.

More cohesive and single-minded than the Sciences Politiques element was the Colonial faction. In fact they overlapped each other as many of the Colonials were graduates of Sciences Politiques and the nationalism of the School was synonymous with colonial expansion. Many of the professors and heroes of the School's students were members of the Colonial movement: for example, Emile Boutmy, Vogüe and Lyautey.[24] Indeed, the School considered colonial expansion to be of sufficient importance to warrant the creation, in 1887, of a whole new section for the training of future colonial administrators. The head of the section, comprising seven professorial chairs, was the well-known intellectual exponent of colonial expansion, Paul Leroy-Beaulieu, who 'made the Ecole Libre the forum for his apology for French expansion, especially in North Africa'.[25] The Colonial faction in the Quai worked for the continual expansion of France's colonial empire, and like other groups in the Ministry had reinforced its position by taking advantage of the disorganisation after 1907 and the weakness of Foreign Ministers. Furthermore, it had the backing of its political wing, the Colonial Party. As the latter had focused its attention on expansion in North Africa, it is not surprising that the Colonial faction had gained a monopoly of the Quai d'Orsay departments which dealt with these affairs: the Moroccan and Tunisian services. It was essentially from these strongholds that they pursued their policies or worked to sabotage others.

Once again Jules Cambon was a prime target. His policy of improving relations with Germany in Europe by making certain concessions to her in the colonies was anathema to the Colonials. He had first crossed swords with them during his days as Governor General in Algeria. Unfortunately, his appointment to Berlin in 1907 had coincided with a growth in their power. In 1908 he was already feverishly writing letters to Pichon warning of the military projects on the Algerian frontiers of Colonials such as General Lyautey, whom he described as 'an apprentice Boulanger but more distinguished than the other'. And he added:'It worries me to rediscover my old adversaries from Algeria.' He complained to his brother that the Colonials were making him lose all moral authority in Berlin[26] but Pichon was too weak to do anything. As Pichon remained Minister until March 1911 their activities went unchecked; but his replacement by Jean Cruppi was disastrous. The spring of 1911 was the climax. Cruppi had no experience of foreign affairs and could be influenced by the anti-German 'bureaux'. Thus Maurice Herbette, *chef de cabinet*, Edmond Bapst, Political Director and Alexandre Conty, Deputy Director, gained ascendancy over the Quai d'Orsay. It was on the shoulders of these intransigent nationalist officials that Cambon and Joseph Caillaux squarely placed the blame for the Agadir crisis.

Just as Pichon, pressed by Jules Cambon, had been willing to respect the letter of the law as far as Franco-German co-operation in Morocco was concerned, so Cruppi, dominated by the 'bureaux', refused. His first move was to deem invalid an agreement with Germany for the construction of a Moroccan railway, which was negotiated under Pichon's ministry and was ready for signature. He blocked all Franco-German co-operation without formally denouncing it. Jules Cambon warned that the Moroccan question was about to flare up. He criticised French intransigence towards Spain and Germany, partners in Morocco according to the Algeciras agreement of 1906. Meanwhile in Morocco, riots against the Sultan among the indigenous population in the principal town, Fez, provided a pretext for a French military expedition to occupy the town to protect the European population. On 17 April, two days before Easter, when members of the government had already dispersed, Cruppi gave the order for the French troops to march, and Jules Cambon wrote to his brother: 'I cannot dismiss from my mind the possibility of war'. He blamed the 'recklessness and impatience of our agents in Morocco' and proposed a more gradual approach than that of the Colonials and the 'war-mongers'.[27] He suggested that Moroccan policy was decided by the Colonial Party and implemented by permanent officials – a cabal he thought 'eminently capable of stupidity in Moroccan affairs because it is the flower of Algerianism and of Colonialism'.[28]

The occupation of Fez placed central Morocco under French control. France continued to postpone any withdrawal of the troops, with the obvious intention of securing a *de facto* protectorate over Morocco and placing a *fait accompli* before Germany. This blatantly flouted the 1906 and 1909 agreements, which guaranteed to Germany a number of rights in Moroccan affairs. The circumstances in which orders had been issued to the expedition and its continuing presence at Fez, in which the feeble Foreign Minister Cruppi could only acquiesce, was evidence of the Colonials' power. Berlin warned of the consequences but the French continued to prevaricate, despite Cambon's reports that Germany should be compensated. The inevitable happened. On 1 July the German gun-boat *Panther* dropped anchor off the south Moroccan port of Agadir and the Agadir Crisis began. France was surprised by this action, Jules Cambon was not. As he told his brother on 16 July 1911: 'I have been warning about the Agadir affair for 6 months.'[29]

The new Caillaux ministry was formed on 27 June. Hearing from Joffre that France did not have the 70 per cent prospect of victory on which Napoleon was said to have insisted before going to battle, Caillaux decided to negotiate. Talks opened on 9 July with Germany demanding the whole of the French Congo and France refusing. The French Cabinet was split between the Prime Minister, Caillaux, favouring a conciliatory attitude and Justin de Selves, the inexperienced Foreign Minister, firmly in the grip of his officials at the Quai. Those officials, including Herbette, whose fanatical Germanophobia was so widely known that the Germans had nicknamed him 'Herr Bête', and the ardent nationalist Conty, whom Caillaux described as mentally unbalanced, wanted to obtain Morocco without any concessions even if it meant going to war with Germany. They pressured de Selves to send a cruiser to Agadir. When Caillaux over-ruled this, with 'certain young officials from the Quai d'Orsay' they began machinations against him and Jules Cambon. Habitual press leaks apart, Conty even took the treacherous step of visiting the German embassy in Paris, without permission, in order to secure his and Herbette's policy.[30] Jules Cambon was so worried about this intrigue that he asked former Foreign Minister Delcassé to intervene, claiming that 'the press is manifestly employed by certain permanent officials to combat what I think are the very intentions of the head of the government'.[31] Caillaux believed that it was possible to come to a general agreement with Germany which would settle all her recent differences with France, the Alsace–Lorraine question apart, by a cession of colonial territories, and that this would be acceptable to public opinion.[32] The final agreement never went this far. In the end, Caillaux resorted to secret and unofficial negotiations with Germany which circumvented both the 'bureaux' and the Foreign Minister, and allowed a more modest agreement to be reached with Berlin on 4 November 1911. But this did not stop the press service at the Quai informing assembled journalists that 'it was war that we needed'.[33]

By the end of 1911 the Colonial faction was at its most powerful within the ministry. George Grahame, First Secretary at the British embassy in Paris, explained the problem that would confront the new Poincaré administration. Moroccan affairs, he explained, were still dominated by Regnault, Minister Plenipotentiary in Fez, who was to chair the interdepartmental committee set up to deal with Morocco.

This is bad for he is 'l'âme damnée' of the Colonial Party. He will be all for bullying Spain, for leaving the door open for harassing her in her zone and for future encroachments as regards Tangiers. Poincaré and the Cabinet may do the right thing, but their resolutions can be deflected by Regnault who will probably bide his time and work 'sournoisement' for the ends which he has in view. A French Cabinet is such a feeble thing when permanent officials in league with 'the colonials' are secretly against its policy.[34]

It was above all Pierre de Margerie, minister in China, and destined to become one of Poincaré's right-hand men in the Quai, who best described the hegemony the Colonial officials exercised over policy-making from their bastion, the Moroccan department. 'It is to be hoped that the Foreign Ministry will be able to follow several affairs at once and will not be reduced so much to being only the "Moroccan Bureau" however important the question might be.'[35] A remark by Jules Cambon was both an accurate appraisal and a fitting epitaph for the 1905–12 era at the Quai. Referring to the 'bureaux' he told his brother: 'All these wretched people are sabotaging foreign policy as they have sabotaged the organisation of the Ministry.'[36] The Agadir crisis was the apogee of power of the 'bureaux', but it also signalled their decline. The aggressive policy they had championed had brought France to the threshold of war. The Government was about to be brought down over the ratification of the Franco-German treaty, which had shored up the incoherent negotiations during the summer of 1911. The factions had become too powerful and too obvious. Hitherto the Quai d'Orsay had managed to eschew public and parliamentary scrutiny, but a succession of scandals in the Ministry meant this was no longer possible. The Political Director, Edmond Bapst, had been suspended. An official in the 'bureaux' named Rouet had been caught copying confidential documents and selling them to the press.[37] The Ministry's Accounting Director, Franz Hamon, had been caught embezzling funds.

Agadir was the last straw. Rumours were circulating in the press about the excessive powers of the Minister's *chef de cabinet*, Herbette, about the role of the 'bureaux' in the negotiations, about the actions of the Colonial faction. An internal disciplinary committee was convened on 18 November 1911 to investigate Herbette's actions. The charges, widely reported in the press, were serious: sending telegrams of protest to a foreign power in conjunction with the *bureau du Maroc* without consulting the Political Director and without ministerial consent; substituting himself for the Political Director; modifying Cabinet instructions to Jules Cambon; communicating alarmist stories to the press; obstructing justice in the 'Hamon affair'.[38] The committee's findings suggest a cover-up – Herbette was acquitted. But any other outcome would have meant a public outcry, parliamentary refusal to ratify the Franco-German treaty, renegotiation and possibly war. Nevertheless justice may be said to have triumphed: Herbette was demoted to Assistant-Director of the subdivision dealing with, amongst other things 'the international union for the protection of useful birds in agriculture'. Nevertheless, someone still had to be held to account for Agadir, and the Foreign Minister could no longer be the convenient scape-goat for the Quai d'Orsay which his predecessors had been. Press and Parliament began to clamour for a stringent review of the Foreign Ministry. The Senate Commission for the ratification of the 4 November Franco-German treaty intended to accomplish that task. Its *rapporteur* was Raymond Poincaré.

THE AMBASSADORS: THE CASE OF JULES CAMBON

Improved Franco-German relations are rarely associated with the years preceding the First World War. Yet from 1907, the date of Jules Cambon's appointment as Ambassador in Berlin, to 1914 a persistent attempt was made to bring about *détente* between Paris and Berlin. Jules Cambon believed that Franco-German *détente* could best serve the two axioms of French diplomacy after 1870: continental security and overseas expansion. He considered the growth of German power in Europe and abroad to be both natural and inevitable and that his policy was the most likely to consolidate and safeguard France's colonial empire and the least likely to end in a continental conflict. His policy involved a transformation of French diplomacy by ending the intransigence which he saw as having characterised it, often with disastrous results, since 1870. He confessed in May 1908 that his ideas were summarised fairly in Clemenceau's remark to him: 'It is said that you have remarked that you want to go neither to Ems nor Fashoda.'[39] These two incidents, the 'Ems telegram' and the Fashoda crisis, symbolised for him the recklessness and inflexibility of France's past diplomacy. In the wake of the First Moroccan Crisis any attempt to alter Franco-German relations along the lines planned by Cambon was bound to meet with considerable opposition. Yet he was often able to circumvent it. He relied on personal correspondence with his Foreign Ministers to offer views on Franco-German relations which by his own admission he would never have dared touch on in official communications for fear of reaction from the nationalistic and hostile 'bureaux' of the Quai d'Orsay.

The 1906 Algeciras Act provided a solution to the First Moroccan Crisis by proclaiming the sovereignty of Morocco and the economic equality of the contracting powers in the area. Following this settlement economic and financial relations between France and Germany, the most important parties to the agreement, enjoyed a boom. Franco-German financial *ententes* in the world were already common in Turkey, Serbia, Rumania, Bulgaria and South America; but from 1906 onwards German firms like AEG increased their interests in France by setting up new subsidiaries or by buying up shares in French firms. Similarly, in order to guarantee long-term supplies of ore German steelmakers, such as Thyssen, Krupp and Hoechst began to take over

French firms in French Lorraine and Normandy. This attitude was matched by French steelmakers like Schneider and Saint-Gobain, who increased their holdings in Lorraine and Ruhr coal, while Michelin and Renault established subsidiaries in Germany. Franco-German coal and steel consortiums were formed. This interpenetration of interests between 1906 and 1910 substantially increased commercial relations, though more in Germany's favour than France's; the former's exports to the latter increasing by 38 per cent between 1905 and 1909.[40] This encouraged business circles to speak out in favour of an economic and financial *rapprochement*.[41]

Jules Cambon's appointment as Ambassador in Berlin, in January 1907, coincided with this new climate. At sixty-two, Cambon's professional experience extended from the prefectoral corps, through the colonial administration, to the embassies of Washington and Madrid. A member of the old generation of republican Ambassadors, he was more moderate than the younger nationalist diplomats who increasingly filled the Foreign Ministry, rather in the way that in the British Foreign Office Thomas Sanderson represented the moderate view against the greater intransigence of Crowe and Nicolson.[42] He admired Jules Ferry's and Delcassé's flexible diplomacy and their willingness in the 1880s and late 1890s, respectively, to negotiate with Germany. Cambon believed that overtures from the German Chancellor, von Bülow, and the Under-Secretary of State, von Mühlberg, to France in late 1906 and early 1907 demanded a constructive response. But economic and financial negotiations quickly encountered the hostility of the nationalist press in both France and Germany. At the Quai d'Orsay diplomats such as Camille Barrère and Paul Cambon, Jules's brother, spoke out against any agreement with Berlin and official negotiations soon ceased.

Jules Cambon's faith in a *rapprochement* with Germany was unshaken, however. Under the acquiescent Stephen Pichon – Foreign Minister in the three consecutive governments from 25 October 1906 to 2 March 1911 – he was able to develop that policy. But this did not guard him from all criticism. In order to discredit him, the 'bureaux' of the Quai d'Orsay had leaked the gist of his ideas to the press. In June 1908 he wrote of how he had been informed that public opinion was beginning to think that he was 'carrying out a humiliating policy'.[43] To circumvent the 'bureaux' he relied increasingly on secret personal correspondence with Pichon to report on Franco-German relations. At the same time he became more and more convinced that it was the intransigent French officials and press who, by their ceaseless provocation of Germany were responsible for the atmosphere of tension between the two countries, making war all the more likely: 'What makes a conflict possible, and even necessary, is not the incident over which it occurs but the atmosphere in which that incident is born.' He attacked France's belief in the inevitability of war after 1905, and cited the genesis of the Franco-Prussian war as a lesson: 'If since 1866 France and Germany had not believed war imminent the Hohenzollern affair would doubtless have resolved itself – that was what von Bismarck meant when he remarked that as a result of painting the devil on the wall he was made to appear.'[44]

Jules did not shy away from criticising his own brother Paul, Ambassador in London. When the German Consul at Casablanca gave refuge to deserters from the French Foreign Legion in September 1908, it provoked a Franco-German diplomatic incident known as the 'Deserters of Casablanca Affair'. Jules claimed his brother had misinterpreted German policy over the affair, seeing in her actions towards France in Morocco and elsewhere mere perfidy, when the true motive as he would so often explain lay elsewhere. 'Economic interest is the principal motive for German policy in the world.' Only by coming to terms with Germany's economic interests could a settlement of the Moroccan question be reached. With characteristic adroitness he was able to reverse the conclusions of his brother's despatch and point them in favour of an *entente* with Germany, citing Paul's diplomacy during the formation of the Entente Cordiale as a lesson in how enemies could be transformed into allies:

> Our Ambassador in London indeed had the honour of playing a considerable role in the bargaining which put an end to the general state of tension generated by local difficulties experienced in many parts of the world with England. He is therefore a better judge than anyone of the benefit of having one's hands free with one's friends, with one's rivals, and even more so with one's enemies.

This led him to what was the crux of his policy: the necessity to encourage German colonial and economic interests in areas likely to divert her gaze from the European continent and from the French Empire.[45]

On 9 February 1909 an agreement was signed between Germany and France over Morocco. Germany acknowledged France's special political interests in the Sherifian Empire on the condition that both countries shared in the economic exploitation of the country.[46] French and German public opinion were generally pleased with the agreement. Financial and business circles, along with Jules Cambon, saw in it a first step to greater things.

After the February 1909 agreement it was hoped that other negotiations which were pending could be settled: notably the longstanding N'Goko Sangha affair involving Franco-German negotiations over the frontier between the Congo and Cameroon and the question of French financial participation in the German-built Baghdad railway. Although Foreign Minister Pichon remained favourable, negotiations made little progress. Leaks to the press from the 'bureaux' continued to criticise Cambon's policy. Cambon realised that the fundamental obstacle to serious *détente* with Germany remained Alsace–Lorraine. In November 1909, after incidents in the 'lost provinces' threatened to excite the 'youngsters in the corridors of the Ministry', he sent a personal letter to Pichon which, if discovered by the 'bureaux', was more than likely to end his career: he seemed to suggest that the question of the 'lost provinces' be left out of account in Franco-German negotiations for they would never be returned of German free will.[47] As he recorded on 21 November 1909: 'The Alsace–Lorraine question is untouchable for Germany, like Rome for Italy; it is the cornerstone of the Empire and the complicity of all the confederated states is after all the link which has united them.'[48] He cited evidence that Alsace and Lorraine themselves were no longer in favour of returning to the French fold. As he explained to Pichon: 'It is a sad thing to say, the French-speaking province is resisting germanisation less than Alsace.'[49] Recent research has endorsed Cambon's analysis.[50] As has already been mentioned, during the 1890s protest movements against Germany in the provinces had weakened, while those in favour of autonomy, from both Germany and France, had gained ground. And because Alsace and Lorraine were dissociating themselves from France so French opinion's interest in the provinces was diminishing. But it was a mere pipe-dream to believe that any politician not bent on committing political suicide would dare to say in public what Cambon wrote in private.

By February 1910 Cambon was speaking frankly of *détente*.

I know that in Paris certain over-heated patriots found it wrong that we should be capable of courtesy towards Germany, and declared that we will get no result from the *détente* pursued for a year. These are the childish views of simple minds who see no middle way between war and alliance.[51]

Which point on that scale between war and alliance Cambon was aiming at is unclear, bearing in mind his earlier reference to the way his brother had transformed an enemy into a friend. What is clear is that he would not always be fortunate in having an acquiescent Pichon as Foreign Minister. That change was just around the corner and it was to come at a most untimely moment.

By the end of 1910 Franco-German relations had worsened. German hopes for joint ventures in central Africa and the Ottoman Empire (strongly encouraged by Cambon) had not materialised. Finally, in Morocco things were turning sour, largely because of overzealous French officials, intent on infiltrating everything from the administration and government to economic and financial affairs. Meanwhile, as has been shown, administrative disorganisation in the Foreign Ministry at the beginning of 1911 had multiplied the intrigues of the 'bureaux'. Cambon was a prime target. He repeatedly complained of the leaks and obstructions from within the Quai d'Orsay. Worse still, on 2 March 1911, the Briand government fell and Pichon's run as Foreign Minister ended. Since the crisis of 1905–6 the Moroccan question had assumed a more serene appearance, marked by the settlements of 1906 and 1909. However, French and German intentions in Morocco had not changed, the former seeking its acquisition, the latter viewing it as a bargaining counter. The formation of the Gabriel Monis cabinet with Cruppi at the Quai d'Orsay led to the hitherto patient and conciliatory attitude of Pichon and Jules Cambon being abandoned for what J.-C. Allain has called 'the diplomacy of adventure'.[52] The new team influenced by the 'bureaux' at the Quai d'Orsay began by reneging on agreements – the Franco-Germany Moroccan railway, the new Moroccan loan, the mining settlement of 1910. This display of ill-will thoroughly contravened the spirit, if not the letter of the 1906 and 1909 agreements, leading Germany, to the joy of the Pan-Germanists, to the conclusion that no agreement with France was possible. When, as has been shown above, native insurrections against the Sultan had broken out in Morocco at the beginning of 1911 France had known that she had a duty to intervene, and an opportunity to seize. A French military column had been despatched to relieve the besieged town of Fez under the pretext of a call for assistance from the Sultan, which in reality was only extracted by French emissaries some three weeks later.[53] For Jules Cambon this new French attitude contradicted all that he had been working for.

> I persist in believing that we must pursue an attentive and good-humoured policy – and not a policy which is aggressive on minor issues and platitudinous on major ones. With my system I arrived at the Moroccan agreement of 1909 – another method is preferred; we shall see.[54]

By 25 April he was convinced that French diplomacy was at its nadir: 'I said when I came here that I did not want to go either to Ems or Fashoda – I believe I was successful: We are in the process of going to Fashoda by way of Ems, which is more stupid than anything.'[55]

Fez was taken on 21 May. Then French troops went on to Meknès, thereby violating the Algeciras Act, which did not give them the right to intervene in the Moroccan interior. Although Germany accepted the expedition she warned that France must not prolong her stay. France did, however, and so presented Germany with an opportunity of her own – a claim for compensation, which Secretary of State, Kiderlen Waechter, intended to back up in what seemed to France to be the characteristic German manner, with a display of force, and which he hoped would double as a diplomatic triumph if France backed down. Jules Cambon, true to his policy of negotiation and attempting to right a situation whose dangerous outcome he rightly forecast, discussed with Kiderlen at Kissingen from 20 to 21 June the possibility of compensation for Germany in exchange for a French protectorate over Morocco. Germany saw the opening and on 1 July the gunboat *Panther* was despatched to Agadir, with Berlin justifiably claiming that the Sultan's independence had been undermined and with it the Algeciras Act which guaranteed it.

Jules Cambon's policy and influence had been negated after March 1911. The presence of Joseph Caillaux at the head of the new French government, and the fact that Germany would overplay her hand in the ensuing negotiations, were to restore much influence to the French Ambassador. German demands for compensation in the form of the entire French Congo, coupled with threats of military action, excited the Colonials and 'bureaux', who pressured the feeble Foreign Minister, de Selves, to suggest a French riposte. But Caillaux refused, having been informed that the French army, lacking heavy artillery, men, and devoid of a Commander-in-Chief, was in no state to risk war. Furthermore Russia had made it clear that she would not go out of her way to support France, thereby repaying Paris for a similar attitude towards St Petersburg during the Bosnian crisis of 1908–9. But what Russia refused, Britain seemed ready to offer in triplicate. She feared that Berlin's action was intended to disrupt the Entente by forcing France into a bargain with Germany over Morocco which could jeopardise Britain's strategic and economic interests in North Africa as well as the balance of power in Europe. A speech at the Mansion House on 21 July by the Chancellor of the Exchequer, Lloyd George, let it be understood that Britain was ready to go to war in order to support France, and the Foreign Secretary, Sir Edward Grey, urged on by those suspicious of Germany in the Foreign Office, promised and gave diplomatic support.[56]

Germany had overplayed her hand. Just as the French military expedition to Fez had produced a German reaction, so German threats had provoked a British riposte. More conciliatory negotiations followed. But agreement was only finally reached in October because Caillaux was able to circumvent the 'bureaux' and the Foreign Minister by secret and unofficial negotiations with Kiderlen Waechter through Jules Cambon and a businessman named Fondère. Cambon deserved a good deal of the credit for the final agreement with Berlin after having fought off so many attempts by the 'bureaux' to sabotage his efforts. The Franco-German treaty of 4 November 1911 detailed and completed the 9 February 1909 agreement. The main clauses gave France the right to establish a protectorate over Morocco, on condition that German economic interests be respected, and that part of the French Congo be ceded to her.[57] Doubtless Cambon believed that all this could have been achieved by his methods at a much lower cost to Franco-German relations. Though the treaty ended the immediate threat of war between the two countries, it unleashed minority nationalist feeling on both sides of the Rhine. In France the revelation of Caillaux's secret negotiations opened him to charges of seeking a *rapprochement* with Germany behind the back of the Foreign Minister and brought his ministry down. A good deal of the blame for his fall and for Agadir rested on the incoherence of French foreign policy.

The general harmony of policy to be found at the British Foreign Office at this time was quite alien to its French counterpart. The unanimity of professional advice offered to the British Foreign Secretary seriously contrasted with what was available to the French Foreign Minister. Whereas in the British Foreign Office a calculated effort had been made between 1905 and 1912 to bring the key European posts into line with London's pro-Entente persuasions,[58] in France the tradition of 'grands ambassadeurs' made individual and independent policies the order of the day, even though these could occasionally, for instance in the case of Jules Cambon, be more sensible than those of weak foreign ministers clearly under the influence of nationalist permanent officials. But what could a mere Foreign Minister do to discipline a Cambon or a Barrère? What was needed was a new breed of Foreign Minister. At last France was about to get one.

3 Raymond Poincaré: A New Style in French Diplomacy

Raymond Poincaré was born in 1860 at Bar-le-Duc in Lorraine of solid bourgeois stock; his father was a state-employed engineer and his cousin was the famous mathematician, Henri Poincaré. From his early youth Raymond demonstrated the fastidiousness that remained a dominant feature of his character for the rest of his life. Few schoolchildren of eleven would have kept a diary as regularly, nor marked the time of their entries so meticulously: '5.05: I played and I wrote this diary.'[1] Too much has been made of his Lorraine origins, supposedly synonymous with *revanche*. Without question the defeat of 1870 had a profound effect on him, a ten-year-old boy uprooted from his home, forced to move from hotel to hotel for three months, only to return to live under German occupation for four years. It inculcated in him a profound mistrust of Germany, an ardent patriotism and a deep feeling of national pride. But this was tempered by his experience of the chaos and destruction of war. If anything, it made him wish to guard against further defeat and further war by ensuring that France would always be prepared militarily and diplomatically.

He obtained brilliant results in his *baccalauréat* at the Lycée Louis-le-Grand in Paris. His capacity for work was extraordinary. Gabriel Hanotaux, his friend for fifty years and a hard worker himself, recorded that Poincaré had 'a passion for work, a persistency in toil which I have never seen surpassed nor even attained by anyone else'. He was said to rise at six or six-thirty and begin his day by reading a page of the four or five languages he knew.[2] Not unnaturally he went on to study law and no doubt found satisfaction in the detail, rigour and order of French legal texts and codes. Having obtained at the age of twenty an arts and a law degree which he read concurrently, he set out on a career as a barrister, doing his articles and preparing a doctoral thesis on a characteristically dry subject, 'On the possession of furniture in Roman Law'. But he also had literary aspirations, and began to write articles for a number of newspapers and literary journals, finally joining the *Voltaire*, where he ran a legal column. Called to the Bar with his friend Alexandre Millerand, he subsequently decided to stand for Parliament. Elected as a deputy in 1887 in his native Meuse, a seat he held until 1903 when he was elected to the Senate, he was able to combine an increasingly successful legal career with a similarly brilliant political career. His intellectual rigour, competence, industry and incorruptibility earned him in 1893 at the age of thirty-three his first portfolio as Minister of Education and Culture. His management of the intricacies of financial matters won him a reputation and the post of Minister of Finance in the Dupuy cabinet of 1894 – a post he held again in 1906. This was to be his last cabinet office before 1912, but not before he had achieved further glory in 1909 with his election to the Académie Française.

Poincaré led his political career under a Progressist label, and championed secularism, but he followed the most tortuous paths in order not to stray from the middle-of-the-road position in politics. During the Dreyfus affair and the Church–State debate he carefully avoided taking an extreme position and was able to displease few people and emerge unscathed. In 1899 he declared his support for Waldeck-Rousseau's government but soon found that his own moderate ideas clashed with its severe anti-clerical policy and he finally refused to vote for the 1901 Law on Associations. This desire for moderation drew Clemenceau's barbed criticism in an article entitled 'Poincarism': 'Fine reckoner, he excels in drawing up for himself and his ideas an account of debit and credit balanced according to all the rules of the art.' And Clemenceau added that in this way all his energies were wasted in 'stating the advantage of what is good or bad rather than what could be'.[3] This was perhaps the mark of a certain self-doubt, his greatest weakness, which led him to agonise for long periods when making crucial political judgements, preferring as often as not to stay as close as possible to the *status quo*. His longstanding friend and colleague, Alexandre Millerand, put it more strongly: 'Civil courage was never the characteristic of Poincaré, he had to a degree which I have rarely seen, a phobia of responsibility.'[4] When his colleagues saw him rushing from the courthouse to the Chamber of Deputies they were said to remark: 'He's hurrying to abstain.'[5] Criticism pushed him into even greater self-doubt and even opened him to manipulation.

The threat of a critical article in the authoritative newspaper *Le Temps* could seriously influence his decisions. Gabriel Hanotaux summarised the problem best: 'He serves public opinion and he makes use of public opinion; it is his strength but he cannot do without it.'[6] It was largely for this reason that after his accession to the Elysée he slowly withdrew from overt intervention in foreign affairs.

His fear of responsibility was doubtless real when the question was one of conscience. Then, like Hamlet, he spent so long weighing the pros and cons of a problem that in the end he often eschewed all action, failing to come down on either side. When the problem was purely administrative his decisions were so precise and swift that they irritated some people. Paul Cambon regularly complained of this seemingly contradictory facet of his character when he attacked Poincaré, saying, 'what M. Poincaré lacks most is guts',[7] but on another occasion could remark: 'There is something Napoleonic in Poincaré's ways.'[8] This could perhaps be explained by the fact that once Poincaré had finally decided on a course of action he was not easily moved from it.

When Poincaré left power in 1906 he had managed to emerge from a number of political crises and incidents unmarked. This ability to stay out of trouble, his intelligence, capacity for hard work, personal integrity and tolerance annoyed others who would love to have found a flaw in 'la blanche Hermine'; hence Clemenceau's bitter pun: 'Il devrait être moins carré' (He shouldn't be so square). Unfortunately people mistook his austerity for insensitivity;[9] but he commanded a general respect which matured during his six years of absence from power.

It is quite remarkable, in view of the importance that foreign affairs would play in his later political career, that Poincaré had never taken any previous interest in them. He belonged to the group of young Republicans with Barthou, who firmly believed in the Russian Alliance, but that was not exceptional. Poincaré had begun his political life when a career was most quickly made in domestic politics. Foreign affairs rarely interested the Chamber, let alone public opinion. The Republic was still vulnerable; Panama and Boulanger had proved that. Here there was plenty of work to be done and a name to be made for high-fliers with clean records.

What provided a clue to the nature of Poincaré's forthcoming diplomatic policy was his character. The qualities which he wished to instil in France – honesty, industry and probity – were the same qualities with which his name was so closely identified. As a programme it was commendable but there was nothing eye-catching about it. This was true of all the tasks he undertook: Poincaré was a manager, not an innovator. This had been demonstrated in the portfolios he had held: no great reforms had been undertaken, he had merely administered efficiently. It would again be demonstrated during his term as Premier and Foreign Minister. Overall in foreign affairs he was able to square that apparent fear of responsibility for making important political decisions with an otherwise administrative decisiveness by stressing the need to maintain the separation of the two European alliance systems, Triple Entente and Triple Alliance, which he carried out to the letter.

As a result of the Agadir crisis parliamentary commissions enjoyed greater authority and power than ever before. The perennial echo of criticism from the budget reports was at last vindicated. The apparent renewal of the German menace and the affront to national pride gave new legitimacy to Parliament in reviewing foreign affairs.

Raymond Poincaré was nominated unanimously *rapporteur* of the Senate Commission called to examine the Franco-German treaty signed on 4 November 1911. Many of the former Premiers and Foreign Ministers in the Senate swelled its ranks. Poincaré had been chosen for his character, authority and competence. Only six months previously he had produced a detailed study of the Quai d'Orsay for the Senate Finance Commission in which he had denounced the 'unbelievable administrative disorder' of the Quai d'Orsay and called for a reorganisation.[10] It was in this critical spirit that he would lead the Senate investigation.

The terms of reference for parliamentary commissions usually concerned only administrative and financial matters, not foreign policy itself. But the new Senate Commission, which had to discuss the treaty resulting from the Agadir crisis, was bound to investigate the role of the Quai d'Orsay. The Quai would no longer be able to mislead the Commission with unimportant documents and blanket refusals of access.

Poincaré's frequent visits to the Quai d'Orsay confirmed his intense disapproval of its organisation and his distaste for its occupants, leading him to speak of his 'pitiful impression of this Ministry'.[11] This patent dislike of the Ministry remained unchanged over the following two years. Yet Poincaré was not opposed to the 4 November treaty in which Germany agreed to a French protectorate over Morocco in exchange for two strips of territory in the French Congo. However, the press was becoming increasingly indignant, less about the content of the treaty than about the way in which Caillaux had conducted secret negotiations with Germany, suspecting him of seeking a *rapprochement*. Proof of this came from a telegram sent from the German embassy in Paris to Berlin intercepted by the *cabinet noir*, the department specialising in the interception and decyphering of diplomatic communications at the Quai d'Orsay. De Selves, annoyed at having been totally disregarded by Caillaux, informed the Germanophobe Clemenceau. On 9 January 1912 Caillaux gave his word to the Senate Commission that no unofficial negotiations had taken place with Germany. Clemenceau immediately asked the Foreign Minister to confirm this declaration. De Selves's refusal to reply was a confession of Caillaux's guilt. De Selves resigned on the grounds that he was not willing to take the responsibility for a foreign policy with which he was not in agreement. Caillaux tried to patch up his Cabinet by offering the portfolios of Foreign Affairs and the Navy to Delcassé and Poincaré respectively. Both refused. Perhaps Poincaré refused in the justified expectation that he would be asked to form a new ministry. The Caillaux government fell on 10 January 1912.

The crisis was now out in the open. France was without a government and unable to ratify a treaty whose rejection could mean war. Public opinion was alarmed by what appeared to be a national and international crisis. The Bonapartist Ernest Judet wrote gleefully in *L'Eclair*: 'It is the débâcle and with it that of the "bloc", of the whole régime.' He was echoed in *La Liberté*: 'A national crisis. M. Fallières should beware: today he is going to play one of the last cards of the Republic.'[12] Experience of public affairs, authority and integrity were the characteristics which the press demanded of President Fallière's choice. Poincaré was clearly designated and accepted the offer to form a ministry. He assumed both the role of Premier and that of Foreign Minister. In assuming the latter office rather than the customary one of the Interior, he clearly indicated his intention to make foreign policy his prime concern.

French national feeling was brimming. From the outset Poincaré intended to harness it to the aims of his policy. The public fervour which acclaimed his ministry gave him a special mandate to restore to France her national prestige and her international role. It also reinforced his position as the sole formulator of foreign policy, and he did not hesitate to re-enlist this confidence when his authority was contested. With this support he possessed the weight necessary to tackle the recalcitrant 'bureaux' and diplomatic corps.

Poincaré's government was immediately recognised as a 'Ministry of all the Talents'. Delcassé took over the Navy, Steeg the Ministry of the Interior, the two eminent ex-Socialists Briand and Millerand Justice and War respectively, with Jean Dupuy at Public Works, Klotz Finance, Lebrun Colonies and Guist'hau at Education. With this strong ministerial team in position Poincaré could concentrate on the Foreign Ministry.

Poincaré probably disliked the personnel of the Foreign Ministry as much as he disliked its organisation. It was a question of incompatibility of character. As has already been shown, the Foreign Ministry cherished its tradition of independence and immunity from parliamentary interference and was the stronghold of social and political customs well-rooted in the aristocracy. Its members were often self-opinionated and pompous, stressing the 'particule' whenever possible and entrenched in frivolous, idiosyncratic tradition, such as the elaborate daily tea ceremony called the 'Ecole du thé';[13] furthermore they often professed a Parisian chauvinism. In this the 'bureaux' and diplomatic corps were the antithesis of all that Poincaré stood for. As a republican, he believed in a certain degree of parliamentary involvement in foreign affairs; middle class and anti-clerical, he was suspicious of the aristocracy and the clerical Right; as an austere lawyer he held frivolity and idiosyncrasy in contempt; as a provincial ascetic he espoused a stern morality compared with the laxity of Parisian morals. Immediately on taking office Poincaré set about reorganising the Quai as an efficient machine to execute his policy.

POINCARÉ'S REORGANISATION OF THE FOREIGN MINISTRY

If public opinion was generally pleased with its new leader and confident of what he would achieve, the most experienced members of the Foreign Ministry were considerably more sceptical. Experience had shown them that pulling the Quai d'Orsay back into line was a daunting task for any Minister, no matter how impressive his government. Pierre de Margerie, head of the Chinese Legation and a future close collaborator with Poincaré, remarked pessimistically:

> Our poor Quai d'Orsay has been tried so much; after four years' absence I found disorder everywhere and a reform will by no means be enough to put things in order. It is the choice of personalities which annoyed me most and it would be wrong to believe that changing one person will be sufficient to assure the normal working of the departments. It is the air of 'the firm'

that needs changing. Is the energy there? Will it be possible to resist the political pressure which will insist on maintaining agents who should have been sent abroad long ago or make them pay for their too rapid recent promotions by a stint abroad?[14]

Geoffray, Ambassador in Madrid, was equally sceptical.

It is said that the Minister intends to make some big reforms and considerable changes among top-ranking personnel. He spoke of it to me himself. . . . But twixt cup and lip. . . . We have heard so much talk of these changes that we can only remain sceptical once again.[15]

The challenge was made and Poincaré was intent on showing that he could meet it. The project to institute a post of Secretary General of the Quai d'Orsay on the lines of the British Permanent Under-Secretary, as recommended by Parliament, did not interest him. He scrapped it, knowing that it was likely to encroach on his own powers. Besides, he had no intention of delegating responsibility: on the contrary, he was resolved to concentrate power in his own hands. His designs for reorganising the Quai were already traced. Firstly, the selection and formation of an inner cabinet of loyal and efficient functionaries to work alone with the Minister on major problems; secondly, a small but selective reorganisation of the central administration; thirdly, the exercise of a quasi-dictatorship in the formulation and execution of foreign policy by making all major decisions personally or with the inner cabinet.

Absence of any previous experience in foreign affairs meant that choosing a competent and loyal team of advisers could be a delicate operation. The restaffing of key posts at the Quai after a change of Minister usually led to jockeying for position and political intervention. Poincaré therefore needed to rely much on the advice of an experienced, responsible and moderate member of the Ministry.

The obvious person to consult was the French Ambassador in London, Paul Cambon, who had recently celebrated twenty-five years in the service, fourteen of them as Ambassador in London. It had almost become a tradition for new Ministers to consult him; he had even been offered the Ministry himself. Poincaré acted quickly. Four days after he took over at the Quai, Paul Cambon was advising him on personnel. For the Ambassadors this was a godsend, as they had seen their influence decline so much in recent years. They were intent on making up the lost ground by packing senior posts with their own men. There were three key appointments to be made straight away: *chef de cabinet*, Political and Commercial Director and the soon to be created post of Associate Director (*directeur-adjoint*). This would constitute Poincaré's inner cabinet. Paul Cambon immediately suggested someone from his own embassy, Emile Daeschner, to be *chef de cabinet* and Poincaré accepted. For Political Director, Cambon advanced the names of two other loyal men:

Albert Legrand from the Rome embassy, a fervent Barrère supporter, and Pierre de Margerie, a protégé of both Paul and Jules Cambon. At first Poincaré appeared to wish to appoint an old schoolfriend, Maurice Paléologue, then serving in Sophia, but eventually decided that Paléologue had 'a little too much imagination' and Legrand was appointed. The Ambassadors' intentions were made indisputably clear when Paul suggested to his brother that, should he so desire, he could also have his own man from the Berlin embassy in Poincaré's cabinet.

> As for Hermite, this excellent chap, who is devoted to you body and soul, only asks for the chance to enter the *cabinet* to provide you with a spokesman. . . . He will do as you like. . . . Weigh up the pros and cons and see what is in your interest.[16]

The language was unequivocal: these men were to be puppets, Daeschner for Paul, Legrand for Barrère and Hermite for Jules.

Unfortunately, things did not run as smoothly as planned. Hermite stayed in Berlin. Although Jules Cambon probably advised this at the time, it was a decision he was later to regret for he would have no spokesman in the Ministry for his Franco-German *détente* policy. More seriously for all three, and above all for Barrère, two days after Paul Cambon's encouraging talk with Poincaré, Legrand, the proposed Director, blotted his copy-book. His mishandling of negotiations during the Carthage and Manouba Affair with Italy[17] led Poincaré to cancel his appointment. A more far-reaching effect of this cancellation was that it foiled Barrère's long-cherished plans for releasing Italy from the bonds of the Triple Alliance, by depriving him of his own man as Director of the Quai. He was furious and felt cheated by Poincaré. This was to play a noteworthy role in the formulation and execution of policy towards Italy.

Things went from bad to worse. Poincaré needed a swift replacement for Legrand. De Margerie was too far away; besides, he was needed in China, where the republican revolution begun by Sun Yat Sen was under way. Thus, the third and last candidate was chosen – Maurice Paléologue. The three Ambassadors must have been dismayed by this choice. Well before his promotion to the Directorship, Paléologue had been singled out as an intriguer. The British Ambassador, Sir Francis Bertie, immediately reported to his Foreign Secretary, Sir Edward Grey, that Paléologue was 'excitable and inclined to spread rumours and that at times his indiscretions were almost incredible'. Sir Eyre Crowe minuted this drily: 'This does not augur very well. We must hope the atmosphere of Paris will have a sedative effect on M. Paléologue but that is not the usual effect of Paris.'[18] The French Ambassador in Madrid, Léon Geoffray, told Bertie that Paléologue was not 'of the right stuff for the Directorship. He is too much of a *marchand de canards* and an alarmist,'[19] while the French Ambassador to Japan, Auguste Gérard, described Paléologue as a 'lamentable choice'.[20]

With Paléologue as Director the hopes of the three Ambassadors appeared shattered. By revoking Legrand and imposing Paléologue, Poincaré had demonstrated his independence. This augured badly for the ambassadors, who now found themselves working against the Foreign Minister.

Nevertheless, Poincaré's initial forebodings about Paléologue's excess of imagination had not disappeared. Too much imagination was certainly a strong criticism when uttered by the legalistic Foreign Minister, as Philippe Crozier, Ambassador in Vienna, was soon to discover.[21] Paléologue's shortcomings hastened Poincaré's decision to create the watch-dog post of Associate Director, which was to be given to de Margerie.[22] A further reason may have been the need to relieve the Director of part of his considerable work-load. Having shelved the idea of instituting the post of Secretary General, which would have lightened the Director's load but which risked posing a threat to the Foreign Minister's power, Poincaré had to find an alternative. But de Margerie had to settle matters with the new Chinese Republic and the post he was to occupy still had to be created. The decree reorganising the Foreign Ministry had not been drafted. Nevertheless Poincaré was already working in closed committee with Paléologue, taking all decisions and drafting most telegrams. In April Margerie was officially offered the post of Associate Director and in July he began work. It was expected that de Margerie would quickly be made Director. But Paléologue maintained Poincaré's confidence and de Margerie only succeeded to the Directorship on 14 January 1914, when Paléologue became Ambassador in St Petersburg. Nevertheless, he quickly proved his worth to the Minister as efficient, hard-working and loyal.

Poincaré now had the three key-men of his inner cabinet in place: Daeschner as head of the *cabinet du ministre*, Paléologue as Political Director and de Margerie as Associate Director. The first step in reorganising the Foreign Ministry – personnel – was complete. The second step was an administrative reorganisation.

It seems at first striking that in view of the disorganisation that had reigned at the Quai d'Orsay in the previous four years the final draft of the administrative reform of the central administration should be so muted. It was enacted on 23 July 1912 to murmurs of disappointment in the French press. However, when the aims of the reform are studied more closely, they give the impression that it was nothing less than tailor-made to Poincaré's designs. As *Le Journal* indicated, the merit of the reform was 'to aim above all at being practicable'.[23] Poincaré was not interested in reorganising the Ministry as an end in itself but as a means for implementing his own foreign policy. He knew that a complete reform of the Ministry would meet considerable opposition and would take a long time to implement. Moreover, it would stir up the hornets' nest of the 'bureaux' more than was necessary or wise. De Margerie had already explained what a stumbling block that could be.

I fear that Paléologue will not be able to do all he would like. It seems that he will have to keep on certain collaborators who, to my way of thinking, should have disappeared, if the foul air of the house was to be renewed. Doubtless he will not have been able to go against certain powerful influences. It is annoying because this time once again we will not be able to get ourselves out of the mire.[24]

This was why Poincaré wanted a quick, selective reorganisation which would allow him to execute his foreign policy with a minimum of fuss. Its aim was patent: to run the Ministry from the top and only from the top.

The first article, the mainstay of the decree, considerably increased the responsibility and authority of the first Assistant Director in the Ministry, making him Associate Director, the post given to de Margerie. Apart from looking after the Europe, Africa and the Orient desks, he was to deputise for the Director and to chair the daily meetings of the Assistant Directors and office chiefs, distributing the work-load and taking control of the interior service of the Political and Commercial Division. Moreover he was given the consummate power of signing on the Minister's behalf. Poincaré had created an almost parallel authority to that of the Director. The Associate Director took his place in the triumvirate of *chef de cabinet* and Director, firmly under the Minister's control. It is significant that he had imposed one important condition on the choice of those collaborators: none were to be of ambassadorial rank. Poincaré knew how French Ambassadors could present a challenge to his authority. Daeschner was a second-class Plenipotentiary Minister, while Paléologue and de Margerie were first-class Plenipotentiary Ministers. Poincaré would take a similar precaution in choosing inexperienced Foreign Ministers when he became President of the Republic. Overall then the essential levers of power were in his own hands; he had broken with the former diffused hierarchical structure; he had found the men for the job or created the jobs for the men. As *Le Journal* concluded, 'henceforth the regime established by M. Poincaré will substantially facilitate the operation of the wheels of the old machine of the Quai d'Orsay'.[25]

Having built the structural platform from which he would direct foreign policy, Poincaré could give his full attention to putting that policy into operation. His nomination after Agadir as a saviour of both the régime and French national pride demanded fast results. He understood that it was politic to achieve as much as possible while the national tide was at its highest and while confidence in him was brimming. With what he knew of the Quai this would be difficult. The attaché's mentor in de Saint Aulaire's memoirs had explained: 'The incompetence of our parliamentary ministers . . . is their principal quality, it puts them at the will of the "bureaux".'[26] Poincaré was by no means incompetent but it was sufficient that the 'bureaux' should think in those terms for him to be the target of intrigue. That he had no previous experience of foreign affairs and combined the Premiership with the Ministry of Foreign Affairs at a time when the 'bureaux' were at the climax of their power, could only strengthen their resolve to grab whatever they could from him. Sir Francis Bertie explained to the Foreign Secretary on 14 January 1912:

> So far as I am aware, M. Poincaré has no special aptitude for foreign affairs. In view of the enormous demands made on the energy and time of the head of Government in France, it is likely that any one holding that post as well as that of Foreign Minister, without previous experience of foreign affairs, will be very dependent on the officials of the Quai d'Orsay.[27]

Geoffray had even asked the British Ambassador to intercede in warning Poincaré of the power of the 'bureaux', a testimony in itself to their strength.[28] So Poincaré was aware of his precarious position. Three things governed the nature of his action. Firstly, there was no immediate chance of subjugating the 'bothersome and meddling bureaux'. Secondly, the 'bureaux' must be kept at arms' length at all times and in particular away from policy-making. Thirdly, the popular acclaim which greeted the formation of his government gave him virtually a free hand to restore French national prestige. This would strengthen his position as he intended to take all major decisions personally. His imperious manner and no-nonsense legal mind complemented his determination to obtain obedience, and this was made easier by his lack of sympathy for the staff of the Ministry.

Concentrating all power in his own hands meant taking on a tremendous work-load. But Poincaré was equal to it. By arriving early in the morning at the Ministry, wishing to see everything himself, studying everything in the original, replying in his own hand to Ambassadors, minuting all dossiers, opening all his post, demanding written notes from all his collaborators before coming to a decision, he managed to keep a firm grip on all affairs. His administrative decisions were taken with rapidity and he addressed them for execution in sharp notes whose sententiousness irritated many. Paul Cambon, who had never been a hard-worker, was ruffled by Poincaré's attention to detail and affinity for work. 'He ends up losing himself in his telegrams, his propositions and his paper-work,'[29] he told his brother. This was untrue as he well knew, for only three weeks before he had stated: 'Poincaré has his dossiers organised like a barrister.'[30] The policy was proving successful. With the help of the inner cabinet the 'bureaux' were being cut out of most important policy-making. Even the normally successful intriguer, Philippe Berthelot, Assistant Director for Asia, noticed the difference two months after Poincaré had taken control: 'The department is calm: the "bureaux" are kept out of things'.[31] Even a renowned gossip like Paléologue was conscious of the necessity to keep everything important from the 'bureaux' and was so successful as to be described by a contemporary French diplomat, quite uncharacteristically, as having a 'passionate affinity for secrecy'. This was a result of conducting all affairs in private with Poincaré in order to thwart any attempt to sabotage policies by the 'bureaux'. Consequently, 'he reserved for his personal secretariat the most confidential dossiers'. Not surprisingly a member of the 'bureaux' recorded in his memoirs that 'the result was an excessive concentration of affairs which was not without inconvenience'.[32]

Ambassadors and diplomats abroad were treated in the same imperious manner by Poincaré. He conceived of Ambassadors as he would have done of a general or *préfet*. Camille Barrère, tainted with 'Italophilie' after the Carthage and Manouba affair, was a prime example. 'He was sent the text of the communications he was to make to the Italian government, and he was ordered not to change one comma.' But he was not alone.

> All the Ambassadors were treated in the same manner by Poincaré. . . . It was like this as soon as he became Minister. I remember the scorn with which he spoke to me of the Cambons and Barrère, when I went to see him at the end of January 1912.[33]

But this was doubtless little more than bitterness on the part of Ambassadors who had grown unaccustomed to receiving orders.

Overall Poincaré's three designs for making the Quai a workable machine were successful, but it was beyond hope to cut out the 'bureaux' completely from all affairs, and they would not give up without a fight when their position was threatened. Poincaré imposed his will with an iron hand. He was the overall master of foreign policy and would remain so until 1914. It remains to be seen to what extent that policy was responsible for the First World War.

4 France and the Triple Alliance in 1912

In their original forms the alliance systems, the Triple Alliance and the Triple Entente, were designed to be defensive. By 1912 members of each opposing camp would have contested that fact and were willing to go to great lengths to break down their opposite numbers' block in order to ensure their own supremacy. Germany had consistently attempted to dislocate the Entente Cordiale and Triple Entente from their inception. Within the Triple Entente France was guilty of the same sin, though using less aggressive means – attempting to woo members of the Triple Alliance to the other side. It was a policy which, like so much of French diplomacy since 1905, had originated outside the Foreign Minister's office, and which its instigators, Ambassadors Barrère in Rome and Philippe Crozier in Vienna, continued to pursue believing it to be in France's interests regardless of Paris. Such policies were to a certain extent both a consequence and a cause of German foreign policy: German aggression invited attempts to parry it by weakening the Triplice, which in turn increased German fears of encirclement and finally completed the vicious circle with further German attempts to divide her opponents. Poincaré fundamentally disagreed with such policies as examples of ambassadorial insubordination and as strategic miscalculations. His own philosophy, as he himself confessed, was perfectly encapsulated in Sir Edward Grey's words:

> We wanted the Entente and Germany's Triple Alliance to live side by side in amity. That was the best that was practicable. If we intrigued to break up the Triple Alliance, our contention that the Entente was defensive and was not directed against Germany would cease to be true. Disturbance and possible war, it was clear, would be the consequence.[1]

Naturally this did not mean giving a free hand to Germany to dominate Europe, which would also mean war. He wished to steer a course between these two dangers. This did not rule out strengthening the Triple Entente in order to contain the Triplice and to guard against the resurrection of a *Dreikaiserbund* or an Anglo-German agreement, both of which would have been fatal to French security. Thus this foreign policy was firmly based on the idea of the balance of power in Europe, which Delcassé had bequeathed him. Indeed, Poincaré's foreign policy overall was little more than a reworking of that of Delcassé.

It was Germany which had forced Delcassé's resignation in 1905. Though the reasons were unrelated, Poincaré resigned from the Radical Sarrien cabinet a year later and forsook politics for the Bar. His six-year absence from political life coincided with a reversal of the Delcassé era at the Quai d'Orsay. Conciliation with and appeasement of Germany followed, at an official level at least. But Agadir was held up as proof that that policy had failed. Delcassé's policy was vindicated. For Poincaré, recalled to restore France's prestige and security, what better than to take up where Delcassé had been forced to leave off? It was a policy which required no innovation, simply good management, clarity and authority, for which the new Foreign Minister was eminently qualified. Maintaining the European balance of power implied little more than abiding by the letters Delcassé had exchanged with his Russian counterpart in 1899 and which made the European equilibrium an aim of the Dual Alliance. However, Delcassé had not been averse to undermining Italy's presence in the Triple Alliance. Poincaré, with characteristic juridical precision, wanted the balance of power observed to the letter – a total separation of the two blocs and a strict refusal to allow any penetration of the alliance systems. His policy towards the Triplice members would be one of peaceful coexistence. But then this would involve undoing the work of the French Ambassadors accredited to these countries.

FRANCE AND ITALY IN 1912

It was common knowledge that since the turn of the century Franco-Italian relations were the 'domaine réservé' of Camille Barrère, Ambassador to Rome after 1897. This strong-minded former Communard, amnestied in 1879, whose horse-riding accidents were desperately regarded as the only way to unseat him from the Palazzo Farnese embassy, was the epitome of independent Ambassadors. Perhaps more than anyone he conformed to Paul Cambon's description of an Ambassador: 'If this gentleman is nothing in himself, he is sacrificed. If he is someone and represents a policy, he is intangible.'[2] Barrère was someone and represented a policy. His Italian policy was founded in 1900 and well on its way to realisation in 1902. As early as 1900 Delcassé had summarised Barrère's ambition as: 'Set on tearing Italy from German domination.'[3] Although not opposed to such a policy, Delcassé conceived of it in a limited context: the future occupation and organisation of Morocco by France. He wished Italy to make the overtures which would lead to an agreement with France on spheres of influence in North Africa. Barrère was afraid that forcing conditions on her would lose for France this opportunity of pulling her from the Triple Alliance. It was Barrère's enthusiasm which finally contributed to the exchange of letters between the Italian Foreign Minister, Marquis Visconti-Venosta and himself on 4 January 1901. The letters, antedated 14 and 16 December 1900, were a statement of Italy's disinterestedness in Morocco and France's disinterestedness in Tripoli. Furthermore if any political or territorial modification was to occur in Morocco Italy reserved the right to develop her influence in Tripolitania–Cyrenaica.[4] The letters euphemistically spoke of being intended to 'consolidate the friendly relations between our two countries', but there was no doubt about their true importance. Visconti had even remarked to Barrère during the negotiations that his greatest desire was to come to a Franco-Italian Mediterranean agreement which would render the Triple Alliance clauses against France obsolete. Delcassé went one step further, claiming that if, as the Italian Minister had said, the Mediterranean question was the sole reason for Italy joining the Triple Alliance then this agreement took away any reason for her continuing in it.[5] Barrère would not let go until he had achieved this. He and Delcassé insisted that the Italians could not count on political and financial friendship with Paris so long as the Triple Alliance was directed against France. He asked for the text of the Triplice to be changed. The Germans, however, were equally insistent that the text should be renewed unchanged. Italy characteristically gave way to both parties. On 28 June 1902 the Triple Alliance was renewed; two days later the Italian Foreign Minister, Giulio Prinetti, exchanged letters with Barrère. They agreed that if either country should be the object of an aggression from a third power the co-signatory would remain neutral. Furthermore, if either country, as a result of direct provocation, should be forced to declare war, she was obliged to notify the other party to the agreement of her intention to enable the latter to judge if there was provocation. Finally, neither of the two parties would be able to conclude any contract, military or otherwise, which contradicted the present arrangement. Barrère was delighted and described the agreement as 'seriously limiting the scope'[6] of the Triple Alliance. This was apparent even to the Italians, who were, as A. J. P. Taylor explains, ashamed of the transaction. The letters were therefore given the fictitious date of 10 July and were subsequently replaced by identical texts dated 1 November 1902. This eased the Italian conscience in what amounted to a repudiation of the obligations of the renewed Triple Alliance before the ink on the treaty was even dry.[7] The fickle nature of the Italians in signing treaties would influence Poincaré's assessment of the importance of the Franco-Italian agreement.

Though Barrère still wished to push the two agreements to their logical conclusion, in the years following Delcassé's ousting from the Quai d'Orsay no further agreement was reached with Italy. She was reluctant to go any further and even showed signs of wishing to be forgiven her infelicities, of which Germany was well aware. Naturally Germany tried to put on a brave face by talking of wives waltzing with men other than their husbands and yet remaining faithful. But no one was more aware than Chancellor von Bülow that Italian flirtations could have more serious consequences, for his wife was an Italian lady who had eloped with him when she was still the wife of the German Ambassador in Rome and von Bülow was on her husband's staff.[8]

However, apart from a brief resurgence in 1906 at the Algeciras conference, when Italy supported France rather than Germany, Franco-Italian relations remained quite unspectacular until 1911.

In 1911 Barrère was given a chance to reactivate his policy. As a result of the Agadir settlement the French had extended their influence over Morocco, thereby bringing into effect the 1900 Franco-Italian agreement. Finding a suitable pretext – the Turkish persecution of Christians in Tripoli – the Italians attacked the Turks with the aim of annexing Tripolitania and Cyrenaica. Italian hopes for an immediate victory were quickly dissipated. Barrère's first thought seems to have been that from an Italian victory would follow the overall Mediterranean agreement with France, which would be the death blow to Italian participation in the Triple Alliance and would lead finally to her incorporation in the Triple Entente.

Unfortunately for Italy, and Barrère, events went badly. Turkish resistance proved greater than estimated. Italy's nervousness increased and with it her susceptibilities. She began to blame other powers for hampering her success. France was accused – not unjustly – of allowing arms to pass from Tunisia into Tripolitania to reinforce the Turks.

It was at this point that Poincaré took over at the Quai d'Orsay. It was inevitable that his Cartesian notion of things, which set the Triple Entente on one side and the Triple Alliance on the other with a great divide in the middle to be crossed by no man, should clash with Barrère's policy. That clash would be the first test of Poincaré's new style of diplomacy, which was intolerant of insubordination, and his new foreign policy, which was punctilious on the separation of the two alliance systems.

There was one other element in Poincaré's make-up which would render acceptance of Barrère's plans difficult from the outset: his estimation of Italy. It amounted to a kind of racialism. Poincaré was a Lorrainer and, while not ignoring the qualities of France's southern neighbour, judged the more fickle side of the Italian character with greater severity. Some historians have argued that this was validated by the nature of her diplomacy during the nineteenth century.[9] Poincaré was certainly aware of her past inconsistencies in diplomacy. Italian diplomacy in the Italo-Turkish war would entrench these views.

Italy's lack of success against the Turks led her to cast around for diplomatic support. None came from the Triple Alliance, and so she turned to the Triple Entente. Russia, who saw that weakening Turkey was a step towards gaining a hold of the Straits, acquiesced. Poincaré did not welcome this as he had evidence that Russia and Italy were putting into effect their 1909 Racconigi agreement, by which Italy acquiesced in Russian designs on the Straits in exchange for Russian approval of Italian ambitions in Tripoli. It also seemed that Austria–Hungary might graft herself on to this arrangement, which would be extended to the Balkans. This threatened the solidity of the already shaky Triple Entente, which Poincaré was committed to strengthening –

Russia, the cornerstone of French security, was working loose from the Dual Alliance and once again Italy was the troublemaker.

The 'Carthage' and 'Manouba' Affair

Barrère was in Paris when passions flared up over the Italian seizure of the French postal ship *Carthage* on 16 January 1912, suspected of carrying an aeroplane destined for the Turks. Albert Legrand was in charge of the French embassy in Rome. Poincaré telegraphed to him to demand the release of the boat. On the 18th another French vessel, the *Manouba*, was seized, carrying twenty-nine Turks who claimed to be members of the Turkish equivalent of the Red Cross, but whom Italy claimed to be soldiers. Public opinion in France was incensed. The next day Poincaré again ordered Legrand to secure the release of the boats. Legrand negotiated with San Giuliano, the Italian Foreign Minister, and was able to secure the release of the *Manouba*, but without the Turks. Poincaré was furious at what he considered a capitulation as well as a demonstration of the Rome embassy's Italophile sentiments and insubordination. Yet he realised how the incident could be used to teach a lesson to those elements in the Foreign Ministry and those powers who were not aware of the form his policy would take. Poincaré received further encouragement from the press, which talked of the Italian incident as an extension of the incompetence which the Ministry had shown during the Agadir crisis, and warned him that if he did not act with firmness his ministry would be discredited.

Poincaré's powerful speech to the Chamber of Deputies on 22 January calling for the release of the Turkish prisoners received a tumultuous ovation and aroused anti-Italian feelings. It angered the Rome embassy almost as much as the Italians. Barrère and his attachés feared that their long-cherished relations with Italy had been harmed. They refused to believe that Italy could be in the wrong as the Hague Court later ruled.

From this point onwards relations between Poincaré and the Rome embassy became severely strained. He began by reversing his decision to appoint Legrand as Political Director. This was as much a blow to Barrère's pride as to the future of his policy, which would no longer have a spokesman in Paris. He appealed to Delcassé for help, but to no avail. The whole French embassy was now tainted with 'Italophilia'.[10] Barrère retaliated by refusing any replacement for Legrand, who was recalled to Paris and effectively demoted – this was also intended to parry the numerous attempts by Poincaré to appoint his own man as chargé d'affaires in Rome. In this Barrère was successful, holding out for over a year until Poincaré had left the Quai d'Orsay.

The affair of the Turkish prisoners had still not been settled. The difference between Minister and Ambassador prolonged it. Barrère complained bitterly to Paris that unless the French press was calmed no settlement would be reached on the release of the prisoners, while Poincaré retorted that unless the Turks were released the press could not be silenced. This led Poincaré to abandon a moderate formula for settlement agreed upon previously with Barrère, leading the latter to adopt a proportionately more conciliatory attitude towards the Italians. But Poincaré was strengthened in his resolve by congratulations from Britain on his handling of the affair. More important still, his attitude had the desired effect of chastening Russia, who immediately declared her willingness to work together with France. Barrère's position was most seriously undermined when on 25 January Poincaré bluntly informed him that he had it on very good authority that the personnel of the Rome embassy had been misrepresenting his orders to the Italians and even shared the feelings of the Italian government.[11] That good authority was nothing less than copies of Italian diplomatic communications between Rome and the Italian embassy in Paris intercepted by the *cabinet noir* deciphering department at the Quai d'Orsay,[12] upon whose services Poincaré was to rely increasingly to determine his policy towards Italy.

The final blow to Barrère's credibility came on 26 January when the Italians seized another French postal vessel, the *Tavignano*, this time in French territorial waters. Still Barrère refused to criticise Italy. It was not until 5 February that France and Italy finally accepted to settle the issue before the Hague Court. However, for Poincaré and Barrère the problems had only just begun. The Rome embassy complained that Poincaré's attitude had seriously affected Franco-Italian relations. This was an exaggeration as a report from the French Consul General in Milan made clear. He explained that even before the *Carthage* and *Manouba* incidents a state of latent Gallophobia had existed in the Italian press, ready to express itself at the slightest pretext. Furthermore Franco-Italian relations had not been as badly affected as they seemed, and French popularity would be restored 'as fast as we had lost it'. This was corroborated by the acting French Vice-Consul in Turin,[13] while Paul Cambon remarked that the incident would do no more than leave 'a slight malaise' between the two countries, which would disappear as soon as Italy was victorious over Turkey and began soliciting international recognition of Tripolitania–Cyrenaica.

The *Carthage* and *Manouba* incident had several results. It confirmed Poincaré's prejudice about Italy's untrustworthy nature. This feeling was reinforced by the machinations of the former Italian Foreign Minister, now Ambassador in Paris, Tomasso Tittoni. His plotting with other ex-Foreign Ministers turned Ambassadors in Paris, namely Alexander Isvolsky of Russia and Baron von Schoen of Germany, was renowned. Tittoni's subsidies to the Paris press and his attempts to secure an Italo-Russian *rapprochement* annoyed Poincaré, who recorded in his memoirs how 'the subtle ambassador . . . attributed to me not only remarks which I had not made, but ulterior motives contrary to my explicit assertions'.[14] The *Carthage* and *Manouba* incident also confirmed Poincaré in his prejudice about French Ambassadors. He was said to have remarked about Barrère: 'We have in Rome an excellent ambassador for Italy.'[15] Consequently he relied increasingly on the Italian intercepts to complement, even replace, official channels of communication between Paris and Rome, a system he would doubtless have willingly seen supplant the Ambassadors in the other foreign capitals had French code-breaking allowed him to do so (the German code was 'lost' following the Agadir crisis). The incident also confirmed him in the righteousness of his policy of the separation of the two blocs. He must have baulked at the challenge presented to his foreign policy on reading Paul Cambon's despatch dated 25 January 1912: 'The question is not new, M. Barrère who enjoys great authority in Rome has been aiming for a long time at pulling Italy out of the Triplice.'[16] But after the Carthage affair the logic of Poincaré's policy had triumphed, as Isvolsky reported to the Russian Foreign Minister, Sergei Sazonov in June.

> As to the question of the formal exit of Italy from the Triple Alliance. Poincaré is totally in agreement with you in believing that there is no motive for aiming at such a result, given that it could only have dangerous complications. It would be best to maintain the present situation, because Italy is an arresting element in the Triple Alliance. Nevertheless France must not forget that Italy belongs to the opposite grouping.[17]

But Barrère would not give up his life's work, or his independent methods of action, just to please one novice Foreign Minister who, according to contemporary parliamentary form, could not be expected to remain in power for long. A further clash took place over a proposed Mediterranean agreement between France, Britain and Italy. Instigated at Barrère's behest, the project gave rise to a detailed appraisal of Italy's worth in the Triplice and her potential worth out of it.

Attempts to Come to a Mediterranean Agreement

As has been seen, Barrère believed that the Mediterranean question was the reason for Italy joining the Triple Alliance, and that therefore a Mediterranean agreement between France and Italy would render the latter's membership of the Triple Alliance redundant while smoothing the way for her passage into the Entente camp. In other words, if France allowed Italy a place in North Africa and provided her with the security she needed in the Mediterranean, then Barrère's dream could come true. As such the Italo-Turkish war was a god-send for the Rome Ambassador. Doubtless Barrère's logic in this matter was flawless, but unfortunately it was based on the premise that Italy's extraction from the Triple Alliance, let alone her inclusion in the Triple Entente, was desirable.

The Italo-Turkish war was a source of concern for Vienna, which feared any increase in Italian influence. It gave rise to a debate between those in favour of Italy remaining in the Triple Alliance and those opposed, which spilled over into French diplomatic circles. Maurice Bompard, Ambassador in Constantinople, noted that taking Italy into the Triple Entente might impress French public opinion, but it would be likely to cause serious problems: 'Liberated from the Triple Alliance and linked to the Triple Entente, she would become aggressive against Austria and oblige us to espouse her quarrel.' More serious still:

> in passing from the Triple Alliance to the Triple Entente Italy would break up, at least in appearance, the balance of forces in Europe; she would at least break it up in the Mediterranean and this rupture of the equilibrium could well lead England to withdraw little by little from the grouping to which she only acceded in order to counter-balance the superior power in her eyes, of the opposite grouping. (Swapping England for Italy would obviously be a fools' deal.)

As such Italian accession to the Triple Entente would be 'a Pyrrhic victory'.[18] Paul Cambon was of the same opinion, remarking prophetically that Italy appeared to be more of an 'embarrassing than useful ally' whose future actions under any circumstances would be dictated solely by her own interests: 'We have reason to believe that in the event of a conflict she would remain neutral or rather would wait for events before taking sides.'[19] But Cambon did believe that the Italo-Turkish war called for a review of traditional thinking about Italy. When she finally beat Turkey, which everyone knew to be a matter of time, and occupied Tripoli, she would have become an important Mediterranean power. Her presence on the North African coast could cause problems for France in Tunisia and for Britain in Egypt, especially if she decided to create a large naval base at Tobruk, which could be placed at Germany's disposal, thereby realising the Kaiser's dream. To guard against any such eventuality Cambon believed that a Mediterranean agreement with Italy was necessary. However, this would need London's consent and participation, for Italy, as a peninsula, felt vulnerable to the Royal Navy and consequently dependent on Britain – a sentiment conveyed to Cambon in the words of a former Italian Ambassador to Paris: 'We will stay in the Triple Alliance so long as England does not tell us to leave.' Barrère was also aware of this[20] and had constantly tried to convert the British Ambassador, Sir Rennell Rodd, to his way of thinking. Now, as a result of the Italo-Turkish conflict the Foreign Office seemed willing to revise its attitude towards Italy, though Sir Edward Grey remained reticent. But Cambon believed that the war would last for quite some time, that Grey's attitude would mellow and that France would have ample opportunities to come to an agreement with Italy.[21] Barrère did not possess the qualities of patience which Cambon and Poincaré were able to demonstrate in relation to Italy. The *Carthage* incident had been a setback for his policy and Italy had to be soothed. He calculated that the best way to do this was to conclude a Mediterranean agreement with her straight away, thereby giving her tacit support against Turkey, winning her good will and preparing her departure from the Triplice.

Sir Rennell Rodd was already converted; only the British Cabinet, and of course Poincaré, remained to be convinced. Barrère hoped that if he could show Britain's conversion, Poincaré would follow. Aware of his 'Italophile' label, he was careful to use Rodd as the mouthpiece for his own ideas, knowing that Poincaré would otherwise have dismissed them out of hand. But Poincaré was not to be fooled and confronted him with Cambon's despatch on his desire to extract Italy from the Triplice. Barrère replied: 'We have never engaged Italy to leave the Triple Alliance; but we have never advised her to stay in it.'[22]

Having been forced to bring his policy out into the open, Barrère worked to defend it. He claimed that if Britain reduced her naval presence in the Mediterranean at a time when Austria was increasing hers then Britain's influence over Italy would decline. And for Britain, to think of Italy's presence in the Triple Alliance as a 'dead-weight' was contemptuous. Why then had Austria and Germany tried so hard to maintain a 'dead-weight' in their alliance? Though Italy might be of less use to the Triple Alliance than before, her presence in it would in the event of a conflict allow Austria to devote more forces to fighting Russia by neutralising Italian forces on Austria's Alpine frontier. Furthermore, Germany was always able to manipulate Austria by her attitude towards Italy and Berlin could be certain, according to Barrère, that in a war with France Italy's presence in the Triplice meant that her help could not be mustered by Germany's enemies. As Britain was the key to Italy's actions, and as Britain and France's destinies were now linked, any reduction of the former's influence in the world would mean a corresponding reduction in the latter's influence.[23]

Barrère continued his campaign to convince Poincaré of the utility of his policy with a report on the 'Origin, value and significance of the 1902 secret agreement between France and Italy', which tried to absolve Italy of her reputation for duplicity in diplomatic circles. But Poincaré countered this with an Italian document, doubtless an intercepted communication, explaining to Germany the value and significance which Italy attached to the 1902 agreement. It contained instructions to the Italian Ambassador in Berlin that he should inform the German Chancellor that no agreement, whether political, military or otherwise, existed between France and Italy which contradicted the Triple Alliance or could diminish Italy's obligations to the allied powers.[24] Little wonder that Poincaré wrote to Barrère questioning with some irony whether 'the pledges given by M. Prinetti, in 1902, still merit on our part, all the confidence that you seem to attribute to them'.[25] Here was irrefutable proof that Barrère's faith in the 1902 agreement was misplaced in that Italian duplicity was not a thing of the past. It further encouraged Poincaré to seek Italy's true policy in the intercepted diplomatic communications and ignore the Ambassador, so that Barrère could be charged with only mild exaggeration when he declared to Pichon 'that all our policy was based on the "verts".[26] Our Ambassador's despatches count for nothing'.[27] Certainly Poincaré was more impressed by the decyphered intercepts than the reports from the Rome embassy. And his estimation of Italy suffered all the more from Tittoni's machinations with Isvolsky. Despite the latter's pledge to work closely with Poincaré, from March onwards demonstrations of Italo-Russian collaboration were far more in evidence: rumours of a visit by the Tsar to Italy, the announcement of a Russian loan on the Milan market; a telegram from Rome to *Le Matin* that a joint demonstration of the Italian and Russian fleets would take place in the Dardanelles to force Turkey's hand caused a slump on the Paris Bourse. By April Poincaré could stand Tittoni's misrepresentations and machinations no longer and instructed Barrère to secure his removal from the Italian Foreign Minister. But the strong possibility that Tittoni might again become Foreign Minister in the near future and harbour an even greater grudge against France led Poincaré to abandon this idea. In these circumstances the Italian intercepts were vital.

Barrère's proselytising of the British Ambassador in Rome began to pay off. London accepted the idea of a mutual guarantee between Italy, Britain and France for their respective possessions in the Mediterranean. Barrère began to think of the next step: for Britain to extend the guarantee to form a similar agreement to the 1902 Franco-Italian one, which France would then develop further – in short a new Triple Entente. However, Barrère wished the Mediterranean agreement to be finalised immediately, while Sir Edward Grey, not wishing to upset Turkey, would only begin negotiations at the end of the Italo-Turkish conflict.

As Great Britain had accepted the idea in principle, Paul Cambon, as was so often the case, followed suit. He informed Poincaré on 13 June that it was time to begin thinking of a Mediterranean agreement to guard against a renewal of the Triple Alliance with new clauses in respect of Tripolitania–Cyrenaica. Poincaré remained sceptical and according to the pencil annotations appears to have approved the cynical remarks of Ambassador Bompard, who stated that Italy was resolved not to commit herself definitively on land or sea, and that whatever agreement was reached with her she 'would not fail to counterbalance the one concluded with England and France by some agreement with Austria relative to the Adriatic'.[28] Poincaré's ideas were best encapsulated in the Madrid Ambassador's comments. Léon Geoffray deemed any Mediterranean agreement unnecessary – a substantial British naval presence in the Mediterranean was enough to prevent Italy and the Triple Alliance from moving into the area. Furthermore, any such agreement would be likely to annoy Germany: 'Will she not see in it an attempt to get Italy to leave the Triple Alliance?' What would France do, he asked, 'faced by a threatening attitude from Germany?' He also thought it unlikely that

Germany would make use of a port on the Tripolitanian coast. After all if she remained on good terms with Italy she could always use ports on the Italian coast. Even then Germany still had to solve the difficult problem of obtaining access to the Mediterranean. Poincaré wholeheartedly approved of these 'very judicious comments'.[29]

Germany discovered the proposed Mediterranean agreement sooner than even Geoffray had expected. The circumstances in which she learnt of it pointed to a deliberate attempt to scuttle the agreement. An article appeared in the English *Daily Graphic* which contained verbatim accounts of a despatch by Paul Cambon about negotiations with Grey on the proposed Mediterranean agreement and which condemned it as pointless. After some preliminary inquiries Paul Cambon blamed the 'bureaux'.[30] The 'bureaux' were certainly Italophobe and would have opposed such an agreement. But Poincaré had an even stronger motive. Barrère's idea of dragging Italy into the Triple Entente was beginning to undermine the very basis of Poincaré's policy on the separation of the two-bloc systems, as well as his authority: Paul Cambon had modified his ideas, Philippe Crozier, French Ambassador in Vienna, was attempting a similar policy to Barrère's with Austria–Hungary, while Jules Cambon in Berlin wanted closer relations with Germany. The Mediterranean agreement was the thin end of the wedge. The fact that only a day or so before Poincaré had wholeheartedly approved of Geoffray's condemnation of the agreement and that the *Daily Graphic* article reflected both his and Bompard's ideas on the untrustworthy nature of Italy further pointed to Poincaré as the culprit. If the motive was there so were the means. Poincaré's closer links with the press, in particular André Tardieu, foreign editor of *Le Temps*, made leaks a perfect means of scuttling the proposal. And this was what further inquiries by the irate Paul Cambon suggested – the Foreign Ministry's press service had communicated his despatch to an editor of *Le Temps*, who had passed it on to an English journalist.[31] Blaming the press service was equivalent to blaming Poincaré himself, as this service came under the authority of the *cabinet du ministre*, which Poincaré had recently made so loyal to himself.

If scuttling the agreement had been the intention it certainly worked. The German press responded immediately to the proposed agreement by warning that Germany would not stand by if it were signed. The *Vossische Zeitung* called it extremely serious and warned that it would lead to a realignment of the powers, while the *Frankfurter Zeitung* remarked that such an agreement would be directed against Germany. The French chargé d'affaires in Berlin advised against the agreement.[32] Negotiations had to be abandoned and the signing of a Mediterranean agreement between France, Italy and Britain was scuppered for good.

Even after the Mediterranean agreement had been abandoned, Poincaré still refused to go out of his way to improve Franco-Italian relations. He had the opportunity for doing so after the peace treaty of Ouchy-Lausanne was signed on 18 October 1912 between Turkey and Italy. Had France made haste in recognising Italian sovereignty over her new possession of Tripolitania, as Barrère urged, she could have removed some of the chill which was affecting relations between Rome and Paris. Instead Poincaré decided to use it as a bargaining counter in settling certain outstanding Franco-Italian colonial issues. Barrère was so annoyed that he appears to have complained to the *Echo de Paris*, for which Poincaré severely castigated him. Poincaré delayed because he had good reason to believe from Paul Cambon's reports that, the Italo-Turkish conflict being over, London was willing to resuscitate the proposed Mediterranean agreement. Thus he intentionally ignored a despatch from Paul Cambon to the latter's considerable annoyance, telling of an overture from London to revive the proposed agreement.

Poincaré's obstinacy in refusing any closer links with Italy did not rest solely on the rigid principle of the separation of the two-bloc systems. It had a more practical foundation. If France was to offer Italy certain guarantees for her security and independence then she must expect Italy to return the favour. And even if Italy could be relied upon, France had to consider how such an agreement would affect the European international system as a whole and, in particular, France's potential enemies. Would their reaction cancel out the potential advantages of such an agreement and, more gravely still, would the overall effects be negative for France. First, Poincaré was not a man to take risks. Second, experience gleaned over the year, in particular from the 'verts', had confirmed Italy's untrustworthiness and undermined the value of the 1900 and 1902 agreements, leading him to conclude that there was no point in extending them. Third, Germany's reactions to the proposed Mediterranean agreement bore out his belief that Berlin would regard it as an act of hostility, and at the same time it would invalidate the claim that the Triple Entente was a defensive agreement. There was no doubt that things were best left as they were, and the First Balkan War merely crowned that belief. On 17 and 18 October Bulgaria, Serbia and Greece, intent on taking advantage of Turkey's weakened position after the Italo-Turkish war, recalled their Ambassadors from Constantinople. Four days later the Bulgarian army routed the Turks. The First Balkan War had begun. Poincaré believed the equilibrium of Europe was threatened. Now there was a chance to sound out Italy's commitment to the 1902 agreements. A conversation with Tittoni on 20 November confirmed his suspicions – in the event of an Austro-Russian conflict over Albania Italy would take up the Austrian cause despite the Racconigi agreement with Russia. When asked by Poincaré whether Italy would respect the 1902 Franco-Italian agreement in the event of Germany intervening and France being led to support Russia, Tittoni replied that the 1902 agreement was subsequent to the 1900 Austro-Italian agreement and could not destroy it. Poincaré immediately informed Barrère that Tittoni had left him 'the very clear impression that eventually we would not be able to rely very much on the agreements undertaken'.[33]

Barrère was astonished by Tittoni's remarks and attempted to gather evidence from the Italian Premier and Foreign Minister which would refute them, but received only more equivocation. Meanwhile, Poincaré checked the content of the Racconigi agreement between Italy and Russia with Isvolsky and found that once again it conflicted with the Austro-Italian agreement of 1900. He made the following prophetic remark to Isvolsky in December 1912:

> neither the Triple Entente nor the Triple Alliance can count on the loyalty of Italy; the Italian Government will employ all its efforts to preserve the peace; and in case of war, it will begin by adopting a waiting attitude and will finally join the camp towards which victory will incline.[34]

Barrère was unable to overcome Poincaré's cynical attitude to Italy, let alone coax him into closer relations with Italy. On 10 December 1912 the Rome Ambassador notified Poincaré of the renewal of the Triple Alliance. San Giuliano, he explained, had stressed that 'neither a comma nor a full-stop of the treaty had been effectively modified'.[35] This was correct: not one comma had been altered in the text. What San Giuliano had failed to say was that a new protocol had been added in respect of Italy's new position in North Africa.[36] Although Poincaré was not aware of this, it was a silent, but fitting, judgement on Barrère's efforts in favour of, and Poincaré's actions against, closer relations with Italy.

One question remains: why did Poincaré not replace Barrère when, after all, Legrand was removed, Crozier ousted and, after a good deal of trouble, George Louis in St Petersburg uprooted, all on Poincaré's orders in 1912. The reason was simply that Barrère was too powerful and too much associated with a specific policy: the Franco-Italian *rapprochement*, the break with the Vatican and consequently the separation of the Church and State in France in 1905. Though Poincaré was unable to remove him, he did keep a tight rein on him. Barrère's embassy was isolated from influence in Paris by the withdrawal of Legrand's appointment to the Directorship, and by using the decyphered Italian telegrams Poincaré could afford to ignore reports from the Rome embassy while issuing Barrère with ready-written communiqués that, according to one French Ambassador, he was told to submit to the Italian government without even altering the punctuation.[37]

Poincaré was successful in imposing the faithful execution of his policy in spite of the traditional independence of a 'grand ambassadeur'. Barrère himself best described the state to which he had been reduced in a private letter to Pichon: 'To tell you the truth I feel like a big bird in a small cage battering itself against the bars each time it wants to spread its wings.'[38]

FRANCE AND GERMANY IN 1912

Franco-German rivalry was a major cause of the two opposing alliance systems in Europe: Paris and Berlin were the two poles which had attracted those countries now constituting the Triple Alliance and Triple Entente. Yet France and Germany, as has been shown, had not always been implacable enemies. Until the signing of the Entente Cordiale in 1904, it was traditionally Britain who was France's hereditary enemy. Contingency plans for a war with her, based on the assumption of German neutrality, were not abandoned until three years later.[39]

The major obstacle to any lasting improvement in Franco-German relations was the Treaty of Frankfurt, by which Germany annexed Alsace and Lorraine. Yet France's attitude towards Germany fluctuated between 1871 and the First World War, partly as a result of who held power in France and partly as a result of Berlin's attitude. From a threatening stance between 1871 and 1875, Bismarck moved to a more conciliatory one for the next ten years. enthusiastically encouraged by the 'peaceful' Republicans. The rise of Boulanger ended the *détente*, which was not fully resumed until 1894. Seven years of *rapprochement* were followed by four years of hostility under Delcassé, only to be followed by a further seven years of *détente* fostered by Ambassador Jules Cambon. The zig-zagging drew to a close with Poincaré's desire to go back to Delcassé's old policy, which was bound to conflict with the incumbent Berlin Ambassador's ideas. The fate of Jules Cambon's policy reveals that Poincaré's more pessimistic view of Germany was shared generally by policy-makers in France in 1912.

Jules Cambon's Attempts to Convince Poincaré of the Need for Franco-German Détente

Initially Jules Cambon was delighted with the new leader of the Quai d'Orsay. Weak Foreign Ministers had allowed the 'bureaux' to impose their will to the detriment of Cambon's diplomacy. Now it seemed that Poincaré would be able to keep them in check. Furthermore, as the Kaiser and the German Chancellor had both explained to the French naval *attaché* just before Agadir, a man of authority was needed at the helm in France to assume the responsibility for *détente* with Germany.[40] Only a month after Poincaré had assumed power the Germans began overtures on *détente*. The Chancellor attempted to make excuses for the Agadir incident by placing the blame squarely on the shoulders of the Secretary of State, Kiderlen Waechter, who, he claimed, was now being squeezed out of power.[41] As Cambon explained to Poincaré, the time was ripe for *détente* and this was symbolised by the Kaiser's request to dine at the French embassy in Berlin.

Cambon's policy of *détente* gathered momentum. He informed Poincaré of a conversation which the Kaiser had wanted passing on to the French: 'I only want and I am only looking for *détente* with France, but I am badly rewarded for my intentions. Every time I take a step towards her France rejects me.' For Cambon this was proof that the Kaiser 'has a persistent tendency for a *rapprochement* with us'.[42] But this growing climate of *détente* was fragile. This was why, when in March 1912 it appeared that the Reichstag's debate on a new Military Law would excite both French and German opinion, Cambon played down its importance and recommended calm. What annoyed him most was the firm and indeed accurate belief that the inevitable outcry from the Parisian nationalist press would be unrepresentative of nationwide public opinion: 'Alas it has been a great misfortune for a number of years that what is called public opinion here should not be the public opinion of France, but the fickleness of Paris and the government of scandal.'[43]

Jules Cambon soon decided that the time had come to explain Germany's motives in wanting *détente* with France. He took the opportunity of using his British colleague's view on the subject as a vehicle for his own ideas. Sir Edward Goschen believed that Germany was uncertain as to whether or not she should begin a *rapprochement* with Britain or France because she was not 'satisfied with her own position as it arises from her alliances'.[44] There was much to be said for this analysis. To Germany's surprise, Agadir, and in particular British diplomatic support for France, had demonstrated the greater unity of the Triple Entente. Conversely the Triple Alliance was showing serious signs of stress: neither Austria–Hungary nor Italy had afforded Germany much support. In the years preceding Agadir, Vienna had been seeking alternative agreements with other powers to lessen her dependence on Berlin; while Italy's flirtations with other partners were common knowledge. Cambon believed that Germany was genuinely seeking *détente*, but Poincaré feared that Germany wished to drive a wedge between the members of the Triple Entente.

The rather nebulous German overtures to France were at last followed by a more tangible proposition. On 23 March 1912 Cambon wrote another personal letter to Poincaré informing him that Charles René, a German subject and former Wilhelmstrasse agent known to be in favour of a Franco-German *rapprochement*, had approached a member of the French embassy in Berlin. René had claimed that the editor of the influential French daily newspaper, *Le Matin*, whose circulation of half a million rivalled that of the *Daily Mail* in Britain, had requested a meeting with him about 'a complete change in French policy . . . in the direction of a *rapprochement* or a formal alliance between France and Germany'. In the subsequent meeting in Paris, the editor of *Le Matin*, Bunau Varilla, had told René that he was willing to influence French opinion towards a Franco-German *entente* provided the problem of Alsace–Lorraine was settled to France's advantage. René had replied that a complete restoration of the 'lost provinces' to France was impossible but that a solution on the lines of almost total autonomy for them could be found. The German Under-Secretary of State at the Wilhelmstrasse let it be understood that Germany 'would be ready to make large concessions regarding the autonomy of Alsace–Lorraine if French policy moved over to the German side'.[45]

Cambon's reaction was non-committal. These proposals went further than anything he had envisaged. He needed instructions from Paris before taking any action. Thus on 27 March, after a second overture had been made to his embassy, Cambon ordered all conversation with René to be stopped. On that last visit René had confirmed that Germany would be willing to make considerable concessions in Alsace–Lorraine but that conversations could only continue 'if the government of the Republic views them in a favourable light'.[46] The limit between unofficial and official conversations had been reached.

However, Cambon's interest in this overture was demonstrated by his immediate invitation to the German Chancellor to dine at the embassy. As he had suspected, Bethmann-Hollweg expressed his desire to see 'appeasement between our two countries'. But Poincaré wanted the René–Varilla conversations terminated immediately, thinking the whole affair a trap in which the German government:

> seems to be pursuing with tireless obstinacy a *rapprochement* which only a complete break with the past would allow. In listening to propositions like those of Mr Charles René, we would fall out with England, and with Russia, we would lose all the benefits of a policy that France has been following for many years, we would obtain for Alsace only illusory satisfactions and we would find ourselves the following day isolated, diminished and disqualified.[47]

From the outset Poincaré had preached the maintenance and separation of the two alliance systems which rendered negotiations for an agreement with Germany out of the question. If Germany was dissatisfied with her alliances France was under no obligation to come to her aid; it made diplomatic sense that the weaker she was the less of a threat she posed. But Cambon reasoned differently. A European conflict could only be averted if Franco-German relations were on a better footing. If Germany, at present, was having problems with her alliances then France should take advantage of her temporary superiority to lay the foundations of better relations for the future. Failure to do so would only result in German frustration, a fear of encirclement and consequently, an even greater effort to build up her military strength, leading inevitably to an arms race and unavoidable European conflict. This was what Cambon meant by the remark: 'By blocking up too many outlets of a boiler does one not cause it to explode?'[48]

Cambon was doubtless disappointed by Poincaré's blunt and blanket refusal to negotiate. While it would be adventurous to suggest that he desired an agreement on the lines Bunau-Varilla proposed, it was at least a basis for negotiation. His disappointment was reflected in the virtual cessation of personal correspondence between the Ambassador and the Minister, though with two notable exceptions: the first, probably despatched by Cambon before he had received Poincaré's order to end all contact with René, explained another conversation with the German Chancellor favourable to *détente*. The second, dated 29 April 1912, reported a further visit from René, now claiming to have learnt personally from the German Under-Secretary of State at the Wilhelmstrasse, the German Ambassador in Paris and Prince Radolin that Germany was in favour of an agreement with France on the basis of neutrality and the complete autonomy of Alsace–Lorraine. The Kaiser wanted peace 'even more than *détente*', but his efforts were often thwarted by the Wilhelmstrasse and men like Kiderlen-Waechter.[49] In the absence of any reply from Paris, Cambon began to adopt a more defensive attitude and tried to guard against any deterioration of relations with Germany. It seems that he wished to keep the German offer of *détente* warm until more favourable circumstances prevailed. Had he already guessed that the evolution of events in the Ottoman Empire would provide a suitable opportunity?

The settlement of the Agadir crisis by the Franco-German treaty of 4 November 1911 confirmed France's protectorate over Morocco. France's colonial aspirations could now be concentrated elsewhere. Syria and Lebanon, in the Ottoman Empire, were traditional areas of French influence which had been badly neglected – Italy was seriously challenging France's religious protectorate and Britain her economic, and even political influence in the area. Jules Cambon, who had ceaselessly crusaded in favour of better Franco-German relations as a passport to French imperial success, thought that Syria could be used to that end.

From June 1912 Cambon began to suggest in his personal correspondence with Poincaré and Paléologue that German and French policies towards the Ottoman Empire had much in common. The Italo-Turkish war, begun in September 1911 following Italy's claim on Tripoli, threatened to undermine the Ottoman Empire if Italy won, as seemed likely. The powers with the largest interests in the Empire were France, then Germany, but neither had made preparations for a liquidation of the Empire and a division of the spoils. Common sense, claimed Cambon, dictated a Franco-German agreement to protect their interests against inevitable Russian and British demands. But the prerequisite was better Franco-German relations, which explained his repeated pleas to Paris to calm the French press and moderate the nationalist actions of French officials at home and abroad. However, relations could always be soured by the slightest incident in Alsace–Lorraine, which was why he was invariably at pains to defuse the situation. He now repeated the suggestion first made to Pichon in 1910, that the question of Alsace–Lorraine should not be allowed to mar Franco-German relations.[50] (In December 1913 he would even tell his brother that 'what these people want is absolute autonomy').[51]

Jules Cambon was probably one of the best-informed Frenchmen on the state of Alsace–Lorraine's feeling for France. He was certainly the most realistic. He knew that the Alsace–Lorraine myth was dying. Most of the generation of '*revanche*' had disappeared, while some secondary school textbooks were even mentioning autonomy for the 'lost provinces'. By 1911 a large part of the Alsatian population had rallied to the German régime, while others believed that the autonomy of Alsace–Lorraine ought to be the basis for a Franco-German *rapprochement*. In the 1912 elections to the Reichstag, the movement of Alsatians closest to French nationalists suffered a defeat. A large majority of the population realised that any future war would once again ravage their homeland and so preferred peace to a conflict. Most were resigned to the *fait accompli* and while maintaining a feeling of piety toward France felt a certain loyalty to the German Empire which their Catholic convictions reinforced, as Church and State in Germany had not undergone the separation that had taken place in France in 1905.[52] But Cambon's realism was not going to make his ideas any more acceptable to Poincaré, or the latter's more right-wing supporters in the Chamber, because they had the added disadvantage of concurring with the policies of the Left. Though Jules Cambon was no man of the Left; the Left, like him, knew that Alsace–Lorraine was the obstacle to a Franco-German *rapprochement*. And also like him, they believed that there were two means of reducing it: by improving Franco-German relations sufficiently to settle the Alsace–Lorraine question, and by searching for a solution to the problem which would lead to a *rapprochement*. But in May of 1913 and 1914 conferences held in Berne by the French and German Left to seek an agreement on the first of these two methods proved fruitless. As for the French Right, though opposed to the idea of a Franco-German *rapprochement* sanctioning the Treaty of Frankfurt, they preferred not to mention Alsace–Lorraine at all. In a curious way the dialogue of the deaf between Cambon and Poincaré over Alsace–Lorraine imitated national politics on the same issue.

Jules Cambon's Conflict with Poincaré

Italy was victorious over Turkey. The Balkan states seized this opportunity to free themselves from the weakened Ottoman Empire by declaring war on Turkey on 18 October 1912 and the First Balkan War began. Cambon renewed his appeals to Poincaré for closer Franco-German relations by stressing the shared commitment to the integrity of the Ottoman Empire and the common interest in settling the war and coming to an agreement on mutual interests in the area. As Cambon told Poincaré on 14 October 1912: 'Force of circumstance has led France and Germany to adopt parallel attitudes in their respective groups on the Eastern question.'[53] The swift defeat of Turkey brought the future of her crumbling Empire into even greater doubt drawing Paris and Berlin even closer together. Though Cambon repeatedly enjoined Poincaré to accept a Franco-German proposal for mediation, Poincaré refused 'all proposals which did not include the participation of Russia and England'. Like Britain he was sceptical of Germany's proposals, whose objective he saw as the formation of a new diplomatic grouping to isolate Russia.[54]

Cambon finally lost his patience. What followed is important in demonstrating the Ambassador's complete isolation in the face of the suspicion and defensive reaction to German foreign policy which characterised Quai d'Orsay thinking before the First World War. In a desperate attempt to force Poincaré's hand, Cambon informed a journalist from *Le Temps* that the French government was making his task impossible by refusing outright all German proposals. The journalist informed the Quai d'Orsay. Poincaré was furious and seriously rebuked the Ambassador, who, nevertheless, remained unrepentant. Following this, Cambon's nephew, Henri, the Political Director's *attaché*, was requested by Paléologue to write to his uncle to explain the danger of his actions and the aims of Poincaré's policy:

> Faced with a Triple Alliance which gives the spectacle of a certain disarray we want the Triple Entente to form an unbreakable bloc. Mr Kiderlen's proposal aims at driving a wedge into our system in order to detach Russia from it. We cannot lend ourselves to the idea of introducing Germany into our system which, from that day, would be broken.[55]

This was unequivocal condemnation of Jules Cambon's policy without mentioning it by name and a clear reaffirmation of Poincaré's ideas on the rigid separation of the two blocs. Before he could have received this letter, Cambon wrote gravely to Paléologue on 1 November warning of the possibility of war with Germany and highlighting Kiderlen Waechter's remarks about France: 'It is impossible to tell you anything in confidence and to talk with you, you interpret everything badly; you want war. We will have it.'[56] Cambon was thoroughly depressed. But the concerted attack against him had not ended. On 4 November his brother, Paul, criticised his stubbornness and impetuosity in a letter thirty-one sides long. He had discussed the matter with Poincaré and wholeheartedly agreed with his policy and his criticism of his brother, whom he now proceeded to rebuke in no uncertain terms: 'As soon as you get an idea that you think is good you become annoyed if it is not immediately shared by others. You do not take sufficient account of the state of mind of the people you are addressing and you lament aloud on their stupidity.' But most of all, Paul's remarks revealed the defensive instinct of French diplomacy during this period. He reminded his brother that he was in fact paid to be suspicious of Germany, and that as a result of Agadir it was futile to want to make the average Frenchman understand anything other than that. He agreed with Poincaré that Jules was too acquiescent towards

Germany, 'opinion in France at the moment does not want to hear talk of an *entente* with Germany . . . you would like to see a policy carried out which no one in France is able to conduct. Take things as they are and do not get anxious about trying to realise the impossible.' Nevertheless, his advice was couched in terms of fraternal sympathy and he attempted to dissuade Jules from carrying out his threat of resignation.[57] Jules Cambon remained unconvinced. He continued to act as a spokesman for Germany's complaints despite further calls to order from his brother and from Poincaré.

The ambassadorial conference which opened in London in December 1912 to settle the Balkan conflict restored a degree of calm to the international scene, and also saw a transformation of Poincaré's ideas. He began to see the importance of safeguarding French interests in the Ottoman Empire. There was now a strong possibility that disaffection within the Empire might spread, leading to an intervention of the great powers, an internationalisation of the area and subsequently a decline in French interests in Syria and the Lebanon. In response to this threat Poincaré developed a Syrian strategy which would gradually draw him closer to Jules Cambon's ideas and closer to Germany.[58]

With hindsight it is easy to feel a good deal of sympathy for Jules Cambon's policy and actions in the pious belief that had they been followed war could have been averted. It certainly took courage to stand alone among French diplomats in stressing Germany's good faith and the idea that an agreement could be reached with her which would reduce tension in Europe. If Eyre Crowe, the Senior Clerk at the Foreign Office, has been described as a product of his times for his cynical views on Germany's development, then Jules Cambon must be seen as at odds with his times for his ideas on *détente*. Certainly his contemporaries, and not the most extreme among them, could point to what was happening in Germany to show that his ideas were at best unsound and at worst foolhardy.

The Nature of Franco-German Animosity

Just as the First Moroccan Crisis had awakened France to the German menace, so the Second Moroccan Crisis undid all that had been repaired afterwards by political, economic and financial agreements and gave futher credence to the idea of the inevitability of war with Germany. On both sides of the Rhine nationalism, at least in ruling circles, fed on the new tensions, which in turn increased it. In Germany dissatisfaction with what was seen as the humiliating Franco-German settlement of 4 November 1911 heightened nationalist sentiments which rested so much on the belief of the superiority of Germany and the German race. The apparent diplomatic triumph of France and Britain over Germany at Agadir exacerbated her fear of encirclement and the feeling that she was being denied her 'place in the sun'. Several leagues were dedicated to the diffusion of these nationalist ideas – the Naval League (Flottenverein) the Military League (Wehrverein) and the Colonial Society (Kolonialgesellschaft) – and between them they commanded a membership of one-and-a-half million members. The influential Pan-German League, linked with those above, could be considered to be the motor of the nationalist agitation with its recruits coming from the liberal and educational professions, as well as from business circles. Some of its more extreme and influential members had no qualms about singling out France as a target for extermination, such as General von Bernhardi, who in his book *Germany and the Next War*, published in 1912, explained that France 'must be slaughtered so that she will never again be able to block our path'.[59]

What was important in this German nationalism was not so much the influence it had in Germany but its impact in France. Many of the pan-Germanist publications were translated into French or analysed in French newspapers. And just as many Germans believed, quite erroneously, that the average Frenchman thought of nothing but *revanche*, so many Frenchmen believed that Germany was out for their blood, even though Jules Cambon went to great lengths to make a distinction between the views of the government and those of the pan-Germanists. In France also, nationalism was heightened after Agadir, though it remained very much the obsession of a minority. Indeed, a good deal of controversy surrounds the actual nature of that nationalism and the degree to which it was widespread. Many contemporaries such as the writer Anatole France and subsequent historians have recorded that from 1905 to 1914 there was a nationalist revival which swept through the whole French population. Claude Digeon has written that during that period war became the great national worry and that the French nation believed it would soon become a reality. The recent monumental study of French public opinion in 1914 by J.-J. Becker disagrees with this thesis and explains that it should only refer to a fraction of the population, with the urban, and especially Parisian, bourgeoisie in the forefront, while the rural world, the clear majority of the nation, was not anti-patriotic but apatriotic. Furthermore, the nature of that nationalism had changed. Although patriotic feeling was buoyant, it was no longer aggressive as it had been at the time of Déroulède or Boulanger, and the theme of *revanche*, inasmuch as it still existed, was more sentimental nostalgia than a political cry.[60] Raoul Girardet describes 'the nationalism of the "nationalists" at the end of the nineteenth and beginning of the twentieth centuries, as firmly attached to the return of Alsace–Lorraine, but no longer a conquering or expansionary nationalism; it is above all the defensive, retrenched and retreating movement of a wounded body'.[61] But even if this nationalism was more benign than in the past its exponents would never contemplate anything along the lines of Jules Cambon's policy of *détente* with Germany. After all, their nationalism remained defensive, and as such could not afford to perform what seemed to them to be acts of generosity towards Germany now that her alliances appeared to be failing her, and all this on the doubtful premise that Germany was not merely attempting to divide the Triple Entente.

Naturally there existed in France an extreme minority whose nationalism was as aggressive as that of the pan-Germanists and who, unfortunately, were given publicity out of all proportion to their numbers. Whether they were part of a nationalist revival is difficult to say because they were often difficult to distinguish from the currents of the traditional French Right, which had professed these ideas since the 1890s. In the arts world there was an undeniably nationalist current, which was reflected in the increase in influence of the Action Française in these *milieux*.[62] After 1911 a certain sort of military literature evoked an imminent Franco-German war, with such books as *La France victorieuse dans la guerre de demain* by Colonel Boucher, *Nos Frontières du Nord et de l'Est* by General Maitrot, or *Vers l'Espérance* by General Cherfils.[63]

Of course the military were almost by profession more sensitive to nationalism then the man in the street. It is sometimes suggested that by reviving the tradition of torch-lit military tattoos the new Minister of War in 1912, Alexandre Millerand, was attempting to encourage greater nationalist feeling in the army and among the people. These tattoos certainly enjoyed great success. But Millerand's motives were quite different. He hoped to restore national sympathy to the army, whose image was still tarnished among certain sections of the population as a result of the Dreyfus trials, which had only really been settled six years before in 1906, with the official declaration of Dreyfus's innocence.

Contemporaries and modern historians have emphasised the virulent nationalist feelings among French youth of the period. The study of Frenchmen aged between eighteen and twenty-five, published in 1912 and entitled *Les jeunes gens d'aujourd'hui*, is regularly cited as irrefutable evidence of this. It reveals the characteristics of a new realistic, sports-loving, adventurous youth, intent on revitalising France and preparing her for a definitive settlement of the Franco-German struggle. In fact this study reveals the temperament of only a fraction of France's youth, the rich Parisian bourgeoisie and in particular students at the Ecole Libre des Sciences Politiques and the Faculty of Law – the 'jeunesse d'élite' who were increasingly filling the French Foreign Ministry. It was to this minority that General Lyautey referred at the end of 1912 when he remarked: 'What I like in the youth of today is that it isn't scared of war, neither of the word nor of the thing itself.'[64]

Recent analyses of the content of French secondary-school history and geography textbooks have shown that they were clearly nationalistic, if not Germanophobe. The author of one of the most widely diffused manuals was Albert Malet, a teacher at the prestigious Lycée Louis-le-Grand in Paris. He has been a tutor to King Alexander of Serbia, which explained his openly expressed pro-Balkan sentiments. He saw the Balkan victories as the forerunners of France's triumph over Germany. In the 1913 edition of his text-book on the contemporary period he spoke of 'repeated German provocations' of France.[65] Though pupils in general did not make great use of these books, the bright young Parisian élite doubtless used them a good deal for cramming. Even the teaching of physical education in schools was given a nationalist flavour as the contemporary weekly sports periodical Le Gymnaste testified,[66] with articles such as 'For the Mother-country' and 'Am I Ready?', which attacked pacifism and exalted the cult of 'la patrie'.

In the fields of finance and economics Franco-German friction increased. French capital, withdrawn from Germany at Caillaux's behest during the Agadir crisis, never returned. However, the main reason for this was French bankers acting cautiously, faced with a worrying international political situation, rather than for any nationalist reason. But whereas before 1911 Franco-German financiers had collaborated on a number of operations a bitter rivalry ensued after 1911, notably in the Balkans. The reason for this was that political pressure, in particular from the French and German foreign ministries, was brought to bear on reluctant financiers. Intense Franco-German economic and financial rivalry developed in Greece. In 1913 the Quai d'Orsay tried to use loans as bait to lure Rumania from the Triple Alliance, but the operation failed because French banks refused to suspend their collaboration with their German counterparts. In 1914 in Bulgaria political motives prevailed in ending years of collaboration between the Deutsche Bank and its French counterpart, Parisbas.[67]

In France in 1912 the nationalist press, such as Le Matin and L'Intransigeant, instituted a campaign against what it saw as the German economic invasion of France and in particular the establishment of German subsidiaries under French names. The French government attempted to prevent this with legislative red tape. Despite this there was no real question of eliminating the long-established, numerous German interests in France, nor could France afford to do so without adversely affecting her economy, dependent as she was to varying degrees on German subsidiaries for mining, dye-stuffs, pharmaceuticals, electrical and mechanical goods, insurance and even the hotel industry. During the period 1911–14 a few French subsidiaries were set up in Germany but many of those already in existence underwent the same harassing tactics meted out to their German counterparts. At the same time a mini-customs war developed between the two countries with amongst other things France demanding the inscription 'fabriqué en Allemagne' on German products and Germany applying stringent legislation on the sulphur content of French wines. Despite this, commercial relations between the two countries continued to improve, with German exports jumping from 606 million francs in 1909 to 1069 in 1913 and with France over the same period managing a more modest increase from 606 to 730 millions. The nationalist campaigns never spoke of these salutary results but concentrated instead on other difficulties which further worsened relations.[68]

It is clear that the myth of French nationalism was greater than the reality. But it was still a major factor in worsening Franco-German relations.

Inextricably bound up with it was military rivalry. From 1912 onwards both countries competed in a fierce arms race. During the first decade of the twentieth century Germany's standing army remained at around 600,000. The principal preoccupation of the German staff at the time was to ensure that they had the capacity to execute the Schlieffen Plan by training an army of reserves which in 1910 stood at 3,700,000. Alfred von Schlieffen had been Chief of the German General Staff from 1891 to 1906 and had based his plan on the idea of an all-out rapid victory over France to be followed by a sustained attack against the giant Russia. Schlieffen believed that a massive German attack across the Franco-German border would fail. His Plan, finally settled in 1905, was for the German armies to move in a giant pincer movement, the considerably larger right wing of which would violate Belgian and Dutch neutrality, swinging round into France in a vast arc to catch the flank of the French forces engaged in an offensive against the slender left wing of the pincer in Alsace–Lorraine. On the eastern front the Austro-Hungarian armies would hold the Russian advanced forces at bay until the bulk of the German army could come to her assistance after crushing France. Schlieffen's plan took into account the intervention of a British expeditionary force to aid France.

Schlieffen's successor, Moltke 'the younger', changed little of the Schlieffen Plan but discarded the idea of violating Dutch neutrality. He predicted a victory over France in six weeks and pressed for an increase in the German standing army which by the law of 14 June 1912 was to be increased by 29,000 men. By the end of 1912 the German General Staff was asking for a further increase, which it justified on the basis of the reinforcement of the Triple Entente, plus the threat of an extension of the Balkan conflict tying up Austro-Hungarian forces in the area. Moltke wanted the numbers increased to 920,000 but Bethmann-Hollweg's bill, presented to the Reichstag at the beginning of 1913, provided for an increase of only 132,000 men. Finally voted on 3 July 1913, it allowed the numbers to be increased to 750,000 by the winter of 1913–14 and 820,000 by October 1914.[69]

French strategy was neither as stable nor as coherent during this period. Mindful of the disastrous lessons of 1870, the French Command had planned for an initial defensive strategy followed by a decisive counterstroke. This had inspired campaign plans XV (1903) and XVI (1909). But a new school of thought became popular, inspired by Colonel de Grandmaison and brought to the fore by the nomination of General Joffre to the newly created post of Chief of the General Staff during the Agadir crisis. It completely overturned the old strategy in favour of the 'outright offensive'. Instead of waiting for the German attack French forces would make a dash into Alsace west of German fortifications around Metz. Despite substantial intelligence evidence to the contrary, including the 'Vengeur' documents allegedly given to French Intelligence in 1904 by a disgruntled German Staff Officer, which explained the German intention to concentrate her attack through Belgium, Joffre refused to take this threat seriously, to France's cost in 1914. His new strategy, incorporated in the notorious plan XVII, which came into force at the beginning of 1914, was based on a double miscalculation about the strength of the German attack and the place of that attack.

Whereas French strategy appeared almost to ignore German strategy in the decade before the First World War, French eyes remained fixed on the increases in the size of the German army. The French High Command constantly worried about the growing gap between the French and German standing armies, which in 1908 was 116,000 men but was 165,000 by 1912. And all this was set against the background of a German population of sixty-five million compared to France's mere thirty-nine million. Since 1905 the Military Service Law compelled all Frenchmen to do two years' service. But by 1912 a campaign had begun in such newspapers as *Le Temps*, *Le Matin* and *L'Echo de Paris* condemning the 1905 law as inadequate. Once the new German increases were known at the beginning of 1913 the French campaign intensified until the famous Three Years' Law debate was finally settled with the Chamber voting for the new law on 16 July and the Senate on 7 August 1913. This raised the French standing army to around 700,000 men. Although calculations differ, at the end of 1913 the gap between the French and German armies was reduced to 50,000 but increased to 120,000 following the latest German measures. In 1914 France, without her colonial empire, could deploy 620 battalions against Germany's 670, but as seventy-two of Germany's total were destined for the Russian front, the military balance was restored. Even so French armaments still left a lot to be desired as the High Command had placed too much faith in its 75-millimetre field-gun while neglecting heavy artillery, which would be so vital when war came.[70]

Jules Cambon was alone among French policy-makers in believing that Franco-German animosity owed more to the irrational than to a cool assessment of either country's perception of the other. He believed that the preconceived ideas and false assumptions of a minority made the idea of Franco-German animosity a self-fulfilling prophecy with an arms race as a further consequence. *Détente* alone, he believed, could provide a solution. But it was not sought on starry-eyed grounds. The trust he was willing to place in Germany was all part of a prudential ends/means policy designed to increase French continental security and consolidate her overseas empire.

In the light of the outbreak of the First World War it is easy to judge Jules Cambon's policy as misguided. The linch-pin of his policy was confidence in Germany, an idea completely at odds with the views of the press and the policy-makers of the time. It was admirably summed up by Paul Cambon when he told his brother:

You must admit all the same that we are paid, you above all, to be suspicious of Kiderlen's [Germany's] suggestions. The Agadir crisis is still present in the minds of all Frenchmen and you must not persist in wanting to make them understand nuances which are beyond their grasp.[71]

Nevertheless Jules Cambon considered his brother to have a short memory. Everything said about Franco-German *détente* after Agadir had been said about Franco-British relations after Fashoda and yet he, Paul Cambon, had managed to reverse this position and bring about the Entente Cordiale.[72] Both examples involved a similar operation: a colonial agreement as a basis for a European settlement. Indeed examples of such diplomacy were abundant. The Entente Cordiale apart, there was the 1902 Franco-Italian agreement brought off by the French Ambassador in Rome, in which a North-African colonial accord became the basis for a continental Franco-Italian non-aggression pact. Likewise the 1907 Anglo-Russian agreement on Persia was one of the main struts of the Triple Entente. Even the Triple Alliance was constructed around a colonial agreement which brought together old enemies by reserving the Mediterranean for Italy and the Balkans for Austria–Hungary. These examples testified to the feasibility of Jules Cambon's strategy. Impetus to implement it came from the tendency in French foreign policy to identify Ambassadors rather than governments with a certain diplomacy. The proverbial transitoriness of pre-war Third Republic cabinets, with an average life-expectancy of nine months was much to blame. They came and went before a policy could be completed. The Ambassadors became the guardians of the stability necessary to complete diplomatic negotiations. Subsequently their names became virtually synonymous with certain treaties or agreements. Of Jules Cambon's colleagues Barrère's name was associated with a policy intent on pulling Italy out of the Triple Alliance and into the Triple Entente; Paul Cambon was associated with the Entente Cordiale.

When Jules Cambon came to Berlin in 1907 his name was associated with no specific policy. This inferiority was made more acute by virtue of the fact that he lived in the shadow of his brother. Although only two years older, Paul Cambon, according to one newspaper, was a household name, whereas Jules Cambon was identified as 'above all the brother of the Other'.[73] The desire to emulate his brother was very strong, so what Paul had achieved with the Entente Cordiale Jules Cambon had hoped to achieve with Germany first in Morocco in 1909, then in the Ottoman Empire and finally in central Africa. He understood the link between a colonial barter and a continental agreement. Germany was France's principal enemy in Europe but in the colonies she was potentially her greatest ally, certainly more so than Great Britain or Russia.[74] He believed an agreement could be reached which would iron out some of the contradictions in that position. Such an agreement could not hope to settle all differences by any means (for instance, Alsace–Lorraine), but then it never had with Great Britain, who, though she was France's friend in Europe, still remained her main rival in the colonies. The same applied to her Russian ally in Europe, who was increasingly a rival abroad.

Why then was his policy of Franco-German *détente* never taken up? The analogy Jules Cambon drew between the formation of the Entente Cordiale and a potentially similar agreement with Germany was acceptable as far as the mechanics of the issue were concerned: a colonial agreement linked to a continental settlement. What it failed to take into consideration was the difference of contexts.

A substantial difference between the pre-1904 and post-1907 periods was the balance of power. Before the signing of the Entente Cordiale, France had been in a position of inferiority *vis-à-vis* the Triple Alliance bloc, with only the Russian Alliance to rely on. France's international position was considerably more secure by the time Cambon arrived in Berlin and the notion of a balance of power existed as a possible safeguard for peace. With such a recent move from an inferior position to an equal one, France was by no means ready to negotiate a change.

Indeed Jules Cambon was perhaps right when he claimed that it was a vociferous minority who latched on to the problem of Alsace–Lorraine for their own bellicose ends. But the problem remained that this powerful minority called the tune. No French Prime Minister in his right mind could have hoped to begin an official policy of *détente* with Germany. Even a man of authority such as Poincaré, whom Jules Cambon believed was the sort of politician needed to assume the responsibility for such a policy, had he wanted to could never have done this after Agadir. His freedom to choose was limited: the Quai d'Orsay was stocked with increasingly aggressive young Germanophobes, as was the press, and even older diplomats in Jules Cambon's entourage, such as Paléologue, were convinced of the inevitability of war, with the old guard of Ambassadors seeing any negotiations with Germany as futile. Finally, there was still good evidence to show that Germany was merely attempting to use *détente* as a means of breaking up the Triple Entente. The only real option open to Poincaré was to declare his attachment to the present alliance systems. It was one thing for Poincaré unofficially to negotiate a colonial settlement with Germany in 1914, it was another to begin a policy of *détente*. Jules Cambon's policy involved a risk. France was not willing to take that risk. In the final hour she did not do so.

FRANCE AND AUSTRIA-HUNGARY IN 1912

Though the Austro-German alliance was the backbone of the Triple Alliance, Vienna and Berlin were not always the loyal allies that one might at first suspect. Well before the Bosnian crisis of 1908 Austro-Russian agreements and *ententes* had flourished on a number of occasions. Ever since 1905 Austria had been much offended by Germany's condescending reference to her as her 'brilliant second' and had begun under Foreign Minister Count Aehrenthal to think of reducing her dependence on her ally. Some people believed that the Triple Entente should take advantage of this opportunity to woo Vienna away from the Triplice, or at least come to some agreement with her on the lines of the Franco-Italian agreement. Philippe Crozier, appointed Ambassador to

Vienna in 1907, was of this belief. He was also guilty of Poincaré's charge that, 'all our representatives accept too easily the point of view of the government to which they are accredited'.[75] As a former Director of Protocol at the Quai d'Orsay and something of a snob into the bargain, he was immediately taken in by the pomp and ceremony of the Viennese court. And with the examples of how Barrère and Paul Cambon had made names for themselves through *rapprochements* with erstwhile enemies at the front of his mind, Crozier embarked on a personal policy of *rapprochement* with Austria–Hungary. The financial troubles of the Dual Monarchy provided him with a golden opportunity.

From the end of the nineteenth century there had been serious indications that the Austro-Hungarian Empire faced dissolution from the resurgent nationalism of the Balkan peoples. The ruthless racial policy of the Hungarians had aroused bitterness among Croats and Serbs. Serbia strove to break her economic dependence on Austria. After the 'Pig War' of 1905 with Austria, from which Serbia emerged victorious, further lessening her economic dependence on Vienna, France replaced Austria as Serbia's principal creditor. Serbia was able to increase her armaments as well as develop her commerce and industry. Two things were apparent from this: if Austria–Hungary could maintain her smaller national states in economic dependence she could calm their irredentism; if France was banker to the Balkans she could perhaps provide Vienna with money too. Thus, ever in need of loans to shore up her creaking régime and unable to find the requisite funds from her German ally, who was almost as desperate for money, the Austro-Hungarian government repeatedly appealed to France for access to the Paris Bourse to float loans. Crozier calculated on tying these loans to conditions which would eventually neutralise Austria–Hungary's position in the Triple Alliance relative to France and possibly bring her into an agreement with the Triple Entente.

Naturally Russia was strongly opposed to any policy of friendship towards her rival in the Balkans. In 1909 she complained to Paris of the 'too Austrophile attitude . . . of Crozier'. Foreign Minister Pichon, unwilling to remove the Vienna Ambassador for fear of upsetting Austria–Hungary, appointed de Saint Aulaire as First Secretary to the Vienna embassy with the mission of moderating Crozier's zeal.[76] This failed. In 1910 Crozier supported Vienna's attempt to negotiate a Hungarian loan. Again Russia complained that the money would be used to float a Bulgarian loan contrary to Russian interests. To begin with Crozier appeared successful. France decided to reject Russian opposition on the grounds of maintaining good Austro-French relations. However British opinion also reacted, protesting strongly that the Triple Alliance had gained another partner in the shape of the Paris Bourse. By January 1910 Germany, fearing the emancipation of Hungary from German political and financial dependency, managed to find some of the money. This was not sufficient and by June 1910 Hungary was again appealing to France. Paris was willing and placed conditions on the use of the loan in spite of renewed Russo-British protests. Ultimately Russian pressure triumphed and France explained to Hungary that the Paris market was not healthy enough to float the loan.[77]

The pro-Balkan 'bureaux', who disliked Vienna for her oppression of national minorities, demonstrated their displeasure over Crozier's policy. Pichon appeared to have summoned up sufficient courage to dismiss the bothersome Ambassador at the beginning of 1911 but the latter was able to side-step. Pichon's successor, Cruppi, spent barely four months in office, knew little and achieved little. De Selves, equally weak, promoted de Saint Aulaire to Plenipotentiary Minister to give him greater authority in the embassy, and hinted at the Ambassador's replacement. But at the end of 1911 Aehrenthal, the Austro-Hungarian Foreign Minister, was attempting to tie a loan on the Paris Bourse to Vienna's recognition of the recently signed Franco-German treaty on Morocco. Crozier approved the request. Russia and the Quai d'Orsay opposed it and in the end the French Foreign Minister was able to secure Austro-Hungarian recognition of the treaty by negotiating directly with the Austrian Ambassador in Paris.[78]

Poincaré's accession to the Quai d'Orsay marked the end of this tradition of ineffectual Foreign Ministers. His brief contact with the Ministry in late 1911 had given him an idea of the power of the Ambassadors. If Ambassador Gérard was to be believed, 'Poincaré arrived at the Ministry in January 1912 with the intention of replacing the majority of ambassadors'.[79] Crozier must have been first on the list. De Saint Aulaire explained that it was above all to Crozier that Poincaré was referring when he said: 'Foreign powers are represented by their Ambassadors and defended by ours.'[80] Poincaré's policy towards Austria–Hungary followed quite unsurprisingly his general policy on the separation of the two opposing alliance systems. Like Sir Edward Grey, Poincaré believed that it was enough for the Triple Entente to contain Germany and that any attempt to isolate her by driving a wedge between her and Austria or Italy could lead to a conflict. Of course if Germany dominated Europe the result would also be war. The solution thus lay with a middle course between these two dangers, in which the defensive but resolute nature of the Triple Entente should be maintained along with the balance of power. Quite obviously Poincaré would not see eye to eye with Crozier. De Saint Aulaire realised this and doubtless saw in Crozier's dismissal promotion for himself and hence intensified his opposition to the Ambassador's policy. Thus at the beginning of 1912 the Vienna embassy was in the curious position of possessing two contradictory policies. During Crozier's rare presence at Vienna (he was absent from the capital for social reasons) communications encouraged closer relations with the Dual Monarchy, during his absence, De Saint Aulaire warned against such a policy.[81]

One of the chargé d'affaire's first telegrams to Poincaré outlined the danger of a loan to Austria–Hungary. The Viennese government was developing its military and naval power to such an extent that it was impossible 'to be mistaken about the true aims of the loans it envisages'.[82] On 3 February Crozier asked Poincaré to grant a loan to Bohemia and Lower Austria. These regional loans, he explained, were quite different from national ones – the money would only go towards the building of railways in inaccessible areas.[83] News of Crozier's dismissal from Vienna was recorded in the press shortly afterwards. He was in fact allowed a stay of execution for six months in which to find alternative employment. But his obstinacy in pursuing his policy would seriously curtail this period.

Foreign Minister Aehrenthal died at the beginning of 1912. His successor Count Berchtold was equally committed to reducing German hegemony of the Triple Alliance. The means he envisaged was a tightening of relations with Rome, an *entente* with France and more seriously an Austro-Russian *rapprochement*, which Crozier appeared to condone, but which Ambassador Georges Louis in St Petersburg warned of as an attempt to resurrect the old *Dreikaiserbünd*.[84] Crozier believed that Barrère's suggestion for a Mediterranean agreement between Britain, France and Italy could be improved by welcoming Austria into it. Paul Cambon was sceptical about any Austro-French *rapprochement* and the price France would have to pay. On 18 March Crozier made an all-out attempt to convince Poincaré of the necessity of such a *rapprochement* in a veritable dissertation thirteen sides long which neither impressed Poincaré by its form nor by its content. Poincaré minuted it with an order to Paléologue to give him his opinion on the dispatch 'in which imagination seems to play a dominant role'. Crozier suggested that the economic necessities of Austria–Hungary could be satisfied in exchange for assurances from Vienna that at the next renewal of the Triple Alliance, France and the Triple Entente could secure 'certain guarantees against the possibility of an aggressive policy by the Triplice, that is to say Germany'. He insisted that a loan would not be spent on armaments and seemed to ignore the fact that building new railways was in itself a strategic action. Nor did he appear to understand that lending money to Vienna, for what he saw as 'non-strategic' expenditure, liberated that much more of Austria's finances for armaments. Furthermore, the finance which France supplied, Germany (the Dual Monarchy's traditional banker) would not have to supply, thereby allowing her to devote more resources to her own armaments. Poincaré minuted that all of this amounted to helping Austria against Russia's will in exchange for a few words of courtesy. The present state of the Near Eastern question meant that little could be done in this direction without upsetting Russia. As for the guarantees of non-aggression by Austria, Poincaré questioned whether Austria would allow them to be made public, and even if she did there was nothing to stop her subsequently signing a new, secret counter-agreement with her Triplice partners.[85]

Twelve days later Crozier received his letters of recall. But undeterred on 18 April he sent another dispatch to Poincaré again encouraging a Mediterranean agreement in which Italy and Austria–Hungary would both be included, and which he expressly stated would be merely the first of a series of agreements with the Triple Entente intended to weaken Vienna's links with Berlin.[86] Little wonder that the French Minister of War, Alexandre Millerand, remarked that to keep Crozier on in Vienna would be 'a public danger'.[87] Poincaré devoted thirty-four pages of his memoirs to Crozier and his policies. The Italo-Turkish war was spreading, trouble was fermenting in Macedonia: 'This was the moment that our Ambassador in Vienna . . . chose to attempt flirtations with Austria.' Describing Crozier's ideas as 'hazy dreams' he added that 'no action was more likely to irritate Emperor William II, if he got to know of it'.[88] In 1921 Crozier attacked his former Minister in an article which attributed his recall to a fundamental difference over policy: 'He and Paléologue were "des Balkaniques". I was French and European: I was sacked.'[89] This was an obvious attempt by the former Ambassador to use the 'Poincaré-la-guerre' polemic of the 1920s to jusitify his own pre-war policy. Criticism of Crozier also came in November 1913 from the head of intelligence at the French War Ministry, who underlined the danger of any loan to Austria–Hungary which would certainly have been used on defence spending. Indeed in 1913 a large increase in the Austro-Hungarian army was voted – the first since 1888. This explained the head of intelligence's sarcastic remark that in the end things had worked out well because Crozier became a banker and was thus able to indulge his financial leanings 'and stopped mixing together two incompatible functions'.[90] But the most pertinent criticism of all came from de Saint Aulaire. His despatch, sent after Crozier's departure from Vienna, described not only Poincaré's policy towards Austria–Hungary but his foreign policy in general and above all his conception of the European states system from 1912 to 1914.

> We could not go any further [than a Mediterranean agreement with Italy and Britain] without falling prey to the deadly system of the penetration of the alliances, of which it has been said, so rightly, that it is 'a cause of international decomposition just as pacifism is a cause of national decomposition'. The penetration of the alliances, in fact, corrupts and dissolves them. By upsetting the balance and by obscuring the clarity of the situation, in reality it leads to ambiguity and instability. In doing so, it eventually weakens the guarantees for peace while claiming to increase them by the chimera of universal harmony.[91]

Philippe Crozier had disobeyed Poincaré from the outset. His method like his policy lacked subtlety. But as he was not backed by powerful political forces, his replacement posed no problems and the French Premier was able to resist the machinations of the *camarillas* and install his own man, Alfred Dumaine, at the Vienna embassy. Dumaine would loyally execute Poincaré's policy up to the First World War – Austria–Hungary would be left to fend for herself in the Triple Alliance.

Poincaré's policy towards the Triple Alliance in 1912, therefore, was clearly conditioned by his conception of contemporary international society, in which Triple Alliance and Triple Entente should exist side by side. In marked contrast to many of his Ambassadors he regarded the inter-penetration of the alliances as an act of provocation and a recipe for disaster.

5 France and the Triple Entente in 1912

Despite the signing of the Anglo-Russian agreement on Persia in 1907, which added the final corner to what became known as the Triple Entente, Europe was not yet unequivocally divided into the two opposing blocs which would confront each other in 1914. Triple Alliance and Triple Entente were as yet relatively flexible. For instance, shortly after concluding the agreement with Britain, Russia balanced it first by an agreement with Japan which weakened the Anglo-Japanese Alliance, then by an agreement with Germany to protect the *status quo* in the Baltic, and finally by proposals to the Austrians to extend the Balkan *entente* of 1897. Flirtations, agreements and *ententes* across the alliances were commonplace. No one as yet knew how far Britain, and indeed France, would go in supporting Russia in the event of a war after the Bosnian crisis of 1908–9. It was not even clear whether Britain would be willing to give military assistance to France. Finally, France's attitude to the Triple Entente since Delcassé's departure was lax and characteristic of the general diplomatic 'laisser-aller' of successive Radical ministries. The Radicals returned to power stronger than ever in the general elections of 1906, but their apparent strength was offset by signs of weakness which encouraged some foreign observers to question the solidity of the régime and to doubt the value of France as an ally.[1] Certainly it was nothing new for domestic problems to dominate French Cabinet policy, but the period between 1906 and 1911 was characterised by a series of new and extremely divisive problems which led to a particular introspection. The régime was still under attack from both flanks. On the Right there was the growth in influence of the extreme nationalist and monarchistic Action Française, devoted to overturning the Republic. More seriously, on the Left, the rise of a revolutionary trades union movement and a united socialist party led to a rise in pacifism and anti-militarism. A large number of violent strikes and disturbances seriously affected many parts of the country and brought the social questions to the fore during this period. In 1910 the Socialists made further gains and the question of the defence of lay schools, electoral reform and income tax completely overshadowed foreign policy. What little time was devoted to foreign affairs did not strengthen France's links with the Triple Entente. The Radicals, and *a fortiori* the Socialists, found the Russian Empire politically and morally repugnant. The former saw the necessity of maintaining the Dual Alliance but could summon little enthusiasm for tighter links with Russia; Joseph Caillaux was even sceptical of supporting Russian finances. They were happier to embark on a policy of *rapprochement* with Germany. As Denis Brogan has written, and as Jules Cambon believed, 'a policy of active collaboration with Germany could, perhaps, have been carried out by a man of great courage, energy and personal dignity'.[2] Unfortunately, there was no one of such stature in the French government during this period, least of all at the Foreign Ministry. Everything was left to a hotch-potch of feeble and inexperienced Foreign Ministers, independent and vain-glorious Ambassadors and finally, as Poincaré almost certainly saw in Caillaux, 'a dangerous diplomatic gambler who was willing to throw away acquired French assets, like the Russian Alliance and the Entente with Britain, for problematic deals with Germany'.[3] In short, from 1906 to 1911 the Radicals had allowed links between France's Triple Entente partners to run down. With Poincaré's accession to the Quai d'Orsay this tendency would be reversed, foreign policy would become pre-eminent, and the importance and value of France's Alliance and Entente would be underlined with Poincaré becoming the 'whip' of Triple Entente solidarity.

FRANCE AND RUSSIA

Just as Franco-German relations were not always bad so Franco-Russian relations were not always good. Ever since the original political *entente* of 1891, reinforced by the military convention of 1893-4, the Dual Alliance had been the cornerstone of French security. The Franco-Russian exchange of letters in August 1899, drafted by Delcassé, reaffirmed the Alliance. The duration of the Dual Alliance in its new form was no longer limited to the life of the Triple Alliance and its objective, formerly the maintenance of peace, now also included the preservation of the European balance of power. But from 1906 the Radicals were less enthusiastic about the Alliance. During the Bosnian crisis of 1908-9, Pichon made it clear to Russia that she could not count on French support in her opposition to Austria–Hungary's annexation of Bosnia–Herzogovinia. Russia's Foreign Minister, Isvolsky, was sufficiently bitter and disappointed to brandish the idea of upturning the alliances, which Pichon correctly understood to be an idle threat. But relations between Paris and St Petersburg were at a low ebb and were reflected in two agreements which gave Paris serious reason for concern. In October 1909 at Racconigi Russia signed a secret agreement with Italy to maintain the *status quo* in the Balkans without informing France. More seriously, the Tsar, accompanied by his Foreign Minister, Sazonov, paid a visit to the Kaiser at Potsdam in November 1910 and signed an agreement on Persia and the Baghdad railway. This led to attacks in the French press on Pichon's foreign policy, which was blamed for weakening the Triple Entente. To cap it all, in a tit for tat stroke for 1909, Russia refused France any real support during the Agadir crisis on the grounds that she would not be willing to go to war to settle a French colonial dispute.

Franco-Russian relations were further complicated at the end of 1911 by events in the Ottoman Empire. Until late 1911 Russia had made a number of unsuccessful attempts to form an alliance with the Ottoman Empire which she had hoped would enhance the possibility of her fulfilling her age-old goal of controlling the Dardanelles Straits, thereby allowing her Black Sea fleet access to the Mediterranean. In fact Turkey was in no real position to negotiate such an alliance principally because Britain refused to allow her route to India via the Suez Canal to be jeopardised by the presence of the Russian fleet in the eastern Mediterranean and the policy failed. The Italo-Turkish war opened the way to a new strategy. St Petersburg gave increasing diplomatic support to Italy, based on the calculation that Turkey would be defeated and the Straits question would be revised in Russia's favour. France disliked this policy for two important reasons: a Turkish defeat could lead to a collapse of the Ottoman Empire and with it French interests in the Levant; Russia might act imprudently, upset Austria or Germany and lead France into a conflict in which she had no direct interest. By January 1912 Russia was soliciting French support in case the Straits question should come up for discussion. De Selves replied to Isvolsky that France would be willing to discuss the subject should such an eventuality arise. However, Russia was willing to hurry along events. Ambassadors Bompard in Constantinople and Louis in St Petersburg, warned that Russia was moving towards an *entente* with Italy and Austria over the Balkans, an extension of the Racconigi agreement, which could weaken her links with France. And Bompard warned that Sazonov 'had shown that he was still the Potsdam man, that is to say careless of the repercussions his policy could have on France'.[4]

This was the situation which confronted Poincaré on his arrival at the Quai d'Orsay on 14 January 1912. As a result of insufficient care and attention the Franco-Russian Alliance was in a precarious state. Russia appeared to be aligned with Italy. This displeased France who, apart from losing her ally, also risked in the meantime being dragged into a conflict in which she had little reason to be involved. The lack of authority in French diplomacy was allowing Russia to treat the Dual Alliance as she liked.

Poincaré was not willing to sacrifice everything for the sake of the Dual Alliance. His objective was to restrain and control Russian actions while maintaining her good will and friendship. But he would quickly discover that the Russian representative in Paris was an unreliable intriguer and that France's man in St Petersburg was old, ailing and inefficient. Poincaré's diplomacy would go through three phases during 1912 on its way to a renovation of relations between the two countries: he would discover the totally unsatisfactory state of Franco-Russian relations; attempts would be made to secure Georges Louis's resignation; and the French Premier would make a trip to Russia to reaffirm the Dual Alliance.

The Unsatisfactory Nature of Franco-Russian Relations

The main preoccupation of Russian foreign policy was the Near East. Russian policy in that area was dictated by a desire to control the Straits. So one of Poincaré's first moves on coming to power was to discover exactly what Russia intended to do in the event of a change in the balance of forces in the area. The French Ambassador in St Petersburg, Georges Louis, was instructed to begin discussions with the Russian Foreign Minister, Sazonov, along these lines. As France was Russia's ally, Poincaré wished to know how such a change could eventually affect France's action. Preliminary discussions with Russia on a three-point agenda concerning possible changes in the balance of power resulting from a governmental crisis in Turkey, Austrian action in the Sandjak of Novi-Bazaar or Albania, or an armed conflict between Turkey and a Balkan state, made Poincaré very anxious. He got the impression that Russia was herself looking for a way of upsetting the balance of forces in the Balkans which would give her control of the Straits. He was already only too well aware that Russia was supporting Italy in her war against the Ottoman Empire for just that reason. He had recently learnt (probably from Italian intercepts) that Italy was pressing Russia to recognise Italian sovereignty over Tripoli and that Russia was likely to join an Italian attack on the Turkish controlled Straits. For this reason Georges Louis was ordered to secure confirmation from Russia that she wished to maintain the integrity of the Ottoman Empire. France was herself firmly committed to maintaining the *status quo* in the area to safeguard her investments and interests, in particular her influence in Syria and the Lebanon. She had not yet evolved a policy to cope with the break up of the Ottoman Empire, which was now beginning to seem inevitable. But throughout this period Louis would be unable to obtain from Sazonov any clear answer about Russia's intended policy in the area.

As if these worries were not enough Poincaré soon began to receive information from envoys abroad which suggested that the European alliances were in a greater state of flux than he had ever imagined. The French diplomatic representative in Munich warned that following the recent death of the Austrian Foreign Minister, Count Aehrenthal, and his replacement by Count Berchtold there was likely to be an improvement in Austro-German relations. Furthermore Berchtold would probably pursue a *rapprochement* with Russia: 'The Potsdam agreement had marked a change in Russian policy toward Germany and this *détente* could easily be converted into an *entente* between the three empires.'[5] The possibility of a resurrection of the old *Dreikaiserbund* was reiterated by the French Ambassadors in Vienna and St Petersburg.

Russian flirtations with Italy and Austria seriously worried Paul Cambon, who warned Poincaré that 'this double game is not without danger'. Russia must be kept well away from Austria. He seriously criticised recent Russian foreign policy: Sazonov was too secretive; at Potsdam Russia had discussed with Germany affairs which had a bearing on the Triple Entente; Sazonov had rejected French proposals to settle the Italo-Turkish war.[6]

Poincaré was furious about what he heard. Intelligence reports about a build-up of Russian troops along the Turkish border were the last straw. On 13 March he summoned the Russian Ambassador, Isvolsky, and stressed to him that according to the terms of the Franco-Russian Alliance, Russia was not allowed to take any major initiative in Near East affairs without having first reached agreement with France. And he warned Isvolsky that 'it is not enough that you inform us, it is necessary that we should have concerted beforehand'.[7] The French embassy in St Petersburg was instructed to remind Sazonov that according to the Franco-Russian agreement of 1899 both countries had agreed to maintain peace and the balance of power in Europe.

Poincaré had now received warnings about Russia from five of the eight French European embassies. Cracks were appearing in the Dual Alliance. The French Ambassador was recalled from St Petersburg for discussions on this state of affairs. Poincaré was angered by Sazonov's evasive tactics and Louis's apparent lack of resolve in countering them. He insisted that he would not be exposed to another unwelcome surprise similar to 'Potsdam'.[8]

Of all the struggles Poincaré had with his Ambassadors the one with Georges Louis, Ambassador in St Petersburg, is the best known. But it was not until after the First World War that the Georges Louis affair, as it became known, reached the apogee of notoriety. It became a focal point in the debate on responsibility for the outbreak of the First World War: 'revisionist' historians claimed that the sacking of the 'peaceable' Louis was proof of Poincaré's 'warmongering'. The stakes in the debate were high. If Germany could show that responsibility did not rest solely with her, she could contest article 231 of the Versailles Treaty, which justified reparations on the basis of German war guilt. Meanwhile, the new Bolshevik régime in Russia was attempting to heap discredit on its Tsarist predecessor to reinforce its own legitimacy. It was more than pleased to show that the Tsar's Ambassador, Isvolsky, and the 'bourgeois' Poincaré had worked for war. Finally, a large section of the post-war intelligentsia, youth and socialist movements were so disgusted by the horrors of the war that they determined to apportion the blame to all the powers who had participated in it in the hope that war would be for ever discredited. Thus, for diplomatic, political and moral reasons facts were manipulated issues became clouded and the question of relations between Poincaré and Georges Louis over Russia assumed unrealistic proportions. It would now seem that Poincaré was more than justified in wishing to replace Louis. Poincaré did not encourage Russia to adopt a belligerent policy against Louis's protests; rather he attempted to restrain Russia because of Louis's lack of resolve in dealing with Sazonov. That lack of vitality was a symptom of the Ambassador's serious ill-health. Poincaré's opponents have always contested that fact, yet Louis was already complaining of poor health to his brother, the writer Pierre Loüys, before 1912. In November 1911 he was suffering from chronic bronchitis, dreaded the cold Russian winters and confessed to living a solitary life and being near to death. By the end of January 1912 he had lost his sight, which stopped him writing, and admitted that had he been asked to carry on as interim Political Director, after Bapst's suspension, he would not have had the energy to do so.[9] To make matters worse, Louis's wife, who was also ill, was forced to remain in France. There was no doubt that Louis was unfit to withstand the pressures that Poincaré's new energetic diplomacy demanded: constant vigilance over Sazonov and Russian political circles to detect the direction of Russian diplomacy; meticulous and extensive reporting of diplomatic conversations; the authority and mental agility to pin the wily Sazonov down to the commitments of the Alliance; and, finally, the physical energy necessary to be able to attend the innumerable social functions of Russian society which so often provided the vital information to an understanding of the Empire's politics.

This unsatisfactory state of affairs was worsened by the presence in Paris of the untrustworthy and intriguing Russian Ambassador, Isvolsky. The situation facing Poincaré was almost a carbon-copy of the problematic lines of communication with Italy – except that he could not fall back on intercepted Russian telegrams as the code had not been broken by the *cabinet noir*. Such imperfect channels of communication left him with no alternative but to make a visit to St Petersburg to settle the problem of the unity of action of the Alliance partners. He probably ordered Louis to arrange this during his visit to Paris, for by 20 March arrangements were already being made.[10] August was probably chosen to allow him to deal with other pressing matters: the Italo-Turkish war, the Haldane Mission and the reorganisation of the Quai d'Orsay. In the meantime Louis was instructed to ask Sazonov to make a public commitment to the Dual Alliance in his forthcoming speech to the Duma.

At the end of March Poincaré received alarming news from Isvolsky about the recent conclusion of a secret Serbo-Bulgarian agreement for mutual aid in the event of aggression, and for the maintenance of the *status quo* in the Balkans. It was confirmed by the French Minister in Sofia, who added that if Italy attacked the Straits, Serbia and Bulgaria would attack Macedonia, which would lead to the intervention of Greece and Montenegro, the surrender of Turkey and the likelihood of Russian action against possible Austrian opposition. Poincaré immediately asked Louis to discover whether the Serbo-Bulgarian treaty contained any clause concerning Russia's role should the *status quo* be broken. Louis replied that Russian public opinion would demand intervention, though Sazonov had remarked that France would be consulted first. According to the Ambassador, the Russian Foreign Minister had no intention of pursuing an adventurous policy in the Balkans. This was perhaps so, but Sazonov's diplomats were far more willing to risk war to secure Russian control of the Straits. Between March and December 1911 Sazonov had been convalescing in Switzerland leaving the Foreign Ministry in the incapable hands of his assistant, Neratov. During this period Russian diplomats, and in particular Isvolsky in Paris, the pan-Slav Nicholas Hartvig in Belgrade and Nekludov in Sofia, had pursued personal policies which had encouraged the formation of a Balkan League, the first stage of which was the Serbo-Bulgarian alliance of 13 March 1912, shortly to be followed by a military convention on 12 May 1912, a Greco-Bulgarian treaty on 12 June and verbal agreements with Montenegro.

Poincaré's alarm quickly turned to anger. Louis was ordered to speak firmly to Sazonov to the effect that Russia had begun the Balkan negotiations without informing France and had then presented her with a *fait accompli*, and Russian attempts to form an Austro-Italo-Russian *entente* could only upset the European balance of power and put the Dual Alliance and the Triple Entente at risk. Finally Sazonov must be warned that 'on such serious questions, we [France] could not be content with *a posteriori* information'.[11] This was certainly not the tone of someone willing to allow Russia *carte blanche* to pursue whatever bellicose policy she chose. This serious rebuke was to be backed up by a series of measures intended to coax Sazonov back into line, ranging from a refusal to float a Bulgarian loan in Paris backed by Russia, to an audience by Louis with the Tsar. By mid-April it was clear that Poincaré had had quite enough of Russian connivance with Italy: 'What does this double game mean? What is the Russian government looking for? We are carrying out the Russian Alliance with scrupulous loyalty, would it be too much to ask her to do the same?'[12]

Matters did not improve. By 16 April Poincaré had discovered that Isvolsky had encouraged Tittoni to press Italy to occupy the islands in the Aegean in her war against Turkey. The conflict, at Russia's behest, was spreading. On 18 April Italy bombarded the Dardanelles and Turkey reacted by closing the Straits to foreign navigation, cutting off vital Russian trade from the Mediterranean. There was now a serious risk that Russia would retaliate. But Louis was still unable to get Sazonov to continue discussions on the three-point agenda concerning Russian action in the event of an upheaval in the Balkans. On 21 April Louis was ordered to seek an audience with the Tsar to complain about Russian policy. Two weeks later that order had still not been carried out. On 8 May a letter was despatched from Paris calling for Louis's resignation.

Attempts to Secure Georges Louis's Resignation

The call for Louis's resignation marked the end of the first phase of Franco-Russian relations under Poincaré. It had been characterised by two issues: the unsatisfactory state of relations between the Dual Alliance partners, and the inadequate diplomatic representation in both capitals. In Poincaré's view the latter was partly responsible for the former. Dogged by ill-health and lack of energy, Louis was unable either to execute the orders issued to him from Paris to calm and control Russia, or to strengthen the links between the two countries. At the same time, Isvolsky, intent on directing Russian foreign policy from Paris, failed to communicate Poincaré's protestations to St Petersburg, and often falsified communications to support his own policy. Poincaré had no other recourse but to demand Louis's resignation and to replace him with a more reliable Ambassador.

The reason why Louis, and not Isvolsky, should be replaced adds to the complexity of the Georges Louis affair. Louis was the subject of a campaign of denigration by Isvolsky as part of a plan to increase his own power and influence in Paris. If the Russian Ambassador could convince Sazonov, and to a certain extent Poincaré, that Louis incorrectly reported the Russian Foreign Minister's conversations then his own position would be reinforced: Sazonov, dissatisfied with Louis, would then refer to Isvolsky's services. The Russian Ambassador would then have virtually all important communications passing through his hands and be able to extract or alter whatever was necessary for his own policy. Isvolsky's machinations combined with Poincaré's dissatisfaction, made Louis's replacement inevitable.

When Louis was acting Political Director in Paris Isvolsky had held him in great esteem. But when it became necessary to dispose of him in the interest of his policy Isvolsky's attitude changed. The change occurred when Louis returned to his post in St Petersburg. On 29 February Isvolsky appealed to Sazonov for more information so he could discuss matters more thoroughly with Poincaré, adding that as 'Georges Louis does not always communicate exactly what he is told in St Petersburg, I do not understand why you prefer to converse with Paris on this question through him rather than me'.[13] The timing of his change of heart was significant. The outbreak of the Italo-Turkish War brought into operation the Racconigi agreements of 1909 between Russia and Italy: St Petersburg contracted to support Italian claims to Tripoli if Rome did likewise for Russian claims to the Straits. The policy had been inaugurated by Isvolsky when he was Foreign Minister, and agreed to by Tittoni, who was Italian Foreign Minister in 1909. Now Ambassadors in Paris, both men saw their agreement coming to fruition and intended to direct their respective countries' foreign policies from Paris along the lines of the 1909 agreements. Furthermore, as Foreign Minister in 1908–9 during the Bosnian crisis, Isvolsky had been intensely humiliated by Austria's annexation of Bosnia–Herzogovinia and was intent on revenge. The recent about-turn of Russian policy from friendship with Turkey to encouragement for the Balkan states had almost certainly received Isvolsky's blessing, if not his connivance. It was a chance to kill two birds with one stone: to put Racconigi into action, and seek revenge from Austria by supporting the Balkan states. Isvolsky's tactic was simple, but effective. When Poincaré ordered Louis to complain of Russia's refusal to keep France informed of her actions and Louis replied that the Russian Foreign Minister refused to comply, Isvolsky merely told Sazonov that Louis had misreported him. Isvolsky could then claim that this was why Poincaré was reluctant to support Russia. What made matters worse was that Isvolsky's reports to Sazonov were often pure fabrication or misrepresentation, as Poincaré pointed out in his memoirs.[14] Little by little, Isvolsky was able virtually to isolate Sazonov and transfer effective power to himself in Paris, from where he could scheme with Tittoni.

Isvolsky's criticisms of Louis increased until in May the Russian Ambassador finally presented Poincaré with a request from his government for Louis's removal. The reason given was Louis's lack of activity in his political and social relations. This provided Poincaré with the perfect pretext for having him replaced. The haste with which Poincaré accepted Isvolsky's claims without first verifying them, when in other circumstances he was always suspicious of them, testified to this. Poincaré attempted, unconvincingly, to justify his actions in his memoirs by explaining that he had expected Louis to defend himself. In fact he was fully warranted in wishing to replace the ailing and inefficient Ambassador who, at sixty-five, had anyway reached retirement age. When asked whether Louis would be offered another embassy the *cabinet du ministre* replied categorically in the negative.

At first Isvolsky's plans appeared to have back-fired. He was shocked by the announcement of Louis's resignation and annoyed with Poincaré for having acted so quickly. It is virtually certain that he had never really wanted Louis replaced, knowing full well that this would restore credibility to the St Petersburg embassy contrary to his own plans. It was very likely to have been Sazonov who, never having liked Louis, had called for his replacement. Isvolsky had probably expected the replacement to have taken some time to be implemented. He even told Sazonov that he had not formally requested Louis's replacement. Isvolsky certainly appears to have done everything to reverse the decision. According to intelligence reports from the *Sûreté Générale* it was Isvolsky who had the affair leaked to the press, probably in the hope that the ensuing stir would force the press-conscious Poincaré to reverse his decision.[15] Sure enough, Louis's dismissal hit the headlines and was immediately followed by a cancellation of his recall. Isvolsky's triumph was greater than even he had calculated. As Louis was to remain in St Petersburg, quite ostensibly against the will of the Foreign Minister, his position would be even weaker than in the past, while Isvolsky's would be reinforced. And Louis's subsequent obsession with trying to prove a conspiracy against himself further undermined his standing. Poincaré wanted the whole affair forgotten, fearing the effect all this would have on the steadily worsening state of Franco-Russian relations. The Tsar and the Kaiser had already arranged to meet in the Gulf of Finland on 3 July and had given political significance to an otherwise private encounter by taking Sazonov and the German Chancellor with them. Poincaré asked Sazonov for a formal assurance that no political questions would be discussed, and insisted that the members of the Triple Entente should agree in advance on solutions to the Italo-Turkish war and that

Sazonov should publicly declare Russia's commitment to the Triple Entente. Sazonov refused on all counts. Poincaré was furious and again ordered Louis to take France's case to the Tsar. But in his audience with the Tsar the Ambassador discussed the Georges Louis affair to the virtual exclusion of anything else.

Poincaré was doubtless relieved to embark upon his voyage to Russia in August. Franco-Russian relations were plainly not as he wished. The signing of a Franco-Russian naval convention in Paris on 16 July 1912 could be seen as a step in the right direction as both navies worked out their joint strategy for a future conflict. The same could be said of the meeting of the Russian and French General Staffs in Paris three days before, which had confirmed the new French military strategy adopted in August 1911, according to which any war should now be conducted offensively and no longer defensively. The Joint Staffs had all agreed that in the first weeks of the war both France and Russia should launch massive offensives against Germany. Russia promised to do so on the twelfth day of her mobilisation and to facilitate this it was agreed that she should do everything to improve her strategic railway network in the west. But these were merely technical arrangements which could only have real value after the Alliance partners had made the decision to activate the alliance, in other words, *after* the *casus foederis* had become operational. What Poincaré wanted was to ensure that Russia did not hesitate in proffering diplomatic support *before* any crisis went that far – he wanted no repetition of Russia's position during Agadir. Thus, like Britain's position in relation to the Franco-British military discussions, these arrangements did not necessarily increase Russia's political commitment to the Alliance. The visit to Russia was therefore a golden opportunity to tidy up the disorder caused by years of dilatory Foreign Ministers and the present unsatisfactory diplomatic representation. Poincaré hoped to make the Russian government aware of France's reluctance to give Russia *carte blanche* in the Balkans but at the same time to reaffirm the Dual Alliance.

Reaffirming the Dual Alliance

The notes made by Poincaré during his official visit to Russia in August 1912 demonstrate by the nature of the affairs discussed the duality of his conception of Franco-Russian relations: cohesion and restraint. The Georges Louis affair had further weakened the cohesion of the Alliance and the discovery of the Serbo-Bulgarian treaty vindicated his desire to restrain Russia. He was reinforced in his conviction that only through closer ties with St Petersburg could Russia be restrained and the strength of the Triple Entente be maintained. When Sazonov showed him the Serbo-Bulgarian treaty Poincaré was shocked and exclaimed: 'But it's an agreement for war!' He asked Sazonov how he could ever have presented such a treaty to France as peaceful and have asked for it to be sanctioned by a loan. Fortunately, Poincaré had delayed floating the loan as soon as he had heard rumours of the treaty.[16] His notes made in St Petersburg, and shown to Louis, state that the treaty contained not only the seeds of a war against Turkey and Austria, but also that Russia seemed to be encouraging the Slav nations.[17] There was little Poincaré could do about the treaty – the Balkan states would never have agreed to its abrogation. Though he was annoyed with Russia this was no time to estrange her further; he could only ask that henceforth she should act with greater prudence.

One of Poincaré's main objectives in Russia was to settle the Georges Louis affair. He attempted to make the best of a bad job by assuring Sazonov that Louis had all the confidence of the French government. Though Sazonov explained that he considered the incident closed Poincaré discussed it with the Russian Premier, Kokovtsov, and the Tsar. Poincaré's meeting with Kokovtsov shows that he would have liked to have had both Louis and Isvolsky replaced, but this was impossible for the moment though it remained an option for the future. Poincaré appears to have been eager to record Kokovtsov's criticisms of Louis, whom he described as 'sad, introspective, unrepresentative' and believing that all Russian policy was made in the Duma.[18] Indeed, during his stay in Russia Poincaré had been able to witness Louis's inefficiency at first hand. The Ambassador was unable to accompany the French Premier to Moscow and had been ignorant of the names of the guests he was supposed to introduce to Poincaré at a reception.

Poincaré considered his visit to Russia to have been a success. The Tsar had reaffirmed his faith in the Alliance, and overall the rickety links between the two countries appeared to have been made good. Yet by no means did this lead him to reduce his vigilance of Russian actions. From August until the outbreak of the First Balkan War Poincaré worked hard to maintain peace, the *status quo* in the Balkans[19] and the cohesion of the Triple Entente. He refused permission for the Bulgarian loan to be floated in Paris and worked to get the powers to pressure Constantinople into instituting reforms which would pacify the Slav states. Furthermore, according to several French diplomats Russia appeared to be co-operating with France in a much more loyal manner. But, as Paul Cambon pointed out, France was likely to be faced with a dilemma over the Near East: Franco-Russian interests in the area were incompatible. If war broke out in the Balkans France might be forced to choose between sacrificing her interests in the Orient and a rupture of the Russian Alliance.[20] Poincaré was determined, however, to maintain the knife-edge balance which would enable him to avoid having to choose one way or the other.

Agitation in the Balkans was reaching boiling point. The national states knew that an Italo-Turkish treaty was about to be signed which would end hostilities between Italy and Turkey. Now was the time to take advantage both of Turkey's weakness after the war and of the hesitation and division of the powers over the Balkan question. French peace proposals were rejected and Russia remained reluctant to restrain her Slav protégés for fear of upsetting domestic public opinion. The members of the Triple Alliance were equally passive. Italy relished the possibility of a Balkan upheaval which would hasten Turkey's acceptance of the peace treaty. Germany, like France, was divided between her traditional patronage of, and interests in, the Turkish Empire and her wish to maintain Austria–Hungary as a great power. A last-ditch attempt was made by Kiderlen-Waechter and Poincaré to forestall the storm; Austria and Russia were ordered to warn the Balkan states in the name of the powers that no change in the *status quo* would be tolerated. Just as the Austro-Russian note was presented on 8 October Montenegro declared war on Turkey. This was followed on 17 October by a similar declaration by Bulgaria, Serbia and Greece. Although a Turkish victory had been expected the opposite happened. Within a few weeks Macedonia was fully liberated, the Greeks were at Salonika, the Bulgarians had besieged Adrianople and were preparing to march on Constantinople. By the end of November Turkey had been driven out of virtually all her European possessions.

The speed and scale of the Balkan victories stunned Europe. The Habsburg Monarchy was immediately made aware of the fragility of its own Empire. For French public opinion the victories were applauded as triumphs for French arms and training over the German-armed and trained Turks. For Russia they were a mixed blessing. Though she had always championed the Slav cause the Straits question was of greater importance to her. Bulgaria was now threatening to invade Constantinople and Russia feared control of the Straits might slip from her grasp. Poincaré was afraid that some rash action by Russia might precipitate a general conflict. As Elie Halévy has remarked: 'An alliance which at the end of the nineteenth century might have been regarded as protecting France against the danger of a German invasion now exposed her to it'.[21] During this period Poincaré kept up constant pressure on Russia to accept French and British proposals for settling the conflict. The unity of the Triple Entente had to be maintained at all costs, which was why he refused Jules Cambon's suggestion for Franco-German mediation, seeing in it a German ploy to divide the Triple Entente. Poincaré believed that the only way to restrain Russia was for Britain and France to keep 'clinging on to her, because it is the only way to maintain her within the bounds of reason or to stop her from carrying out a settlement with others'.[22]

The international tension and the extra work it created was more than Georges Louis could cope with. On 31 October he wrote to his brother that his illness had confined him to his room. His judgement and capabilities were so severely impaired that in mid-November he completely misconstrued one of Poincaré's despatches and made the serious mistake of presenting to the Russians as a formal proposal something Poincaré had merely wished to discuss with the Ambassador, and Russia had proceeded to execute it. Poincaré was furious. Though Louis considered his own state of health sufficiently bad to contemplate resigning, in the end he decided to soldier on,[23] thereby becoming a serious handicap for French diplomacy. Millerand, the Minister of War was so alarmed by Louis's inefficiency that he claimed it was imperative he be brought back to Paris.

Historians have often pointed to Poincaré as continually acquiescing to Russian demands. It should now be clear that this was untrue. Indeed, in November, when Paul Cambon, who was usually severely critical of Russia, insisted that France could do none other than assure Russia of her support in the event of a conflict if the Dual Alliance was to be maintained, Poincaré refused until Russia first made clear her intentions should Austria take action in the Balkans.[24] Russia was worried by this, for she had learnt that Britain was also reluctant to support her. Poincaré attempted to quell Russia's anxiety by explaining the situation clearly to Isvolsky. He pointed out that although the French government wished to know of Russia's plans in advance of their execution, 'in the meantime she had neither said nor implied anything which could be considered as failing in her support'.[25] It was a natural statement to make at a time when one's ally was under pressure from an enemy power. It was a conditional reassurance that certainly went no further than the Alliance itself: France confirmed that she would not abandon her ally and merely encouraged her to inform Paris of her intentions. Some observers have taken this statement out of the context of the other calls to heel by Poincaré and used it unfairly as evidence that he gave *carte blanche* to Russia – an idea encouraged by Isvolsky's totally inaccurate account of what Poincaré allegedly told him, and who he records as saying: 'All this means is that if Russia makes war France will do the same.' Poincaré firmly denies this in his memoirs.[26] It certainly contradicted all of his previous calls for restraint and he was not in the habit of contradicting himself. On the other hand, Isvolsky was just the man to alter the meaning of a conversation as he had so often done in the past. Only the day before, Poincaré had complained to Louis that Isvolsky had misrepresented his thoughts to St Petersburg and asked him to set the record straight.[27]

Poincaré's position *vis-à-vis* Russia was certainly a delicate one. He was walking a tight-rope – falling on one side would give Russia leave to go to war, on the other encouragement to desert the Dual Alliance. The statement to Isvolsky was an attempt to maintain his balance by the use of intentionally equivocal language which, unfortunately, the Russian Ambassador was easily able to deform. Poincaré guessed this might happen and decided to define precisely under what circumstances the military side of the Alliance would be activated. He was so worried about this that he even recalled Isvolsky the following day to alter the definition of when France would march: in the event of Germany giving armed support to Austria.[28] A day later he altered it again, finding it 'too general'. He finally told Isvolsky that France would respect the alliance treaty and would if necessary support Russia militarily should the *casus foederis* arise,[29] which involved an attack on Russia by Austria supported by Germany. In the end, Poincaré's statement to Russia was nothing more than a reiteration of the original alliance. To see in it evidence of war-mongering is to ignore all Poincaré's attempts to restrain France's ally.

The powers remained divided over a settlement of the Balkan war. By 15 November Serbian troops had reached the Adriatic. In order to shore up her shaky position Austria–Hungary refused to allow Serbia a port on the Adriatic and called for the creation of an independent Albania to block Serbian access to the sea, which met with Italian approval. Russia backed the Serbian claim. Until 18 November, when Bulgaria's advance was stopped before it reached Constantinople, Russia had appeared prepared to go to war to prevent her gaining control of the Straits. The Germans urged Britain and France to co-operate in keeping Russia out of Constantinople. Grey agreed, wanting Constantinople to be made a free city if the Turkish Empire fell – a solution abhorrent to Russia. Poincaré could not support this proposal as the Alliance would be jeopardised. Thus he played along with Russia while refusing her any definite support.

Too many of France's interests conflicted over any settlement of the Balkan war: on the one hand, outright support for Russia could mean war, or a disintegration of the Ottoman Empire, while failure to support her could lead to a collapse of the Dual Alliance; on the other hand, support for Germany, whose interest in the integrity of the Ottoman Empire coincided with France's, risked estranging Russia, while failure to work with Berlin risked developing an incipient Anglo-German partnership. In characteristic fashion Poincaré avoided any one choice and plumped for a middle-of-the-road solution by reiterating his proposal of 15 October for an international conference in Paris to settle the Balkan imbroglio. This would have the added advantage of doubling as a platform for his candidature in the forthcoming French presidential elections.

Meanwhile, Russia continued to worry Poincaré by again raising the question of the future of the Straits. Poincaré refused to discuss the subject until Russia first made clear her desiderata. Fortunately, the Bulgarians failed to take Adrianople, let alone Constantinople. Unable to make further progress, the Balkan states concluded an armistice with Turkey on 3 December. This immediately removed any urgency on Russia's part to settle the Straits question, she could return to her traditional patronage of Balkan nationalism without risk to her own interests.

The powers, led by Sir Edward Grey, agreed that an ambassadorial conference should be called. But the venue, to Poincaré's considerable dismay, was switched from Paris to London, which was considered to be a more neutral and more discreet capital. Meanwhile, in London, Turkey and the Balkan states began negotiating a peace treaty. Preparations for the coming peace conference, which finally opened on 17 December 1912, were marked by a good deal of muscle-flexing on Germany's part intended to frighten the powers into greater concessions for the Triple Alliance. Bethmann-Hollweg declared publicly that Germany would support Austria militarily if she were attacked by a third power. Poincaré immediately wished to know of Britain's attitude should France be forced to protect Russia. Grey was non-committal, though he warned the German Ambassador that if Germany intervened to protect her interests in Europe Britain could do the same. Official reports reached Paris of minor German mobilisation procedures. On 5 December, as a mark of solidarity before the conference opened, the Triple Alliance was renewed. This further encouraged Poincaré to maintain the cohesion of the Triple Entente. Overall, however, Russia remained remarkably calm in the face of Vienna's primary preparations for mobilisation. St Petersburg regarded such action as a bluff to force her hand in the conference negotiations. But the French Premier still recommended restraint from Russia, whose leaders were under tremendous pressure from the press to adopt a more aggressive stance at the conference.

Poincaré's mandate as Minister of Foreign Affairs and Prime Minister was drawing to a close. He had been elected President of the Republic and would occupy the Elysée on 17 February. The constitution provided for him to dispatch current business matters in between leaving the Quai and the installation of a new Foreign Minister. He was to make full use of that prerogative to deal with Georges Louis. Meanwhile Russia had been restrained, the peace conference was in session and a serious threat of war had been averted. It was Austria–Hungary's failure to intervene against Serbia, but also Russia's refusal to support the Serb claim to the port of Scutari on the Adriatic which had spared Europe a general conflict. It was during this period that Poincaré's restraint had been the firmest and the most effective. The conference of Ambassadors could do little more than make the result of the Balkan war palatable to Russia and Austria–Hungary. Russia merely sought to keep the Bulgarians from Constantinople. But as the Turks were strong enough to do this alone Petersburg remained conciliatory. The only other serious task of the conference was to put into practice the establishment of an independent Albania agreed upon by both Vienna and St Petersburg. However, Turkey's refusal to cede Adrianople led to a renewal of fighting in February. Only after new victories by the Balkan allies was the Treaty of London signed on 30 May 1913.

Poincaré had restrained Russia during the critical period at the beginning of the Balkan war. And he had managed to do so in spite of the ailing and ineffectual Georges Louis. The serious relapse in Louis's health in mid-November 1912 could only be remedied by convalescence. Far from providing a period of rest the Balkan negotiations were mercilessly extended over the Christmas and New Year vacations, placing an ever greater strain on the Ambassador's frail constitution. Georges Louis had become a liability. His blundering in February 1913 was the last straw. Although Charles Jonnart had taken over at the Foreign Ministry Poincaré was still in command. When he discovered that Sazonov had informed Louis of his intention to make certain declarations to Rumania and Bulgaria without first consulting the other powers and the Ambassador had not deterred him, Poincaré was furious both with Louis and Russia.[30] Ten days later Louis was asked to resign on account of his health, and on 20 February 1913 the French Cabinet sanctioned Delcassé's nomination as Ambassador to St Petersburg. Delcassé had in fact been chosen by Poincaré to replace Louis on 1 June 1912.[31]

Since 1894 France's diplomatic security had rested on the Alliance with Russia. When Poincaré came to power that alliance was in a state of disrepair. And with Russia pursuing a more active Balkan policy it seemed that France might end up paying all the costs of the alliance and gaining none of the benefits for her security. Poincaré wished to rectify that position. His policy was an exercise in maintaining a delicate balance between too great a show of French support for her ally, which risked encouraging her to enter a Balkan war likely to end in conflict with Germany; and too little support, which could lead Russia to forsake the Dual Alliance and leave France at Germany's mercy. Georges Louis's presence in St Petersburg was a threat to that policy. A man of authority was needed to implement a policy which demanded fine tuning, immediate responses to orders from Paris and the confidence of the Russians. Louis's replacement by Delcassé and later Paléologue would unfortunately tilt the balance in favour of strong links with Russia to the detriment of restraint.

FRANCE AND GREAT BRITAIN IN 1912

> One must take the French as they are and not as one would wish them to be. They have an instinctive dread of Germany and an hereditary distrust of England, and with these characteristics they are easily lead to believe that they may be deserted by England and fallen upon by Germany.[32]

Sir Francis Bertie's words perfectly summarised France's feeling of insecurity in the decade before the Great War and explain her incessant attempts to transform the Entente Cordiale into an alliance. Paul Cambon never abandoned the hope that this could be realised and often mistook his desires for realities. Ever since May 1905 he had been under the mistaken impression that Lord Lansdowne was ready to begin discussions which would lead to an Anglo-French alliance. He did not consider the formation of the Liberal government in December 1905 as likely to change that state of affairs. The backing which London gave to Paris during the Algeciras conference was proof of her commitment to resist Germany and support the Entente. But try as he might Cambon was unable to get the British Foreign Secretary to contravene Britain's traditional policy of refusing any continental alliances.

Paradoxically, the success with which Britain and France had worked together at Algeciras may have lessened the possibility of an alliance by demonstrating that the present state of the Entente was quite enough to maintain the balance of power in Europe. There was, however, an influential group at the Foreign Office, led mainly by Sir Arthur Nicolson (Permanent Under-Secretary from 1910), Eyre Crowe (Senior Clerk and later, Assistant Under-Secretary) and Sir Francis Bertie (Ambassador in Paris), who believed that a much closer understanding, even an alliance, with France was necessary to combat growing German hegemony. On the other hand, in France there were many critics of the Entente. There were those who believed that the military support which insular Britain could offer to continental France was derisory, her strength resting on her navy, which, as Prime Minister Rouvier sardonically remarked, 'does not run on wheels'. Men such as the influential foreign editor of Le Temps, André Tardieu, or the pro-Entente Prime Minister Clemenceau, tried to convince Britain, in vain, that she must adopt conscription. Others believed that France could enjoy greater benefits from political and economic co-operation with Germany, especially in the imperial field. After all, despite the Entente of 1904 Britain was still France's major rival overseas – there were substantial differences between the two countries in North Africa, Newfoundland, Egypt, the Ottoman Empire and China. Many Frenchmen, not least in the Quai d'Orsay, would still after 1904 have echoed the words of the embittered colonialist who had written in 1900 'that France gets colonies so that England may take them over'.[33] A Franco-German agreement seemed a more logical means of consolidating France's position in North Africa and the Near and Middle East. Sir Francis Bertie was ever wary of such an agreement which he warned could lead to France abandoning the Entente.

But Franco-British relations had been consolidated to a certain extent by the commencement in December 1905 of secret conversations between the British and French General Staffs on possible joint action in a conflict in which both countries might become involved. Perhaps intended only as a temporary measure to provide for a possible conflict during the Algeciras conference, they became a permanent part of the Entente. Though Britain maintained her previous position of refusing to commit herself to France in the event of war, the French, and in particular Paul Cambon, came to view such help as virtually certain. Military conversations lapsed from 1906 to 1910, but then flourished when Brigadier-General Henry Wilson became Director of Military Operations in August 1910 and fostered increasingly intimate relations with the new French High Command in 1911. Nevertheless, as late as August 1911 Wilson was obliged to admit to the Committee of Imperial Defence that he had no precise details of French war plans. This was perhaps not surprising for at that time the French War Ministry itself had very little idea of its strategic intentions. These were in a serious state of flux as the new Chief of General Staff, General Joffre, was in the process of switching the strategy from the defensive to the 'outright offensive'. Prompted by Agadir, Joffre gave more attention to Britain's assistance then his predecessors, for his new plan contained detailed provisions for the concentration of the British

Expeditionary Force of 150,000 men in north-east France.[34] However, as Grey ceaselessly pointed out to the French, who thought differently, these talks in no way bound either country to come to the other's assistance in the event of war. Though they gave some substance to what was really nothing more than a colonial barter, the talks were so secret that very few people knew of their existence, including up until 1912 most of the British Cabinet, who would probably never have approved their instigation. This secrecy meant that critics could not be silenced by pointing to the conversations as proof that the Entente was more substantial than it appeared.

This was the case during the summer and autumn of 1911. Britain and France successfully worked together to counter the German challenge at Agadir when their interests coincided, but were soon in dispute over the future of Morocco. That friction threatened to undermine the whole basis of the Entente. Nationalist French officials sought to compensate France in Morocco at Spain's expense for her losses in the Congo. At the same time Britain attempted to defend the Spanish presence on the North African coastline, which surveyed the Straits of Gibraltar to ensure for strategic reasons that it was not dominated by a naval power like France. Caillaux went as far as to complain to Bertie on 4 November that had it not been for the Entente with Britain 'France might long ago have come to terms with Germany'.[35] This was enough to upset even the strongest of supporters of the Entente in London. It was worsened by publication in the same month in *Le Temps* of what was claimed to be the secret clauses of the Franco-British 1904 agreement. This forced Grey to publish the treaties in full in order to allay severe criticism from the radicals in the government. Grey's publication of the treaties further weakened the standing of the Franco-British agreement by making it clear to the French public that Britain was in no way bound to come to France's assistance in the event of her being involved in a conflict.[36] This was the shaky state of relations with Britain that Poincaré inherited from Caillaux. As with Russia, he wished to rectify that position. His Ambassador in London, Paul Cambon, relished such an idea, but unfortunately overestimated Britain's commitment to France. In doing so he perhaps misled Poincaré as to Britain's likely action if France went to war with Germany.

Paul Cambon had been Ambassador in London since 21 September 1898 and was the *doyen* of France's diplomatic corps. He represented a certain continuity and stability which patently contrasted with that of the Foreign Ministers, who came and went with the proverbial transience of French Cabinets, and which instilled in him a certain condescension towards them. This was increased by his actually having rejected Charles Dupuy's offer of the portfolio in 1894. As a newspaper acknowledged in January 1912: 'He is the Nestor of French diplomacy, his advice has the force of law; that is perhaps why there is no law for him.'[37] Cambon was certainly aware of this as he told his brother when speaking of Ambassadors: 'If the gentleman is nothing himself, he is sacrificed. If he is somebody and represents a policy, he is untouchable. Your retirement or mine would be political events which would create a certain fuss for our government whichever it might be.'[38] Little wonder that the *Cri de Paris* should talk of the Cambon brothers' clan dominating the Quai d'Orsay. A clash of personalities was inevitable between the self-important Paul Cambon and the austere and meticulous Poincaré. The Foreign Minister set the tone of their relations by recalling the Ambassador from London to subject him to detailed and spontaneous questioning on the most intricate and baffling issue facing French diplomacy before the war – the political status of Tangier. Cambon was speechless, and Poincaré did not hide the fact that he had found the Ambassador 'tired' – a veiled reference to his future replacement?

Differences between the two men did not exist solely on a personal level. Paul Cambon belonged to the old school of diplomacy in which the role of the Ambassador was paramount. His watchwords were secrecy and independence. He perceived his task to be establishing personal contacts in the country to which he was accredited based on confidence, negotiating in a private capacity and decanting the distilled product to the Minister. The Ambassador alone conducted affairs with his country of residence; the Minister merely haggled with Parliament and synthesised general policy.[39] Poincaré, on the other hand, had a more modern view of diplomacy. The Ambassador was expected to respond to orders from the minister like a general or prefect. All negotiations were to be communicated in their minutest details to the Foreign Minister, who made the decisions and issued instructions to be executed to the letter. Paul Cambon's refusal to adhere to these ideas, indeed his reaction against them, would have serious consequences. The fact that he saw the 'Entente Cordiale' as a tribute to his own ability and as marking a personal domain further led him to disregard any ideas emanating from Paris. He perhaps also suffered from a degree of complacency in his understanding of British domestic and foreign policies, which was even less warranted given his habits, education and outlook.

In the best Gallic tradition Cambon was convinced of the superiority of French culture. He admired its rationality and overlooked its inflexibility; the idea was so often superior to the fact. In the country of pragmatism *par excellence* this could be a handicap. The fact that he never spoke English and, as his son records, did not feel at home in Britain, leaving for Paris every fifteen days if not every week, without a doubt isolated him from English life.[40] The counsellor at the German embassy in London claimed that his social life was hampered by his lack of English. The Francophile Lord Esher was more critical: 'Shrewd and pliant he gives an impression of possessing powers of mind that are in truth lacking.'[41] Things did not improve when the Liberals came to power in 1905 with Sir Edward Grey as Foreign Secretary. Grey neither spoke a word of French nor had he ever set foot on the continent. During diplomatic audiences Grey spoke in English, Cambon in French, both paying attention to articulate clearly. Henri Cambon noted in respect of Grey that many nuances must have escaped him.[42] Would it be unfair to suggest that some may also have escaped his interlocutor?

This state of affairs was not improved by Cambon's reliance on Sir Arthur Nicolson, Permanent Under-Secretary of State at the Foreign Office. Both men had entertained good relations since their postings to Constantinople several years before. Unfortunately, Cambon tended to think of Nicolson as the voice of Grey and the British Government, which he certainly was not. Nicolson represented only one current of opinion in the Foreign Office and the government, which was not the most powerful, advocating ever closer ties with France and even Russia. His narrow, inflexible appraisal of the international scene was rejected by Lord Loreburn (Lord Chancellor), Lord Morley and the radical wing of the Cabinet, many of whom preferred a *rapprochement* with Germany, as did Grey's very influential private secretary, Sir William Tyrrell.[43] Thus, a number of factors, not least the unrepresentative nature of Paul Cambon's British contracts, as well as his unwillingness to consider, or ignorance of, the role of the Cabinet in British policy-making, invariably led him to make wrong assumptions, the most serious of which was his over-confidence in Britain's commitment to France.

The Haldane Mission

The first weeks in February 1912 witnessed growing apprehension in diplomatic circles about the European situation, resulting from the growth of German armaments and Britain's reactions to it. The radicals were alarmed at how close Britain had come to war during the Agadir crisis and criticised Sir Edward Grey for having adopted such a provocative attitude toward Germany. The support their case received meant some form of *détente* with Berlin was bound to follow. Ever cautious about maintaining the unity of the Cabinet, Grey decided that an arrangement with Germany on naval rivalry, which had dominated relations between the two countries since 1908, would silence his critics and avert a costly arms race which risked devouring the finances needed for the liberal Cabinet's social reform programme.[44] The British desire for *détente* dovetailed with a similar dream by Chancellor Bethmann-Hollweg, who, for both diplomatic and domestic reasons, wished to reduce the threat of war with Britain. When the French were informed in early February of the Minister of War, Lord Haldane's mission to Germany to discuss such an agreement they grew anxious. To a large extent the Entente's survival rested on British and French distrust of Germany's ambitions. If one partner sought an accommodation with her the other inevitably became restless. At the beginning of 1912 the new French leadership was particularly sensitive to any such move as relations with London were already in need of repair after Caillaux's imprudent statements and quarrels with Sir Francis Bertie. Supporters of the Anglo-French understanding on both sides of the

Channel were worried about the Haldane Mission. Paul Cambon appeared remarkably unperturbed, claiming that nothing would come of it. He called for complete confidence in Britain. That confidence was in fact the main strut of his policy. Flattering though it may have been for France's partner, it was short-sighted.

On 13 February Grey presented Cambon with a summary of the points Haldane would discuss: naval expenditure, the Baghdad railway and a possible formula on the absence of any aggressive British policy against Germany except in the case of an attack against France. According to Grey, Cambon merely remarked that the last point would be satisfactory to his government and did not even bother to comment on the other points.[45] Neither was he worried by a speech by Prime Minister Asquith which welcomed an arrangement with Berlin. Public opinion in France did not share his confidence and Poincaré informed Cambon that he would have to make a public statement to counter the arguments of the Entente's adversaries, and asked him to discuss it with Grey. This was Poincaré's way of reminding Grey of the Anglo-French understanding while negotiations were in train with Berlin, though Cambon immediately criticised it as unnecessary. Nevertheless, Poincaré continued to receive news from other embassies of the dangerous nature of the talks. Jules Cambon explained that Bethmann-Hollweg and Foreign Minister Kiderlen Waechter had probably risked a good deal on these talks to combat the Tirpitz, anti-British element in the German government. They needed success and in order to save face would probably accept the vaguest formula which would be presented by the British radicals as the beginning of Anglo-German *détente* and which could prejudice France's relations with Germany. What worried Poincaré most was France's relations with Britain. He was willing to go to serious lengths to tighten links with her. On 21 February he had summoned an informal group to the Quai for a review of France's defence posture. Joffre advocated a French offensive across lower Belgium should France be threatened by Germany. But whereas the Ministers of War and of the Navy supported that strategy, Poincaré rejected it. He was clearly aware that its adoption would lose for France any hope of gaining British support in a war against Germany.[46]

By 15 March events had taken a more serious turn. Cambon was shown a copy of the formula Britain was willing to exchange with Germany if the naval agreement was satisfactory. It stated that Britain would not attack Germany without provocation, would not pursue an aggressive policy against her, and was not party to an agreement or treaty of aggression against her, nor ever would be. According to Grey, 'Cambon read the words and seemed satisfied with them.'[47] He certainly showed no sign of apprehension when he telegraphed the formula to Poincaré. He appears not to have grasped its significance. Neither did he comprehend that the formula was to be a written exchange with Germany and not simply a declaration.[48] It was not so much the content of the formula, which he communicated precisely, but oddly for him the form which he neglected. Ironically Cambon would claim eight months later that a written exchange of formulae had a good deal more diplomatic significance than a mere declaration. This could have serious implications for the credibility of the Entente Cordiale. Thus Poincaré was misled. Furthermore, Cambon's display of satisfaction with the formula was tantamount to condoning Britain's desire for such an arrangement and risked encouraging greater conciliation toward Germany. The radicals might consider this to be French approval. Though Grey desired improved relations with Berlin, this was not to be at the expense of the Entente and if the French did not protest he would not be adequately armed to combat the radicals.

A week later Cambon again misinterpreted an interview with Grey. He notified Poincaré that Grey had refused to give Germany an assurance of benevolent neutrality should she be at war, in exchange for naval limitation talks. Consequently, said Cambon, the Germans had called off the talks, thus putting an end to the fears of 'uninformed minds'.[49] In fact this was quite untrue. Grey told Bertie that Cambon had been informed that the matter had been suspended and could be revived at any time. Again Cambon had appeared satisfied. Poincaré was now so misled about the whole affair that he even asked Cambon to thank Grey on behalf of the French government for having ended talks with Germany.

Poincaré may often have claimed that he was not well served by his own Ambassadors but he was at least well served by one foreign Ambassador. Sir Francis Bertie was the only person who reacted to Paul Cambon's acquiescence. Having learnt of Cambon's satisfaction from Grey, he visited Poincaré and asked to speak to him as if he were not an Ambassador. Bertie was shocked by Cambon's acquiescence and attempted to make the French more keenly aware of its dangers, in the hope that this would bring additional pressure to bear on the British government to break off the negotiations. Referring to the London Ambassador's 'satisfaction', he remarked gravely that he was very surprised by it for the declaration had not been rejected definitively. Grey's position was much weakened. He was under a good deal of pressure from the partisans of a rapprochement with Germany, and Bertie stated quite candidly: 'I no longer understand his policy and I am worried.'[50] He insisted that under no circumstances should the declaration be allowed to be exchanged. And he pointed out what Cambon had overlooked all along in a British declaration of neutrality should Germany be attacked – the Entente Cordiale could be destroyed. Who could guarantee that France, provoked or threatened by a German mobilisation along her frontiers, would not be forced to take the offensive to defend herself. Would Britain then have to remain neutral? He concluded by insisting that it was indispensable that Cambon should not look satisfied and advised that if Poincaré spoke to London with 'a little firmness' Britain would not commit the mistake he feared.[51]

Poincaré immediately communicated the text of this conversation to the London embassy. As if this were not a serious enough rebuke for Cambon, he also cast aside his calls for confidence in Britain by ordering him to explain to London that although no diplomatic convention tied Britain to France and though she had maintained her freedom in spite of the conversations between General Staffs, 'there would be the most annoying contradiction should she alienate this freedom *against us and to Germany's profit*'.[52]

From this point onwards Poincaré took great care to pester Cambon with communications ordering him to put pressure on Grey to abandon talks with Germany. Cambon's attitude still remained surprisingly cavalier. Fortunately there was increasing activity among the pro-Entente protagonists in the Foreign Office to put a halt to the talks and to ensure that not even the most platitudinous formula was accepted by Britain. But Grey insisted that 'it was not reasonable that tension should be permanently greater between Germany and England than between Germany and France or Germany and Russia'.[53] In other words French protests were unfair. On 10 April Asquith agreed with Grey that the French were unduly nervous.

Bertie continued to maintain the vigilance that was so absent from Paul Cambon's communications – Cambon had even decided to take an eight-day holiday. On 10 April Bertie again visited Poincaré to insist that France must speak with greater energy if Britain was to renounce her dangerous project. Poincaré followed this with an order to the London embassy to warn Grey that the proposed declaration would be interpreted in France as a voluntary abandonment by Britain 'of all the policy pursued since 1904'.[54] Anglo-German talks on a formula finally ended, but more as a result of German greed than British reluctance. Had Berlin contented herself with a colourless formula, yet one she could brandish as evidence of a crack in the Entente Cordiale or of British perfidy, France could have been in a precarious position. On 12 April the French chargé d'affaires in London, de Fleuriau, was informed that the German government had found the British formula insufficient, negotiations were at an end, the German naval budget would be voted. But as de Fleuriau pointed out, Grey had accepted a German proposal to continue Anglo-German negotiations on colonial matters.[55] Poincaré could perhaps be grateful to Paul Cambon for having taken his holidays when he did, for it is doubtful whether he would have received such a clear explanation of this last point had de Fleuriau not been in charge of the embassy. In his memoirs Poincaré acknowledged his debt to Bertie, without whom France would never have learnt of 'the most serious aspect of the German manoeuvre'.[56]

On his return to the London embassy Paul Cambon attempted to justify his position throughout the Anglo-German talks, but this only made his ineptitude more apparent. Claiming that Admiral von Tirpitz and his supporters had found the conversations ridiculous, he failed to mention that this group was only a minority. He insisted that the failure of the talks showed the 'inanity' of the affair and appeared to suggest quite incorrectly that Germany had relinquished all attempts in this direction – the coming

appointment of Baron Marschall von Bieberstein to replace Metternich as
German Ambassador in London would show she had not. He continued to
insist that Grey 'would never have consented to a written arrangement
however inoffensive it might be' – this was not the opinion of Crowe
Nicolson, Bertie and Sir Edward Goschen, Ambassador in Berlin. He
characteristically borrowed words from Nicolson to dismiss the coming
Anglo-German colonial negotiations as 'a few territorial exchanges on the
borders of the South African Dominion'[57] – yet France would soon become
seriously worried about the nature of these conversations, in particular the
discussions on the future of the Portuguese colonies. Even Sir Arthur Nicolson
could not understand how Cambon could have been so unmoved by the
talks.[58]

One salutary effect of the Haldane Mission was to underline the shaky
nature of the Entente Cordiale, which now more than ever appeared to be
dependent upon personalities and the whims of the British government
France, already anxious about German military preparations and plans as well
as the unsatisfactory nature of relations with Russia, now appeared to be
losing her only other major effective deterrent against German aggression
This was not all, there was further reason to suspect the value of the Entente
Cordiale. As Samuel Williamson has pointed out, the Moroccan crisis of 1911
exerted a profound impact upon Anglo-French relations. The shock of the
Agadir incident prompted both governments to reconsider every aspect of the
Entente relationship – diplomatic, military, naval. But whereas the military
and naval conversations emerged from the crisis with new substance and
importance, diplomatic relations were relieved of some of their force. 'The
termination of the second Moroccan dispute', says Williamson, 'settled more
than a Franco-German question; it also saw France collect its share of the 1904
Anglo-French accord. The act of collection ended Britain's formal obligation
to render France diplomatic support', even though the community of interests
extended further then ever before.[59] Paul Cambon desired some form of
agreement which would cover this deficit. But he knew that Britain had to be
in the right frame of mind to accept. Was the inordinate confidence he placed
in Britain after Agadir an attempt not to upset her in order to woo her into
more substantial commitment? Thus, convinced of Britain's loyalty and
single-mindedly pursuing that aim, he had paid but scant attention to the
Anglo-German conversations. In the end he had come through more by luck
than judgement. Now more than ever he was intent on clinching an
agreement with Britain.

The Grey-Cambon Letters

What had prompted Cambon to think that an agreement with Britain was
possible were the Anglo-French naval conversations. These had been resumed

in December 1911 when the French naval attaché, Count Gouz de Saint-Seine, had had his first meeting with the British First Sea Lord. The talks on the division of respective fleets in the Channel were, however, considerably retarded by the intricacies and Anglophobia of French naval bureaucracy. Cambon was forced to intervene directly with Delcassé, the Naval Minister, in January 1912. But the talks failed to gain momentum and de Saint-Seine was still complaining in March. Yet Cambon must have seen here the seeds of a possible agreement. He was determined that the Haldane Mission, now under way, should not jeopardise a potential accord by prompting France to upset Britain with cries of perfidy. Hence his appeals for total confidence in her. He could see she was faced with the prospect of a further increase in German naval strength and the development by Italy and Austria–Hungary of their fleets, thereby placing the British fleet in the Mediterranean in a difficult position should war break out with the Triple Alliance. Cambon was aware of the reorganisation of the fleets proposed by the Admiralty and outlined by Churchill to the Commons on 18 March. The London Ambassador also fully understood that Britain recognised that without French assistance British interests in the Mediterranean would be dangerously exposed in time of conflict. Thus it was Paul Cambon who, as soon as the Anglo-German conversations had failed, broached the question of an alliance.[60]

On 18 April Cambon visited Nicolson to demonstrate to him the need for closer Franco-British relations. Recent events had shown the fragility of the present arrangements and he asked Nicolson quite bluntly for a new agreement, which need not be a signed treaty. 'We could content ourselves with an exchange of verbal declarations in the form of notes.'[61] Remarkably, Cambon now saw the importance of such an exchange when only a week or so before he had paid little attention to a similar demand by Germany. Furthermore, Nicolson refused precisely on the grounds that the pro-German element in the Cabinet would not accept limitations on their freedom to act in any contingency.

After this disappointment, some two weeks later Cambon returned to the Anglo-French naval conversations as a means to a more binding agreement with Britain. On 4 May 1912 he suggested to Nicolson that the talks be intensified and that Britain join France and Russia in a naval convention. What France desired was for Britain to look after the Channel and France's northern coasts while the French undertook care of the Mediterranean. After all France was the world's fourth largest naval power and such an agreement involved no major reorganisation of either country's naval policy. Ever since 1907 and 1908 British war-planners had seen the possibility of gaining French aid in the Mediterranean, where the bulk of her fleet was already concentrated, and this had been mentioned to the French naval attaché in December 1908. As for the Royal Navy, its main force was already concentrated in home waters. With the collapse of the Haldane talks and the substantial increase in the German navy the Cabinet was forced to reconsider Britain's naval strategy. The Admiralty was already drafting proposals to denude the Mediterranean still further with the transfer of ships from Malta to Gibraltar, where a new battle squadron would have to cover for the Mediterranean or be able to move into the Atlantic and up into the North Sea according to circumstances. Cambon could see that Britain's navy was overstretched. This provided France with a perfect opportunity for strengthening the Entente by proposing French naval assistance to Britain in the Mediterranean. Both Grey and the First Lord of the Admiralty, Winston Churchill, refused to begin any talks on the subject before the government had looked at the Admiralty's proposals.[62]

Meanwhile, Cambon had learnt that the replacement for the German Ambassador in London was to be Baron Marshall von Bieberstein, a shrewd diplomat known to be in favour of a *rapprochement* with Britain. Whereas Nicolson was worried by this, Cambon once again preached calm and confidence in Britain. He was worried about upsetting London at a time when there was a likelihood of getting her to increase her commitment to France. But other French Ambassadors had serious misgivings about the new appointment, as had Bertie, who was becoming a regular French Ambassador himself by keeping Poincaré informed of the true state of Anglo-German relations.

The debate on the reorganisation of the British fleet continued. The pro-French element in the Foreign Office called for an arrangement with France in the Mediterranean. The radicals in the Cabinet opposed both a reorganisation of the British fleet and an accord with France, fearing that the former would be dependent upon the latter. Grey preferred an increase in naval expenditure – which would have averted both solutions – to a split with his colleagues. At a meeting of the Committee of Imperial Defence on 4 July, Churchill's proposals for a greater concentration of the fleet in home waters at the expense of the Mediterranean were defeated. However, it was decided that, subject to a reasonable margin of superior strength in home waters, the Admiralty should maintain a battle fleet in the Mediterranean only equal to a one-power Mediterranean standard excluding France. Thus Churchill's defeat was more apparent than real, as the decision made an appeal to the French for assistance in the Mediterranean inevitable.[63]

The French intended to make all the diplomatic capital they could out of their knowledge of the Admiralty's future plans, encouraged by the British and French press, who generally appeared to favour closer Franco-British relations. The question of French assistance for Britain in the Mediterranean provided France with the lever she had lacked for seven years. In Samuel Williamson's words: 'What Morocco had once been to the entente the Mediterranean now became.' The fact that in the same month the French Navy Board decided to concentrate the French first-line forces in the Mediterranean and her second-line forces in the Atlantic and North Sea increased France's bargaining position *vis-à-vis* Britain.[64] The British Cabinet's sanctioning of the resumption of Anglo-French naval conversations on 16 July (albeit so long as Britain's liberty of action was not impeded), and the possibility that plans might be arranged for co-operation in the Mediterranean, prompted Cambon to open the bidding. But Grey at once made clear to him on 22 July that the Anglo-French naval conversations would not prejudice the freedom of decision of the governments so as to commit either to assist the other in the event of war. He stressed that there was no formal Entente between France and Britain. Cambon was quick to retort that there was a moral Entente, 'which might however be transformed into a formal "Entente" if the two Governments desired, when an occasion arose'.[65] Two days later, in discussing the draft agreement on the positioning of the British and French fleets, he noted cunningly to Nicolson that sending nine-tenths of the French fleet to the Mediterranean would expose France's Channel and Atlantic ports to an attack by Germany. Poincaré and the French Admiralty were likely to object unless France had some assurance that British naval aid would be forthcoming for the Channel and Atlantic coasts.[66] Paul Cambon now had his foot in the negotiating door.

Churchill objected that the agreements were being made by each government quite independently of the other. Cambon replied that this was an error; it was necessary to have some understanding between the two governments that they would at least communicate if there was a threat of war, and concert beforehand. He suggested notes, but Grey objected that a leak would cause trouble. What the Foreign Secretary said of the nature of the Entente was significant. 'It was now what it had been for several years past, why could it not be left as it was?'[67] The clash of national characters was becoming apparent. Grey insisted, and would continue to do so until the war, that Britain had not made and would not make a commitment to France to come to her aid in the event of war – the pragmatic approach was dominant, Britain would 'wait and see'. Yet for Cambon the rational approach triumphed – what was written was somehow more positive, even if it only repeated a verbal declaration. Here lay the basis for the misunderstanding over the British commitment to France in the event of war. If London refused to commit herself to Paris, confirming that in writing would hardly reverse that decision. Cambon's misunderstanding of British character would lead him to misunderstand her actions.

Talks continued through the August holidays, and Grey and Churchill were assailed from all sides: Cambon in London, Poincaré and Bertie in Paris. But the French were making progress. Although Churchill warned Asquith on 23 August, 'Everyone must feel who knows the facts that we have all the obligations of an alliance without its advantages and above all without its precise definitions',[68] he was prepared to abandon the draft declaration which upset the French.

On 19 September it was again plain how different traits of national character were affecting the way in which either side viewed the talks.

Cambon proposed a formula (the product of his own initiative) whereby, on fear of aggression by a third power or a menace to peace, the two governments would discuss and search for a means of averting it. Grey replied that 'this was what would happen under the existing conditions if either of us had reason to fear an attack by a third Power'. Cambon 'agreed that this was so in fact, but said that there was no written understanding.'[69] Each party was making its own assumptions about the value of an eventual declaration without realising that its opposite number had a totally different picture of its worth. The same would be true of the Grey–Cambon letters. For Grey the existing de facto case was no different from the written de jure case. Cambon said he agreed; but in preferring the written example he was demonstrating that he afforded it more importance. If reflected the dominance in French thinking of the form of things, over the substance. Obtaining a written formula from Britain altered the nature of the agreement for Paul Cambon, despite the British government's insistence to the contrary and prompted him to interpret the coming exchange of notes as a virtual commitment by Britain to France in the event of war. Furthermore, his reliance on Nicolson and neglect of the power of the radical Cabinet Ministers reinforced this misapprehension and almost gave France a serious shock in August 1914.

Grey told Cambon he would show the formula to Asquith on his return to London in October. Meanwhile, Paul Cambon returned with another formula on 25 September, which Grey agreed to put before the Prime Minister. Pressed both by Sazonov, who was visiting Balmoral, and Cambon, Grey now had few doubts that he would have to give France something tangible for looking after the Mediterranean, or risk disruption of the Entente and possibly isolation in the face of Germany.

The Prime Minister's remark on seeing the formula on 11 October was significant: 'I don't see any harm in Cambon's formula; indeed it is almost a platitude.'[70] Like Grey, Asquith did not believe that the formula committed Britain any more than in the past. On 16 October Grey again told Cambon that there was no need to convert verbal assurances into writing. But Cambon countered by a tactic (not reported to Paris), that the frequent changes in the French government required that some written accord 'to bind France . . . be on the record'.[71]

On 31 October Cambon explained that Poincaré would only accept an exchange of documents if they took the form of private letters approved by the Cabinet. A small amount of wrangling in the Cabinet led Grey to draft another formula, accepted by Poincaré and finally accepted by the Cabinet on 20 November. On 22 and 23 November Sir Edward Grey and Paul Cambon exchanged their letters. These set down that although in recent years British and French military and naval experts had consulted together, it had always been understood that this did not restrict the freedom of either government to decide at any future time whether or not to assist the other by armed force and that the dispositions of the French and British fleets were not based on an engagement to co-operate in war. But if either government had reason to expect an unprovoked attack by a third power or a threat to the general peace, it should discuss with the other whether both governments should act together to prevent aggression, preserve peace, and decide on measures to be taken. If action was necessary the plans of the General Staffs would be taken into consideration.[72]

For the French, the letters shored up the Entente Cordiale. Poincaré thanked Paul Cambon for the authority he had demonstrated in the negotiations and, in complete contrast to Asquith's description of them as a 'platitude', recognised their 'great value'.[73] Much has been written recently about the extent to which the British government had compromised her liberty of action by these notes, the staff talks and the disposition of the fleets. Certainly it can be claimed that when on 1 August 1914 Cambon insisted that Britain had a moral obligation to defend France's northern coastline because France had transferred her fleet to the Mediterranean as part of an agreement with Britain, there was nothing written down to contest this. It was also true that, as a result of the notes, talks and fleet dispositions, the countries had been drawn closer together. Furthermore, plans for co-operation were worked out during the autumn and winter of 1912–13. By April 1913 agreements had been reached on the defence of the Straits of Dover and the western Channel and for joint operations in the Mediterranean. Even war orders for the contingency of an alliance with France had been sealed and distributed to appropriate commanders.[74] Nevertheless, the essential question is not whether Britain had or had not compromised her freedom of action, but whether she *believed* she had or had not done so. And the fact is that she truly believed that she had not done so. And what the British government believed, she would act upon. As Williamson clearly explains:

> For the radicals the letters constituted definite, unmistakable, written recognition that the highly irregular staff talks did not obligate the British government and that the Cabinet retained 'the freedom of decision unfettered . . . Furthermore, in agreeing to consultation, the Cabinet clearly believed that it had promised nothing beyond what the Cabinet would do in a crisis. When compared with the variety and sweep of the various French demands made since May, the letters looked positively innocuous.

Precisely for this reason there was no real crisis within the Cabinet in late 1912.[75] The ultimate question of what Britain's attitude would be in the event of war was, as Grey had repeatedly insisted to Cambon, dependent upon public opinion and Parliament. In this, as with so much, Cambon relied on Nicolson's idea 'that public opinion would not hesitate to pronounce itself in favour of immediate intervention'.[76]

Because Paul Cambon was ignorant of, or misunderstood the nature of, radical opposition in the Cabinet or was overconfident of Britain's commitment to France, Poincaré was misinformed and France was misled. In the last days of July and the first days of August 1914, Cambon was to discover that his optimism about the Entente was not warranted. Britain's refusal to commit herself straight away to France, almost led him to despair. He called 2 August 1914 'the day through which I passed the darkest moments of my life'.[77] In the end it was not really the Entente which decided Britain to go to war but Germany's violation of Belgian neutrality, of which Britain was a guarantor, and fear of German sea power. Had Cambon kept Paris properly informed of Britain's position, France might have been more prepared for Britain's hesitation. In a confidential despatch to Delcassé in December 1914 on the reasons for Britain's attitude in August 1914, Cambon explained how he had feared that Britain might make up her mind to side with France much too late.[78] As it turned out France could count her blessings that 'the Cabinet's agreement about Belgium was, at least in retrospect, the watershed for Britain between war and peace'.[79]

From the beginning of 1912 Poincaré had set about tightening the bonds of the Triple Entente upon which France's security ultimately depended. Before the end of the year that policy had met with much success: relations with Russia were on a sounder basis and links with Britain had been improved. With that grand design on its way to completion he could, from the Elysée turn his attention to another preoccupation: consolidating France's Empire.

6 Poincaré President of the Republic and French Foreign Policy, 1913–14

The crisis of 16 May 1877 taught the embryonic Third Republic a lesson: henceforth Presidents of the Republic were expected to be feeble creatures. Despite the fact that nearly thirty-six years later when Poincaré became President the Republic was firmly established in France, the tradition remained unchanged. But the three constitutional laws of 1875 had never been altered. They endowed the President with considerable powers, though certain of these necessitated a ministerial countersignature. It was probably in the realm of international affairs that these powers were greatest. The President commanded the armed forces; he appointed to military and civil posts (which included Ambassadors); foreign envoys and Ambassadors were accredited to him; he negotiated and ratified treaties, and informed Parliament of them only when the interests and security of the state permitted it.

Before his election to the Elysée Poincaré was known to have supported a campaign for strengthening the executive *vis-à-vis* the legislature.[1] In 1912 the publishers Hachette brought out a book on political science by Poincaré intended for schools entitled, *Ce que demande la Cité*. It demonstrated his belief in an increase in presidential powers to temper the excesses of a *régime d'assemblée* and to allow the will of the people to be properly expressed. It praised the President's right to dissolve the Chambers, stating: 'The use to which it was put in 1877 has since cast on this part of the constitution a shadow and discredit. *It does not deserve it.*'[2] More important still, Poincaré underlined the pre-eminent role of the President in international affairs. There was no doubt on 17 January 1913, the day of the presidential elections, that if elected Poincaré's training and knowledge of the constitution would enable him to interpret legally in his favour the articles of the constitution. This is precisely what worried Clemenceau when he unfairly attacked Poincaré as a neo-Boulangist who dreamed of imposing by 'force and dissolution his arrogant infallibility and his regal scorn for the constitution'.[3]

The electoral college of Deputies and Senators which finally chose Poincaré to be President of the Republic for the next seven years did so principally because he had safeguarded and even bolstered France's international position over the preceding year. The French press was convinced that Poincaré would be a strong President and generally acclaimed his election. A more sentimental indication of his popularity was the substantial increase in the number of

117

babies christened 'Raymond'. Yet the day after his election Paléologue, his old school friend, recorded that Poincaré appeared to be in a quandary as to his future role as President. He had reflected all night on the subject and feared that 'the principle of constitutional irresponsibility will divest me of all initiative and condemn me for seven years to silence and inaction'.[4] This was evidence of his habitual self-doubt and proof that he was well aware of the limitations of his powers. But the circumstances of his accession played a substantial part in coaxing him in the direction of a strong presidential role.

Poincaré was the first example in the history of the Republic of an elected candidate being a serving Prime Minister. It would be difficult to adapt to an office which traditionally had little power, but much potential, without wishing to use the presidential powers that lay dormant. This was particularly so when that candidate was also Foreign Minister at a time of international tension – a certain continuity in French foreign policy was imperative. Indeed, the constitution allowed for the usual dispatching of business matters during the changeover period. There was every reason for the new President to maintain his presence at the helm of foreign policy.

Foreign affairs had been by far the most important issue of Poincaré's term of office in 1912 and the crowds who now acclaimed the new President did not want any change. The prerogative which the constitution conferred upon him for choosing the Prime Minister to form the next government would be used to preserve this. One other factor would be important in assuring the continuation of his foreign policy: the choice of Foreign Ministers. Although it was not in the President's power to choose the Foreign Minister directly, he could exercise considerable influence by the conditions he imposed on the appointment of his Premier, who would be accepted only if he gave his word to implement the President's choice. What conditioned that choice was the Foreign Minister's prior agreement to continue to execute the grand designs of Poincaré's diplomacy. As a further precaution he tried to pick men with as little character as knowledge of foreign affairs to ensure that they would continue to depend on him after their nomination. Consequently after 1912 the grand designs of French foreign policy continued to be motivated by the need to strengthen France's position on the international stage through reinforcing her militarily, through tightening the links of the Triple Entente, and through refusing any penetration of the alliance systems. But a new factor would emerge after the First Balkan War: France would turn her attention increasingly to protecting and consolidating her position in the Ottoman Empire.

The settlement of the Agadir crisis by the Franco-German treaty of 4 November 1911 confirmed France's protectorate over Morocco. France's colonial aspirations could now be focused elsewhere. Syria and the Lebanon were traditional areas of French influence which had been badly neglected until 1912 – Italy was seriously challenging France's religious protectorate and Britain her economic, and even political influence. Now that the Moroccan question was settled in France's favour diplomats like Paul and Jules Cambon and Maurice Bompard pressed the Quai d'Orsay to regain the lost ground. The outbreak of the First Balkan War in October 1912 was the jolt that France needed to take up this policy with greater purpose. Fearing that disaffection within the Ottoman Empire might spread to Syria, lead to an intervention of the great powers, an internationalisation of the region, and subsequently a decline in French influence, Poincaré was forced to define publicly France's policy towards Syria, which explains his remark at the end of 1912: 'The time will come when the partition [of the Ottoman Empire] will take place . . . and we will have to organise ourselves in advance so as not to be absent.'⁵ Paul Cambon was instructed by Poincaré to discuss with Sir Edward Grey Britain's growing influence in the area and obtain some guarantee that it would be curbed. During the talks, which lasted from 26 November to 5 December 1912, Grey committed himself by saying that Britain had no designs on Syria. In turn Poincaré was prompted to make a speech in the Senate on 21 December 1912 dispelling the widespread rumours of British ambitions in Syria, emphasising French belief in the integrity of the Ottoman Empire, and making clear her opposition to any attempt by a third power to undermine her special position there. Syria was now an important issue in French diplomacy.

CHARLES JONNART

In choosing Aristide Briand, his former Interior Minister, as the new Premier, Poincaré could be confident his policy would continue unchanged. There is little doubt that they decided together on the choice of Charles Jonnart as Foreign Minister. Whereas Poincaré was in close contact with the Asian wing of the colonialist movement, was one of the founder members of the *Comité de Défense des Intérêts Français en Orient* and was a member of the *Comité de l'Asie Française*, Jonnart was President of the *Comité de l'Afrique Française* and a 'patron' of the *Comité de l'Orient*, a colonial association bent on increasing French influence in the Levant.⁶ With these qualifications the new Foreign Minister could be counted on to encourage France's new drive in Syria and the Lebanon. It was an added bonus for Poincaré that apart from the Governor Generalship of Algeria, very much an administrative post, Jonnart had no knowledge of foreign affairs and was ill into the bargain. Indeed, he stated publicly that he would have to rely on Poincaré up to the date of his investiture as President on 17 February 1913 and even afterwards. According to the Austrian Ambassador in Paris, Poincaré had assured him that after his election to the Presidency: 'I will see to it that a man is put in my place who will follow my policy. It will be as if I were still at the Quai d'Orsay.'⁷

Poincaré Continues to Control the Quai d'Orsay

The formation of Briand's Cabinet was completed on 21 January 1912. On 22 January Poincaré was expected to hand over the running of the Ministry to Jonnart. But he found him 'drowsy or absent-minded'. This was the excuse he needed to square his conscience with a continued intervention in foreign affairs. As he confessed in his diary: 'I still command Jonnart, I go to the Quai d'Orsay every morning.'[8] As the constitution was sacrosanct to him Poincaré was often at pains to justify to himself his continued direction of foreign affairs. Hence his detailed explanations in his diaries of Jonnart's ignorance of foreign affairs of which Poincaré was fully aware before appointing him, his ignorance of the Balkan towns, of Balkan statesmen, and his depressed state, brought about by his love for his neice, who was his only subject of conversation and whose daily visits to place flowers on his desk, he awaited impatiently.[9] It was evidence of the dilemma with which Poincaré would live for the next eighteen months: a fear of overstepping his constitutional prerogatives, and a fear of leaving France adrift. Nowhere in his extremely personal diaries (which he considered so confidential that he refused to take them on holiday for fear of indiscretions) did he ever confess to overstepping that constitutional role. He sincerely believed that he was interpreting the constitution correctly, albeit in favour of a strong presidency.[10] But then he saw nothing wrong with that as 'the 16 May' did not hold for him the emotional value it held for older politicians like Clemenceau.

It was now apparent to the Quai d'Orsay and the diplomatic corps that Poincaré's elevation to the Elysée would not make him loosen his grip on foreign policy. Paul Cambon, who saw that this could further undermine his own independence, remarked bitterly: 'There is in Poincaré's ways something Napoleonic and if he begins to get infatuated with himself nineteen days before his coronation what will it be like when he is on the throne after a few years?'[11] In his inaugural address to the French Parliament on 20 February, Poincaré stated quite clearly that a reduction in the powers of the executive was not desired by the French people. He told Paléologue that he would not be 'a simple signing machine', and made this clear by telling Isvolsky to deal directly with him at the Elysée whenever necessary. Some polemicists have seen this as an indication of the President's bellicose intentions. But as has been shown, Poincaré was well aware of Isvolsky's shortcomings and Machiavellian character, and thought it more sensible to keep a close eye on him, particularly as it was common knowledge that he played a prominent role in formulating Russian policy and that there was still a strong possibility that he would regain his former post as Foreign Minister. The same invitation was extended to the Austrian Ambassador, and even to his German colleague. Von Schoen was in fact startled by this offer and regarded such personal interviews as a break with tradition and a possible source of embarrassment. He told the German Chancellor he would only use it sparingly and only for acts of courtesy. The German envoy's apparent concern for the French constitution was flattering if unfounded. Poincaré could claim, in line with the constitution, that all foreign envoys were accredited to him and he could receive them at will.

The constitution also provided for the President to negotiate and ratify treaties. This could be interpreted very widely. Where did one draw the line between negotiating treaties and executing foreign policy? The whole of the Balkan negotiations taking place at the time were intended to reach a peace treaty to which France would be a party. This explains why so many of the dispatches arriving at the Quai were passed on to the Elysée with Cabinet approval. Presiding over the French Cabinet meetings was a further presidential prerogative which provided more opportunity for intervention, particularly as 'most cabinets were', as Jules Cambon noted, 'as ignorant as carp in foreign policy'.[12] Chairing the Higher War Council, whose job it was to prepare the country for an eventual war, was yet another presidential privilege, which Poincaré had himself conferred on the President in 1912 and which some have seen as preparation for his term at the Elysée. Of course there were less formal and more subtle means of influencing foreign policy, such as behind-the-scenes discussions with foreign and French envoys and Cabinet Ministers, not to mention the Foreign Minister himself. It can be taken for granted that someone so well versed in foreign affairs as Poincaré could easily make this a formidable means of influence. Furthermore two members of Poincaré's old inner cabinet were still in position: Paléologue, the Political Director, and de Margerie, the Associate Director, both of whom shared his views and could be relied upon to ensure that they prevailed in the Quai d'Orsay. Paléologue openly admitted to tutoring successive Foreign Ministers until his departure for St Petersburg in the spring in 1914.

Conflicting French Interests over a Balkan Settlement

Poincaré had informed Sir Francis Bertie that his election to the Presidency 'would enable him to give steadiness and "suite" to the foreign policy of France'.[13] One issue which called for continuity in French policy was the London ambassadorial conference which continued to deliberate into the New Year. The problem of settling the Balkan conflict, because of its implications for the future of the Ottoman Empire, cut across the existing European alliances. French interests clashed with Russia's and to a certain extent Britain's, but coincided with Germany's. Though it was possible for the three major powers to restrain Russia and Austria–Hungary, they had less influence over the Balkan states.

Turkey was willing to abandon Macedonia and the Albanian provinces but she refused to cede Adrianople to Bulgaria. After a palace revolution, which brought to power more intransigent elements, the Ottoman government broke off negotiations. War between Bulgaria and Turkey was resumed on 3 February 1913, again awakening fears in Europe of a general conflict. Sir Edward Grey was hard pressed to keep the European Concert going by serving as an intermediary between Russia and Austria. In Vienna the military wished to take this opportunity to crush Serbia, while Russia again grew anxious about the Straits when on 26 March the Bulgarians took Adrianople. Montenegro, which had claimed Scutari against the will of the powers, laid siege to the port and was able to hold out for six weeks against European diplomatic opposition. On 4 May she finally evacuated the city, thereby lifting the threat of a general war which Austrian military intervention and Russian counter-measures could have provoked. On 30 May the Treaty of London was signed, with Turkey ceding to the Balkan allies all the territories west of a line running from Enos to Midia, and Crete – the Albanian boundaries and the furture of the Aegean were to be settled by the powers. The First Balkan War was at an end. But the seeds of another were already germinating. The Balkan allies were to fall out among themselves over the division of the spoils.

During this period, in which Poincaré continued to dominate the Quai d'Orsay, France, because of her conflicting interests in any Balkan settlement, was intent on appearing disinterested. For this reason the French were willing to concede the initiative for a solution to Sir Edward Grey, which would keep them off the spot and save them from upsetting any party. When in March 1913 Paul Cambon, who was France's representative at the peace conference, decided quite independently of Paris that he would stray from that 'disinterested' position, he was seriously rebuked: 'Poincaré who is still running the Quai d'Orsay had me called to order by saying that we are abandoning our programme, that we have no decisions to take.' When Cambon had denied the charge and protested that he had only been putting forward a view, back had come the retort, ' "Those are not views which you are formulating", replied Paléologue, inspired by Poincaré, "you are adopting motions!" '[14]

The conflict of French interests over the Balkan settlement was further reflected in Poincaré's attitude to Germany, which, according to Jules Cambon on 8 February 1913, had undergone something of a revolution. The Berlin Ambassador claimed that the President was now attempting to improve relations with Germany and that his former anti-German attitude had been merely an election tactic to whip up support for himself in the campaign for the presidential elections: 'how benign he has become since his election'. Poincaré, he remarked, 'had flung the motors of an anti-German policy into reverse.'[15] Poincaré's attitude to Germany had certainly changed, but the reasons for the change lay elsewhere. Again the explanation seems to be France's conflicting interests in Near Eastern affairs and, in particular, the future of the Ottoman Empire and the new importance of Syria and Lebanon in the President's foreign policy. Despite the guarantees Paul Cambon had been able to squeeze from Sir Edward Grey in December 1912 on British ambitions in Syria, during the first half of 1913 the Quai d'Orsay continued to receive reports of growing Anglophile sentiments in the area. The British appeared to be encouraging Syrian separatists. The virtual certainty of a renewal of hostilities in the Balkans due to Turkish intransigence over the ceding of Adrianople to the Balkan allies, further threatened France's Syrian interests. France could expect no support from Britain or Italy, who hoped to gain from her losses, nor from Russia, who rejoiced at any weakening of the Ottoman Empire if it increased the chances of achieving her age-old goal of controlling the Straits. Thus German interests increasingly appeared to square with France's. Was it not, therefore, commonsense to seek German good will in support of French interests in the event of a partition of the Turkish empire? Such a move was a perfect example of the 'reactive nationalism' of French imperial policy, which, when convinced that Britain was about to replace France in the Levant, was willing to go to any lengths to combat her.[16] Jules Cambon even feared that Poincaré's clumsy diplomacy would over-react to Britain's actions, lead to a 'cooling' of relations with London and a revival of relations with Berlin.[17] Though he was in favour of improved relations with Berlin, this was not to be at the expense of relations with Britain. Furthermore, he appeared to be worried that the Quai d'Orsay would suspect him of pursuing this policy: 'What amuses me are the imbeciles who believe that I am pursuing *it* when I am only trying to gain our freedom from her [Germany] by courtesy towards her and the consideration that is owed to a great power. No one in France understands any more the power of courtesy.'[18]

The Three Years' Law

A more benign attitude towards Germany did not mean under any circumstances lowering France's guard: Germany remained France's main potential enemy. A major item in the President's inaugural programme was a promise to strengthen the armed forces to insure the country against threats or humiliation. It was the continuation of a policy begun in 1912 and further encouraged by the German army Bills, in particular the one under discussion in the Reichstag in early 1913. The Turkish defeat in the Balkan War weakened the military position of both Austria and Germany and prompted the latter to discuss a new army Bill which vastly increased her armed forces and, according to Taylor, 'first created the mass army'.[19] By the summer of 1914 German preparations for war would be at a peak and the temptation to use that superiority against France and Russia would be substantial. This was all the more worrying for France as Russia's military strength and readiness were in doubt. During the Agadir crisis the French military command had been sceptical of Russia's efficiency, with Caillaux replying to those who encouraged him to take a tough line, 'you forget that the Russian Army is worth nothing'.[20] Although Russia was supposed to have begun a great programme of military reforms and the size of her standing army and trained reserves appeared impressive, at the Franco-Russian General Staff conference on 31 August 1911 it was stated that it would be two years before Russia would have the slightest hope of success in a war against Germany.

The situation barely seemed to have improved nearly a year later when, at a similar conference on 13 July 1912, the Russian representative, General Jhilinski, underlined the inadequacy of Russia's strategic railways and the slowness of her mobilisation. Poincaré had been made keenly aware of this during his visit to St Petersburg in August 1912, and consented to very large loans for Russia in 1913 for the improvement of her western strategic railways. But this alone could not offset the forthcoming increase in German military manpower, and France's overall inferiority. France had a population only two-thirds the size of Germany's; she had already lowered her standard of physical fitness to keep her regiments full. There was no alternative but to increase the term of service with the colours from two, Germany's level, to three years. Even Jules Cambon, who was so convinced of the necessity for *détente* with Germany, repeatedly counselled a return to the Three Years' Law to demonstrate France's strength because *'the German people have respect only for strength'*. He maintained: 'Without it Germany will become insolent and we shall have acquiesced in our own downfall.'[21] Poincaré did not need much convincing and called a meeting of the Higher War Council on 4 March 1913 to discuss the subject. With some encouragement from the President the generals unanimously demanded a return to the Three Years' Service. When an article in the *Kölnische Zeitung* inveighed against what it called 'France's threatening policy towards Germany', Poincaré called this an 'audacious lie' and wrote indignantly in his diary that for forty-three years France had been peaceful, while Germany had threatened her without provocation in 1875, 1887, 1905, 1908 and 1911. Fortunately, he remarked, France's youth was aware of this: 'For them it is no longer a question of "revanche", it is a question of threats. And it is against this threat that they want our peaceful country to be militarily armed.'[22]

The project was a political bombshell. Reducing the term of service had been a major part of the military policy of the Republic and had been almost the only tangible result of the victory over the army in the Dreyfus case. It immediately met with tremendous opposition from the Socialists and a growing number of Radicals. The leader of the campaign against the Bill was the head of the French Socialist party and brilliant orator, Jean Jaurès, who had already written an impressive work calling for 'the New Army'. Jaurès held to the Radical Republican view that a truly Republican army should not be a professional force but should consist only of 'the nation in arms', in other words, a citizens' militia. He believed that the leaders of the existing French army wanted a long period of service with the colours, because they thought that the war would be of short duration and decided by front-line troops. His system proposed a better defensive force at a greatly reduced cost, to be carried out in conjunction with a policy of Franco-German *rapprochement*. Though much of Jaurès's criticism of French army mentality, training and strategy was justified, as the first months of the First World War would show, it lost much of its force through being associated with the less intelligent elements of anti-militarism and anti-patriotism. Less than three months before Jaurès's campaign of criticism of French military strategy was to go into full swing, on 18 April 1913, after nearly twenty-one months of study, Joffre presented the War Board with an outline of the new offensive, and almost catastrophic, Plan XVII.

As Denis Brogan has written, 'it was idle to pretend, as was pretended then and has been asserted since, that the reorganisation of the German army could be a matter of indifference to France'; there was a real disparity of forces between Germany and France.[23] The only other possible course of action would have been a reorientation of French foreign policy in favour of a *rapprochement* with Germany, which was both risky and, as has been mentioned, perhaps too difficult after Agadir. Not surprisingly the debate in the French Chamber, which was in full swing by 2 June 1913, was a heated one. But the Bill was finally adopted on 7 August 1913, despite the opposition of the Socialists and many Radicals. However, this was by no means the end of the matter. The Law appeared to be very unpopular. Some troops revolted when told they would have to serve for another year; some of the middle classes believed it would reduce the supply of labour and increase the cost of living; the peasantry were said to hate the Law because it took away its sons, who were so often its only source of labour. The Radical party believed this and, at its party conference at Pau from 16 to 21 October 1913, chose as its leader Joseph Caillaux, who was to lead the campaign in favour of a return to two years' service. This campaign was given further impetus by the outbreak of a smallpox epidemic which spread through the barracks and which was blamed on the overcrowding resulting from the retention of the conscripts for an extra year.[24] The question of the Three Years' Law would remain the running sore of French political life until the war, making Poincaré's task of choosing subservient French Cabinets particularly difficult.

French Assessment of her Potential Enemy - Germany

What was striking about this prolonged debate was the degree to which assessment of the German army was overshadowed by the political question raised by Jaurès of the role of the French army. This was unfortunate because France's assessment of her potential enemy was far from accurate. The French High Command misjudged both the strength and direction of the German attack and quite wrongly based French strategy on an early victory. These serious errors of judgement, as Christopher Andrew has pointed out, resulted from weaknesses in three distinct areas: in intelligence collection, in intelligence analysis and policy-making, and in France's self-assessment.[25]

Lack of information was not the main reason for the miscalculations of government and High Command. One of the speakers in a Senate debate on the eve of war was able to document, from mainly public sources, the 'flagrant inferiority of our military equipment compared to that of Germany'.[26] Even Joffre admitted in his memoirs that German military writers had publicly discussed the possibility of a German attack through Belgium. All the same the weaknesses of France's highly fragmented intelligence collection were partly to blame for the errors of 1914.

Although France had a substantial lead over other great powers in the field of communications intelligence, the benefits open to her were sadly squandered by irresponsible Ministers, interdepartmental rivalry between codebreakers and delay in extending the art to the War Ministry. French 'human intelligence' gathering suffered from a similar fragmented organisation as well as from a lack of funds. Even that money was often misspent with a sizeable sum of the War Ministry's secret fund being allotted until 1911 to a large Bastille Day lunch. Military intelligence was reorganised after its disreputable behaviour in the Dreyfus affair, with intelligence gathering being transferred to a Section de Renseignements attached to the Deuxième Bureau of the General Staff (effectively the peacetime headquarters of military intelligence). Its ineffectiveness was shown at the time of the First Moroccan Crisis when the Section had five officers at headquarters and seven at frontier posts along France's eastern frontier from Nancy to Nice, collecting German, Italian and Austrian intelligence. But no field intelligence officer was stationed north of Nancy and none was responsible for Belgian or Dutch intelligence. Not until 1913 was an intelligence post created for the first time at Mézières on the Belgian border, but this was too late to provide anything but negligible information on German preparations for the attack on Belgium.

If the collection of intelligence about France's main potential enemy was inadequate the use to which it was put was even worse. This had a good deal to do with the general incoherence of French foreign and defence policy-making in the decade before the First World War. Before Agadir the Foreign and War Ministries lived in a state of almost mutual ignorance. It was seven years before military planners were even informed of the 1902 secret Franco-Italian convention, thereby wasting two French army corps on the Alpine frontier. Similarly the War Ministry had never received an official diplomatic appraisal of Anglo-French relations. Though slightly improved after 1911, this poor co-ordination had not really been overcome by the time of the July crisis.[27] The role of assessing Germany as a potential enemy devolved mainly on the Ministry of War, but the Ministry was not up to the task. The legendary instability of other major Ministries was partly compensated for by the stability of their Ministers, who were often returned in successive governments. Not only did the Ministry of War change hands more than any other in the Third Republic but most of the office holders were of modest ability. On rare occasions when the Ministry was lucky enough to attract a capable Minister, it was quite impossible for him, as one of the members of the Senate Army Commission explained in February 1914, to master the fourteen separate departments of the Ministry and the eleven standing and about a hundred *ad hoc* committees of the High Command. Though the appointment of General Joffre to the new post of Chief of the General Staff in July 1911 improved control over the French army, nothing at all was done to improve the use made of intelligence within the General Staff. In August 1914 the Deuxième Bureau and the Troisième Bureau (Operations) were still operating as 'watertight compartments' and the rivalry between the two was a serious handicap in assessing Germany. Moreover it would seem that in the final years of peace, as Christopher Andrew suggests, 'intelligence assessments were accepted by Operations and by Joffre only when they reinforced their "preconceived ideas"'.[28] This was true of intelligence on the Schlieffen plan and France's grossly misjudged and nearly catastrophic assessment of Germany's use of reserves and heavy artillery.

The third area which contributed to France's miscalculations about Germany as her potential enemy was France's assessment of herself. Though less than a month before the outbreak of war Senator Humbert caused a parliamentary uproar when he gave a devastating account of France's inferiority in armaments to Germany, and though the Senate debate was well-publicised, it had no visible affect on morale. When the French government and people went to war three weeks later it was with a greater confidence in victory than at any time since the Franco-Prussian War.

That confidence in victory had been on the increase since 1905. At the time of the First Moroccan Crisis the vast majority of the Cabinet and High Command believed that a war with Germany would lead to a defeat similar to that of 1870. By the time of the Agadir crisis, Germany was considered to be much less formidable. Though the idea of going to war with her was turned down, it was no longer because France believed in inevitable defeat, but rather because she did not yet believe she had a 70 per cent chance of victory. French confidence continued its exponential growth, for in the following year a General Staff report forecast a victory of the Triple Entente over the Triple Alliance in the event of an Austrian offensive in the Balkans. During the July crisis, Joffre was completely confident that victory would be swift and certain; in the event France was only saved from swift defeat by the 'miracle of the Marne'.

What was striking about this amazing transformation of French confidence in less than a decade, was that it did not reflect any belief in German military decline. Indeed, Germany in 1914 was even more of a formidable opponent than in 1905. France's growing confidence in victory, as Christopher Andrew explains, reflected less a changing assessment of her enemy than a changing assessment of herself. And this changed self-assessment found its ultimate expression in the new strategic doctrine of the offensive adopted by the French High Command at Joffre's behest after Agadir. That doctrine placed the greatest emphasis on the *élan* of the French army, with the enemy's intentions being relegated to a very poor second. Adhering to Napoleon's dictum 'the moral is to the physical as three to one', Joffre believed that France had the capacity to snatch the initiative from Germany's hands at the outbreak of war through a vigorous offensive.

Some of France's confidence derived from her improved diplomatic position after 1905. But she could not expect much military back-up from Russia and Britain in the early stages of the war. France might have confidence in the sheer mass of the Russian army, but as the General Staff calculated in July 1913, Russian troops would not make contact with the Germans until fifteen days after mobilisation and could not launch a general offensive until the twenty-third day. Russia would therefore be of no direct assistance for two to three weeks during the crucial early battles of what was expected to be a short war. With Britain the opposite was true. The British Expeditionary Force could intervene quickly but with little might. Though the Anglo-French military conversations were in all more regular and more fruitful in terms of potential co-operation should Britain decide to fight alongside France, their execution remained hypothetical until the night of 3 August 1914. She again seemed to reason only in terms of confidence. Paul Cambon placed excessive confidence in an immediate British intervention. And to a large extent British intervention in the first stages of the war was valued more as a morale booster than as military back-up. When Henry Wilson asked General Foch in 1909: 'What would you say was the smallest British military force that would be of any practical assistance to you in the event of a contest such as we have been considering?' Foch replied immediately, 'One single private soldier and we would take good care that he was killed.'[29]

Certainly, during the first few weeks of the war France did not expect much assistance from her Triple Entente partners. She believed that on her own she could gain a substantial advantage over Germany on the Western Front which would allow her to win the war, despite having no numerical superiority over the German army and inferior armaments. Christopher Andrew concludes: 'Her confidence had a psychological rather than a material origin.'[30] It rested on the traditional belief that France, all said and done, was superior to Germany. Just as French public opinion in 1914 held to the irrational belief that war would be short because they wanted it to be short, so the French government and High Command's assessment of Germany as a potential enemy was based less on concrete evidence than on wishful thinking.

STEPHEN PICHON

Another of those recurrent debates of French political life which must have contributed to an acute sense of *déjà vu* in most politicians, the question of electoral reform,[31] brought down the short-lived Briand Cabinet on 18 March 1913 by a vote in the Senate. Poincaré immediately began negotiations for the formation of a new government. The criteria which had conditioned the selection of the last one were again in the front line. After much wrangling, Poincaré's long-standing nationalist colleague and member of the *Comité de l'Orient*,[32] Louis Barthou, was chosen. Poincaré and Barthou had been the 'boy-wonders' of politics in the 1890s, though Jules Cambon saw them more as 'young crocodiles'. Poincaré doubtless had a hand in choosing Stephen Pichon to lead the Quai d'Orsay in the new Cabinet from 22 March 1913.

Pichon, like Jonnart, was a nationalist and ex-President (1911–12) of the Comité de l'Orient. Poincaré was confident that the new Foreign Minister would respect the tenets of his policy in Europe and attempt to arrest the decline of France's presence in the Levant – a decline becoming increasingly accute in the first half of 1913 as pro-British sentiment continued to develop in Syria in spite of Grey's December declaration. Britain was encouraging the Syrian separatists not because she wanted a dissolution of the Ottoman Empire, but simply to maintain her influence there as a bargaining counter with France in the event of the Empire collapsing. During Pichon's term of office, Poincaré kept a lower profile in foreign affairs, though his overall influence was maintained. He engineered the temporary shift of priorities in French diplomacy from the European to the Levantine theatre. The most notable effect of this diplomacy was a continued improvement in relations with Germany and growing evidence of the incompatibility of French and Russian interests in the Ottoman Empire.

Franco-German Détente and the Future of the Ottoman Empire

Ambassadors Paul and Jules Cambon and Camille Barrère were delighted with Pichon's appointment as they had enjoyed such close relations with him in the past. Jules Cambon was particularly pleased when in early April he received a letter from the new Foreign Minister explaining that his whole policy would be one of *détente* with Germany. But he feared that an overzealous attitude towards Berlin might earn him blame from the 'bureaux' in Paris. Already Pichon's zeal in wishing to negotiate with Germany had been discovered by the 'bureaux', in the same way as Caillaux's secret negotiations had been discovered during the Agadir crisis. Pichon had spoken of better relations with the German Ambassador, who had translated the Minister's words as *rapprochement* in a communication to Berlin, which had been intercepted by the *cabinet noir* and discovered by the 'bureaux', causing an uproar.[33] Jules was worried enough to stress to Pichon that the best policy to adopt towards Germany was one which took a middle path 'between unwarranted eagerness and offensive bluster' – to speak of *rapprochement* could produce 'painful and sometimes dangerous reactions'. And he cited the recent courteous settlement of the potentially explosive Lunéville incident, in which a German Zeppelin had accidentally landed on French soil, as an example of what France's attitude should be.[34] But most important of all Cambon had no doubts about who had inspired such a policy: 'Pichon has dropped Clemenceau and has become completely "poincariste".' Again what he feared most was that Poincaré, whom he described as 'the least diplomatic mind I have encountered in my life', would seek better relations with Germany and upset Britain.[35]

The Syrian strategy apart, Poincaré's willingness to negotiate with Germany was probably given added impetus by the already discussed mood of confidence which characterised the French government and High Command at the end of 1912. It was sustained by the victory of the French-trained and armed Balkan states over German-trained and armed Turkey, which some observers saw, rather naïvely, as a dummy run for a future European war. What better time to capitalise on that assumed position of strength? The settlement of the First Balkan War in May 1913 gave France another opportunity to shore up her position in the Middle East. Jules Cambon pressed Pichon to come to an agreement with Germany on the future of Turkey-in-Asia. This involved adopting a conciliatory attitude towards her over the Baghdad Railway.

The question of the construction of a railway, which the Sultan hoped would unite the far-flung parts of the Ottoman Empire, had affected French, German and British relations since 1892. Germany had obtained the concession for the construction of the railway from Istanbul to Baghdad. But from the outset, the Deutsche Bank, which controlled the affair, realised that it would need the financial assistance of the Imperial Ottoman Bank, which was dominated by French banks. Until 1899 the Quai d'Orsay had refused to sanction any such collaboration. But from that date until 1903 Franco-German collaboration was fruitful in setting up the Baghdad Railway Company. However, Delcassé's switch to a more Germanophobic policy blocked any floating of the shares on the Paris Bourse in 1903, thereby seriously affecting the progress of the enterprise. Subsequently, the Railway became the subject of a series of diplomatic confrontations between Germany, who wished to use it as an instrument of economic penetration of Asiatic Turkey; France, who had similar interests; Britain, who feared that a German presence there would adversely affect Britain's strategic position in the Mediterranean and the Persian Gulf; and Russia, who feared that such a railway could undermine her security along her southern Caucasian border. But in 1911 at Potsdam Germany gained Russian acquiescence in the project and Britain and Germany resumed negotiations, which reached fruition in the early months of 1913. The line was split into two sections. Britain took control of the southern half from Basra to Kuwait, thereby protecting her strategic position in the Persian Gulf, while Germany was responsible for the line from Baghdad to Basra. The Anglo-German negotiations of 1913 increased France's feeling of being left out of the vital claim-staking in the Ottoman Empire and encouraged her to re-open negotiations with Germany.

France, however, had also to be careful not to bully Turkey in the parallel negotiations she had begun with her in May 1913 to obtain railway concessions in the Empire in exchange for loans. Intimidation would only annoy Germany, Turkey's protector, and lead her to refuse her blessing for the French sphere of influence in Syria.[36] Hence, Jules Cambon's remark about Franco-German relations: 'Never have we had so many opportunities as at present, not for a *rapprochement* between us, but for bringing about *détente*.'[37] But outbursts from the 'bureaux' and the actions of Germanophobe French officials abroad continued to threaten *détente*. It was probably this which led Cambon to attempt to justify his policy by expounding for the first time in detail in an official despatch his theory on Franco-German relations. He asked whether it was reasonable to keep an expanding nation of seventy millions with a flourishing industry confined within a country until recently occupied by a population only half that size, since the result would be an explosion: 'Would it not be more prudent' he added, 'not to block everywhere an inevitable expansion?' On the contrary, why did not France revert to Bismarckian tactics to dissipate the strength of her rival. 'It would perhaps be a good thing if Germany also had to expend her energy in far-off places . . . and that her fleet had things to defend other than her North Sea coasts.' It was shortsighted to wish to oppose Germany everywhere in the world. On the contrary:

> we ought, it seems to me, to confine ourselves to areas where, as in Syria, we have interests to maintain and perhaps make more real effort than we are doing by concentrating our economic and moral forces there. It is senseless to wish to be everywhere when one does not have an expanding population.[38]

It was on this issue that there were clear divisions in the Quai d'Orsay. The 'generalists' favoured the expansion of French interests everywhere, while the 'regionalists' or 'Syrians', such as Jules Cambon, only envisaged French expansion in certain privileged areas of the French Empire, such as Syria.[39]

Between August and November 1913, France was given an even greater incentive to come to an agreement with Germany. In August the French Parliament voted for a return to the Three Years' Law, thereby strengthening France's negotiating position with Germany. In the same month, on 10 August 1913, the belligerents of the Second Balkan War made peace at Bucharest giving France perhaps her final opportunity to consolidate her possessions in the reprieved Ottoman Empire. During that war, which began on 26 June as a result of squabbling between the Balkan allies, Bulgaria,

encouraged by Vienna, attacked Greece and Serbia, who were soon joined by
Rumania and Turkey. Against such numbers Bulgaria was quickly defeated.
Once again the war cut across the existing great-power alliances. Germany
and Italy worked to restrain Austria, who wished to support Bulgaria against
Serbia, while Germany, Britain and France worked together to ensure that
Russia did not attempt to bring about the demise of the Ottoman Empire.
With the ending of the Balkan Wars, the future of Turkey-in-Asia was
becoming the decisive question in international relations. And the great-
power alliances began to feel the strain. Already in April, Maurice Paléologue,
the Political Director at the Quai d'Orsay, had stressed to Isvolsky the
conflicting policies of Paris and St Petersburg in the Near East when he told
him: 'You want to exhaust Turkey: we want her to be capable of still living
and even of recovering in Asia.'[40] Rivalry also continued to increase with
France's other Triple Entente partner, Britain, over oil concessions in the
Middle East. *Détente* with Germany was becoming an important issue in
French foreign policy. Poincaré was spurred on to be more conciliatory
towards her over the Baghdad railway.[41] Jules Cambon, who was adamant
that such an opportunity should not be missed, even began to take issue with
his own colleagues for blindly criticising Germany. It was to Delcassé that he
referred when he remarked: 'Some of our compatriots imagine that when it
hails on our vineyards it is Germany's doing, but she does not yet play the role
of the political Almighty God that is too easily attributed to her.'[42]

On 15 November 1913 negotiations with Berlin began in earnest. But
Germany warned France that she would be unwise to come to a final
settlement with Turkey before Berlin had achieved satisfaction on the
Baghdad question. Jules Cambon told the Under-Secretary of State in the
German Foreign Office, Arthur Zimmermann, that this was 'an affair of
general interest whose settlement will later have consequences for the relations
of the two countries and the peace of Europe'.[43] Their importance was
certainly demonstrated by the fact that even such serious nationalist outbursts
as the Saverne incident, arising from a young German officer's insults to
Alsatian recruits and the French flag in November 1913, failed to alter the
course on which Poincaré had set French diplomacy. Even when Cambon was
told of a conversation between King Albert of Belgium and the Kaiser, in
which the Kaiser had explained that 'war with France is inevitable' because of
her desire for revenge, the Berlin Ambassador merely advised calm and the
need for France to 'keep her powder dry'.[44] He told his brother that in spite
of this, in Berlin there was a tendency towards *détente*, 'and in Paris more than
a tendency'. He even told the German Chancellor that the hostile elements of
1911 'would this time be with us and that an *entente* on Asia Minor would be
welcomed'. Moreover, he confirmed that Poincaré was personally 'in the best
of frames of mind'.[45]

Not even the Liman von Sanders affair was able to divert France from her
desire for an agreement with Germany, even though it provoked considerable

unrest, not least with Jules Cambon. Shortly after it became known on 27 November 1913 that the Turkish government had appointed as Inspector-General of the Ottoman Army and Commander of the First Ottoman Army Corps in Constantinople the German General, Liman von Sanders, Russia protested strongly at the prospect of a German controlling the Bosphorus garrison and called on France to support her. Jules Cambon immediately complained to Pichon that Russia was using this incident as a pretext for upsetting French negotiations with Germany because she feared the Baghdad railway would pose a threat to her Caucasian frontier. To stop negotiations with Berlin in order to satisfy Russia would merely allow Germany to supplant France in Syria.[46]

Despite Cambon's repeated warnings to Paris, negotiations with Germany were interrupted as international tension mounted. Consequently, France was unable to put her final signature to the agreement reached with Turkey on 11 and 18 December 1913. The loan to Turkey had to be delayed until Germany was satisfied on the Baghdad question, which the von Sanders affair now jeopardised. But Cambon's continuous calls to resist Russian appeals for help soon found support with Poincaré. At a Cabinet meeting on 13 January 1914 he successfully put pressure on the new Doumergue Cabinet to turn Russia down.[47] Poincaré's action refutes two commonly held beliefs: that he unfailingly acquiesced to Russian demands, and that he was unconditionally opposed to Germany. Here, indeed, was a clear case of Poincaré opposing Russia in order not to upset Germany.

The affair was finally settled on 15 January when Germany agreed to a compromise in which von Sanders kept his rank of Inspector-General of the Turkish Army but relinquished direct command of the Constantinople Corps. Russia was satisfied. But in the time it had taken to reach a settlement an important change had taken place in French domestic politics – the Barthou ministry had fallen on 2 December 1913 and with it Pichon. Jules Cambon was anxious about the effect this would have on the Franco-German negotiations. He made a desperate appeal to Pichon to remain at the Quai d'Orsay at all costs. 'Remember 1911: if you had not fallen we would have signed the agreement on the Moroccan railways, we would have executed the 1909 arrangement – and we would have averted Agadir and its consequences.' And he concluded: 'Stay, you must, and if necessary make some sacrifices in order to stay.'[48] It was to no avail.

There is no doubt that at the end of 1913 Franco-German relations were on a better footing than for years. Even the Russian Prime Minister was able to report to the Tsar on 13 December 1913: 'All French statesmen want quiet and peace. They are willing to work with Germany and are much more peaceful than two years ago.'[49] Clearly a good deal of the credit belonged to Jules Cambon for his patience and perseverance in pursuing it through his personal correspondence with Pichon. But in the end it was only possible to carry out a policy of improved relations with Germany because Poincaré sanctioned it. In doing so he was in no way compromising his position on the separation of the alliance systems: that applied to European matters. What was at stake here were imperial interests where France and Germany could work together for their mutual benefit.

Poincaré's choice of a successor to Barthou proved difficult. In the end he turned to Gaston Doumergue. But Doumergue, who took over both the premiership and the Foreign Ministry, soon showed signs of wishing to follow his own policy. His pro-Russian stance in the von Sanders affair had risked undermining Franco-German negotiations until Poincaré had intervened. Negotiations with Berlin were resumed after the affair was settled on 15 January 1914. To mark his willingness to work with Germany, Poincaré made a gesture unprecedented by a French President of the Republic after 1870 – he accepted an invitation to dine at the German embassy in Paris on 20 January 1914.

Less than a month later, on 15 February 1914, Franco-German negotiations came to fruition on French participation in financing the Baghdad railway. It was the first step towards a partition of Asiatic Turkey. The French were given northern Anatolia and Syria for development of their railways. In exchange, France agreed to German terms for railway links at Aleppo and Alexandretta and recognised the German sphere of influence in the area crossed by the Anatolian and Baghdad railways. The agreement opened the way for the conclusion of negotiations with Turkey on 9 April 1914, thus cementing France's economic and religious presence in the area and making France, as Jules Cambon had predicted, 'the definite master of Syria'.[50] However, in Paris the agreement got a mixed reception, with *Le Temps* complaining that France had been evicted from the Baghdad project. Once again this was the reaction of the influential nationalist minority in France, which instinctively found any negotiation with Germany distasteful. This time Cambon had stolen a victory over them but he remained pessimistic about the future.

> Since the Dreyfus Affair, we have in France a militarist and nationalist party which will not brook a *rapprochement* with Germany at any price, and which excites the aggressive tones of a great number of newspapers. The government will have to take them into account, and also the party they represent, should another incident break out between the two nations. The majority of Germans and Frenchmen want to live in peace, that cannot be denied. But a powerful minority in both countries dreams only battles, conquests, or revenge. That is the danger beside which we must live as if next to a powder-barrel which the slightest imprudence might blow up.[51]

Since 1907 Cambon had believed that the possibility of war with Germany could be averted if only France would concentrate her imperial efforts in areas where she already had an interest and allow Germany to expand elsewhere. Negotiations between the two countries would have mutual imperial benefits with the added bonus of bringing about *détente* and reducing the risk of war in

Europe. Thus it comes as no surprise that as soon as he had secured the agreement on Asia Minor, Cambon appeared ready to embark on another deal with Germany on central Africa. On 13 April 1914 he informed the Political Director at the Quai of the private talks he had had with the German Secretary of State. Von Jagow had suggested that if France, Britain and Germany could agree on the exploitation of central Africa 'all chance of war would be averted for many long years' because Germany would have a sufficiently large theatre of operations to keep her occupied.[52] Cambon obviously agreed, but the suggestion never in fact went further than private talks. This was the last move in favour of Franco-German *détente*. In just over two months the European nations would turn from colonial preoccupations to infinitely more serious problems nearer home. War, instead of being averted for many years, was just three-and-half months away.

Poincaré's Low Profile in Foreign Affairs

Though Poincaré continued to influence Foreign Minister Pichon, his influence was a good deal less conspicuous than it had been under Jonnart. The first reason for this must have been Pichon's experience of foreign affairs. Pichon had experience whereas Jonnart had had none. Poincaré was left with no valid excuse for direct intervention at the Quai d'Orsay. Secondly, the Radicals were intent on bringing about Poincaré's downfall. They were certain to seize on any evidence of direct intervention in foreign affairs to achieve this. During the presidential election campaign, led by Clemenceau they had mounted a particularly ignoble campaign to discredit him. Scurrilous rumours were circulated about Poincaré's wife Henriette, who had divorced her first husband in 1890 and had remarried. Her second husband had died in 1892 and she had married Poincaré in 1904 in a strictly civil ceremony which had upset his pious mother, but which had reinforced his standing as a *laïc*. Henriette subsequently discovered that her first husband had died in 1909. Both Poincaré's mother, who died on 11 April 1913, and his wife had wanted the marriage to be celebrated by a religious ceremony. This represented a considerable risk for the anti-clerical President. He none the less agreed out of respect for his mother to be married in secret on 5 May, claiming afterwards that it was the best action of his life. The inevitable happened, the secret began to leak out providing obvious material for unscrupulous Radicals. Poincaré knew full well that if an anti-clerical campaign was started against him, his popularity would quickly dissolve. This was a further reason for not provoking his political opponents unnecessarily by overstepping his constitutional prerogatives.

A third and similar reason for keeping a low profile derived from an incident which had taken place in April and May 1913, which concerned the Vatican. The suspected imminent death of Pope Pius X in April 1913 led

Paléologue to encourage both Pichon and Poincaré to advise the French Cardinals on the necessity to elect one of their number who would support France in the future. In particular, it was hoped that such an appointment would redress France's influence over her religious protectorates in the Levant to the detriment of her rivals. Doubtless Poincaré agreed for this reason. However, he was aware of the risk he was taking and expressed concern about a meeting with the Cardinal Archbishop of Paris lest Clemenceau should hear of it. On 30 April it was decided that Armand Nisard, France's former Ambassador to the Vatican, be despatched to gain official contact with the French Cardinals. Orders were given to him officially on 5 May 1913.[53] However, in April and May 1913 the cryptographic services of the Sûreté at the Ministry of the Interior decyphered three telegrams from the Italian Ambassador in Paris revealing the Poincaré–Pichon secret negotiations with the Vatican.[54] On 6 May 1913 Klotz, Minister of the Interior, produced the telegrams at the meeting of the Cabinet. There was uproar, with Pichon threatening to resign if the Ministry of the Interior continued to intercept communications. Interceptions by the Sûreté were stopped, but here was more incriminating evidence which in the hands of the unscrupulous could topple Poincaré from the presidency. Poincaré's fear of the Radicals was becoming so acute that, according to Jules Cambon, the President was now attempting to patch up differences with their leaders. He had even offered the London embassy to the Anglophile Clemenceau, much to Jules Cambon's distress. As the power of the Radicals grew, so Poincaré would maintain an increasingly low profile in foreign affairs.

GASTON DOUMERGUE

Poincaré's choice of a successor to the Barthou government had been conditioned by his desire to see French foreign policy maintained on its present path and to keep the Radicals, opposed to the Three Years' Law, from power. However, his popularity had declined considerably since what some had called the Boulangist fervour of his election to the Elysée. His parliamentary support had also dwindled and this had led Paul Deschanel and two other nationalists, Alexandre Ribot and Charles Dupuy, to decline his offer to form a new ministry, for fear that it would be shortlived. As the possibility of forming a centre government had been ruled out, on 6 December 1913 Poincaré had turned to a Radical of the centre, Gaston Doumergue; but it was not on any terms that Doumergue had been offered the premiership. Firstly, his credentials were good: as a former Colonial Minister, a member of numerous colonial movements and a past-president of the *Mission Laïque*, devoted to the expansion of French secular education above all in the Middle East, it was believed that he could be relied upon to continue Poincaré's policy in the Levant. Secondly, Poincaré had stated quite frankly to Doumergue that his selection would be conditional on his agreeing beforehand to maintain the Three Years' Law and France's present foreign policy. Doumergue accepted without disagreement. As a final guarantee, the President had persuaded him to accept the post of Foreign Minister, fully aware that he had no experience of foreign policy. Once again Poincaré had chosen a straw-man to head the Quai d'Orsay, in the belief that he would have to refer to the President for advice.

However, Poincaré was not able to stop Doumergue including Joseph Caillaux, Poincaré's arch-rival, in the Cabinet as Minister of Finance. Caillaux has launched the Radical programme at the party conference in Pau with a call for an income tax and a return to the Two Years' Law. In domestic policy Caillaux would increasingly prove to be the real power in the government as the Radicals' popularity in the country continued to increase, backed by a real, though informal, alliance with the Socialists. In order to stem that popularity before the parliamentary elections of April–May 1914, some of the most able parliamentarians, who supported the Three Years' Law, united under Briand's leadership to form the *Fédération des gauches*. The new party's label was typically untypical of its political leanings, the new grouping having greater affinities with the Centre and Right then the Left. The battle lines were drawn for the forthcoming elections.

Doumergue, as has been shown, did not turn out to be the docile creature the President had hoped for. Franco-German negotiations over the Baghdad railway broke down partly as a result of his stance in the Liman von Sanders affair. He had been intent on disproving the traditional belief that the Radicals were opposed to the Franco-Russian Alliance and had pandered to Russian appeals for action against Germany until Poincaré openly intervened in a Cabinet debate in January to counter this policy. But Poincaré's influence was none the less on the wane. He had considered the last ministerial crisis serious enough to contemplate resignation from the Elysée. Paul Cambon was surprised by Poincaré's new-found sympathy towards him and his brother and attributed it to the plots of the Radicals, and in particular 'those two adventurers who are after him, Clemenceau and Caillaux, [who] do not hide their aim of slitting his throat'.[55] Doubtless Poincaré believed that through close contacts with the Cambon brothers he would be able to maintain his influence in foreign affairs. But under the protective wing of the Radicals Doumergue felt safe to act independently. Poincaré was soon complaining that the Foreign Minister no longer felt the need to consult him. It was Doumergue who, on learning of Russia's desire for a state visit from the French President of the Republic, sprang at the opportunity. His desire to display pro-Russian sentiments seemed to know no bounds. At a Cabinet meeting on 12 January he even claimed the credit for the Franco-Russian agreement for a loan to build railways in Russia, agreed upon during Kokovtsov's visit to Paris during the previous ministry. His room for independent manoeuvre was further encouraged by the fact that the Cabinet was now only rarely allowed to discuss foreign affairs, which reduced the President's power of influence. Poincaré lamented to himself: 'Where is the time when all the Cabinet meetings which I chaired were for three-quarters of the time given over to the study of foreign affairs?'[56] On 16 January, aware of his impotence, Poincaré reflected nostalgically on the euphoria which had surrounded his election a year before and what had happened since: 'A year has passed! My good mother is no longer here, the last ministerial crisis has broken the charm and smashed the national movement; a large part of those wonderful hopes has already withered up and the constitution imposes on me the cruel duty of not interfering.'[57]

The Replacement of Delcassé as Ambassador to St Petersburg

If anyone had encouraged Russia irresponsibly, it was the Germanophile French Ambassador in St Petersburg, Delcassé. Paléologue claimed that the former Foreign Minister had told him, on leaving for the Russian capital at the beginning of 1913, that his sole aim would be to ensure that the Tsar's armies would be prepared to make any necessary offensive in fifteen days: 'As for the diplomatic twaddle and old nonsense about the European equilibrium, I shall bother with it as little as possible: it is no longer anything but verbiage.'[58] Even given Paléologue's habitual exaggeration, this was worrying. When Sazonov visited France in October 1913, he appeared surprised at her peaceful intentions, which led Paléologue to wonder whether Delcassé had been misleading the Russian government and whether he had been executing his orders faithfully. On 18 November the Grand Duke Nicholas Michaïlovitch complained of Delcassé's over-secretive manner and his failure to mingle with Russian society. By Christmas 1913 Paléologue was complaining that Delcassé's 'patriotism is turning into a fixation, an obsessive exaltation, I would even say to monomania'.[59] Pichon had earlier expressed concern about this and had suggested that Delcassé's request for retirement be accepted immediately. Poincaré had also been critical of Delcassé's role. He recorded in his diaries how he had pandered to Russian demands, often to the detriment of France's interests, and claimed that had all his suggestions been accepted, France would have sacrificed all her interests in the Orient.[60]

Poincaré's first choice for a replacement for Delcassé was Pierre de Margerie. The President was bitterly disappointed when de Margerie declined the offer on grounds of ill-health and insufficient wealth. Some of the disappointment was relieved, however, when he discovered that Doumergue was reserving de Margerie for the political directorship. Only then did he agree with Doumergue that Paléologue should take over the St Petersburg embassy in February 1914. The Russians were not enthusiastic about Paléologue's nomination. Given Delcassé's excessive support for Russia in the past, this was not surprising. But Paléologue would prove to be as great a supporter of Russia as Delcassé had been. Entranced by the pomp and ceremony of the Russian court, impatient to be accepted and to impress, Paléologue would pledge support to St Petersburg which over-reached his orders from Paris.

The Caillaux Trial

The plotting and increasing popularity of the Radicals pushed Poincaré into greater isolation from mid-January to the April–May general elections. It was a period in which his presidential influence was at its lowest. He was keenly aware of this, but his failing popularity increased his self-doubt and led him to avoid taking any action to improve his position. In March 1914 he was encouraged by his political associates to take the politically explosive, yet constitutional, step of intervening, by means of an official presidential note, in a Chamber debate on the vital issue of the reorganisation of the officer corps, which looked like going against the government. For several days he hesitated about what to do. 'The present Cabinet has taken away much of my popularity, I was elected in order to act. I cannot be a President like Fallières and Loubet.'[61] But in the end he abstained from any action.

Poincaré was not helped by the fact that the spring and summer of 1914 were marked in Europe by a period of exceptional calm. He had been elected on the strength of his ability to make France's position felt in any international crisis. Since the beginning of 1913 he had been seen to be doing just that. But now the absence of international tension to a large extent took away his *raison d'être*, and gave him no opportunity to restore his popularity. Worse still, a number of unsavoury scandals concentrated public opinion on domestic affairs in which Poincaré felt powerless to act. Those scandals, which, true to French standards, possessed all the ingredients of crime, passion, money and politics, were dominated by the assassination of the editor of the newspaper *Le Figaro* by the wife of the Finance Minister, Joseph Caillaux. Madame Caillaux's motive for entering Gaston Calmette's office on 16 March and shooting him six times was the bitter campaign he was running against her husband, which included the publication of her love letters to Caillaux, written while he was still married to his first wife. A further dimension was added to the scandal when rumours began to circulate about copies of two decyphered German telegrams in Calmette's possession, which revealed Caillaux's secret negotiations with Germany during the Agadir crisis. The German Ambassador learnt of these rumours and called at the Quai d'Orsay to protest. It was serious enough that the French had intercepted German communications. But if the affair became public, continued the German Ambassador threateningly, 'a bomb would explode'.[62] And there was a very real chance of that happening at Madame Caillaux's trial, which was set to open on 20 July. But even more worrying for France was the prospect of a diplomatic scandal involving countries other than Germany. Caillaux, who had resigned from the government, was adamant that his position would not be undermined still further by the revelation of his dealings with Germany. He was ready to retaliate by threatening publication of a number of Italian intercepts which he had in his possession, having had them burgled from the Ministry of the Interior. These could incriminate Poincaré for his dealings with the Vatican. He also threatened to produce copies of Spanish intercepts which showed that Calmette was in the pay of Spain. Thus it was the prospect of a mammoth diplomatic scandal rather than the prospect of war with Germany which preoccupied the French government for most of the July crisis. In the end an international scandal was avoided as the government issued an official lie denying that German intercepts existed. Caillaux's blackmail had paid off and he felt no need to retaliate. His good fortune continued when his wife was acquitted. France may have averted an international scandal but she had not emerged unscathed. Most major Foreign ministries had been alerted to the activities of French cryptographers. Consequently, they changed their codes leaving the Quai d'Orsay, on the eve of war, unable to decypher any diplomatic telegrams.[63]

King George V's State Visit To France

The atmosphere of domestic and potential international scandal could do nothing less than bring the institutions of the Republic into disrepute. Crowds had taken to the streets of Paris. They expressed their contempt for politicians by boos and chants. There were violent scenes. The President's declining popularity suffered further. There is no doubt that Poincaré viewed the forthcoming state visit to France by King George V from 21 to 25 April as a very welcome distraction for public opinion from sordid domestic affairs. It would also provide an opportunity for drawing attention to himself as the guardian of France's Entente and Alliance and perhaps restore some of his popularity. Protests had already been made about the state visit taking place too near to the April–May general elections. The King's visit also provided Poincaré with an opportunity for tightening still further the bonds of the Triple Entente. With the Syrian negotiations finally tucked away on 9 April 1914, Poincaré wished to smooth out some of the creases which France's concentration on the Middle East question had occasioned with London and St Petersburg over the last eighteen months. Some two weeks before the visit he had been shown a telegram from Paléologue in St Petersburg, explaining a campaign by the influential Count Witte in favour of a Russo-Franco-German alliance backed by the Kaiser. Paléologue and Sazonov saw in it a ploy by Germany to divide the Triple Entente. Poincaré stated that he would use the King's visit and his own forthcoming state visit to Russia to thwart these intrigues.[64]

Russia believed that a strong alliance with Great Britain and France would quell any warlike intention on Germany's part. She had tried to consolidate the Triple Entente in December 1913, but France had refused. Now, two weeks before George V's visit, Russia asked France to foster a Russo-British alliance. Paul Cambon, briefed by Sir Francis Bertie, informed Poincaré that Britain would never accept an alliance, but that she might accept a military agreement analogous to the Franco-British exchange of letters.

The visit to Paris by the King, accompanied by Sir Edward Grey, placed Poincaré in his element. He immediately took control of affairs. In discussions Doumergue concentrated on questions of detail to which he obtained few replies, while Poincaré took the helm in discussing general policy,[65] which to a large extent reflected the overall conduct of French foreign affairs from 1913 to the July crisis. A Russo-British agreement was touched on in discussions, but it was Poincaré who quite independently, it would seem, ordered Paul Cambon to encourage Britain to begin naval conversations with Russia. As Cambon remarked, 'it is he, and he alone, who is the Minister of Foreign Affairs'.[66] Grey conceded to Anglo-Russian naval talks along the lines of the 1912 discussions with France, though more to please the French than the Russians. This was less than Russia had wanted, but she was still pleased and showed it in the substantial concessions she made to Britain in Persia, though the discussions had not even begun by June. Poincaré would doubtless have liked something a little more substantial to have come from the King's visit just before the elections, but he had all the same, tightened up the Triple Entente that much more. And that success could be measured by Germany's displeasure when she discovered the proposed naval talks through her spy in the Russian embassy in London.

The 1914 General Elections

A victory for the Left in the forthcoming general elections had been predicted for some time. The seeming unpopularity of the Three Years' Law and the general ascendancy of the Socialists encouraged that belief. It was further aided by the absence of any international tension which could strike the nationalist chord and make the Right's policies appear more attractive. Contemporary analyses of the election results under the two-round majority system, which took place on 26 April and 10 May 1914, nearly all agree that they show substantial opposition to the Three Years' Law. As such they have traditionally been seen as a rejection of Poincaré's diplomacy. However, Jean-Jacques Becker's monumental study of French public opinion in 1914 suggests that these analyses are inaccurate. An analysis of election manifestos shows that only two groups had trenchant opinions on the question of the Law: the Socialists were vehemently opposed; the *Fédération des gauches* was adamantly in favour. The other parties were a good deal more discreet – the Radical party's manifesto neither rejected nor reiterated the party conference's decision to oppose the Law. It remained intentionally ambiguous. Of the 2451 candidates who stood for election in 590 of the 602 constituencies over half (1265) were supporters of the Law, while less than half (1085) were opponents.[67] Thus in terms of candidates for or against the Law, both camps were fairly evenly balanced. Candidates in favour of the Law obtained in the first round a nationwide score of 55 per cent of polled votes, while those opposed polled only 43 per cent. The picture is thus one of public opinion divided into two roughly equivalent groups. Analysis of the attitudes to the Law of candidates elected to the Chamber as portrayed in their official election manifestos again show two finely balanced camps for and against. It is clear from this that the supporters of the Law constituted half of the newly elected deputies. Overall the Socialists were the real victors in the elections, gaining some 30 seats to give them 100 deputies. The Radicals returned some 260 deputies, though this, as has been shown, cannot be seen as an indication of opposition to the Law. Neither is the fact that both the Centre and Right lost deputies a sign of opposition to the Law. The election results show support for the Law in terms of votes rather than in terms of seats. This apparent anomaly is merely a consequence of the two-round majority system exaggerating one side's victory in terms of deputies out of all proportion to the number of votes it polled.

It should now be clear why contempories saw in the election results a defeat for the defenders of the Law. They drew their conclusions from the general swing in the number of seats rather than the votes polled. Instead of seeing little change in the former political balance their attention was caught by the spectacular progression of the one party which had the most marked views on the Law – the Socialists. Becker's overall conclusion is that there was probably a majority in the country resigned to the Three Years' Law, but that that majority was shrinking. Thus the significance of the 1914 elections is less simple than it has hitherto been portrayed. The vast majority of Frenchmen in 1914 might be more accurately described as being characterised by a pacifism which did not exclude patriotism but which rejected both the extremes of nationalism and anti-patriotism.[68]

RENÉ VIVIANI

Though the country as a whole was uncertain in its attitude to the Law, it appeared to contemporaries that the new Chamber was not. The Three Years' Law seemed doomed. Poincaré was pressed by political affiliates to force the Doumergue Cabinet to resign so that a new government could be formed which would defend the Law with greater resolve.[69] Typically, Poincaré's fear of responsibility threw him into confusion as to his course of action. He hesitated, wondering whether he would be overstepping his constitutional role. In the end it was Doumergue who decided to resign on 2 June. There followed a two-week-long governmental crisis, during which Poincaré did all he could to safeguard the Three Years' Law. When his old political associate, Léon Bourgeois, declined to form a ministry, Poincaré turned to the ex-Socialist, René Viviani. The President first made sure that Viviani did not equivocate about maintaining the military Law, which made his task of forming a ministry difficult. Poincaré, himself, believed that the Radical-Socialist bloc was likely to reject any ministry not chosen by them. Viviani was eventually successful in getting together a ministerial team. But disagreement in the Cabinet-elect on the question of the Three Years' Law broke up the team before it even got to the Chamber and the crisis was on again.

The Radicals' attacks against Poincaré were stepped up. Two emissaries had been sent to the United States to glean information about – and if possible bring back – Madame Poincaré's first husband, hitherto presumed dead. Poincaré could only shrug his shoulders in despair when he learned of a letter allegedly sent to the Queen of England giving details of the First Lady of France's past. The press began to follow up these rumours propagated by Caillaux. Threats were made to publish love letters from Madame Poincaré's first husband to her.

As Viviani's attempt had failed on 8 June, Poincaré naïvely called on a man of the Centre Right, Alexandre Ribot, to form a new government. Four days later the ministry collapsed ignominiously on a Chamber vote. Poincaré again turned to Viviani. He was once more contemplating resignation if Viviani failed, on the grounds that he would not be a party, directly or indirectly, to the abrogation of the Law. This he believed would leave 'the way clear for the opponents of the Russian Alliance and the perfidious artisans of a Franco-German *rapprochement*',[70] which as far as Europe was concerned was anathema to him.

Viviani completed his Cabinet on 12 June. He took on the Premiership and the Foreign Ministry. That evening Poincaré once again reflected pessimistically on his political future: 'My constitutional powerlessness will bring me new attacks, my declining popularity will disappear altogether, unpopularity will triumph, but I will have made the effort right until the end to save the country.' On 16 June Viviani's government won a majority in the Chamber.

The fact that it did win a majority shows that the Three Years' Law was not such a crucial issue. Not only was the new government committed to upholding the Law, but the vast majority of its members had clearly voted for it in the previous year. Out of seventeen Ministers ten had voted in favour, only five had voted against, and two had abstained. The Law was not the cause either for the failure of Ribot's government. That had failed because it had appeared as right wing, and therefore in contradiction to the new Chamber. A new government was now in place, an embarrassing political crisis had been solved and the Law was for the moment safe. Yet again President Poincaré had had his way. He had done so unaware of the looming shadow of war.

Raymond Poincaré was one of the strongest presidents of the Third Republic. His power was based on a judicious reading of the constitution, which allowed the President considerable influence in international affairs. During his ministry in 1912 he had built a reputation for having a clear-cut view of French diplomacy and international affairs which, following his election to the Elysée, he imposed on subsequent Foreign Ministers. Though his influence in foreign affairs was always considerable it did fluctuate, partly according to the state of international tension – the greater it was the more he could justify his intervention – and partly as a result of his vulnerability *vis-à-vis* the Radicals. However, despite the eclipsing of his direct role during late 1913 and early 1914, Poincaré ensured that the main tenets of his foreign policy were respected: military preparedness in the form of the Three Years' Law, a stronger and more cohesive Triple Entente and the separation of the alliance systems. But these were by no means the only issues of French policy during 1913 and 1914. In many ways, hindsight has led us to assume that because war was only a short time away the problems which brought it about were constantly on the minds of the statesmen of the day. Certainly this was not true of France. To a large extent it could be said that during 1913 and 1914 France was more concerned with Syria than Bosnia, and more preoccupied with reaching an agreement with Germany over the future of the Ottoman Empire than with supporting her ally, Russia, in the Near East. And again it was Poincaré who developed and directed these policies, when, ironically, he has traditionally been cast as the bigoted anti-German and pro-Russian. Thus from 1913 to 1914 French foreign policy was characterised by a firm attitude to Germany on continental issues but a conciliatory one on extra-European matters. If Poincaré remained the determining influence in French diplomacy, what then was his role during the July crisis?

7 The July Crisis

For French public opinion in 1914 the July crisis, as we know it today, never really existed. Had the average French contemporary been asked what he thought the July crisis was, he would doubtless have replied: the Caillaux trial. Analysis of press coverage of the European diplomatic crisis and Madame Caillaux's trial shows that certainly until 24 July 1914 the latter totally dominated newspaper columns. Even until three days before France began general mobilisation the trial rivalled the European crisis, if not surpassed it, in importance. On 29 July France's most respected newspaper renowned for its authoritative coverage of international relations, *Le Temps*, devoted over twice as much space to the final verdict of acquittal in the trial as to the European crisis. It was no different for newspapers with the widest circulation, such as *Le Petit Parisien* and *L'Echo de Paris*.[1] The French population as a whole had for a month been virtually unaware of the intense diplomatic wrangling which had taken place since the assassination of the Archduke Franz Ferdinand of Austria. They were now in the last days of July about to go to war and yet virtually oblivious to any danger.

French newspaper editors could, however, be excused for devoting so much attention to the Caillaux trial rather than to the European crisis. Even for normally well-informed contempories it was by no means obvious that the assassination at Sarajevo on 28 June 1914 of Archduke Franz Ferdinand, heir to the Austro-Hungarian throne, would be the beginning of a European crisis. Only with hindsight does it appear so. Indeed, by the summer of 1914, a European war was beginning to seem anachronistic. France and Germany had not been at war for forty-four years, Austria for nearly half a century, and Russia and Britain for sixty years. More serious crises than the assassination, such as the Bosnian and Agadir crises, had come to nothing in recent years. More encouraging still, two Balkan wars had just been contained and settled by the mechanism of the old Concert of Europe, thereby providing hope for a settlement, if need be, of a third. Moreover the lull in international relations in the spring and early summer of 1914 did not escape contemporaries. Once again only hindsight shows us that the lull prefaced the storm. For many this 'exceptional tranquillity', as Winston Churchill called it, may have appeared as the beginning of the return of the fat years of peace after the lean years of hectic diplomacy since Agadir. In the wake of the Franco-German Asia Minor settlement even Jules Cambon appeared optimistic: 'I am far from believing that at this moment there is anything in the air which could be a threat to us, on the contrary.'[2] The arch-pessimist – Sir Arthur Nicolson – had never seen such 'calm waters'.[3] A measure of the relaxation felt in the European chancelleries was provided by Britain, who in June 1914 had permitted eight of her precious dreadnought battleships to sail into the heavily German-patrolled waters of the Baltic: four were to make a courtesy call to the Russian harbour of Kronstadt, while the other four were to anchor in the midst of the German fleet for the ceremonies at Kiel to mark the re-opening of the canal.[4]

In France the new Viviani Cabinet was settling down to its duties, relieved at having secured the vote of the Chamber, but clearly anxious about the Caillaux trial. Viviani, like Doumergue, had no previous experience of foreign affairs. Like his predecessor he combined the foreign affairs' portfolio with the premiership. Once again Poincaré had taken the customary precautions to maintain his influence over foreign policy. He had however, admitted to one change: a new post of Under-Secretary of State for Foreign Affairs was created at the Quai d'Orsay. But the new appointee, Abel Ferry, was as ignorant of foreign affairs as his Minister. In fact, two days after the formation of the new Cabinet at the first sign of a diplomatic problem, the new Under-Secretary was hastily despatched by Viviani to seek Poincaré's advice. After the partial eclipse of his influence under Doumergue, Poincaré would soon resume control of affairs.

A telegram announcing the assassination of Archduke Franz Ferdinand and his wife in the Bosnian capital of Sarajevo by a young Serbian nationalist, Gavrilo Princip, was passed to Poincaré on the Sunday afternoon of 28 June 1914. The President was attending the Grand Prix at the Longchamp race-course together with the diplomatic corps. Understandably, the news caused consternation and the Austrian Ambassador withdrew. But the President and the other members of the diplomatic corps remained to watch the afternoon's racing. It was some time before the incident became a crisis.

If the July crisis never existed for French public opinion, it did not really exist for French political and diplomatic decision-makers either. The assassination of the Austrian heir to the Dual Monarchy caused relatively little consternation, at least in the chancelleries of the Triple Entente powers. Franz Ferdinand and his morganatic wife were known to be unpopular in Austro-Hungarian ruling circles, partly because of their more liberal views on the treatment of minorities in the Empire. This was evident at the funeral, which was only attended by the Emperor and the Court. The only flowers were those sent by the diplomatic corps and the Hohenberg children, who, however, were not allowed to attend their parents' funeral service.[5] Of course no one believed that the incident would be ignored by Austria. On the other hand there is little evidence to show that many diplomats thought that Vienna would issue such a forceful ultimatum to Serbia on 23 July. In France during the first three weeks of July the subjects dealt with in diplomatic correspondence were by and large the same as before 28 June. Indeed, compilers of the collection of French Diplomatic Documents decided to advance the ending of their work to 23 July precisely because the assassination did not have the effect on French politics which has so often been attributed to it.

The Triple Entente's ignorance of the events taking place between Vienna and Berlin in the first weeks of July was one thing; the near-total isolation of France's principal diplomatic decision-makers from 15 July until three days before French mobilisation is certainly another. On the morning of Wednesday 15 July Poincaré, Viviani and de Margerie, the Political Director at the Quai d'Orsay, left the Gare du Nord for Dunkirk to begin a state cruise to Russia and the Scandinavian countries, which was scheduled to end on 31 July. Their trip, arranged several months previously, involved spending most of the time at sea during a period when radio-cabling was in its infancy. The men left in charge at the Quai d'Orsay were either inexperienced or completely ignorant of foreign affairs: the Minister of Justice, Bienvenu-Martin, became interim Foreign Minister and Abel Ferry continued as Under-Secretary of State for Foreign Affairs. Third in the hierarchy was the only man with any experience of diplomacy at all: Philippe Berthelot, who stood in for de Margerie as Political Director. Thus, as one historian has written: 'It is hard to imagine the leaders of the country indulging in the joys of tourism, even political, having plotted the outbreak of a European war.'⁶ The Austrians, with German backing, purposefully withheld issuing the ultimatum to Serbia until Poincaré and his party had left Russia on 23 July and set sail for Sweden. On the eve of war, French leaders were literally and metaphorically at sea. Until the party finally cut short its trip and returned to Dunkirk on 29 July, French leaders were less well informed of events, less able to communicate with other powers, in short, less able to influence the course of events than any of their counterparts. By the time they returned to French soil it was probably too late to stop the outbreak of war. To a large extent their action could only be reactive not preventive.

What, then, was the course of events after the assassination as we now know them? As far as France is concerned they fall into two parts: before, and after, Poincaré's arrival in Russia. In the first French Cabinet meeting which followed the assassination, on Tuesday 30 June, there was hardly any talk of Austria–Hungary. Poincaré continued to follow a very heavy time-table of honorary functions ranging from artists' dinners to the cycling grand prix at Vincennes. But he remained preoccupied with the behind-the-scenes machinations in the Caillaux trial and the continuing attacks and plots against him orchestrated by the Radicals, who were still bent on forcing his resignation. Poincaré had heard that according to an article in the *New York Times* emissaries had been sent to America to find his wife's first husband, and that she had once been a music-hall actress whom Poincaré had defended in divorce proceedings before marrying her. Caillaux even attempted to blackmail Poincaré into encouraging the judges to acquit Madame Caillaux by threatening to produce witnesses ready to say that the President had backed Calmette's campaign. It was all quite untrue and naturally Poincaré refused.⁷

He continued to receive representations from journalists and politicians blaming his declining popularity on his earlier failure to dissolve the Chamber to safeguard the Three Years' Law and French foreign policy in general.

Meanwhile in Vienna, Austria–Hungary had decided on her course of action. She believed Serbian irredentism was behind the Sarajevo assassination and that it posed an open threat to the Dual Monarchy. If she failed to take serious action then her already rapidly declining position as a great power would pass beyond recovery. She already had the unenviable reputation as the sick-man of Europe and disintegration of the Dual Empire was a regular topic of conversation in diplomatic circles. Delcassé had made contingency plans for such an eventuality in his agreement with Russia on the balance of power in Europe in 1899. Vienna's immediate source of weakness was the Balkans. She could no longer be content with diplomatic victories as in 1909 or 1913, which had been shown to be mere palliatives against the South Slav nationalism in Serbia. An independent Serbia would be a constant source of trouble: there was no other solution but to reduce her, once and for all, to the satellite status she had occupied in the 1880s. In short, Austria was determined to seize on the assassination as one of the few remaining opportunities for creating a situation in which a war against Serbia would be possible. She hoped that such a war would be localised. But in order to deter Russia from intervening as the protector of the Slavs she had to obtain German backing. If Russia could be forced to remain on the sidelines the victory against Serbia would be doubled with a dramatic blow to Russian prestige, which it was hoped would lead to the elimination of her influence in the Balkans for a long time. Of course this involved a number of obvious risks. But Austria–Hungary viewed such action as defensive and intended to guarantee her survival within the European states system. As such it was worth the gamble.

It was predictable that Germany would support such a move. Her own security and future were inextricably bound up with that of her strongest and perhaps only remaining ally. On 6 July the Austrian Ambassador in Berlin was informed by the German Chancellor, Bethmann-Hollweg, that Germany would back Austria in any action she wished to take against Serbia. Thus armed, Count Berchtold, the Austrian Foreign Minister, drafted an ultimatum so constructed that Serbia could do nothing but reject it. Nevertheless, both Austria–Hungary and Germany still hoped at this point that the war could be localised. This is suggested by the fact that Germany made no serious military or economic preparations for war between 6 and 23 July, and by the Kaiser's decision taken on the advice of Bethmann-Hollweg to depart on the imperial yacht *Hohenzollern* for a three-week cruise in Norwegian waters. It is confirmed by the letter from the German Secretary of State for Foreign Affairs, von Jagow, to Lichnowsky, Ambassador in London on 18 July:

We must attempt to localise the conflict between Austria and Serbia.

Whether this is possible will depend in the first place on Russia and in the second place on the moderating influence of the other members of the Entente. The more boldness Austria displays the more strongly we support her, the more likely is Russia to keep quiet. There is certain to be some blustering in St Petersburg, but at bottom Russia is not now ready to strike. Nor will France and England be anxious for war at the present time.[8]

Moreover, before Austria presented the ultimatum to Serbia on 23 July, there was no top-level discussion among German army leaders. Even the Chief of the General Staff, von Moltke, was not thinking in terms of a European war when on 13 July he commented to the German military attaché in Vienna that 'Austria must beat the Serbs and then make peace quickly, demanding an Austro-Serbian alliance as the sole condition. Like Prussia did with Austria in 1866.'[9] He did not even bother to return to Berlin from his 'cure' in Carlsbad, where he had been since 28 June and where he would remain until the evening of 25 July. Germany calculated that France and Russia were unprepared for war. This certainly appeared to be France's case as the Senate debate of June–July 1914 clearly demonstrated. Great Britain had serious domestic problems to contend with in Ireland, which many saw as leading her to the brink of civil war. The important colonial agreements which Germany had recently signed with both Britain and France stood out as evidence of improved relations with them. There was also a belief that the restraint which Britain, and France in particular, had exercised over Russia of late, would again prevail. Finally, great hopes were placed on the feeling of monarchical solidarity which, it was thought, would deter the Tsar from taking the side of regicides. However, the likelihood of Austria being allowed to crush Serbia in a localised Balkan conflict was a mixture of miscalculation and wishful thinking: Russia had far too much to lose if she stood by.

In France the government and Foreign Ministry were blithely unaware of what was taking place in central Europe. The Caillaux trial and its ramifications apart, Poincaré was extremely anxious about the parliamentary uproar which had followed a recent and very damning Senate report by Charles Humbert on France's inferiority in armamemts to Germany. It appeared at first that the Senate would withhold approval for the government's military budget. Poincaré even seriously contemplated cancelling his trip to Russia, something which the Sarajevo incident had never prompted him to do. Approval was only obtained after a marathon Senate debate, uncustomarily held on France's national holiday, and only concluded at 10.30 the same evening when the government reluctantly agreed to a parliamentary inquiry on the state of French armaments. Though the Senate debate had received wide publication and was monitored by Germany, astonishingly it had no visible effect on morale in France.

Small wonder then that Poincaré was singularly relieved to embark on his trip to Russia, Sweden, Denmark and Norway and escape from the Caillaux trial and the seamy side of French domestic politics. At 11.30 p.m. on Wednesday 15 July the presidential train left the Gare du Nord for Dunkirk, from where the President, accompanied by Viviani and de Margerie, was to set sail aboard the battleship *France* the following day at 5.00 a.m. Poincaré spent most of the four-day voyage to Kronstadt either relaxing or giving foreign-affairs lessons to Viviani, whose ignorance on the subject he found frightening.[10] He thought it useful to brief him on a number of questions before they arrived in Russia, 'details about the alliance, about different subjects dealt with at Petersburg in 1912, about the Chinese consortium, Franco-Russian military conversations; Anglo-Russian negotiations on the proposed naval convention; relations with Germany'. Furthermore, he insisted on the necessity of maintaining the Three Years' Law and explained how he 'had never had any serious difficulties with Germany because I have always used great firmness with her'.[11] But Viviani was more preoccupied with other things: the possible divulging of the intercepted foreign telegrams at the Caillaux trial, and, as rumour had it, the whereabouts of his unfaithful mistress at the *Comédie Française*. A mark of Poincaré's peace of mind during the voyage was that his only irritation was caused by the admittedly embarrassing incident in which, in Russian territorial waters, the battleship *France*, pride of the French fleet, piloted by an Admiral and aboard which the President of France was travelling, collided with a Russian tug and narrowly missed crashing into the accompanying French battleship *Jean Bart*.[12]

The Austrian ultimatum to Serbia was drafted and ready by 14 July. But the Austro-Hungarian Council of Ministers decided that it should be despatched only when the French President had left Russia on 23 July, to ensure that the two allies were unable to organise any action, thereby lessening the possibility of joint military intervention. However, approximate news of Austria's intentions had been reaching the Russian Foreign Minister, Sazonov, since 14 July from diplomatic sources and from intercepted Austrian telegrams decoded by Russia. It was only natural that he should wish to discuss them with Poincaré.

Early on the afternoon of Monday 20 July Poincaré arrived at Kronstadt, where he was greeted by Tsar Nicholas II aboard the imperial yacht *Alexandria*. The two heads of state then sailed to Peterhof. Before that evening's banquet at the palace, when toasts and speeches were made about the mutual benefits of the Dual Alliance, Poincaré and the Tsar, on the one hand, and Viviani and Sazonov on the other, began diplomatic conversations. The compilers of the French Diplomatic Documents made all possible investigations to discover the minutes of these and subsequent discussions, though to no avail. Telegrams exchanged between Paris and St Petersburg during the visit concern French domestic affairs exclusively. But Poincaré's extremely personal and candid diaries do reveal the nature of some of those talks. On 20 July the Tsar explained to Poincaré that he hoped that the Three

Years' Law would not be altered. The French President replied that in recently voting by a majority of 150 to fund the new Law, the Chamber had demonstrated its true will.[13] The Tsar also informed Poincaré, who knew already, that Joseph Caillaux had been in contact with the Russian, Count Witte, the proponent of an alliance between France, Russia and Germany.[14]

The following morning talks continued between the two heads of state on the subject of Anglo-Russian difficulties in Persia. The Tsar wanted talks on the naval agreement with Britain speeded up. He sympathised with British complaints about Russian action in Persia, but blamed overzealous Russian functionaries. Discussions then moved to the subject of the Balkans, in which the Tsar expressed anxiety about Austria and Bulgaria.[15] But he had no fear of war when he expressed a desire to return Poincaré's state visit with a similar one to France in the summer of 1915.[16] That afternoon Poincaré left on the imperial yacht for St Petersburg, where extensive strikes, together with those in other large cities, demonstrated the widespread social unrest and gave further credence to the idea that Russia was unprepared for war. Poincaré was introduced to French expatriates at the French embassy and then went on to meet members of the diplomatic corps at the Winter Palace. The British Ambassador, Sir George Buchanan, expressed the fear that Vienna would send an aggressive note to Belgrade and proposed direct conversations between Vienna and St Petersburg to avert any difficulties. Poincaré replied that this could be a dangerous move and suggested that France and Britain should counsel moderation to Austria. He left the meeting feeling pessimistic. His conversation with the Austrian Ambassador, Count Szapary, did nothing to improve matters. Szapary made it plain that his country was about to take serious measures against Serbia. Poincaré advised caution as complications could result from the fact that Serbia's friend was Russia and that Russia's ally was France. To see in Poincaré's words a threatening attitude, as the Austrian Ambassador did, is quite unwarranted. To warn of a possible escalation of events made sense and made Austria aware of her responsibilities. To have said nothing would have been, as Poincaré himself subsequently noted, tantamount to approving Austria's action.[17]

That evening Poincaré gave a dinner at the French embassy for the Russian government, Foreign Ministry officials and a few military. He and Viviani were by now informed of a telegram from the usually cautious Jules Cambon, forwarded to them that afternoon by Paris, warning that Germany would support Austria in her *démarche* at Belgrade and had no intention of acting as mediator. In talks with the President and Foreign Minister, Sazonov appeared far more worried than before. He even confessed to Poincaré that if things turned sour Russia would have great difficulty mobilising as the peasants were all busy in the fields.[18]

What little part Viviani had played so far during the visit was further reduced when on Wednesday 22 July he received a telegram about developments in the Caillaux trial. It threw the French Premier into a neurasthenic state. *Le Figaro* had mentioned the diplomatic intercepts and Caillaux was threatening to produce them at the trial with obvious diplomatic consequences. The Premier's sad and nervous state was noticed by everyone, not least the Tsar, whose questions to him met with silence. Viviani's state of mind was affected to such an extent that during the presidential inspection of the imperial regiments he spent his time grumbling, cursing and swearing in full view of everyone. In the end, the French Ambassador, Paléologue, tired of trying to calm him, convinced him he had a liver attack and called the doctor. For the rest of the day Viviani continued to sulk, though by now the Russians were also convinced he had a liver complaint.[19] That afternoon the text of the Austrian ultimatum was communicated to the German Foreign Minister, von Jagow. Unaware of this, Sazonov telegraphed instructions that night to the Russian chargé d'affaires in Vienna to warn the Austrian Foreign Minister cordially, but firmly, of the dangerous consequences which could result from Austrian demands on Serbia. Nevertheless, he still believed that as a result of warnings from the great powers Austria would see reason.

The 23rd was the last day of the state visit to Russia. That evening the Tsar, Tsarina and members of the imperial Court were invited to dine on board the *France*. Dinner completed, the President and his party prepared to set sail for Sweden. The timing of Poincaré's departure was of vital importance for the *dénouement* of subsequent events. On it hung the despatch of the ultimatum to Serbia. When the Germans discovered that Poincaré was to depart on the 23rd, not at 10 but 11 p.m. local time from Kronstadt, they calculated with typical efficiency that if the Austrian ultimatum was delivered at 5 p.m., it might become known at St Petersburg before Poincaré left because of the difference of central European time. On learning of this the Austrians relayed instructions to their representative in Belgrade to deliver the ultimatum at 6 p.m. on 23 July.

The extreme nature of the Austrian ultimatum surprised everyone. Sir Edward Grey found it 'the most formidable document I have ever seen addressed by one state to another that was independent'.[20] Poincaré learned of it, as intended, at sea through a series of garbled radio messages on 24 July. He, Viviani and de Margerie discussed action, though it seems that Poincaré's ideas dominated. That action was remarkably restrained. Viviani telegraphed four suggestions to St Petersburg for relay to Paris and London: Serbia should accept as many of the Austrian conditions as honour would allow; she should seek prolongation of the forty-eight-hour deadline by twenty-four hours; France should support this request at Vienna; and the Triple Entente should try to substitute an international inquest on the assassination for the Austro-Serbian one.[21]

Poincaré was still admirably composed when the state party reached Stockholm on Saturday 25 July. Despite his habitual self-interrogation, this time on the pros and cons of continuing his state visit or returning to France, he was still able to enjoy the beauty of the fjords. But news from abroad was increasingly pessimistic. A telegram from Paris explained that on the 24 July the German ambassador, von Schoen, had visited the acting Foreign Minister, Bienvenu-Martin, to support the Austrian note and to insist that the affair be localised, as any intervention by another power would activate the alliances and bring about incalculable consequences. Viviani, de Margerie and Poincaré regarded this step as extremely grave, as it showed that Germany was in effect rejecting the method of settlement of past disputes: the Concert of Europe. Doubts about continuing the state tour returned. Poincaré calculated that interrupting his visit would only excite French opinion and give the impression that France was mixed up in the conflict. What more could be done in Paris, he asked himself. And to demonstrate how far that was true, he instructed Viviani to inform the Havas news agency that the French Premier and Foreign Minister had taken over from Paris the control of foreign affairs. Poincaré was effectively running affairs, though on the following day as he sailed towards Copenhagen he confessed to being powerless,[22] all the more so for having learnt from the King of Sweden that at 6 p.m. on the 25th the Austrian ultimatum had expired followed by the departure from Belgrade of the Austrian envoy.[23]

On 27 July, as the state party was sailing to Denmark, telegrams were received from members of the government requesting their return home. The Kaiser had interrupted his cruise and had returned to Kiel the day before. The visit to Denmark and Norway was broken off and the *France* sailed for Dunkirk. The same day a telegram informed Poincaré that Sir Edward Grey had stated that if war broke out in the Near East no nation could remain disinterested. Poincaré held this up as an example to the worried and confused Viviani and encouraged him to telegraph to Sazonov

that France, appreciating, no less than Russia, the high importance for both countries of affirming their perfect mutual understanding in regard to the other powers and to the need for neglecting no effort in view of a solution of the conflict, is ready in the interests of the general peace wholeheartedly to second the action of the Imperial Government.

Poincaré had in fact asked de Margerie to prepare a telegram to this effect beforehand and Viviani, after more hesitation, now consented to its despatch.[24] Poincaré's aim in offering such support was consistent with his policy towards Russia since 1912: Russia must be constantly aware of the loyalty of her ally to enable France to influence her actions; if she felt abandoned the consequences could be disastrous. Sazonov's position was not secure and if he fell from power his replacement could foreseeably come from the strong pro-German faction at the court and in the army. The growing danger of revolution, so evident in the strikes which had greeted Poincaré's visit, risked accelerating that eventuality by leading the Russian government to turn for support to Germany, in the hope of bolstering her monarchical institutions by reviving the old understanding between the two nations.[25] More palpable was the telegram Poincaré received from Paléologue on 25 July informing him that Sazonov was acting peacefully in asking Serbia not to riposte if she were attacked.[26]

That evening Austria began mobilisation. Poincaré believed that the only way to deal with Germany was through firmness. On learning that Bienvenu-Martin had had several audiences with von Schoen, the President noted in his diary: 'So long as Bienvenu-Martin in his desire to maintain peace did not show himself to be too weak!' And he warned Viviani that in dealing with Germany it was necessary to remain calm but firm. But both Poincaré and de Margerie were extremely anxious about Viviani's continuing nervous state, which made him incapable of running foreign affairs: 'He is nervous, agitated, never ceases pronouncing imprudent words or sentences which show a complete ignorance of foreign affairs.'[27]

When he landed on French soil on Wednesday 29 July Poincaré was at the climax of his presidential power. The scenes which greeted him filled him with a profound sense of calling comparable to that of another French leader at a similar moment some twenty-five years later: 'It was no longer to a person that these acclamations were addressed; it was to the representative of France *vis-à-vis* the world.' There was no more tergiversation. Poincaré straighforwardly took over the direction of affairs, fearing that Viviani would be 'hesitant and pusillanimous'. He ordered Cabinet meetings to be held every morning.[28] But there was little that he could do to stop the tragic course of events now in train. Two weeks had passed in which the diplomatic and political masters of France had been absent and, to a large extent, intentionally isolated from that chain of events known as the July crisis. The German government had even sent instructions to its radio transmission service at Metz to jam all Franco-Russian radio communications as well as those between the *France* and Paris.[29] Poincaré could merely familiarise himself with much of the news of events and communications which had been kept from him since his departure from Russia five days previously.

While Poincaré had been sailing the Gulf of Finland crucial events had been taking place in St Petersburg. Sazonov had learnt of the content of the Austrian note on the morning of the 24 July and immediately decided to ask the consent of the Ministers and of the Tsar to a partial mobilisation against Austria. But it would only be put into operation at the necessary moment, which might never arise if Austria stayed her hand.

The Council of Ministers was to meet that afternoon at 3 p.m. In the meantime Sazonov went to lunch with the British and French Ambassadors. He held firmly to the belief that war could be prevented if only the British government would make a clear statement to Germany of her intention to support France and Russia, if necessary militarily, in a war against the Central Powers. Sir George Buchanan made it clear that British public opinion would never sanction a war on Serbia's behalf. Of course Britain was free to act as she pleased, being neither the ally of France nor Russia. France was not. The cohesion of the Alliance rested on French support of Russia. When in 1909 that support had not been forthcoming not only had the Alliance suffered but France had been repaid in kind during the Agadir crisis. Furthermore Russian support for Serbia seemed increasingly justified in the face of Austrian intransigence. Finally the terms of the Alliance stated clearly that if Russia was attacked by Austria supported by Germany, France would employ all her available forces to fight Germany. Too much should not therefore be made of Paléologue's pledge to Sazonov of French diplomatic support and a commitment, if necessary, to fulfil the obligations imposed on her by the alliance, which, after all, was a statement of the obvious. But Paléologue can perhaps be criticised for profering such support so readily and apparently without specific orders to do so. He can certainly be criticised for what he did not do later that day – telegraph to Paris the Council of Ministers' decision in principle to call a partial mobilisation, of which Sazonov had informed him. On 25 July the Tsar approved that decision, stating that mobilisation would only begin when Austrian troops had crossed the Serbian frontier and even then, as operations were to be confined to action against Austria, only four military districts were to be mobilised, and the rest were to be only if Germany joined Austria. But as Russia claimed to have information of Austrian preparatory measures for mobilisation, 'the pre-mobilisation period' was to begin in the night of 25–6 July. Unfortunately, this last measure, which involved the call up of reservists to bring the frontier troop divisions up to strength, had been designed for the whole of Russian territory, without distinguishing between Austria and German frontiers, which explains the alarm of German military authorities and Bethmann's subsequent protest to Sazonov. Paléologue only telegraphed this news to Paris on the evening of 25 July, while Poincaré confesses to having learnt of it on the 27th. But there is no trace in the French Diplomatic Documents of a conversation Sazonov had with Buchanan and Paléologue that afternoon when they were informed of the measures. According to the British Ambassador, Paléologue told Sazonov that France unreservedly placed herself on Russia's side. It seems clear, however, that Sazonov was peaceful and that the threat of mobilisation was merely intended to deter Austria and Germany from their dangerous action.

If Paléologue displayed characteristic impulsiveness in expressing French support for Russia in a bid to stiffen Sazonov's resolve to deter the Central Powers by firmness, Bienvenu-Martin was correspondingly weak. Not surprisingly, decapitated as it was, the Quai d'Orsay was in a state of confusion. The acting Foreign Minister even appeared at first favourable to Austria–Hungary, giving the Austrian and German Ambassadors the impression that France would place no obstacle in the way of Austrian measures against Serbia.[30] On 24 July in London at the close of Cabinet discussions on Ulster, Sir Edward Grey brought up the Serbian crisis. It was the first time in a month that the Cabinet had discussed foreign policy.

Though well intentioned the British Foreign Secretary seemed to lack any sense of urgency. He suggested that the four less interested powers should intervene diplomatically in the event of severe tension between Russia and Austria. But as Paul Cambon reminded him afterwards the forty-eight hour ultimatum expired the following day and Austria would march into Serbia because the Serbians would never accept the Austrian demands, at which point mediation would be too late. Following this, Grey received the German Ambassador, Prince Lichnowsky, to whom he recommended a joint proposal at Vienna to extend the time limit of the ultimatum, and the idea of four-power mediation. But Germany purposefully delayed passing on Grey's suggestion to Austria in order that it reach Vienna after the time limit had expired. Albertini criticises Grey for not realising that 'it was a foolish waste of time to call for the help of Berlin by means other than those which put the fear of God into Germany'.[31] One wonders why then Albertini is so scathing in his criticism of Poincaré for wishing to be firm with Germany.

Grey's proposals for mediation seem to have been both naïve and to have ignored the time factor. That weekend he set off for his fishing lodge. On the evening of Saturday 25 July news reached London of Austria's mobilisation against Serbia. With Grey still fishing it was Sir Arthur Nicolson, Permanent Under-Secretary at the Foreign Office, who came up with the idea for mediation by means of a conference of Ambassadors similar to the one which had settled the Balkan disputes of 1912–13. Informed on 26 July, Bethmann-Hollweg rejected it on the 27th. A further proposal made by Grey to Lichnowsky on the 27th for Berlin to induce Vienna to accept the Serbian reply as a basis for negotiations, was passed on to Austria with strong hints that it be rejected. Not surprisingly it was. Of course, acceptance of any proposal for mediation by the powers automatically robbed Vienna of her golden, and perhaps last, opportunity to restore some of her prestige as a great power by crushing Serbia, which after all was the whole object of the Austro-German exercise since Sarajevo. Yet it seems that few diplomats understood this. And because they did not understand it, no real warnings went out from London, Rome or Paris to Berlin that were likely to shatter the German illusion that Austria could bring off her *coup de force* without upsetting the general peace. On the contrary, news continued to arrive in the Austrian and German capitals reinforcing the idea that the Triple Entente would not allow general war to break out for the sake of Serbia.[32]

Poincaré was right to doubt whether Bienvenu-Martin was dealing with the German Ambassador in a firm manner. Von Schoen was given the impression that the acting Foreign Minister had no objection in principle to urging moderation on St Petersburg.[33] This could only encourage Germany still further. Already on 16 July the Chancellor had explained:

We have grounds to assume and cannot but wish, that France, at the moment burdened with all sorts of cares, will do everthing to restrain

Russia from intervention . . . If we succeed in not only keeping France quiet herself but in getting her to enjoin peace on St Petersburg, this will have a repurcussion on the Franco-Russian alliance highly favourable to ourselves.[34]

Indeed, Germany continued to believe until as late as 29 July that France was 'setting all levers in motion at St Petersburg to exercise a moderating influence there'.[35] Even Sazonov gave the impression of being very conciliatory when he talked to the Austrian and German Ambassadors on the 27th. He even set Grey's proposal for an ambassadorial conference aside in the hope that the direct talks he had begun with Austria would be fruitful. However, on the 28th Austria declared war on Serbia and the talks ceased. The point of no return had almost been reached.

The Austrian declaration of war incensed Russian popular feeling. In the most serious of games of 'tit for tat' Sazonov telegraphed to Berlin on the evening of the 28th that Russia felt compelled to proclaim for the next day mobilisation of the military districts of Odessa, Kiev, Moscow and Kazan, though he stressed that Russia had no intention of attacking Germany. That order for partial mobilisation still had to be signed by the Tsar. But right across Europe military precautions were beginning to constrain diplomatic action and gather a momentum of their own. It is an exaggeration to claim that in 1914 mobilisation meant war, for just as no war is inevitable until it breaks out so any mobilised army can be stopped before it crosses a frontier. But by requiring a rapid victory against France in order for Germany to be able to turn against Russia before she was completely prepared for war, the Schlieffen Plan set the tone for rapid mobilisations in Europe. In doing so it seriously increased the nervousness of the competitors in the race to mobilise. France began precautionary measures on the 26th as a reaction to similar German measures in Alsace. Adolphe Messimy, the Minister of War, recalled all officers from leave and took steps to protect the railways. The following morning in Britain the Admiralty postponed the dispersal of the First and Second Fleets. Even Belgium called up its reservists on the 29th. More gravely still, on the morning of the 29th the Tsar signed the two mobilisation *ukazes*, one for partial, the other for general mobilisation, though they were to be executed only when circumstances demanded it. That day Sazonov informed the German Ambassador that Russia would straight away issue the order for partial mobilisation because Austria had mobilised eight army corps. He did stress, however, that in Russia mobilisation was far from being the same as war, for the Russian army could stand at ease for weeks without crossing the frontier. This was perfectly true. The agreed statement made by Russia and France in 1892 during negotiations for the military convention, immortalised in General Boisdeffre's words to the Tsar that 'mobilisation is the declaration of war', was by November 1912 obsolete. On 21 November the Russian General Staff revoked orders stating that the mobilisation began hostilities and the Tsar expressly confirmed that principle on the 26th.[36]

As yet, Sazonov was still thinking of declaring only partial mobilisation. But events on 29 July pressed him towards general mobilisation. The Russian Foreign Minister received further representations from the Minister of War and Chief of General Staff that there was no plan for partial mobilisation and that such action could only seriously disorganise general mobilisation, with the likelihood of disaster for the Russian armies should war break out. Furthermore, Austria's refusal of direct conversations with Russia, her bombardment of Belgrade on the 29th and Bethmann Hollweg's threat that further Russian mobilisation would lead to German mobilisation and a European war, which Sazonov took to be an ultimatum, convinced him that general mobilisation must be announced. The Tsar agreed that evening. But shortly after, just as the mobilisation order was about to be despatched, the Tsar countermanded it and ordered partial mobilisation instead. He had received a telegram from the Kaiser appealing for his help in averting a catastrophe.

This was only a temporary respite. The Russian military continued to emphasise the technical reasons against partial mobilisation. And though Sazonov continued to work for peace by proposing a further formula for mediation to the German Ambassador on the 30th, late that afternoon he was insisting to the Tsar that general mobilisation had to be declared. The Tsar reluctantly agreed, and at 5 p.m. on the 30th the order was issued for mobilisation to begin the following day. But already in the night of 30–1 July the red mobilisation notices had been posted on the walls in St Petersburg.

Too much has been made of the idea that Russian mobilisation provoked the war. This is unjust. Sazonov sincerely believed that mobilisation was not war. What option other than general mobilisation was open to Russia? As Albertini stresses, Germany and Austria–Hungary believed that they could bring off their *coup de force* against Serbia because they would encounter no opposition. Such a *coup* would wipe out the results of the Balkan Wars and the decisions arrived at through the international conferences; it would damage the prestige of the other powers, not to mention their interests in the Balkans, with incalculable consequences for the balance of power and the fate of European and Asiatic Turkey.[37] And Russia stood to lose most by this. Albertini insists that the Triple Entente powers should have dealt more forcefully with Germany in order to overawe her. Sazonov had acted with restraint, genuinely seeking a peaceful solution. Austria–Hungary, with German backing, had ignored his efforts and had continued to escalate her action against Serbia to the point where physical hostilities had begun against her. As Sazonov firmly believed that the Central Powers would only back down if confronted with firmness (which explains his appeals to Britain to threaten Germany with intervention), he had to match their military escalation with similar Russian action. In this classic spiral of escalation, by 30 July he had exhausted all steps other than general mobilisation.

But as he told Paléologue that day he would go on negotiating until the last moment.

What is important in the Russian general mobilisation is how it affected France. However, the French Ambassador in St Petersburg did not keep Paris sufficiently well informed of events for her to influence them. An extrovert eager to be accepted by the Russian aristocracy, Paléologue had begun, since his appointment, to give himself airs by repeating to everyone that he was Poincaré's intimate friend.[38] Consequently, his personal opinions, which in France were known to tend towards exaggeration, assumed in Russia a more official status and particularly so during Poincaré's isolation at sea. Thus, the unofficial encouragement he gave Russia appeared official in St Petersburg. Furthermore, though informed of the events of the 29th and 30th leading to Russian general mobilisation, Paléologue preferred to keep Paris in the dark for fear the Quai d'Orsay should oppose it. Paris was merely informed at 9.15 p.m. on the 30th that the Russian government had resolved only to 'proceed secretly to the first measures of general mobilisation'. And it was only the following morning, on the 31st, after the mobilisation order had been published for several hours, that he telegraphed to Paris that 'general mobilisation of the Russian army has been ordered.' That telegram only reached Paris that evening at 8.30 p.m.[39]

The mood of French public opinion, by contrast, was still calm up to the 29th, as the British and Austrian Ambassadors noted. This was not surprising as the final verdict on the Caillaux trial, the main subject of popular preoccupation, had only been reached the day before with Mme Caillaux's surprising acquittal. The 29th was the day Poincaré had arrived back in France. He quickly discovered from despatches that the situation was worse than he had thought: Germany was that day attempting to secure British neutrality in the event of a European conflict, while Grey was making a last-ditch attempt to mediate on the basis of a temporary Austrian occupation of Belgrade. At 5 p.m. that afternoon the German Ambassador told Viviani that if France continued to arm, Germany would proclaim *Kriegsgefahr*, the 'danger of war' period which preceded general mobilisation. Nevertheless, von Schoen was still able to report to Berlin that Viviani and France sincerely desired peace. This was clearly demonstrated in the night of the 29th–30th. Isvolsky received instructions from Sazonov to tell the French government that Germany was threatening to order mobilisation unless Russia suspended hers, and that Russia was going to ignore this on the grounds that Austria had herself mobilised and rejected all settlement proposals. Russia was, he went on, speeding up her military preparations and reckoning on the imminence of war. He was therefore to thank the French government 'for the declaration, which the French Ambassador made to me in his government's name, that we may count completely on the allied support of France'.[40] Isvolsky despatched his counsellor to communicate this to Viviani that night. Viviani was so disturbed by the message that he called on the Minister of War and together they left to waken Poincaré at the Elysée. What is of great significance in Sazonov's telegram is the fact that he made no mention of any promise of support for Russia by Poincaré or Viviani during their visit to St Petersburg, which he would certainly have done had one been given. Poincaré suggests that Sazonov had merely given too wide a meaning to Viviani's telegram of the 27th, which was an assurance of support in the interests of peace. It is also possible that Paléologue was to blame for Sazonov's misinterpretation. But Poincaré and Viviani quickly corrected it by a telegram despatched at 7 a.m. on the 30th, which stated quite clearly that Russia 'should not immediately proceed to any measure which might offer Germany a pretext for a total or partial mobilisation of her forces'.[41] Similar instructions were given to Isvolsky and his military attaché shortly afterwards. Here is clear evidence that Poincaré and Viviani were exercising a restraining influence on Russia. Unfortunately, Isvolsky's telegram to St Petersburg arrived after general mobilisation had been decreed. Not that it would in the end have made much difference, because before knowing of the Russian general mobilisation Germany, on the evening of 30 July, had taken the decision to send St Petersburg an ultimatum demanding the withdrawal of even partial mobilisation.

It has been shown conclusively by Albertini that Paléologue, by a mixture of concealment and belated information, kept Paris in the dark about the Russian mobilisation.[42] But to proceed from this to saddle France with substantial blame for the outbreak of the First World War, as some historians have done, is quite unfounded. First, it is clear that Paléologue was acting independently of Paris. He certainly has a lot to answer for in overstepping his orders by encouraging Russia to take a firm line, and especially for failing to keep Paris properly informed of her ally's actions. But the fact that he did do this independently, and even contrary to orders from Paris, shows by the same token that France was not to blame. Secondly, given that Paléologue did encourage Sazonov to take a firmer line, what were the consequences of such action? It was certainly not merely on the strength of Paléologue's encouragement that Sazonov ordered mobilisation. The technical reasons apart, what alternative did the Russian Foreign Minister have, given that he was quite convinced that only by firm action would the Central Powers back down? If he did not go ahead with general mobilisation Berlin and Vienna would believe that their bluff had paid off and continue their action. If he did, the Central Powers might reciprocate. Sazonov was confronted with a major dilemma. Superficially the choice he finally made appears crucial. In reality it mattered little. Vienna and Berlin were adamant about going through with their action against Serbia because failure to do so would signal their decline as great powers. So even if Paléologue had exercised restraint on Sazonov, with the doubtful effect that mobilisation had been postponed, it now seems certain that Germany and Austria would have continued to reject any mediation proposals, let alone a compromise, leaving Russia in the same predicament.

As soon as Germany learnt of Russian general mobilisation on the morning of 31 July, *Kriegsgefahr* was immediately proclaimed. The Chancellor despatched an ultimatum to St Petersburg demanding that Russia cease all military measures against Germany and Austria within twelve hours. Receiving no reply, Germany declared war on Russia at 6 p.m. on 1 August.

If Russia's action was the single most important factor conditioning French foreign policy on the eve of war, Britain's was the second. Like Sazonov many French diplomats believed that the preservation of peace was in Britain's hands, for Germany would certainly modify her attitude if Britain made a clear declaration to come to France's aid if she was attacked. Despite Paul Cambon's pressing appeals, Sir Edward Grey refused to give any such assurance without the approval of the Cabinet, which thus far was bitterly divided. Even though on the 30th Grey had rejected a last desperate offer from Germany to the effect that she would not annex any French territory in a war in which Britain remained neutral,[43] the French remained extremely anxious. Tired of Grey's tergiversations, on the 31st, Poincaré, backed by the government, made a direct personal appeal by letter to King George V. It was to no avail. The Cabinet and British public opinion were still greatly divided over intervention in a continental war resulting from an incident in the Balkans.

While waiting all this time for London to make a decision whose outcome she was now seriously beginning to fear, France had to take some military precautions. Rumours from Berlin of German mobilisation hastened such action. That day the French Cabinet, while specifically refusing any mobilisation measures, agreed that covering troops be ordered to take up positions along the Luxembourg–Vosges borders. But strict instructions were issued to the troops not to approach closer than ten kilometres to the frontier. This was to avoid any contact with German patrols offering a pretext for war. Moreover, the 'ten kilometre withdrawal' was above all a gesture to influence British public opinion, as Paul Cambon emphasised to Grey on 1 August. He also insisted to the Foreign Secretary that France had, in line with the joint naval arrangements of 1912, concentrated her fleet in the Mediterranean to help Britain, thereby leaving her northern and western ports exposed. However, strictly in keeping with what he had always maintained, Grey denied that the naval arrangements put Britain under any obligation to fight. Cambon was now paying the price for his overconfidence in a British commitment. Nevertheless Grey agreed to discuss the matter with the Cabinet on Sunday 2 August.

French anxiety further increased when on 1 August the German Ambassador called at the Quai d'Orsay to learn what France would do if war broke out between Russia and Germany. Berlin insisted that even if France pledged to remain neutral she would still have to surrender the principal fortresses on her eastern frontier as a guarantee of 'her sincerity'. Viviani replied that France would act in accordance with her interests. That evening

France declared general mobilisation. Attempts were made to reshuffle the Cabinet to bring Briand and Delcassé into the government – but the Socialists refused.[44] It was only on 3 August that Viviani was finally persuaded to abandon the foreign affairs portfolio to Gaston Doumergue, much to the relief of senior diplomats at the Quai d'Orsay and Poincaré in particular. It was the confused Viviani who had 'not once been able, when reading a telegram from Vienna, to speak of the Ballplatz without saying the Boliplatz or the Baloplatz'.[45]

On 2 August the British Cabinet, realising that a Franco-German naval conflict in the Channel could threaten the safety of Britain, agreed to promise the French, and warn the Germans, that no German naval action in the Channel or against the French coasts would be tolerated.[46] This calmed Paul Cambon, who was already asking 'whether the word "honour" should not be struck out of the English vocabulary'.[47] In fact this commitment was of little value as the Germans subsequently promised to refrain from such operations.[48] As it turned out the decision taken by the Cabinet later that evening was of far greater importance to France: any violation of Belgian neutrality would oblige Britain to intervene. That same day German troops had entered Luxembourg and demanded free passage through Belgium. King Albert and the Belgian government rejected the demand the following morning. At 6.45 p.m. on 3 August, on the false pretext that French areoplanes had bombed Nuremberg, Germany declared war on France. On the morning of the 4th, treating their solemn guarantee of her neutrality as a 'scrap of paper', German troops crossed the Belgian frontier; a British ultimatum demanding their withdrawal was disregarded and as Big Ben struck 11 a.m. Britain and Germany were at war. The invasion of Belgium also provided Italy with the necessary pretext for declaring herself neutral; her alliance obliged her to support her partners only if they were attacked by a third power. As of 4 August the Triple Entente powers were at war with Germany and Austria–Hungary.

For the third time within a century France was faced with a German invasion. But whereas in 1815 and 1870 she had been alone, she was now supported by two powerful allies. The country which had annexed Alsace and Lorraine in 1871 and threatened France again in 1875, 1887, 1905 and 1911 once more appeared as the aggressor. Many observers and historians have spoken of an enormous groundswell of opinion which responded to Poincaré's appeal on the 4th for a *union sacrée* against the enemy. They have pointed to it as the culmination of the years of nationalist revival since 1905. But as has been shown the idea of a nationalist revival with Germany as the focal point is an exaggeration. French public opinion was surprised by the conflict. The reason historians have written of a general feeling of the inevitability of war is because many people tried to say so *a posteriori*, to justify their actions and embellish their statesmanlike qualities. Although in early August patriotic feeling was buoyant, no one really wanted war. Becker's study shows that the movement of protest against the war was greater than is often believed. But the protesters, the trades unions and the Socialist Party, were both divided on possible action and caught unawares by events. At its general congress in July 1914, half of the Socialist Party had rejected the idea of a general strike against war, while the other half had only defended it with reservations. The C.G.T. trade union should have been the motor of protest because its stance against war was unambiguous. But most of its leaders were at the time attending the Belgian trades union congress, and anyway its *comité conféderal* had at the last minute abandoned the idea of a general strike on 31 July. The assassination on 31 July of the Socialist leader, Jean Jaurès by a half-witted fanatic driven to action by the vituperative attacks in the nationalist press against the 'pro-German Socialist traitor', symbolised the failure of the opposition to war. The government's wise decision not to arrest trade-unionists, pacifists, anti-militarists and suspected spies, named in the black list compiled by the authorities and known as the 'Carnet B', helped to rally support to their cause. The idea that they were fighting for a just cause united what otherwise appeared to be a divided France.

The *union sacrée* is perhaps best described as merely a truce for the duration of hostilities in order to win the war. There was no abandoning of convictions on either side. The Left fought a war it saw as in defence of the rights of man and democracy; the Right fought to defend its own conception of France. Of course the *union sacrée* was given greater impetus by the belief, common to Europe as a whole, that the war would be over by Christmas. The *union sacrée* was not then a myth created by the leaders of the time, but neither was it the climax of nationalist feeling and an enthusiastic welcoming of war. After mobilisation was decreed on the afternoon of Saturday 1 August, nationalism was not in evidence, *revanche* was hardly evoked, and Alsace–Lorraine even less. A fitting epitaph to that erroneous belief was the reaction of the Alsatian population as French troops arrived in the province: it was, to say the least, reserved, if not ambiguous. Even the semi-official newspaper, *Le Temps*, noted the reserve. It was obvious that the Alsatians would rather have been left out of the conflict.[49]

France entered the war with total national unity behind the man who had been her effective leader from January 1912. Poincaré's diplomatic efforts to strengthen the bonds of the Triple Entente to protect against future German aggression survived the final test of fire. During the July crisis Poincaré remained the principal decision-maker. However, because of his isolation from events during the trip to Russia, he more than any other European statesmen responded to events more than he influenced them. His principal preoccupation remained Russia. Much speculation has centred on whether during his three-day visit to St Petersburg, he encouraged Russia along the path of intransigence or even bellicosity. At the time the Austrian ultimatum had not even been delivered. Though he doubtless discussed the Serbian crisis, a natural thing to do with one's ally, it seems certain from other evidence, and unlikely from a logical point of view, that he encouraged Russia to take a hard line. Mention has already been made of the telegram Sazonov sent to Paris on the night of 29–30 July which, while referring to Paléologue's declaration of French support for Russia, makes no mention of any similar promise by Poincaré during his visit to St Petersburg. Similarly, the attitude of Russian military circles after the visit shows that they were still uncertain of French support. Five days after the visit, the Russian military attaché in Paris even asked Joffre whether, according to the Franco-Russian agreement, in the event of Germany mobilising part of her forces against Russia, France would mobilise. Pierre Renouvin has seen this as proof that Poincaré in his talks in St Petersburg did not go any further than a simple statement of fidelity to the Russian alliance.[50]

When looked at in the general context of Poincaré's policy towards Russia since 1912, unconditional support for her would have been illogical. For two-and-a-half years he perfected a balancing act in his dealings with Russia which he has summarised well:

> not to break up an alliance on which French policy has been based for a quarter of a century and the break-up of which would leave us in isolation at the mercy of our rivals; and nevertheless to do what lay in our power to induce our ally to exercise moderation in matters in which we are much less directly concerned than herself.[51]

Given that when he finally returned to Paris his efforts continued in this direction, the likelihood of him having given a blank cheque to Russia in St Petersburg seems even more remote.

A last comment on Poincaré's role during the July crisis might be the unjust way in which commentators and historians alike have treated him in particular. It should now be clear that during the July crisis Poincaré was the principal decision-maker in foreign policy, with Viviani acting as a mere puppet. Yet historians, such as Albertini and Jules Isaac, praise Viviani's consistency, correctness throughout, and moderating influence on Russia, while attempting to attribute to Poincaré all manner of evil when, more often than not, he was the instigator of such a policy.[52]

Poincaré, like Sir Edward Grey, was finally constrained by events into taking his country into war – a defensive war. Both believed it was for a just cause. But whereas Grey made plain his hatred of war, his fear of it, and was for many reasons ill-suited to deal with it, Poincaré, because he acted with firmness, resolution and confidence, gave the impression he accepted it without regret. This was not true. On 3 August he reflected deeply on the toll in human lives the war would take.[53] But in peace he had prepared resolutely for any eventuality. War was now a reality and he faced it with equal resolve.

Conclusion

Any study of France and the origins of the First World War must highlight the role of Raymond Poincaré. His was the major influence on French diplomacy during the last two-and-a-half years of peace. The control he exercised was probably greater than that enjoyed by any of his European counterparts. In Germany no single person consistently controlled foreign policy: the Kaiser, the Chancellor, the Secretary of State, the military and a host of domestic pressure groups were active, whether directly or indirectly. In Russia the Tsar, the Prime Minister, the Foreign Minister, the faction-ridden bureaucracy and the military all struggled to influence foreign policy. In pre-war Britain the Foreign Secretary exercised more effective control over diplomacy than in the authoritarian states. But even though he remained the overall master of foreign-policy decisions, which continued to be conducted in isolation from the parliamentary currents of the day, he still faced certain constraints. The first of these was public opinion; second was the Cabinet, certain of whose members held radical ideas which Grey was obliged to take into account when any major decision was being made. However, it was in democratic and Republican France that one-man control of foreign policy was able to develop further than anywhere else. The 'abominable venality'[1] of the French press was such that it could be bought or rigged sufficiently to lessen its influence on foreign affairs. Moreover, internal Cabinet opposition on foreign-policy matters was virtually unheard of in the run up to the war. In Britain a Foreign Secretary was forced to live with Cabinet opposition virtually unchanged from one parliamentary term to the next. A Cabinet reshuffle would elicit careful scrutiny and debate in the press. By contrast, the endemic instability of French governments could be a source of strength for an astute Prime Minister or President of the Republic intent on weeding out opponents within the government and replacing them with allies or yes-men. There was ample opportunity for doing this before the First World War, with seven different governments and six Prime Ministers between January 1912 and June 1914. Poincaré perfected it to an art, so that foreign-policy decisions taken in Cabinet when he was Prime Minister and President were nearly always unanimous.

Poincaré set out to make French foreign policy a one-man affair and was completely successful. His methods and style were a complete break with the past. Whereas the success of Delcassé's foreign policy may in part be attributed to the loyalty and efficiency of his permanent officials and Ambassadors, Poincaré's foreign policy was imposed in spite of many of his

165

permanent officials and Ambassadors. He succeeded by adapting the French diplomatic machine to his own ideas rather than the reverse, as had been the case with previous Foreign Ministers. In many ways in the wake of Agadir, being new on the European scene, with no experience in foreign affairs, and with a new vigorous style and forthright policies, Poincaré was bound to attract attention and certain suspicions that his Lorraine origins could only reinforce.

Poincaré's diplomacy was in reality far more passive than has often been alleged. Although he was indubitably suspicious of Germany, he did not act aggressively or intransigently toward her. He merely sought to consolidate France's position in Europe and the Empire and to prepare for any eventuality. Indeed, from 1912 to 1914 Franco-German colonial relations were good, the occasional over-zealousness of a nationalist functionary notwithstanding. Franco-British colonial relations, by contrast, were bad. In no way was Poincaré's foreign policy intended to provoke war; indeed it was a good deal more restrained than those of Germany, Austria–Hungary or Russia. For Poincaré, peace was best safeguarded by the balance of power inherent in the rigid separation of the two alliance systems. He conceived of no alternative international order. Nor was there much likelihood of French public opinion accepting one. France more than any other European nation understood the necessity for strong alliances. Ever since 1871 she had attempted to break out of the diplomatic isolation Bismarck had imposed on her. The process had been a long and painful one, which had only really been completed in 1907 with the formation of the Triple Entente, the fruits of which, principally international security, were only just being tasted. To a large extent then, the balance of power inherent in the European international system after 1907 was arguably of even greater importance to France than to Britain, its traditional champion. However, Britain had a more flexible approach to it. Sir Edward Grey was opposed to any inter-penetration of the alliance systems but willing to negotiate agreements with the Triple Alliance bloc. In contrast to French governments from 1907 to 1912, and despite considerable opposition from French diplomats, Poincaré ruled out any such move, though his attitude softened in 1913 and 1914, notably towards Germany. Overall, however, his inflexibility in applying the notion of the strict separation of the two alliance systems inevitably built into it the inflexibility which was its greatest weakness in times of crisis. In this manner, Poincaré's foreign policy seriously contributed to crystallising still further the two blocs. Thus in the words of one historian, whereas in 1907 Triple Alliance and Triple Entente 'had stood side by side; in 1914 they stood face to face'.[2]

A balance of power is by definition fragile. For it to be maintained nations would have to remain inert. It is, therefore, virtually in the nature of a balance of power that politicians should prepare for the eventuality of the balance being upset. They do so by attempting to gain and maintain a margin of superiority over their rivals which they perceive as a guarantee of safety but which their opponents see as a threat. By 1914 it appeared to most French politicians and soldiers that France, after having lived for decades with the balance firmly tipped against her, had gained that superiority through her membership of the Triple Entente. This appeared to be confirmed by a War Ministry report of September 1912 which predicted a victory of the Triple Entente in a conflict against the Triple Alliance. It was therefore in France's national interest to maintain that margin of superiority not for any bellicose end but as a guarantee of safety.

France's decision to support Russia was not taken out of blind obedience to the Franco-Russian Alliance, but because France's margin of safety was at risk. To have held Russia back from entering the war, had that been possible, would have allowed Austria–Hungary to regain some of her prestige, while seriously reducing that of Russia, thus altering the balance between Triple Entente and Triple Alliance to the disadvantage of the former. The alternative of allowing Russia to fight alone would have condemned her to certain defeat by Germany and Austria–Hungary, thus ever more gravely jeopardising France's international security, perhaps even returning her to her isolation of the 1880s. Even if in the end the final decision had not been made for France by Germany's declaration of war on her, she would still have felt compelled to fight alongside Russia. In the end, like Britain, she entered the war for negative reasons – because not to have done so would have been a certain blow to her national security as it was generally perceived. And just as Britain's decision to go to war was not primarily to uphold the 1839 treaty of guarantee of Belgian neutrality, but because she feared the consequence of German domination of the continent, so France did not decide to go to war because of the Franco-Russian Alliance, but because she was not willing to live again in the shadow of a mighty Germany.

A striking feature of the July crisis is the extent to which the decision-makers were unwittingly reacting to situations which had already substantially altered; for instance, by the time Sir Edward Grey realised what the Austro-Hungarian government was intending to do, the ultimatum to Serbia had been despatched, leaving him with no prospect of influencing Vienna as he had hoped to do. This was more true of the French, for Poincaré and Viviani were absent and out of touch with Paris until only three days before mobilisation. By the time a telegram from Paris reached St Petersburg on 31 July recommending a delay in mobilising in order not to offer Germany a pretext to mobilise, the Tsar could only remark that it had 'come too late'. Russia had already ordered general mobilisation.[3] France more than any other power in July 1914 was following events rather than leading them. In the end the choices open to her leaders were narrowly limited. Even then the final decision for war was taken for them when in the evening of Monday 3 August Ambassador von Schoen handed to Foreign Minister Viviani the German declaration of war on France.

Chronological Table

1870	2 July	Hohenzollern candidature for Spanish throne
	13 July	Ems telegram
	19 July	France declares war on Prussia
	30 August–	
	2 September	Battle of Sedan
	4 September	Fall of Napoleon III and proclamation of French Republic
	19 September	Beginning of siege of Paris
1871	18 January	Foundation of German Empire
	28 January	Franco-German armistice
	8 February	Election of National Assembly
	17 February	Thiers becomes head of the government
	18 March–	
	28 May	Paris Commune
	10 May	Frankfurt peace treaty between France and Germany
1873	24 May	Fall of Thiers, Macmahon President of the Republic
	16 September	End of German occupation
	October	Three Emperors' League formed
1875	24 February–	
	16 July	Constitutional Laws of Third Republic passed
	April	War scare in France
1877	16 May	Macmahon attempted 'coup d'état'
	14 October	Republican electoral victory
1878	June–July	Congress of Berlin
1879	7 October	Austro-German Dual Alliance
1881	18 June	Dreikaiserbund between Russia, Germany and Austria–Hungary
1882	20 May–	
	September	Triple Alliance, British occupation of Egypt ends Anglo-French condominium
1883		French occupation of Annam and Tonkin
1885	March	Collapse of Jules Ferry ministry after fall of Tonkin

1886	1 July	Boulanger Minister of War
1887	20 February	Triple Alliance renewed
	20 April	Schnaebelé Incident
	18 June	Reinsurance Treaty between Russia and Germany
1888	15 June	Accession of Kaiser William II
	November	First French loan to Russia
1890	18 March	Dismissal of Bismarck
1891	May	Pre-term renewal of Triple Alliance
	27 August	Franco-Russian Entente
1892	17 August	Franco-Russian military convention
1893–		
1894		Panama scandal
1893	27 December	Russia ratifies Franco-Russian Alliance
1894	4 January	France ratifies Franco-Russian Alliance
	December	First Dreyfus trial
1896	June	Marchand expedition
1898	September–	
	December	Fashoda crisis
1899		Second Dreyfus trial
	9 August	Addition of secret clauses to Franco-Russian Alliance
	12 October	Outbreak of Boer war
1900	16 December	Secret Franco-Italian agreement
1901	22 January	Death of Queen Victoria; accession of Edward VII
1902	30 January	Anglo-Japanese Treaty
	28 June	Triple Alliance renewed
	30 June	Secret Franco-Italian neutrality agreement
1903	1–4 May	Edward VII's state visit to Paris
	6–9 July	Visit of President Loubet and Delcassé to London
1904	8 February	Outbreak of Russo-Japanese war
	8 April	Entente Cordiale
	30 July	Ending of French diplomatic relations with the Vatican
	21 October	Dogger Bank Incident
	23 November	Russo-German alliance negotiations break down
1905	2 January	Fall of Port Arthur to Japanese
	22 January	Outbreak of revolution in Russia
	31 March	William II visits Tangiers; First Moroccan crisis
	27 May	Destruction of Russian fleet at Tsushima
	6 June	Delcassé resigns

1905	24 July	German and Russian Emperors sign agreement at Björkö
	12 August	Anglo-Japanese Alliance renewed
	5 September	Treaty of Portsmouth ends Russo-Japanese war
	28 September	Morocco conference agreed between France and Germany
	9 December	Separation of Church and State in France
	11 December	Campbell-Bannerman forms Liberal administration
	15 December	Anglo-French staff talks begin
1906	January	Liberal victory in British general election
	1 January	Moltke succeeds Schlieffen as Chief of German General Staff
	16 January	Algeciras conference opens
	7 April	Algeciras Act signed
	5 June	German Third Naval Law ratified
	17 July	Rehabilitation of Dreyfus
	October	Radical victory in French elections; formation of Clemenceau ministry
1907	31 August	Anglo-Russian convention
1908	5 April	Asquith becomes Prime Minister
	14 June	Fourth German Naval Law ratified
	25 September	'Deserters of Casablanca' affair between Germany and France
	6 October	Austrian annexation of Bosnia and Herzegovina
1909	9 February	Franco-German agreement over Morocco
	July	Briand succeeds Clemenceau
	14 July	Bethmann-Hollweg replaces Bülow as German Chancellor
	24 October	Racconigi agreement between Italy and Russia
1910	15 January	Liberal administration retained in British General Election
	6 May	Death of Edward VII; accession of George V
	4–5 November	William II and Nicholas II meet at Potsdam
1911	21 May	French occupy Fez
	27 June	Caillaux becomes French Premier
	1 July	Panther sent to Agadir; second Moroccan crisis
	21 July	Lloyd George's Mansion House speech
	August	Strategy of the 'offensive' becomes French military policy
	28 September	Outbreak of Italo-Turkish War

1911	4 November	Franco-German agreement over Morocco
1912	January	'Carthage' and 'Manouba' affair
	14 January	Poincaré becomes French Premier
	7 February	Kaiser announces Army and Navy bills
	8 February	Haldane mission to Berlin
	13 March	Serbia and Bulgaria form Balkan League
	18 March	Churchill proposes redistribution of fleet
	29 May	Greece joins Balkan League
	30 May	French protectorate over Morocco proclaimed
	16 July	Franco-Russian naval convention signed
	22 July	French fleet transferred from Brest to Toulon
	August	Poincaré visits Russia
	15 October	Treaty of Lausanne ends Italo-Turkish War
	17 October	First Balkan War
	22–23 November	Grey-Cambon letters exchanged
	3 December	Armistice between Turkey and Balkan states
	5 December	Triple Alliance renewed
	16 December	Ambassadorial conference opens in London
1913	5 January	Jagow succeeds Kiderlen-Waechter in German Foreign Office
	17 January	Poincaré elected President of the Republic; Briand ministry formed
	22 March	Barthou forms new ministry
	30 May	Treaty of London ends First Balkan War
	29 June	Outbreak of Second Balkan War
	30 June	German Army Bill ratified
	7 August	French Army Bill ratified (3-year military service)
	10 August	Peace of Bucharest ends Second Balkan War
	November	Saverne Affair
	November–December	Liman von Sanders Affair
	6 December	Doumergue forms new ministry
1914	15 February	Franco-German agreement on Baghdad Railway
	16 March	Madame Caillaux assassinates Calmette
	9 April	Franco-Turkish agreement on Ottoman Empire
	21–24 April	George V and Grey visit Paris
	26 April–10 May	French general elections; swing to left
	May	Anglo-Russian naval talks begin
	2 June	Fall of Doumergue ministry
	9–13 June	Formation and collapse of Ribot ministry

1914	16 June	Formation of Viviani ministry
	28 June	Assassination of Archduke Franz Ferdinand at Sarajevo
	15 July	Poincaré and Viviani leave on state visit to Russia and Scandinavia
	20 July	Poincaré arrives in Russia; opening of Caillaux trial
	23 July	Austrian ultimatum to Serbia
	25 July	Poincaré arrives in Sweden
	27 July	State visit to Denmark and Norway cancelled
	28 July	Austria-Hungary declares war on Serbia. William II appeals to Tsar's monarchical solidarity. Russia orders mobilisation of four western military districts for 29 July
	29 July	Poincaré arrives in Paris. Russian general mobilisation ordered but revoked by Tsar late that same evening
	30 July	Austria-Hungary orders general mobilisation for 31 July. Russian general mobilisation ordered for 31 July
	31 July	Kaiser proclaims 'state of imminent war'. Jaurès assassinated, Germany refuses to mediate and issues ultimatum to Russia. French Ministerial Council orders 'ten-kolometre withdrawal'
	1 August	German ultimatum to Russia expires; Germany declares war on Russia and mobilises. France orders general mobilisation
	2 August	British cabinet agrees to protect north coast of France and Channel against German attack. Germany invades Luxembourg and sends ultimatum to Belgium
	3 August	Italy remains neutral. Germany declares war on France. Belgium rejects German demands. British mobilise army. British Cabinet agrees to send ultimatum to Berlin
	4 August	Germany invades Belgium. British ultimatum transmitted to Berlin. Ultimatum expires at midnight; British ambassador asks for passport
	6 August	Austria-Hungary declares war on Russia. British Cabinet agrees to send British Expeditionary Force to France
	12 August	Great Britain and France declare war on Austria-Hungary.

Bibliography

1. BASIC BACKGROUND READING

For further information on the general diplomatic background of the First World War students should refer to the following studies:

L. ALBERTINI, *The Origins of the War of 1914*, 3 vols (London, 1965).

V. R. BERGHAHN, *Germany and the Approach of War in 1914* (London, 1973).

R. GIRAULT, *Diplomatie européene et impérialismes, 1871-1914* (Paris, 1979).

F. H. HINSLEY (ed.) *British Foreign Policy under Sir Edward Grey* (Cambridge, 1977).

R. T. B. LANGHORNE, *The Collapse of the Concert of Europe: International Politics, 1890-1914* (London, 1981).

R. POIDEVIN and J. BARIÉTY, *Les relations franco-allemandes, 1815-1975* (Paris, 1977).

Z. STEINER, *Britain and the Origins of the First World War* (London, 1977).

A. J. P. TAYLOR, *The Struggle for Mastery in Europe, 1848-1918* (Oxford, 1954).

L. C. F. TURNER, *Origins of the First World War* (London, 1970).

S. R. WILLIAMSON, *The Politics of Grand Strategy: Britain and France Prepare for War, 1904-1914* (Cambridge, Mass., 1969).

There is no recent major study of the role of French diplomacy in the outbreak of the War. The following French monographs provide the most up to date research on particular aspects of French international relations:

J.-C. ALLAIN, *Agadir 1911, une crise impérialiste en Europe pour la conquête du Maroc* (Paris, 1976).

J.-J. BECKER, *1914, comment les Français sont entrés dans la guerre* (Paris, 1977).

R. GIRAULT, *Emprunts russes et investissements français en Russie, 1887-1914* (Paris, 1973).

R. POIDEVIN, *Les relations économiques et financières entre la France et l'Allemagne de 1898 a 1914* (Paris, 1969).

J. THOBIE, *Intérêts et impérialisme français dans l'Empire Ottoman (1895-1914)* (Paris, 1977).

2. GENERAL BIBLIOGRAPHY

This list includes autobiographies, biographies and works containing source material. Books of particular interest (in addition to those listed in section 1) are marked with an asterisk (*).

AGATHON [pseud. H. MASSIS and A. De TARDES] *Les jeunes gens d'aujourd'hui* (Paris, 1913).

*J. C. ALLAIN, *Joseph Caillaux - le défi victorieux, 1863-1914* (Paris, 1978).

*R. D. ANDERSON, *France, 1870-1914, Politics and Society* (London, 1977).

*C. M. ANDREW, *Theophile Delcassé and the Making of the Entente Cordiale, 1898-1905* (London, 1968).

*C. M. ANDREW and A. S. KANYA-FORSTNER, *France Overseas: the Great War and the Climax of French Imperial Expansion* (London and Stanford, 1981).

B. AUFFRAY, *Pierre de Margerie et la vie diplomatique de son temps* (Paris, 1976).

J. BARTHÉLEMY, *Démocratie et politique étrangère* (Paris, 1917).

C. BENOIST, *Souvenirs*, vol. III (Paris, 1934).

R. BINION, *Defeated Leaders* (Columbia, 1960).

J.-F. BLONDEL, *Au fil de la carrière, récit d'un diplomate, 1911-38* (Paris, n.d.).

*R. J. B. BOSWORTH, *Italy the Least of the Great Powers: Italian Foreign Policy before the First World War* (Cambridge, 1979).

*J. BOUVIER and R. GIRAULT (eds), *L'impérialisme français d'avant 1914* (Paris, 1976).

F. R. BRIDGE and R. BULLEN, *The Great Powers and the European States System, 1815-1914* (London, 1980).

*D. W. BROGAN, *The Development of Modern France, 1870-1939* (London, 1940).

H. BRUNSCHWIG, *French Colonialism, 1871-1914: Myths and Realities* (London, 1966).

*J. P. T. BURY, *France, 1814-1940* (4th edn, London, 1969).

J. CAILLAUX, *Agadir: ma politique extérieure* (Paris, 1919).

——, *Mes mémoires*, 3 vols (Paris, 1942-7).

J. CAMBON, *The Diplomat* (London, 1931).

P. CAMBON, *Correspondance, 1870-1924*, ed. H. Cambon, 3 vols (Paris, 1940-6).

F. CARON, *An Economic History of Modern France* (London, 1979).

*E. M. CARROLL, *French Public Opinion and Foreign Affairs, 1870-1914* (London, 1931).

C. CHARLE (ed.), *Les hauts fonctionnaires en France au XIXe siècle* (Paris, 1980).

F. CHARLES-ROUX, *Souvenirs diplomatiques d'un âge révolu* (Paris, 1956).

——, *Souvenirs diplomatiques, Rome-Quirinal, 1916-19* (Paris, 1958).

J. CHASTENET, *Raymond Poincaré* (Paris, 1948).

——, *La France de Monsieur Fallières* (Paris, 1949).

——, *Histoire de la Troisième République*, 7 vols (Paris, 1952-63).

J.-J. CHEVALLIER, *Histoire des institutions et des régimes politiques de la France de 1789 à nos jours* (5th ed., Paris, 1977).

WINSTON S. CHURCHILL, *The World Crisis, 1911-18*, 2 vols (repr. London, 1968).

*H. CONTAMINE, *La Revanche, 1871-1914* (Paris, 1957).

E. DECLEVA, *Da Adua a Sarajevo. La Politica estera italiana e la Francia 1896-1914* (Bari, 1971).

*C. DIGEON, *La crise allemande de la pensée française* (Paris, 1959).

UN DIPLOMATE [H. CAMBON] *Paul Cambon, ambassadeur de France* (Paris, 1937).

*J. DROZ, *Les causes de la première guerre mondiale, essai d'historiographie* (Paris, 1973).

*J.-B. DUROSELLE, *La France et les Français, 1900-1914* (Paris, 1972).

K. EUBANK, *Paul Cambon, Master Diplomatist* (Oklahoma, 1960).

S. B. FAY, *The Origins of the World War*, 2 vols (New York, 1928).

A. FERRY, *Les carnets secrets d'Abel Ferry, 1914-1918* (Paris, 1958).

*F. FISCHER, *Germany's War Aims in the First World War* (London, 1967).

*——, *War of Illusions* (London, 1973).

J. GANIAGE, *L'expansion coloniale de la France sous la Troisième République 1871-1914* (Paris, 1968).

A. GÉRARD, *Mémoires d'Auguste Gérard* (Paris, 1928).

*R. GIRARDET, *Le nationalisme français, 1871-1914* (Paris, 1966).

——, *L'idée coloniale en France de 1871 à 1962* (Paris, 1972).

J. GIRAUDOUX, *Bella* (Paris, 1926 edn).

*G. P. GOOCH, *Franco-German Relations, 1871-1914* (New York, 1923).

——, *Before the War: Studies in Diplomacy and Statecraft*, 2 vols (London, 1936-8).

VISCOUNT [SIR EDWARD] GREY OF FALLODON, *Twenty-five Years, 1892-1916*, 2 vols (London, 1925).

E. HALÉVY, *The Rule of Democracy, 1905-14* (4th edn, London, 1970).

G. HANOTAUX, *Raymond Poincaré* (Paris, 1934).

*F. H. HINSLEY, *Power and the Pursuit of Peace* (Cambridge, 1963).

M. HURST, *Key Treaties for the Great Powers, 1870-1914*, 2 vols (Newton Abbot, 1972).

*J. ISAAC, *Un débat historique, 1914: le problème des origines de la guerre* (Paris, 1933).

E. JAECKH, *Kiderlen-Waechter intime, d'après ses notes et sa correspondance* (French trans., Paris, 1926).

*J. JOLL, *The Unspoken Assumptions* (London, 1968).

E. JUDET, *Georges Louis* (Paris, 1925).

*P. M. KENNEDY, *The War Plans of the Great Powers, 1880-1914* (London, 1979).

H. W. KOCH (ed.), *The Origins of the First World War: Great Power Rivalry and German War Aims* (London, 1972).

A. KRIEGEL and J.-J. BECKER, *1914: la guerre et le mouvement ouvrier français* (Paris, 1964).

*W. L. LANGER, *European Alliances and Alignments, 1871-1890* (2nd edn, New York, 1950).

J. LAROCHE, *Quinze ans à Rome avec Camille Barrère (1898-1913)* (Paris, 1948).

——, *Au quai d'Orsay avec Briand et Poincaré, 1913-1926* (Paris, 1957).

P. G. LAUREN, *Diplomats and Bureaucrats: the First Institutional Responses to Twentieth-century Diplomacy in France and Germany* (Stanford, 1976).

G. LOUIS, *Les carnets de Georges Louis*, 2 vols (Paris, 1926).

R. MARCHAND (ed.), *Un livre noir: diplomatie d'avant guerre d'après les documents des archives russes (1910-1917)* (Paris, 1922).

E. MAY (ed.), *Potential Enemies* (Harvard, forthcoming).

A. MESSIMY, *Mes souvenirs* (Paris, 1937).

A. MILLERAND, 'Mes souvenirs', unpublished memoirs in the possession of Mme M. Millerand.

*P. MILZA, *Les relations internationales de 1871 à 1914* (Paris, 1968).

P. MIQUEL, *Poincaré* (Paris, 1961).

M. MISOFFE, *La vie volontaire d'André Tardieu* (Paris, 1930).

M. PALÉOLOGUE, *Un grand tournant de la politique mondiale, 1904-6* (Paris, 1934).

F. PAYEN, *Poincaré chez lui, au parlement, au palais* (Paris, 1936).

H. POGNON, *Lettre à M. Doumergue au sujet d'une réforme du Ministère des Affaires Étrangères* (Paris, 1913).

*R. POIDEVIN, *Finances et relations internationales, 1887-1914* (Paris, 1970).

——, *Les origines de la première guerre mondiale* (Paris, 1975).

R. POINCARÉ, *Au service de la France*, 11 vols (Paris, 1928–74).

——, *Comment fut declarée la guerre de 1914* (Paris, 1939).

*D. PORCH, *The March to the Marne* (Cambridge, 1981).

A. G. RAFFALOVICH, *L'abominable vénalité de la presse* (Paris, 1921).

D. B. RALSTON, *The Army of the Republic* (Cambridge, Mass., 1967).

*J. REMAK (ed.), *The Origins of World War I, 1870-1914* (New York, 1967).

*——, *The First World War, Causes, Conduct, Consequences* (New York, 1971).

*P. RENOUVIN, *Les origines immédiates de la guerre 28 juin-4 aout 1914* (Paris, 1925).

——, *L'époque contemporaine II. La paix armée et la Grande Guerre* (Paris, 1939).

*——, *Histoire des relations internationales*, vol. VI, *1871-1914* (Paris, 1955).

*——, *La crise européenne et la première guerre mondiale* (4th edn, Paris, 1962).

*P. RENOUVIN and J.-B. DUROSELLE, *Introduction à l'histoire des relations internationales* (Paris, 1965).

COUNT DE SAINT AULAIRE, *Confession d'un vieux diplomate* (Paris, 1953).

B. E. SCHMITT, *The Coming of the War, 1914*, 2 vols (New York, 1930).

——, *The Triple Alliance and the Triple Entente* (New York, 1947).

*F. L. SCHUMAN, *War and Diplomacy in the French Republic* (London, 1931).

W. I. SHORROCK, *French Imperialism in the Middle East* (London, 1976).

*J. STEINBERG, *Yesterday's Deterrent: Tirpitz and the Birth of the German Battle Fleet* (London, 1965).

*Z. STEINER, *The Foreign Office and Foreign Policy, 1898-1914* (Cambridge, 1969).

G. TABOUIS, *Jules Cambon* (English trans., London, 1938).

*A. J. P. TAYLOR, *War by Time-Table: How the First World War Began* (London, 1969).

A. THIERRY, *L'Angleterre au temps de Paul Cambon* (Paris, 1961).

M. TOSCANO, *The History of Treaties and International Politics*, vol. I (Baltimore, 1966).

N. WAITES (ed.), *Troubled Neighbours: Franco-British Relations in the Twentieth Century* (London, 1971).

D. WATSON, *Georges Clemenceau: a political Biography* (London, 1974).

*E. WEBER, The Nationalist Revival in France, 1905-1914 (Berkeley, Calif., 1959).

*G. WRIGHT, *Raymond Poincaré and the French Presidency* (California, 1942).

T. ZELDIN, *France, 1848-1945* (Oxford, 1973-7).

3. ARTICLES AND ESSAYS

J.-C. ALLAIN, 'L'expansion française au Maroc de 1902 à 1912', in J. Bouvier and R. Girault (eds), *L'impérialisme français d'avant 1914* (Paris, 1976).

C. M. ANDREW, 'German World Policy and the Reshaping of the Dual Alliance', *Journal of Contemporary History*, I, 3 (1966).

——, 'The Entente Cordiale from its Origins to 1914', in N. Waites, (ed), *Troubled Neighbours* (London, 1971).

——, 'Déchiffrement et diplomatie: le cabinet noir du quai d'Orsay sous la Troisième République', *Relations Internationales*, no. 5 (1976).

——, 'The French Colonialist Movement during the Third Republic: The Unofficial Mind of Imperialism', *Transactions of the Royal Historical Society*, 5th ser., XXVI (1976).

——, 'La France à la recherche de la Syrie intégrale, 1914-20', *Relations Internationales*, no. 19 (1979).

C. M. ANDREW and A. S. KANYA-FORSTNER, 'The French "Colonial Party": Its Composition, Aims and Influence, 1885-1914', *The Historical Journal*, XIV (1971).

——, 'Gabriel Hanotaux, the Colonial Party and the Fashoda Strategy', *Journal of Imperial and Commonwealth History*, III, 1 (1974).

C. M. ANDREW, P. GRUPP, and A. S. KANYA-FORSTNER, 'Le mouvement colonial français et ses principales personnalités, 1890-1914' *Revue Française d'Histoire d'Outre-mer*, LXII (1975).

I. V. BESTUZHEV, 'Russian Foreign Policy, February–June 1914', *Journal of Contemporary History*, I, 3 (1966).

V. I. BOVYKIN, 'The Franco-Russian Alliance', *History*, LXIV (1979).

J. C. CAIRNS, 'International Politics and the Military Mind: the Case of the French Republic, 1911-14', *Journal of Modern History* (Sep 1953).

R. D. CHALLENER, 'The French Foreign Office: The Era of Philippe Berthelot', in G. A. Craig and F. Gilbert (eds), *The Diplomats* (Princeton, 1953).

P. CROZIER, 'L'Autriche et l'avant-guerre', *La Revue de France* (May–June 1921).

I. GEISS, 'The Outbreak of the First World War and German War Aims', *Journal of Contemporary History*, I, 3 (1966).

R. GIRAULT, 'Les Balkans dans les relations franco-russes en 1912', *La Revue Historique* (Jan–Mar 1975).

P. G. GUILLEN, 'Les questions coloniales dans les relations franco-allemandes à la veille de la première guerre mondiale', *La Revue Historique*, no. 248 (1972).

J. JOLL, 'The 1914 Debate Continues: Fritz Fischer and his Critics', *Past and Present*, 34 (1966); reprinted in Koch (ed.), *Origins of the First World War*.

——, 'Politicians and the Freedom to Choose: the Case of July 1914', in A. Ryan (ed.) *The Idea of Freedom, Essays in Honour of Isaiah Berlin* (Oxford, 1979).

A. OUTREY, 'Histoire et principes de l'administration française des affaires étrangères', *Revue Française de Science Politique*, III (1953).

W. R. SHARP, 'Public Personnel Management in France', in W. R. Sharp, ed., *Civil Service Abroad* (New York, 1935).

D. STEVENSON, 'French War Aims and the American Challenge, 1914–18', *The Historical Journal*, XXII, 4 (1979).

L. C. F. TURNER, 'The Russian Mobilisation in 1914', *Journal of Contemporary History*, III, 1 (1968).

T. WILSON, 'Britain's "Moral Commitment" to France in August 1914', *History*, LXIV (1979).

4. UNPUBLISHED SOURCES

A *Private Papers*

BERTIE MSS., Public Record Office

BILLY (DE) MSS., Archives du Ministère des Affaires Etrangères

JULES CAMBON MSS., Archives du Ministère des Affaires Etrangères

PAUL CAMBON MSS., Archives du Ministère des Affaires Etrangères

PAUL CAMBON MSS., Correspondence in the possession of M. Louis Cambon

DELCASSÉ MSS., Archives du Ministère des Affaires Etrangères

GÉRARD MSS., Archives Nationales

GOUT MSS., Archives du Ministère des Affaires Etrangères

GREY MSS., Public Record Office

LOUIS MSS., Archives du Ministère des Affaires Etrangères

MARGERIE (Jacquin de) MSS., Archives du Ministère des Affaires Etrangères

NICOLSON MSS., Public Record Office
PICHON MSS., Bibliothèque de l'Institut de France
POINCARÉ MSS., Bibliothèque Nationale (n.a.fr. 16024–16034)
REINACH MSS., Bibliothèque Nationale (n.a.fr.)

B   *Official Papers*

Archives du Ministère des Affaires Etrangères
   Volumes in the 'Nouvelle Série Reliée' for years 1905–14
Archives Nationales
   Dossier on G. Louis F^7 Police Générale
Public Record Office
   Volumes on France in FO 371 series

Notes and References

ABBREVIATIONS

AN	Archives Nationales
B.D.	*British Documents on the Origins of the War, 1898-1914*, ed. G. P. Gooch and H. Temperley, 11 vols (London, 1926–38).
BN	Bibliothèque Nationale
D.D.F.	*Documents diplomatiques français, 1871-1914*, Ministère des Affaires Etrangères, 2ᵉ and 3ᵉ séries (Paris, 1930–53).
FO	Foreign Office Papers
Inst. de Fr.	Bibliothèque de l'Institut de France
JODebPC	*Journal Officiel de la République Française, Débats Parlementaires (Chambre des Députés)*
JODebPS	*Journal Officiel . . . Débats Parlementaires (Sénat)*
JODocPC	*Journal Officiel . . . Documents Parlementaires (Chambre des Députés)*
JODocPS	*Journal Officiel . . . Documents Parlementaires (Sénat)*
L.N.	*Un livre noir: diplomatie d'avant-guerre d'après les documents des archives russes (1910-1917)* 2 vols, ed. R. Marchand (Paris, 1922).
MAE	Archives du Ministère des Affaires Étrangères

INTRODUCTION

1. For a brief introduction to this question, see H. W. Koch (ed.), *The Origins of the First World War* (London, 1972) pp. 3–6.

2. For bibliographical references, see the very comprehensive and excellent historiographical survey of the debate from its origins to the present in J. Droz, *Les causes de la première guerre mondiale* (Paris, 1973).

1. THE SEARCH FOR SECURITY

1. A. J. P. Taylor, *The Struggle for Mastery in Europe, 1848-1918* (Oxford 1954; paperback edn, 1971) p. xxx. This work carries detailed tables of the might and fortunes of the great powers from 1850 to 1914, pp. xxiv–xxxi.

2. Quoted in W. L. Langer, *European Alliances and Alignments, 1871-90* (2nd edn, New York, 1950) p. 11.

3. F. R. Bridge and R. Bullen, *The Great Powers and the European States System, 1815-1914* (London, 1980) p. 111.

4. G. P. Gooch, *Franco-German Relations, 1871-1914. The Creighton Lecture, 1923* (New York, 1923) p. 4.

5. Bridge and Bullen, *The Great Powers*, p. 111.

6. R. Poidevin and J. Bariéty, *Les relations franco-allemandes, 1815-1975* (Paris, 1977) pp. 123–4.

7. Ibid., pp. 125–6.

8. Ibid., pp. 126–35.

9. R. D. Anderson, *France, 1870-1914, Politics and Society* (London, 1977) p. 146. For a detailed analysis of the importance of the Empire in the French economy, see C. M. Andrew and

A. S. Kanya-Forstner, *France Overseas: the Great War and the Climax of French Imperial Expansion* (London and Stanford, 1981) pp. 14–17.

10. Andrew and Kanya-Forstner, *France Overseas*, p. 10.
11. E. M. Carroll, *French Public Opinion and Foreign Affairs, 1870-1914* (London, 1931) p. 87.
12. Quoted in Gooch, *Franco-German Relations*, p. 21.
13. Ibid., p. 22.
14. Ibid., p. 21.
15. Ibid., p. 24.
16. Ibid., p. 28.
17. R. Girault, *Diplomatie européenne et impérialismes, 1871-1914* (Paris, 1979) pp. 122–6.
18. P. Renouvin, *Histoire des relations internationales*, vol. VI, *1871-1914* (Paris, 1955) p. 121.
19. Quoted in Andrew and Kanya-Forstner, *France Overseas*, p. 17.
20. Ibid.
21. Poidevin and Bariéty, *Relations franco-allemandes*, p. 151.
22. Ibid., pp. 151–2.
23. Ibid., pp. 153–4.
24. Quoted in Renouvin, *Relations internationales*, vol. VI, p. 169.
25. Ibid., pp. 167–70.
26. Poidevin and Bariéty, *Relations franco-allemandes*, pp. 163–6.
27. Quoted in C. M. Andrew and A. S. Kanya-Forstner, 'Gabriel Hanotaux, the Colonial Party and the Fashoda Strategy', *Journal of Imperial and Commonwealth History*, III, 1 (1974) p. 94.
28. Ibid., pp. 92–3.
29. Ibid.
30. C. M. Andrew, *Theophile Delcassé and the Making of the Entente Cordiale, 1898-1905* (London, 1968) pp. 51–2.
31. Poidevin and Bariéty, *Relations franco-allemandes*, pp. 167–8.
32. For a fuller explanation see Andrew, *Delcassé and the Entente Cordiale*, pp. 119–35.
33. For further details see Ch. 4, pp. 56–7.
34. Andrew, *Delcassé and the Entente Cordiale*, pp. 180–215.
35. Ibid., pp. 201–12.
36. Ibid., pp. 228–48.
37. Ibid., pp. 250–2.
38. Ibid., pp. 268–9.
39. Ibid., pp. 273–301.
40. Ibid., p. 302.
41. Quoted in Renouvin, *Relations internationales*, vol. VI, p. 221.
42. Ibid., pp. 221–2.
43. Andrew, *Delcassé and the Entente Cordiale*, p. 306.

2. BUREAUCRATS AND DIPLOMATS

1. Count de Saint Aulaire, *Confession d'un vieux diplomate* (Paris, 1953) p. 29.
2. Reinach to Bertie, 12 Jan 1916, FO 800/60.
3. *JODocPC*, 1914, no. 3318.
4. Great Britain and Germany began in 1906. See Z. Steiner, *The Foreign Office and Foreign Policy, 1898-1914* (Cambridge, 1969), and P. G. Lauren, *Diplomats and Bureaucrats: the First Institutional Responses to Twentieth-century Diplomacy in France and Germany* (Stanford, 1976). Italy began in 1908. R. J. B. Bosworth, *Italy, the Least of the Great Powers: Italian Foreign Policy before the First World War* (Cambridge, 1979) p. 115.
5. *JODebPC*, 10 Mar 1914.
6. *JODocPC*, 1912, no. 1237.
7. Lindenlaub to Gérard, 14 Nov 1911, AN Gérard Mss., 329 AP 19.

8.   Jules Cambon to Paul Cambon, 8 Feb 1908, MAE Jules Cambon Mss., 25 (1908). He was still calling for a return to the old organisation in 1911.

9.   H. Pognon, *Lettre à M. Doumergue au sujet d'une réforme du Ministère des Affaires Etrangères* (Paris, 1913) p. 37.

10.   The Colonial Party, which was the official political grouping, has been the subject of studies by C. M. Andrew and A. S. Kanya-Forstner. For example, 'The French "Colonial Party"': Its Composition, Aims and Influence, 1885–1914', *The Historical Journal*, XIV (1971); with P. Grupp, 'Le Mouvement colonial français et ses principales personnalités, 1890–1914', *La Revue Française d'Histoire d'Outre-mer*, LXII (1975).

11.   W. R. Sharp, 'Public Personnel Management in France', in W. R. Sharp, *Civil Service Abroad* (New York, 1935) p. 105.

12.   See Z. Steiner, *The Foreign Office and Foreign Policy, 1898-1914* (Cambridge, 1969).

13.   Z. Steiner, *Britain and the Origins of the First World War* (London, 1977) p. 171.

14.   It is interesting that the defeat of France in the Second World War had the same effect, giving rise to the Ecole Nationale d'Administration in 1945. Indeed the parallels between Sciences Po and the present day ENA are striking.

15.   The early history and the influence of the School on the French administrative élite is dealt with in T. R. Osborne, 'The Recruitment of the Administrative Elite in the Third French Republic, 1870–1905: the System of the Ecole Libre des Sciences Politiques' Ph.D. thesis, University of Connecticut, 1974.

16.   See de Saint Aulaire, *Confession*, p. 7 and R. de Billy, 'Souvenirs' (unpublished) pp. 2–6, MAE de Billy Mss., 3.

17.   Jules Cambon to Paul Cambon, 14 Dec 1912, MAE Jules Cambon Mss., 25.

18.   Agathon (pseud. H. Massis and A. de Tardes – graduate of the school) *Les jeunes gens d'aujourd'hui* (Paris, 1913) p. 29.

19.   Jules Cambon to Pichon, 21 Nov 1909, Inst. de Fr., Pichon Mss., 4396.

20.   Jules Cambon to Paul Cambon, 16 July 1911, ibid., p. 192.

21.   See the section on Italy, Ch. 4, pp. 55–67.

22.   Pognon, *Lettre à M. Doumergue*.

23.   MAE de Billy Mss., Souvenirs, Dos. 3, p. 6.

24.   For further examples of colonial academics and the groups to which they belonged see Andrew, Grupp, and Kanya-Forstner, 'Mouvement colonial et ses personnalités, p. 651.

25.   Osborne, 'École des Sciences Politiques', pp. 208–9. The colonial section of the School was abolished in 1892 after the creation in 1889, by Eugène Etienne, of the state-sponsored École Coloniale Française, see ibid.

26.   Jules Cambon to Paul Cambon, 18 May 1908, MAE Jules Cambon Mss., 25.

27.   Jules Cambon to Paul Cambon, 17 and 21 Apr 1911, MAE Jules Cambon Mss., 25.

28.   Jules Cambon to Paul Cambon, 21 Apr 1911, ibid. For further examples of Jules Cambon's reaction to this policy and more details about Agadir see pp. 40–3.

29.   Jules Cambon to Paul Cambon, 16 July 1911, ibid.

30.   J. Caillaux, *Mes mémoires*, vol. II (Paris, 1943) pp. 148–52.

31.   Jules Cambon to Delcassé, 4 Oct 1911, MAE Jules Cambon Mss., 14, dos. D-G.

32.   Caillaux, *Mémoires*, vol. II, p. 159.

33.   Ibid., p. 152. Herbette attempted to harangue the *rapporteur* of the French foreign affairs commission to get the treaty rejected, which Kiderlen had explained would mean war, ibid., pp. 175–9.

34.   Grahame to Tyrrell, 23 Jan 1912, FO 800/53.

35.   Margerie to Reinach, 25 Feb 1912, BN Reinach Mss., n.a.fr. 13,547.

36.   Jules Cambon to Paul Cambon, 17 Apr 1911, MAE Jules Cambon Mss., 25.

37.   See MAE Jean Gout Mss., 'Affaire Rouet', pp. 67–86.

38.   *Le Matin*, *Le Temps*, 13 Nov 1911, in MAE, 'Dossier personnel' Maurice Herbette, réservé. The incomplete nature of the dossier suggests a cover-up.

39.   Jules Cambon to Paul Cambon, 19 May 1908, MAE Jules Cambon Mss., 25, dossier Jules to Paul, II. Foreign Minister Pichon criticised this as an obsession: '"M. Cambon would be

perfection itself if he were not so haunted by the memory of Benedetti'' (allusion to your: Always twixt Ems and Fashoda).' Mermeix to Jules Cambon, 8 Mar 1912, MAE Jules Cambon Mss., 15, dossier Lu-Pc.

40.   R. Poidevin and J. Baréty, *Les relations franco-allemandes, 1815-1975* (Paris, 1977) pp. 177–80.

41.   For further examples of *détente* see ibid., pp. 147–69.

42.   See Steiner, *Britain and the Origins*, p. 45.

43.   Jules Cambon to Pichon, 1 June 1908, MAE Jules Cambon Mss., 16.

44.   Jules Cambon to Pichon, 17 May 1909, ibid., dossier Pichon – Z.

45.   Jules Cambon to Paris, Dec (?) 1908, MAE Jules Cambon Mss., 12, correspondance officielle 1907–8.

46.   For a detailed analysis of the treaty see J.-C. Allain, *Agadir 1911* (Paris, 1976) pp. 233–46.

47.   Jules Cambon to Pichon, 21 Nov 1909, Inst. de Fr., Pichon Mss., 4396.

48.   Jules Cambon memorandum to himself, 21 Nov 1909, MAE Jules Cambon Mss., 16, dossier Pichon – Z.

49.   Jules Cambon to Pichon, 21 Nov 1909, Inst. de Fr., Pichon Mss., 4396. See also telegrams Jules Cambon to Pichon dated 10, 20 and 25 Mar 1911 and the very secret report by the Berlin commercial attaché on the 'State of mind of the Alsatians', with Jules Cambon's cover-note: 'It is only through silence that another future can be prepared', dated 14 June 1910, and Pichon's reply to Jules Cambon dated 23 June 1910, all in MAE. N. S. Allemagne 10, Alsace–Lorraine 1906–10. The estrangement of Alsace–Lorraine was such that when the First World War broke out the French government opposed settling the provinces' fate by a plebiscite for fear it would not show a majority for reunion with France. On this see D. Stevenson, 'French War Aims and the American Challenge, 1914–18', *The Historical Journal*, XXII, 4 (1979) pp. 877–94.

50.   See for example the excellent work by J.-J. Becker, *1914: comment les Français sont entrés dans la guerre* (Paris, 1977) pp. 53–62, and Poidevin and Bariéty, *Relations franco-allemandes*, pp. 150–4

51.   Jules Cambon to Pichon, 3 Feb 1910, MAE Jules Cambon Mss., 16, dossier Pichon – Z.

52.   For further explanation see Allain, *Agadir*.

53.   J.-B. Duroselle, preface in ibid., p. x.

54.   Jules Cambon to Paul Cambon, 17 Apr 1911, MAE Jules Cambon Mss., 15, dossier H – Loub.

55.   Jules Cambon to Paul Cambon, 25 Apr 1911, ibid.

56.   For details, see Steiner, *Britain and the Origins*, pp. 70–8.

57.   For details, see Poidevin and Bariéty, *Relations franco-allemandes*, p. 188.

58.   Steiner, *Britain and the Origins*, p. 177.

3.   RAYMOND POINCARÉ

1.   Quoted in J. Chastenet, *Raymond Poincaré* (Paris, 1948) p. 14.

2.   G. Hanotaux, *Raymond Poincaré* (Paris, 1934) p. 11.

3.   *Le Bloc* (15 Mar 1902) quoted in P. Miquel, *Poincaré* (Paris 1961) p. 179.

4.   Alexandre Millerand, 'Mes souvenirs, 1859–1914', unpublished memoirs in the possession of Mme M. Millerand.

5.   Miquel, *Poincaré*, p. 175.

6.   Hanotaux, *Poincaré*, p. 57.

7.   Paul Cambon to de Fleuriau, 29 Dec 1913, P. Cambon, *Correspondance, 1870-1924*, ed. H. Cambon, vol. III (Paris, 1946) p. 59.

8.   Paul Cambon to Jules Cambon, 6 Feb 1913, Paul Cambon correspondence in the hands of M. Louis Cambon.

9.   See for example, the romantic novel by J. Giraudoux, *Bella* (Paris, 1926) in which Poincaré is depicted as the callous and thoroughly dislikeable Rebendart.

10.   *JODocPS*, 1911, no. 165, p. 640.

11.   G. Louis, *Les carnets de Georges Louis*, vol. II (Paris, 1926) p. 125, and A. Gérard, *Mémoires d'Auguste Gérard* (Paris, 1928) p. 449.

12.   Quoted in Miquel, *Poincaré*, p. 249.

13.   Count de Saint Aulaire, *Confession d'un vieux diplomate* (Paris, 1953) p. 31.

14.   Margerie to Reinach, 26 Jan 1912, BN Reinach Mss., n.a.fr., 13,547.

15.   Geoffray to Margerie, 29 Feb 1912, MAE Margerie Mss., Carton 'Lettres particulières de diplomates', Dos. Geoffray.

16.   Paul Cambon to Jules Cambon, 19 Jan 1912, MAE Jules Cambon Mss., 25, Dos. Paul to Jules.

17.   For details, see Ch. 4, pp. 59–61.

18.   Bertie to Grey, 26 Jan 1912, FO 371, France 3958.

19.   Bertie to Nicolson, 26 Jan 1912, FO 800/165.

20   Louis, *carnets*, II, p. 125.

21.   For details, see Ch. 4, pp. 81–6.

22.   B. Auffray, *Pierre de Margerie et la vie diplomatique de son temps* (Paris, 1976) p. 230.

23.   *Le Journal* (23 July 1912). See also minute on Carnegie (British embassy, Paris) to FO, 26 July 1912, FO 371, France, 1368. 'The proposed reorganisation of the Ministry for Foreign Affairs appears to have resolved itself into a mere redistribution of the work of the sub-directors.'

24.   Margerie to Reinach, 25 Feb 1912, BN Reinach Mss., n.a.fr., 13,547.

25.   *Le Journal* (23 July 1912).

26.   De Saint Aulaire, *Confession*, p. 31.

27.   Bertie to Grey, 14 Jan 1912, FO 371/366, France.

28.   Bertie to Nicolson, 1 Feb 1912, FO 800/165.

29.   Paul Cambon to Jules Cambon, 28 Nov 1912, Cambon, *Correspondance*, vol. III, p. 30.

30.   Paul Cambon to Jules Cambon, 4 Nov 1912, MAE Jules Cambon Mss., 25, Dos. Paul to Jules.

31.   Berthelot to Gérard, 26 Mar 1912, AN Gérard Mss., 329 AP 20.

32.   Jules Laroche, *Au quai d'Orsay avec Briand et Poincaré, 1913-1926* (Paris, 1957) pp. 14–15.

33   Louis, *carnets*, II, p. 212.

4. FRANCE AND THE TRIPLE ALLIANCE

1.   Viscount Grey of Fallodon, *Twenty-five Years, 1892-1916*, vol. I (London, 1925) quoted by R. Poincaré in *Au service de la France*, vol. I (Paris, 1926) pp. 247–8.

2.   P. Cambon, *Correspondance, 1870-1924*, ed. H. Cambon vol. III (Paris, 1946), p. 17.

3.   Delcassé to Barrère, 28 Feb 1900, MAE Delcassé Mss., 12.

4.   For a detailed account of these negotiations see C. M. Andrew, *Theophile Delcassé and the Making of the Entente Cordiale* (London, 1968) pp. 138–46.

5.   Barrère to Delcassé, 21 May 1900, MAE Delcassé Mss., 12, and Delcassé to Barrère, 30 May, ibid.

6.   Barrère to Delcassé, 10 July 1902, *D.D.F.*, 2e série, II, no. 329.

7.   See A. J. P. Taylor, *The Struggle for Mastery in Europe, 1848-1918* (Oxford, 1954; paperback edn, 1971), pp. 406–7.

8.   D. W. Brogan, *The Development of Modern France, 1870-1939* (London, 1940) p. 392.

9.   See Taylor, *Struggle for Mastery*, p. xxiii.

10.   J. Laroche, *Quinze ans à Rome avec Camille Barrère (1893-1913)* (Paris, 1948) p. 261.

11.   Poincaré to Barrère, 25 Jan 1912, MAE N.S. Turkey 216.

12.   For a detailed account of the French decyphering department or *cabinet noir* see C. M. Andrew, 'Déchiffrement et diplomatie: le cabinet noir du Quai d'Orsay sous la Troisième République', *Relations Internationales*, no. 5 (1976).

13.   Consul General Milan, 7 Feb 1912, MAE N.S. Italy 22; Consulate Turin, 10 Feb 1912, ibid.

14.   Poincaré, *Au service*, vol. I, p. 51.

15. F. Charles-Roux, *Souvenirs diplomatiques, Rome-Quirinal* (Paris, 1958) p. 30.

16. Paul Cambon to Poincaré, 25 Jan 1912, MAE Paul Cambon Mss., Correspondance officielle, 9, Dos. 3.

17. Isvolsky to Sazonov, 24 May/16 June 1912, *L.N.*, I, p. 266.

18. Bompard to de Selves, 28 Dec 1911, *D.D.F.*, 3ᵉ série, I, no. 400.

19. Paul Cambon to Poincaré, 25 Jan 1912, MAE N.S. Italy 11.

20. This is what Barrère meant when he said: 'There are times . . . when the route from Paris to Rome goes through London.' Charles-Roux, *Souvenirs diplomatiques, Rome-Quirinal*, p. 28.

21. Paul Cambon to Poincaré, 25 Jan 1912, MAE Paul Cambon Mss., Correspondance officielle, 9, Dos. 3.

22. Barrère to Poincaré, 21 Feb 1912, MAE N.S. Italy 11.

23. Barrère to Poincaré, 1 Mar 1912, ibid.

24. Barrère to Poincaré, 10 Mar 1912, ibid.

25. Poincaré to Barrère, 18 Mar 1912, MAE N.S. Italy 22, see also the *D.D.F.* editors' note on Poincaré to Barrère, 18 Mar 1912, *D.D.F.*, 3ᵉ série, II, no. 218.

26. Both the Quai d'Orsay and the Ministry of the Interior possessed *cabinets noirs*. The communications intercepted by the Quai were transcribed on to slips of green paper, 'les verts', and those of the Sûreté Nationale, at the Interior, on to pink paper, 'les roses'. See Andrew, 'cabinet noir'.

27. G. Louis, *Les carnets de G. Louis*, vol. II, (Paris, 1926) 21 May 1912. Quoted in Andrew, 'cabinet noir'.

28. Bompard to Poincaré, 14 June 1912, MAE N.S. Italy 11.

29. Geoffray to Poincaré, 6 July 1912, MAE N.S. Italy 12.

30. Paul Cambon to Poincaré, 8 July 1912, ibid.

31. Paul Cambon to Poincaré, 25 July 1912, MAE Paul Cambon Mss., correspondance officielle, ix, 1912. Cambon was in fact at pains to find a formula to express his annoyance, as this manuscript draft shows. For the final version see Paul Cambon to Poincaré, 25 July 1912, MAE N.S. Italy 12.

32. De Manneville to Poincaré, 10 July 1912, ibid.

33. Poincaré to Barrère, 20 Nov 1912, MAE N.S. Italy 23.

34. L.N.; I p. 356, qouted in S. B. Fay, *The Origins of the World War*, vol. I (New York, 1928) p. 148.

35. Barrère to Poincaré, 10 Dec 1912, MAE N.S. Italy 23.

36. See for details the fifth treaty of the Triple Alliance. Second final protocol concerning North Africa, Albania, Novi Bazar. Michael Hurst, *Key Treaties for the Great Powers, 1870-1914*, vol. II (London, 1972) no. 184, pp. 837-8.

37. Louis, *carnets*, II, 5 Oct 1915, p. 212.

38. Barrère to Pichon, 20 June 1912, Inst. de Fr., Pichon Mss., 4396.

39. See C. M. Andrew, 'France and the German Menace' in Ernest May (ed.), *Potential Enemies* (Harvard University Press, forthcoming).

40. 'Notes sur les voyages à Paris du 22 juin-8 juillet 1911' MAE Jules Cambon Mss., 13.

41. Kiderlen in fact remained in power until his death in December 1912.

42. Jules Cambon to Poincaré, 3 Mar 1912, MAE Jules Cambon Mss., 16, dos. Pichon – Z.

43. Jules Cambon to Mermeix, 24 Feb 1912, ibid., 15, dos. H – Loub.

44. Jules Cambon to Poincaré, 23 Mar 1912, ibid., 16, dos. Pic – Z.

45. Jules Cambon to Poincaré, 27 Mar 1912 (bis), ibid.

46. Jules Cambon to Poincaré, 27 Mar 1912, ibid.

47. Poincaré to Jules Cambon, 27 Mar 1912, ibid.

48. Jules Cambon to Pichon, 8 July 1913, ibid., 13, repeated in Jules Cambon to Paris, 28 Jan 1914, *D.D.F.*, 3ᵉ série, IX, no. 177.

49. Jules Cambon to Poincaré, 29 Apr 1912, MAE Jules Cambon Mss., 16, dos. Pic – Z.

50. Jules Cambon to Poincaré, draft letter (n.d.) July (?) ibid., dos. Bethmann-Hollweg, July–Sep 1912.

51. Jules Cambon to Paul Cambon, 21 Dec 1913, letter in the possession of M. Louis Cambon.

52. J.-J. Becker, *1914: comment les Français sont entrés dans la guerre* (Paris, 1977) pp. 53–6.

53. Jules Cambon to Poincaré, 14 Oct 1912, MAE Jules Cambon Mss., 16, dos. Pic – Z.

54. Poincaré to Jules Cambon, 26 Oct 1912, *D.D.F.*, 3ᵉ série, IX, no. 246.

55. Henri Cambon to Jules Cambon, 31 Oct 1912, letter in the possession of M. Louis Cambon. Paléologue also asked Henri to tell his uncle that 'the French government's system of *ententes* is so firm that no unilateral action can be taken'.

56. Jules Cambon to Paléologue, 1 Nov 1912, MAE Jules Cambon Mss., 15.

57. Paul Cambon to Jules Cambon, 4 Nov 1912, ibid., 25, dos. Paul-Jules.

58. For a detailed account of France's policy in Syria and the Lebanon from 1912 to 1914, see C. M. Andrew and A. S. Kanya-Forstner, *France Overseas, The Great War and the Climax of French Imperial Expansion* (London and Stanford, 1981) pp. 31, 40–54; W. I. Shorrock, *French Imperialism in the Middle East* (London, 1976) pp. 83–165; P. G. Guillen, 'Les questions coloniales dans les relations franco-allemandes à la veille de la première guerre mondiale', *La Revue Historique*, no. 248 (1972) 98–105; J. Thobie, *Intérêts et impérialisme français dans l'Empire Ottoman (1895-1914)* (Paris, 1977) pp. 647–724.

59. Quoted in R. Poidevin and J. Bariéty, *Les relations franco-allemandes, 1815-1975* (Paris, 1977) p. 195.

60. Becker, *1914*, pp. 5, 38.

61. Quoted in ibid., p. 21.

62. Ibid., pp. 39, 52.

63. Poidevin and Bariéty, *Relations franco-allemandes*, p. 198.

64. Quoted in ibid., p. 119.

65. Becker, *1914*, pp. 34–6.

66. Ibid., p. 36.

67. Poidevin and Bariéty, *Relations franco-allemandes*, pp. 203–5.

68. Ibid., pp. 205–7.

69. Ibid., pp. 208–9.

70. For details, see ibid., pp. 209–11.

71. Paul Cambon to Jules Cambon, 4 Nov 1912, MAE Jules Cambon Mss., 25, dos. Paul-Jules.

72. Jules Cambon to Paris, Dec (?) 1908, ibid., 12, dos. correspondance officielle 1907–8.

73. *Action Nationale* (?) (Jan, 1912) 'Ce que sont les neuf ambassadeurs de France', in AN, Gérard Mss., 329 AP 1.

74. For fuller details, see K. I. Hamilton, 'Great Britain and France, 1911–14', in F. H. Hinsley (ed.), *British Foreign Policy under Sir Edward Grey* (Cambridge, 1977) pp. 328 et seq.

75. Poincaré carnets, 29 Jan 1914, BN n.a.fr., 16,026.

76. Count de Saint Aulaire, *Confession d'un vieux diplomate* (Paris, 1953), pp. 208–9.

77. See R. Poidevin, *Les relations économiques et financières entre la France et l'Allemagne de 1898 à 1914* (Paris, 1969) pp. 550–3.

78. De Saint Aulaire, *Confession*, p. 230; Poidevin, *Les relations économiques et financières* p. 702.

79. Quoted in E. Judet, *Georges Louis* (Paris, 1925) p. 121.

80. De Saint Aulaire, *Confession*, p. 230.

81. Ibid., p. 230.

82. De Saint Aulaire to Poincaré, 17 Jan 1912, *D.D.F.*, 3ᵉ série, I, no. 480.

83. Crozier to Poincaré, 3 Feb 1912, MAE N.S. Austria–Hungary 28.

84. Crozier to Poincaré, 16 Feb 1912, *D.D.F.*, 3ᵉ série, II, no. 47; Crozier to Poincaré, 20 Feb 1912, ibid., no. 68; Louis to Poincaré, 23 Feb 1912, ibid., no. 84.

85. Crozier to Poincaré, 18 Mar 1912, MAE N.S. Austria–Hungary, 28.

86. Crozier to Poincaré, 18 Apr 1912, *D.D.F.*, 3ᵉ série, II, no. 364.

87. Louis, *carnets*, I, p. 139.

88. Poincaré, *Au service*, I, pp. 236–7, 263, 270.

89. P. Crozier, 'L'Autriche et l'avant-guerre', *La Revue de France* (May–June, 1921) pp. 589–90.

90. Report 20 Nov 1913, MAE N.S. Austria–Hungary, 28.

91. De Saint Aulaire to Poincaré, 17 May 1912, *D.D.F.*, 3ᵉ série, III, no. 17.

5. FRANCE AND THE TRIPLE ENTENTE

1. J. P. T. Bury, *France, 1814–1940* (London, 1949; paperback edn, London, 1969) pp. 210–11.

2. D. W. Brogan, *The Development of Modern France, 1870–1939* (London, 1945) p. 443.

3. Ibid., p. 444.

4. Bompard to Minister, 13 Jan 1912, *D.D.F.*, 3ᵉ série, I, no. 465.

5. Allizé to Poincaré, 20 Feb 1912, ibid., II, no. 70.

6. Paul Cambon to Poincaré, 7 Mar 1912, ibid., no. 168.

7. Poincaré to Paul Cambon, 13 Mar 1912, ibid., no. 193.

8. Poincaré to Louis, 24 Mar 1912, ibid., no. 254.

9. See for example, Louis to P. Loüys, 28 Nov 1911, 30 Jan 1912(?) MAE G. Louis Mss., 3.

10. Louis to Poincaré, 20 Mar 1912, MAE N.S. Russia 41.

11. Poincaré to Louis, 8 Apr 1912, ibid., no. 310.

12. Poincaré to Louis, 11 Apr 1912, MAE N.S. Russia 41.

13. Isvolsky to Sazonov, 29 Feb 1912, *L.N.*, I, pp. 203–4.

14. R. Poincaré, *Au service de la France*, vol. I (Paris, 1926) pp. 301, 322 et seq., 359.

15. See Isvolsky to Sazonov, 17 and 23 May 1912, *L.N.*, I; Poincaré to Barrère, 20 May 1912, MAE N.S. Russia 41; G. Louis, *Les carnets de G. Louis*, vol. II (Paris, 1926) 21 May 1912, p. 19; Bertie to Nicolson, 18 May 1912, FO 800/356; M. Paléologue, *Au quai d'Orsay à la veille de la tourmente* (Paris, 1947) p. 53.

16. Poincaré to Paul Cambon, 15 Oct 1912, *D.D.F.*, 3ᵉ série, IV, no. 170.

17. Notes, meeting with Sazonov on Serbo-Bulgarian treaty. MAE N.S. Russia 41.

18. Notes, MAE N.S. Russia 41, pp. 273 et seq.

19. R. Girault believes that in order to safeguard the Alliance, Poincaré abandoned the principle of the *status quo* in the Near East. R. Girault, 'Les Balkans dans les relations franco-russes en 1912', *La Revue Historique*, no. 513 (1975) 175. This is not so, see Poincaré to London, Vienna, Berlin, 4 Oct 1912, *D.D.F.*, 3ᵉ série, IV, no. 41; Poincaré to Paul Cambon, 8 Oct 1912, ibid., no. 92.

20. Paul Cambon to Poincaré, 9 Oct 1912, *D.D.F.*, 3ᵉ série, IV, no. 107.

21. E. Halévy, *A History of the English People in the Nineteenth Century*, vol. VI, *The Rule of Democracy, 1905-14* (English trans., 1934; paperback edn, London, 1961) p. 628.

22. Henri Cambon (on Paléologue's and Poincaré's behalf) to Jules Cambon, 31 Oct 1912, in the possession of M. Louis Cambon.

23. Georges Louis to Pierre Loüys, 31 Oct 1912, MAE G. Louis Mss., 3; Poincaré to Louis, 10 Nov 1912, *D.D.F.*, 3ᵉ série, IV, no. 413; Louis to Pierre Loüys, 19 Nov 1912, MAE Louis Mss., 3.

24. Paul Cambon to Poincaré, 12 Nov 1912, *D.D.F.*, 3ᵉ série, IV, no. 434; Poincaré to Louis, 13 Nov 1912, ibid., IV, no. 443.

25. Poincaré to Isvolsky, 16 Nov 1912, ibid., no. 468. Poincaré explained to Louis what he was trying to do. He had abstained from any words which could be interpreted as a 'failing in support' for he knew that in 1908-9 Isvolsky had attributed the failure of his policy to the hesitation of France. 'I want to be quite sure that reproaches of this type cannot be levelled at us and that responsibilities which are not our own are not attributed to us.' Poincaré to Louis, 16 Nov 1912, ibid., no. 469.

26. Poincaré, *Au service*, II, pp. 334–8.

27. Poincaré to Louis, 16 Nov 1912, *D.D.F.*, 3ᵉ série, IV, no. 469.

28. Isvolsky to Sazonov, 17 Nov 1912, Mezhdunarodyne otnosheniya, 2nd ser., xxi (i) no. 280, quoted in Taylor, *Struggle for Mastery*, p. 493.

29. Poincaré to Louis, 19 Nov 1912, *D.D.F.*, 3e série, IV, no. 494.

30. Paul Cambon to Jules Cambon, 6 Feb 1913, letter in the possession of M. Louis Cambon. Prime Minister Briand described Louis as 'a wreck', in Paléologue, *A la veille de la tourmente*, 11 Feb 1913, pp. 32-3; 17 Feb 1913, pp. 50-1.

31. AN Paul Deschanel Mss., 151 AP 44, Poincaré notes.

32. Bertie to Grey, 17 Mar 1906, FO 800/164, quoted by K. I. Hamilton in F. H. Hinsley (ed.), *British Foreign Policy under Sir Edward Grey* (Cambridge, 1977) p. 118.

33. Quoted in C. M. Andrew and A. S. Kanya-Forstner, *France Overseas, the Great War and the Climax of French Imperial Expansion* (London and Stanford, 1981) p. 9. In late 1904, well after the signing of the Entente Cordiale, the War Office was still perfecting amphibious operations against French colonies. S. R. Williamson, *The Politics of Grand Strategy*, (Cambridge Mass., 1969) pp. 20-1.

34. For fuller details, see Williamson, *Politics of Grand Strategy*, pp. 61-89, 125-6. Williamson makes extensive use of French archives.

35. Quoted by Hamilton, 'Britain and France', in Hinsley (ed.), *British Foreign Policy*, pp. 324-5.

36. Williamson, *Politics of Grand Strategy*, p. 165.

37. *Action Nationale* (Jan ? 1912).

38. Paul Cambon to Jules Cambon, 6 June 1912, *Correspondance*, III, p. 17. For accounts of his independence see Andrew, *Delcassé and the Entente Cordiale*, p. 180; K. Eubank, *Paul Cambon, Master Diplomatist* (Oklahoma, 1960).

39. F. Charles-Roux, *Souvenirs diplomatiques d'un âge révolu* (Paris, 1956) p. 257.

40. Un diplomate (H. Cambon), *Paul Cambon, ambassadeur de France* (Paris, 1937) p. 182.

41. Eubank, *Paul Cambon*, p. 201. A recent unpublished dissertation also mentions Paul Cambon's lack of familiarity with British society and customs, his ignorance of the strength of radical opposition in the Cabinet and Foreign Office, and his overestimation of the speed and unanimity with which Britain would give its support to France. P. E. Prestwich, 'French Attitudes towards Britain, 1911-14' (Ph.D. thesis, Stanford, 1973) pp. 239-45.

42. (H. Cambon), *Paul Cambon, ambassadeur de France*, p. 234.

43. Williamson, *Politics of Grand Strategy*, pp. 144-5; Halévy, *History of the English People*, p. 631; Z. Steiner, *Britain and the Origins of the First World War* (London, 1977) pp. 181-6.

44. For fuller details of Anglo-German rivalry see Steiner, *Britain and the Origins*, pp. 48-59. For full accounts of the Haldane Mission see Williamson, *Politics of Grand Strategy*, pp. 249-63; R. T. B. Langhorne, 'Great Britain and Germany, 1911-1914', in Hinsley (ed.), *British Foreign Policy*, pp. 288-308.

45. Grey to Bertie, 13 Feb 1912, *B.D.*, VI, no. 519.

46. Williamson, *Politics of Grand Strategy*, p. 212.

47. Grey to Bertie, 15 Mar 1912, *B.D.*, VI, no. 540.

48. Paul Cambon to Poincaré, 15 Mar 1912, *D.D.F.*, 3e série, II, no. 205.

49. Paul Cambon to Poincaré, 22 Mar 1912, ibid., no. 244.

50. Grey to Bertie, 22 Mar 1912, *B.D.*, VI, no. 550.

51. Minute by Poincaré, 27 Mar 1912, *D.D.F.*, 3e série, II, no. 266; see also, Poincaré, *Au service*, I, p. 171.

52. Minute by Poincaré, 27 Mar 1912, *D.D.F.*, 3e série, II, no. 266, underlined in the original.

53. Minute on Bertie to Grey, 3 Apr 1912, *B.D.*, VI, no. 564.

54. Poincaré to Paul Cambon, 11 Apr 1912, *D.D.F.*, 3e série, II, no. 329.

55. De Fleuriau to Poincaré, 12 Apr 1912, ibid., no. 332.

56. Poincaré, *Au service*, I, p. 180.

57. Paul Cambon to Poincaré, 18 Apr 1912, *D.D.F.*, 3e série, II, no. 363.

58. Nicolson to Goschen, 9 Apr 1912, *B.D.*, VI, no. 568.

59. Williamson, *Politics of Grand Strategy*, p. 166, see also pp. 132-248.

60.   For a detailed account of the Anglo-French Mediterranean naval agreement and the Grey–Cambon letters, see Williamson, *Politics of Grand Strategy*, pp. 264–83, 284–99 respectively, and Hamilton in Hinsley (ed.), *British Foreign Policy*, pp. 324–8.

61.   Paul Cambon to Poincaré, 18 Apr 1912, *D.D.F.*, 3e série, II, no. 363.

62.   See Hamilton in Hinsley (ed.), *British Foreign Policy*, pp. 328–9.

63.   Ibid., pp. 330–1.

64.   Williamson, *Politics of Grand Strategy*, pp. 263, 234.

65.   Grey to Carnegie, 22 July 1912, *B.D.*, VII, no. 400.

66.   Nicolson to Grey, 24 July 1912, ibid., no. 401.

67.   Grey to Carnegie, 26 July 1912, ibid., no. 402.

68.   Quoted by Hamilton in Hinsley (ed.), *British Foreign Policy*, p. 334.

69.   Grey to Bertie, 19 Sep 1912, *B.D.*, VII, no. 410.

70.   Asquith to Grey, 11 Oct 1912, *B.D.*, VII, no. 412.

71.   Quoted in Williamson, *Politics of Grand Strategy*, p. 296.

72.   Paul Cambon to Poincaré, 23 Nov 1912, *D.D.F.*, 3e série, IV, annexes 1,2; Grey to Cambon, 22 Nov 1912, *B.D.*, X, no. 416; Cambon to Grey, 23 Nov 1912, ibid., no. 417.

73.   Poincaré to Paul Cambon, 25 Nov 1912, *D.D.F.*, 3e série, IV, no. 562.

74.   Steiner, *Britain and the Origins*, p. 104. Zara Steiner explains that the Cabinet believed it had not incurred any obligation. Harcourt spoke of 'our unfettered policy and discretion'; Nicolson and Crowe criticised the ambiguity of the Entente, which left Britain with a choice; and both the radicals and the Foreign Office believed, correctly, that the question of war rested with the Cabinet. See ibid.

75.   Williamson, *Politics of Grand Strategy*, p. 298.

76.   Paul Cambon to Poincaré, 4 Dec 1912, *D.D.F.*, 3e série, IV, no. 622.

77.   Eubank, *Paul Cambon*, p. 181.

78.   P. Cambon to Delcassé, 22 Dec 1914, in A. Thierry, *L'Angleterre au temps de Paul Cambon* (Paris, 1961) p. 203.

79.   Williamson, *Politics of Grand Strategy*, p. 353.

6. POINCARÉ PRESIDENT

1.   See, G. W. Chapman, 'Decision for War: The Domestic Political Context of French Diplomacy, 1911–1914', Ph.D thesis, University of Princeton, 1971, p. 71.

2.   Quoted in P. Miquel, *Poincaré* (Paris, 1961) pp. 287–90.

3.   Ibid., pp. 298–9.

4.   M. Paléologue, *Au Quai d'Orsay à la veille de la tourmente* (Paris, 1947) p. 12.

5.   Quoted in C. M. Andrew and A. S. Kanya-Forstner, 'La France à la recherche de la Syrie intégrale, 1914–20', *Relations Internationales*, no. 19 (1979) 263.

6.   C. M. Andrew and A. S. Kanya-Forstner, *France Overseas*, p. 50.

7.   Quoted in E. M. Carroll, *French Public Opinion and Foreign Affairs, 1870-1914* (London, 1931) p. 258.

8.   Poincaré carnets, 26 Jan 1913, BN n.a.fr., 16,024.

9.   Ibid.

10.   Poincaré told Bertie that 'he had no intention of being locked up at the Elysée and being confined to state functions'. Bertie to Grey, 21 Jan 1913, FO 800/166.

11.   Paul Cambon to Jules Cambon, 6 Feb 1913, letter in the possession of M. Louis Cambon.

12.   Jules Cambon to Paul Cambon, 8 Feb 1913, letter in the possession of M. Louis Cambon.

13.   Bertie to Grey, 21 Jan 1913, FO 800/166.

14.   Paul Cambon to Jules Cambon, 12 Mar 1913, P. Cambon, *Correspondance, 1870-1924*, ed. H. Cambon, vol. III (Paris, 1946) p. 43.

15.   Jules Cambon to Paul Cambon, 8 Feb 1913, letter in the possession of M. Louis Cambon.

16.   Andrew and Kanya-Forstner, *France Overseas*, p. 50.

17.   Jules Cambon to Paul Cambon, (n.d.) 25 Jan 1913(?), letter in the possession of M. Louis Cambon. On 8 Feb Jules Cambon again explained that Poincaré had moved from his anti-German stance and warned that he might upset England. Jules Cambon to Paul Cambon, 8 Feb 1913, ibid.

18.   Jules Cambon to Paul Cambon, (n.d.) 25 Jan 1913(?) ibid.

19.   Taylor, *Struggle for Mastery*, p. 496.

20.   Quoted in L.C.F. Turner, *Origins of the First World War* (London, 1980) p. 31.

21.   Jules Cambon to Pichon, 30 and 28 Mar 1913 respectively, MAE Jules Cambon Mss., 13 (underlined in the original).

22.   Poincaré carnets, 9 Mar 1913, BN n.a.fr., 16,024.

23.   D. W. Brogan, *The Development of Modern France, 1870-1939* (London, 1945) pp. 448-9.

24.   For further details, see J.-J. Becker, *1914*, pp. 63-4.

25.   I am indebted to Christopher Andrew for a typescript copy of his suggestive article, 'France and the German Menace', in E. May (ed.) *Potential Enemies*, on which this section is heavily dependent.

26.   Quoted in ibid.

27.   For further details, see S. Williamson, 'Joffre Reshapes French Strategy, 1911-13', in P. Kennedy (ed.), *The War Plans of the Great Powers, 1880-1914* (London, 1979) pp. 136-7.

28.   Andrew, 'France and the German Menace'.

29.   Quoted by Williamson in Kennedy (ed.), *War Plans*, p. 150.

30.   Quoted in C. M. Andrew, 'France and the German Menace' in E. May (ed.) *Potential Enemies*.

31.   The debate centred on the question of whether the single-member constituency system should be retained or replaced by proportional representation. As usual the Senate blocked any change and the 1914 elections were held under the old system.

32.   See C. M. Andrew, P. Grupp and A. S. Kanya-Forstner, 'Le mouvement colonial français et ses principales personnalités, 1890-1914', *Revue Française d'Histoire d'Outre-Mer*, LXII (1975) p. 659.

33.   Jules Cambon to Paul Cambon, 5 Apr 1913, letter in the possession of M. Louis Cambon.

34.   Jules Cambon to Pichon, 5 Apr 1913, Inst. de Fr., Pichon Mss., 4396.

35.   Jules Cambon to Paul Cambon, 5 Apr 1913, letter in the possession of M. Louis Cambon.

36.   See W. I. Shorrock, *French Imperialism in the Middle East* (London, 1976) p. 160, and R. Poidevin, *Les relations économiques et financières entre la France et l'Allemagne de 1898 à 1914* (Paris, 1969) pp. 690-701.

37.   Jules Cambon to Paul Cambon, 7 June 1913, letter in the possession of M. Louis Cambon.

38.   Ibid.

39.   See J. Thobie, *Intérêts et impérialisme français dans l'Empire Ottoman* (Paris, 1977) pp. 706-10.

40.   Quoted in Turner, *Origins*, p. 65.

41.   On 6 Nov 1913, Poincaré held a meeting at the Elysée in which he, Pichon, Barthou and Jules Cambon decided on the strategy to be adopted in negotiations with Germany. P. G. Guillen, 'Les questions coloniales . . . à la veille de la première guerre mondiale', *La Revue Historique*, no. 248 (1972) 99.

42.   Jules Cambon to Pichon, 28 Sep 1913, MAE Jules Cambon Mss., 16, Dos. Pichon – Z.

43.   Report by J. Cambon, 9 Dec 1913, MAE N.S., Turkey, 349, quoted in Guillen, 'Les questions coloniales', pp. 100-1.

44.   Jules Cambon's letter informing Pichon of this conversation was drafted on 10 Nov 1913, but Cambon hesitated about despatching it, probably because he feared it could upset negotiations with Berlin. It was finally sent as a private letter dated 22 Nov 1913, with instructions for it to be locked in the Ministry's safe. Jules Cambon to Pichon, 10 Nov 1913, MAE Jules Cambon Mss., 13, and Jules Cambon to Pichon, 22 Nov 1913, *D.D.F.*, 3e série, VII, no. 522, respectively.

45. Jules Cambon to Paul Cambon, 15 Nov 1913, letter in the possession of M. Louis Cambon.

46. Jules Cambon to Pichon, 27 Nov 1913, *D.D.F.*, 3e série, VIII, no. 537.

47. Poincaré carnets, 13 Jan 1914, BN n.a.fr., 16,026.

48. Jules Cambon to Pichon, 3 Dec 1913, MAE Jules Cambon Mss., 16, dos. Pichon – Z.

49. Kokovtsov to Nicholas II, 13 Dec 1913, quoted in Taylor, *Struggle for Mastery*, p. 501.

50. Jules Cambon to Margerie (Political Director at the Quai) 18 Feb 1914, MAE Margerie Mss., dos. Jules Cambon.

51. *Amtliche Aktenstucke zur Geschichte der Europaïschen Politik, 1885-1914*, Belgische Weltkriege, VI (Erster Erganzungsband) 303, 20 Feb 1914, quoted in E. Weber, *The Nationalist Revival in France, 1905-1914* (Berkeley, Cal., 1959) p. 159.

52. Jules Cambon to Margerie, 13 Apr 1914, MAE Margerie Mss., dos. Jules Cambon.

53. Paléologue, *A la veille de la tourmente*, pp. 100–24.

54. C. M. Andrew, 'Déchiffrements et diplomatie: le cabinet noir du Quai d'Orsay sous la Troisième République', *Relations Internationales*, no. 5 (1976).

55. Paul Cambon to de Fleuriau, 29 Dec 1913, *Correspondance*, III, pp. 59–61.

56. Poincaré carnets, 13 Jan 1914, BN n.a.fr., 16,026.

57. Ibid., 16 Jan 1914.

58. Paléologue, *À la veille de la tourmente*, 16 Mar 1913, p. 78.

59. Ibid., 26 Dec 1913, p. 263.

60. Poincaré carnets, 26 and 29 Jan 1914, BN n.a.fr., 16,026.

61. Ibid., 4 Mar 1914, 16,027.

62. Quoted in Andrew, 'France and the German Menace'.

63. Ibid.

64. Poincaré carnets, 26 Mar 1914, BN n.a.fr., 16,027.

65. Paul Cambon to Jules Cambon, 29 Apr 1914, Cambon, *Correspondance*, III, pp. 64–5.

66. Ibid.

67. The position of some fifty candidates is difficult to ascertain. For further details, see J.-J. Becker, *1914*, pp. 68–80.

68. Ibid.

69. Poincaré carnets, 19 May 1914, BN n.a.fr., 16,027.

70. Poincaré carnets, 2–13 June 1914, BN n.a.fr., 16,027.

7. THE JULY CRISIS

1. J.-J. Becker, *1914*, pp. 131–5.

2. Quoted in ibid., p. 127.

3. Z. Steiner, *Britain and the Origins*, p. 215.

4. See L. C. F. Turner, *Origins*, p. 78.

5. See L. Albertini, *The Origins of the War of 1914*, vol. II (London, 1965) p. 117.

6. Becker, *1914*, p. 140.

7. Poincaré carnets, 2 and 11 July, BN n.a.fr., 16,027.

8. Quoted in Turner, *Origins*, p. 85.

9. Quoted in ibid., p. 86.

10. Poincaré carnets, 18 July 1914, BN n.a.fr., 16,027.

11. Ibid., 16 July.

12. Ibid., 20 July 1914.

13. It is sometimes believed that on his trip to Russia in 1912, Poincaré promised the Tsar that he would restore the Three Years' Law. Poincaré states explicitly in his diaries that neither he nor Millerand, Minister of War, nor any of their colleagues were thinking at that time of restoring the Three Year's Law. Ibid., 19 June 1914.

14. Ibid., 20 July 1914.

15. Ibid., 21 July 1914.

16. R. Poincaré, *Comment fut déclarée la guerre de 1914* (Paris, 1939) p. 32.

17. Poincaré, *Comment*, pp. 34–5; Poincaré carnets, 21 July 1914, BN n.a.fr., 16,027. The Japanese Ambassador expressed a desire to see the Triple Entente made Quadruple with the association of Japan. Poincaré replied that because of the Russo-Japanese and Anglo-Japanese *ententes* Japan could be assured of French support.

18. Poincaré, *Comment*, p. 36.

19. Poincaré carnets, 22 July 1914, BN n.a.fr., 16,027.

20. Quoted in Steiner, *Britain and the Origins*, pp. 221–2.

21. Poincaré carnets, 24 July 1914, BN n.a.fr., 16,027.

22. Poincaré carnets, 26 July 1914, BN n.a.fr., 16,027.

23. Poincaré, *Comment*, p. 54.

24. Poincaré carnets, 27 July 1914, BN n.a.fr., 16,027. Full text of telegram in Poincaré, *Comment*, p. 68. Interestingly, Albertini, who was not aware that the telegram was Poincaré's work, remarks that it was 'timely, unexceptionable in tone and indicative of a level-headed, pacific attitude on the part of Viviani'. Albertini, *Origins*, II, p. 593.

25. This was the reason why the British refused to put too much pressure on St Petersburg, see ibid., p. 206.

26. Poincaré carnets, 25 July 1914, BN n.a.fr., 16,027.

27. Ibid., 27 July 1914.

28. Ibid., 29 July 1914.

29. Instructions in service log of Metz wireless transmission centre, 27 and 28 July 1914, in Poincaré, *Comment*, p. 64.

30. For details, see Albertini, *Origins*, II, pp. 322–5.

31. Ibid., p. 332.

32. See ibid., p. 458.

33. Ibid., pp. 395–7.

34. Quoted in ibid., p. 160.

35. Quoted in ibid., p. 161.

36. Ibid., pp. 579–80.

37. See ibid., pp. 577–8.

38. Poincaré carnets, 10 Mar 1914, BN n.a.fr., 16,027.

39. Albertini, *Origins*, II, pp. 620–2.

40. Poincaré, *Comment*, p. 88.

41. Quoted in Albertini, *Origins*, II, p. 604.

42. For a full discussion of this point, see ibid., pp. 619–27.

43. However Germany refused a similar assurance with regard to the French colonial empire.

44. Poincaré carnets, 1 Aug 1914, BN n.a.fr., 16,027.

45. Ibid., 3 Aug 1914.

46. Steiner, *Britain and the Origins*, p. 230.

47. Quoted in Turner, *Origins*, p. 111.

48. See Steiner, *Britain and the Origins*, p. 230.

49. For a full discussion of the above-mentioned points, see Becker, *1914*, pp. 6–9, 99–117, 123–6, 130–1, 190, 249, 367.

50. P. Renouvin in *Le Monde* (29 July 1964).

51. Poincaré, *Comment*, p. 100.

52. See for example, Albertini, *Origins*, II, pp. 604–7; Jules Isaac, *Un débat historique, 1914: le problème des origines de la guerre* (Paris, 1933) pp. 201–2.

53. Poincaré, *Comment*, p. 152.

CONCLUSION

1. See A. G. Raffalovich, *L'abominable vénalité de la presse* (Paris, 1921).

2. Quoted in S. B. Fay, *Origins of the First World War*, vol. II (New York, 1929) p. 226.

3.   L. Albertini, *Origins*, II, p. 611, cited in J. Joll, 'Politicians and the Freedom to Choose: the case of July 1914', in A. Ryan (ed.) *The Idea of Freedom: Essays in Honour of Isaiah Berlin* (Oxford, 1979) pp. 108–9. Professor Joll's excellent essay is a refreshing challenge to observers of this period who forget the constraints on the political leaders of the day and castigate them all too easily for failing to have taken totally different courses of action.

Index

The 1998–1999 Traveler's Companions
ARGENTINA • AUSTRALIA • BALI • CALIFORNIA • CANADA EAST • CANADA WEST • CANADA •
CHINA • COSTA RICA • CUBA • EQUADOR • FLORIDA • HAWAII • HONG KONG • INDIA • INDONESIA •
JAPAN • KENYA • MALAYSIA & SINGAPORE • MEDITERRANEAN FRANCE • MEXICO • NEPAL •
NEW ENGLAND • NEW ZEALAND • PERU • PHILIPPINES • PORTUGAL • RUSSIA • SPAIN •
THAILAND • TURKEY • VENEZUELA • VIETNAM, LAOS AND CAMBODIA

Traveler's NEPAL Companion
First Published 1998
The Globe Pequot Press
6 Business Park Road, P.O. Box 833,
Old Saybrook, CT 06475-0833
www.globe.pequot.com

ISBN: 0 7627 0231 1

By arrangement with Kümmerly+Frey, AG, Switzerland
© 1998 Kümmerly+Frey, AG, Switzerland

Created, edited and produced by
Allan Amsel Publishing, 53 rue Beaudouin,
27700 Les Andelys, France. E-mail: aamsel@aol.com
Editor in Chief: Allan Amsel
Editor: Laura Purdom
Original design concept: Hon Bing-wah
Picture editor and designer: David Henry

Printed by Samhwa Printing Co. Ltd., Seoul, Korea

TRAVELER'S NEPAL COMPANION

By Chris Taylor
Photographed by Mohamed Amin and
Duncan Willetts

Kümmerly+Frey

The
Globe
Pequot
Press

Old Saybrook

Contents

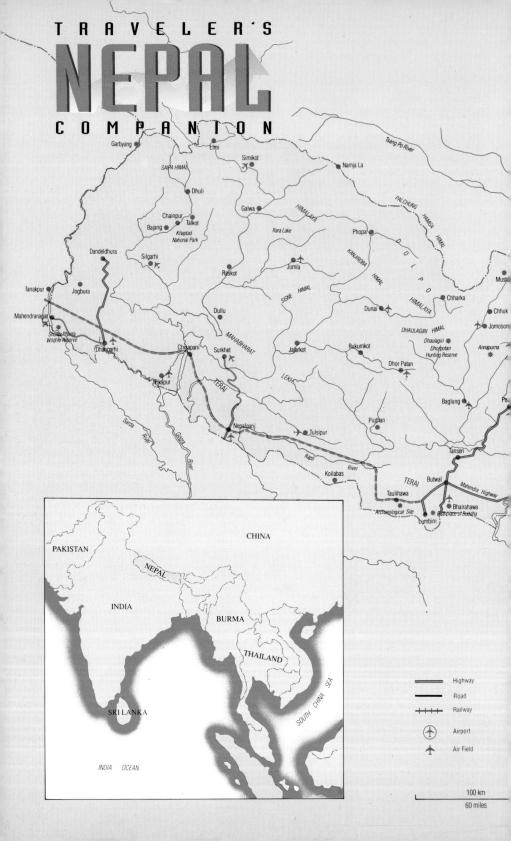

TRAVELER'S
NEPAL
COMPANION

Garbyang

Limi

Simikot

Namja La

Tsang Po River

SAIPA HIMAL

Dhuli

Galwa

HIMALAYA

PALCHUNG

HAMGA HIMAL

Chainpur

Talkot

Rara Lake

Phopa

Bajang

*Khaptad
National Park*

Dandeldhura

Silgarhi

Jumla

KANJIROBA HIMAL

D O L P O

Musta

Raskot

SIGNE HIMAL

Chharka

Tanakpur

Jogbura

HIMALAYA

Dunai

Chhuk

Dullu

DHAULAGIRI HIMAL

Jomoson

Mahendranagar

MAHABHARAT

Jajarkot

Rukumkot

Dhaulagiri
*Dhorpotan
Hunting Reserve*

Annapurna

*Shukla Phanta
Wildlife Reserve*

Dhangarhi

Chisapani

Surkhet

Dhor Patan

Tikapur

TERAI

LEKH

Baglung

Po

Piuthan

Sarda

Nepalganj

Tulsipur

Tansen

River

Koshi River

Koilabas

Rapti

River

TERAI

Butwal

Mahendra Highway

Taulihawa

Bhairahawa

Archaeological Site

Birthplace of Buddha

Lumbini

CHINA

PAKISTAN

NEPAL

INDIA

BURMA

THAILAND

SRI LANKA

SOUTH CHINA SEA

INDIA   OCEAN

	Highway
	Road
	Railway
	Airport
	Air Field

100 km

60 miles

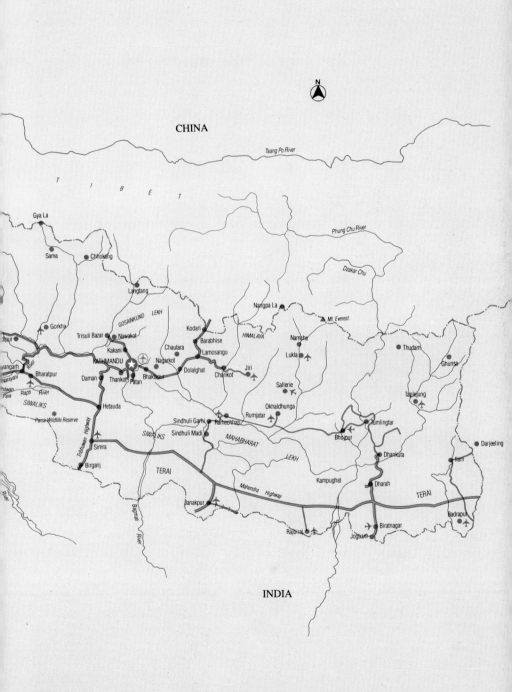

TOP SPOTS

Cruise the Himalayan Skyline

THE LURE OF EVEREST MIGHT BE IRRESISTIBLE IF IT WERE NOT FOR THE SMALL FACT of 15 days of walking at altitudes that reach over 5,000 m (16,400 ft) — a fabulous trek for those with the endurance, energy and the time, but one that many visitors decide to decline. Fortunately there's an easy option: every morning from September to May Royal Nepal Airlines and other domestic carriers offer a mountain-hugging cruise past Everest and two dozen more great peaks.

The **Mountain Flight** heads east of Kathmandu for 160 km (99 miles), in what is an unparalleled spectacle: ice-encrusted peaks on one side; a verdant patchwork of cultivated fields on the other. In the course of the flight, you pass just 25 km (16 miles) from the world's

highest mountains. And at a flight altitude of 7,500 to 8,500 m (24,600 to 27,900 ft), you see them at eye-level. If weather conditions obscure the peaks, you get your money back.

If the Mountain Flight sounds a little too jet-age, the soft option is **Balloon Sunrise Nepal (** (01) 418214 FAX (01) 424157, P.O. Box 1273, Hattisar, Kathmandu, an Australian company that offers hot-air balloon flights over Kathmandu valley.

Starting shortly after sunrise, when the light is at its best and the air is clearest, the balloon ascends from Kirtipur to a height of around 3,000 m (10,000 ft), where you find yourself in a large wicker basket with a small group of strangers gazing out on the world's most impressive skyline and trying not to think about how far you are from the ground. If nothing else, it's exhilarating.

Gaze on the Eyes of Buddha

THERE IS NO IMAGE MORE EVOCATIVE OF NEPAL THAN THE HEAVY-LIDDED, SUMMER-SKY-BLUE EYES OF THE BUDDHA at **Swayambhunath temple**, near Kathmandu. The question-mark nose that sits beneath them is in fact the

OPPOSITE: The heavy-lidded eyes and question-mark nose of the Buddha at Swayambhunath temple is, along with the Annapurna skyline, the most evocative image of Nepal. ABOVE: Machhapuchhare, the holy fishtail peak of the Annapurna range, wreathed in clouds, is an unforgettable sight for those who've trekked in its shadow.

Nepal numeral "one", symbolic both of unity and the one path to salvation as preached by the Buddha. If you look carefully, you'll see a delicate whorl rising from the gilt background above the eyes — the third eye, all-seeing, symbolic of Buddha's omniscience.

There can be few more pleasant ways to while away a late afternoon in Kathmandu than to walk out to Swayambhunath. Start the walk from Durbar square. Behind the Kasthamandap, in the south-west corner of the square is **Pie Alley** or Maru Tole, although the pie shops for which it was once famed are now all gone. Follow it down to the river and cross via a footbridge that rocks and sways with the continuous passage of local pedestrian commuters. A path leads up to a road lined with houses and shops, where you turn left towards the green at the foot of Swayambhunath hill.

The climb to the temple involves puffing up more than 300 steps — some sources claim 365, a number that is disputed but you can check yourself if you wish. Along the way sellers of Tibetan jewelry, their wares spread out on rugs, will call to you. Look in particular for the carvers of miniature *mani* stones. Mani stones are inscribed with prayers and are usually seen at the tops of passes, where they are laid in thanks for a successful journey. Watch out too for the monkeys, which scamper about mischievously, and are best kept at a distance. Manjushri, the Tibetan Buddha of Discriminative Awareness, is said to have once had his hair cut here: the shorn hairs became trees; the lice became monkeys.

After you've recaptured your breath at the summit, choose a quiet spot to survey the scene. At your feet is spread a fabulous view of Kathmandu, while circling the stupa in a clockwise direction, one outstretched hand slapping the prayer wheels into a devotional spin, lips muttering a mantra, is a Tibetan monk or two. All around, prayer flags flutter in the breeze, scattering their prayers

heavenward for the salvation of all beings.

The famous eyes gaze out in the four cardinal directions. Over them is a staggered cone of 13 gilded rings, representing the 13 steps to enlightenment. At the summit the "umbrella" with its saffron skirt, represents enlightenment itself.

It's almost chastening, the air of antique devotion that hangs about this place, particularly late in the afternoon as the warm light deepens into the searing reds and lambent shadows of sunset. But then, before you know it, worldly concerns sweep such thoughts aside: it's getting dark and time to turn back to Kathmandu for dinner.

Little Tibet

NEPAL IS A PATCHWORK OF ETHNIC GROUPS, EACH WITH THEIR OWN RELIGION, LANGUAGE AND DRESS. But if most of these ethnic groups are obscure to the nonspecialist, the one that everyone has heard of is the Tibetans.

In October 1950 the Chinese People's Liberation Army rolled into Tibet, sweeping aside the poorly equipped Tibetan forces. For the Chinese, Tibet was in this way "liberated"; for most Tibetans, their country had been invaded. And with their religious and other individual rights suppressed in their own country, many have made their way to the more tolerant soil of Nepal.

There are probably around 100,000 Tibetans in Nepal, and many of them have settled around **Bodhnath,** a stupa that long has had a Tibetan connection. Walking around Bodhnath you momentarily leave Nepal and find yourself in Tibet. The many new temples here are known as *gompa* and were built with help of donations from overseas.

The gompa are active places of worship; although you may enter, it is always polite to ask permission of one of the many maroon-cloaked monks. Don't

The weaving of colorful Tibetan carpets, a tradition near extinction in Tibet, has found a new lease of life in Nepal.

forget to remove your shoes and hat
before entering the main chapel.
If you wish to take photographs, a
small donation or a gift — the white
kata scarf is the customary Tibetan
gift for monks — is appreciated.

Entering a gompa when a service is
in progress is a unique, mysteriously
atmospheric experience that you will
never forget. The interior is dark, shifting
with flickering pools of luminescence
thrown off by innumerable candles.
In Tibet these candles are made of yak
butter, making the air heavy with a
slightly rancid, slightly sweet smell,
but in Nepal vegetable ghee is usually
substituted. Add to this the rolling
drone of meditating monks kneeling
on cushions and muttering a tape-loop
mantra, and you have a heady concoction.

If you're lucky, your visit to Bodhnath
may coincide with a ceremony that
requires a musical accompaniment.
Such performances are not melodious;
but the crashing of cymbals, pounding
of drums and the booming of the three-
meter (10-ft) *radung* — something like
a cross between a Swiss horn and a
didgeridoo — combine to create a
haunting cacophony of sound.

Trekking with the Royals

*PRINCE CHARLES HAS DONE IT;
MICK JAGGER HAS IT DONE IT*; there's
no reason why you can't.

A long, arduous trek is not for
everyone; in fact only around 10
percent of Nepal visitors go trekking.
But trekking doesn't necessarily entail
weeks in the wilderness, and Nepal is
also blessed with numerous short and
less taxing walks in the hills. The most
famous is the so-called **Royal trek** from
Pokhara. Combining rugged scenes of
the world's highest mountains with all
the effort of a strenuous amble in the
countryside, the only drawback of
the Royal trek is that it doesn't offer
tea house accommodation en route.

The reward of an arduous uphill climb.

But then again this drawback is precisely what keeps the crowds at bay.

The three- to five-day trek never goes above 2,000 m (6,600 ft), and the climbs are of the gentle variety, making it a perfect trek for children or anyone who is not as fit as they might be.

It begins with a short taxi ride from Pokhara to **Biyajapur** (an army camp), from where a trail ascends through rice fields, past a small village to a resting place under a pipal tree. Such trees were planted long ago with the purpose of providing shade for travelers, and often — like this one — have a stone bench, or *chautara*, beneath them.

The trail follows a ridge, providing stunning views (weather permitting) of Machhapuchhare and Annapurna. A late afternoon camp in the vicinity allows you to feast your eyes on the mountains in the glow of sunset while you enjoy a meal cooked over a campfire.

The second day involves a gradual climb, passing through villages where it is possible to buy an average *dahl bhat* (rice and lentils) lunch — of interest if you haven't tried one before. The Gurung village of **Shakhlung**, at 1,750 m (5,740 ft), is the usual place to overnight.

By the third day, the ground you've covered even in this short time means that the skyline is changing. As the trail descends steeply, Annapurna II and Himalchuli come into view. After pausing at a checkpoint, which also has a couple of tea shops, the trail ascends once again, making for **Chisophani**, a village with a small temple and a campsite that commands beautiful mountain views.

With the exception of a final ridge, just before entering the Pokhara valley again, you spend most of the final day of the trek descending, first along a ridge and then sharply down a series of steps. The walk ends, as it began, through rice fields. At the village of **Begnas** you can catch a taxi 12 km (7 miles) back to Pokhara.

Safari on Elephant-Back

THE INDIAN RHINOCEROS IS A MASSIVE LUMBERING CREATURE that stands at around 1.7 m (5.6 ft) and weighs around two tons. Combine this with notoriously poor eyesight and a tendency to charge anything that moves, and you have a dangerous beast indeed. If you find yourself in the path of a charging rhino, you are advised to make a dash for it (in a curve), dropping an item of clothing as you go. Better still, do your rhino-seeing on the back of an elephant.

ABOVE: The safest way to see Nepal's animal life is on elephant-back. LEFT: An elephant is about the only thing a 300-kg (650-lb) rhino will leave alone. OPPOSITE: Fording the tals of the Terai (top), a favored rhino haunt, is not something you'd want to do on foot. Rare gurials bask in the sunny waters of Chitwan National Park (bottom).

Rhinos leave elephants alone, as do tigers, making elephants the safest mode of transport for a safari in the **Royal Chitwan National Park**. The elephants themselves are curious enough, munching their way through up to 300 kg (660 lb) of food and quaffing 200 liters (52 gallons) of water per day, not to mention resignedly obeying the commands of their diminutive human masters — the mahout or, in Nepali, *pahit*; but the real attraction of Chitwan — and other national parks of Nepal's lowland Terai — is its wild animals.

From your railed *howdah* — the platform "saddle" used on elephants — you have a sweeping view of the marshy grasslands, the preferred habitat of the Indian one-horned rhino. More often than not, you'll find them wallowing muddily in the *tals* — lakes formed by the monsoonal shifts in river courses — of the Terai.

Almost everyone is on the lookout for a Bengal tiger. You will have to keep your eyes peeled. With just 120 (or so) of them spread out over an area of nearly 2,000 sq km (760 sq miles), this shy creature bestows the gift of a sighting on only the luckiest of visitors.

But if tigers are scarce, other animals are not. The chital is the most numerous of the park's four species of deer; others include the barking deer. Golden jackals scavenge on the plains. The gaur is the world's largest species of wild ox, growing to a maximum height of 2.2 m (7.2 ft). Sloth bears, langur monkeys and wild pigs may also be seen, along with a host of smaller mammals such as squirrels, leopard cats and porcupines. And if you weren't worried enough about the rhinos, the rivers harbor two species of crocodile; while lurking in the tall grass is the world's most venomous snake, the king cobra.

At Chitwan, it's a world of discovery aboard an elephant. For many first-timers, however, an unwelcome discovery is that, while riding an elephant may be the safest way to search out horned rhinoceroses and rare Bengal

tigers, it is by no means painless: a couple of hours on the back of an elephant will leave you feeling the following day as if you had done an unaccustomed workout in the gym.

Bazaar Experiences

DON'T SPEND YOUR TIME IN KATHMANDU BEING FERRIED AROUND IN RICKSHAWS AND TAXIS: get out and walk.

One of Kathmandu's best strolls is from Indra Chowk to Asan Tole, taking you through the heart of the **Old Bazaar**, once the start of the long trade route to Tibet.

Chowk means "intersection", and **Indra Chowk** is an intersection *par excellence,* a swirling juncture of six bustling streets and alleys. Presiding over the shops and shoppers is the upstairs shrine of **Akash Bhairav** — *akash* means "sky", which is where this bhairav (a ferocious manifestation of Shiva)

On Kathmandu's Durbar square, amongst the temples and statuary, a young woman OPPOSITE sells fruit. While ABOVE, a Newari woman vends fresh fruit on a curbside.

is supposed to have miraculously fallen from. Opposite the shrine, in a narrow alley is the **bead bazaar,** where stalls glitter with the glass beads much coveted by Nepali women for use in necklaces. Also on Indra Chowk is a **Shiva temple**, its platform cluttered with woolen rugs and shawls for sale.

The walk from Indra Chowk is short but brimming with interest. Try and keep to a slow amble, and pause when you reach **Kel Tole**, where you will find the **Seto Machhendranath temple**, dedicated to the patron saint of Kathmandu's Buddhists. Wander into the temple courtyard and linger in a quiet corner for a few moments to take in the scene: women make *puja* (ritual offerings) of flowers and incense; a few children dash in and out of the shadows; a sacred cow lumbers sleepily out into the street; shopkeepers preside hopefully over small piles of grain and domestic items. At night, from around 9 PM, musicians often perform here.

From here continue your walk up to **Asan Tole**. If you have not been long in Nepal, chances are you will be suffering from a kind of sensory overload by now. This bazaar area in the heart of old Kathmandu is so chock-a-block with the unfamiliar that before long it becomes difficult to process it all. A sacred goat bleats from inside the pushing crowd; you pause over a pile of brown vegetative bricks wondering what they

are (Tibetan tea) and are nearly knocked aside by two hurrying porters, vast, overstuffed sacks hanging from their crowns; in the square are sacks of mysterious spices and baskets of vegetables.

In amidst all this buying and selling, pushing and shoving, stands the delightful **Annapurna temple**, and beside it smaller temples to **Ganesh** and **Vishnu**. The Annapurna temple is home to a manifestation of Lakshmi, the Goddess of Wealth. Watch the never-ending flow of worshippers calling upon her favor in this most secular of places, a bazaar that wakes before the sun and continues long after it has set.

Toothache Gods and Child-Devouring Demons

A MYRIAD OF DISCOVERIES AWAIT YOU IN KATHMANDU. Myths, legend and superstition have nested in the most unlikely corners of the city, and for those who know how to seek them

out there are countless tiny shrines and temples that mark their presence.

In **Asan Tole**, that busy square where vegetable and spice sellers hawk their goods, is a paving stone with an impression of a fish that fell from the sky one day. The story goes that an astrologer was once awaiting the tolling of a bell that would announce the birth of his son. When at last the bell rang, he immediately cast the boy's horoscope and discovered that he was not after all the father. In horror and anger he quit town.

Years later he returned to study under a gifted young astrologer, who asked him to make a prediction. He duly predicted a fish would fall from the sky, stating the time and even the precise spot where it would fall. "Surely," suggested the younger astrologer, "you've failed to account for the wind." Sure enough, he repeated his sums and discovered that his calculations were slightly off. And in the same moment he remembered another time he had failed to account for the wind. He cast that horoscope of

so many years ago again, and discovered the boy whose birth he had been awaiting was his after all; indeed he was no other than the gifted young astrologer who now sat before him.

If fish falling from the sky and leaving dents in the paving stones isn't curious enough for you, take the road that leads west out of Asan Tole. About halfway along before you reach the next crossroads, on the left, is the **Ugratara temple**, where locals come to pray when their eyes are troubling them. Stroll up to the crossroads, turn left and look to your left for a piece of wood that has had thousands of nails hammered into it. If you look carefully amongst all the coins, you will find an image of the **toothache god** — sooner a prayer and a coin for him than a visit to the dentist.

OPPOSITE: Shiva in his most terrifying aspect as an incarnation of Bhairav, on a mask carved in the eighteenth century. ABOVE: The accomplishment of Newar woodcarving in the Royal Palace of Kathmandu is breathtaking — there are sections where you might stand transfixed for an hour and still discover new details.

It is this mixture of the surreal and fanciful that makes Kathmandu so bewitching. In the area around the toothache god, in amongst the shops and houses, you can find shrines to Ganesh and Vishnu, stone lions, a miniature replica of Swayambhunath — those unable to mount the 300-odd stairs of the real thing may instead circumambulate this one — and dozens of small pagodas and temples. Best of all is the **Kichandra Bahal**, an erstwhile Buddhist monastery west of Kel Tole. Its unassuming courtyard, complete with a small stupa and pagoda sanctuary is noted for four brass plaques, one of which shows the demon Gurumapa devouring a small child whole. This demon's hunger for children is insatiable and must be appeased with an annual festival in which a buffalo is slaughtered for fear that the demon will start on the local infants.

Funny Business

IF YOU'RE THE PRUDISH SORT, IT WON'T DO TO LOOK TOO CLOSELY AT THE CARVINGS THAT ADORN SOME TEMPLES OF THE KATHMANDU VALLEY — if there's bliss here, it's certainly not the spiritual kind.

Erotic carvings can be seen on the slanting wooden struts that support the curved roofs of pagodas. Usually the images carved onto the struts are of manifestations of the deity to which the pagoda is dedicated, ferocious protective griffins at the far corners. But from time to time you will find a concourse of sexual athletics, in which everybody — from the servants to the pets — gets a turn. It's dizzying stuff, particularly when you consider you're looking at a place of worship.

The explanations are legion; yet no theory seems more compelling than another. Scholars point to the influence of Tantric practices, in which sexuality is used as a stepping stone to higher states of consciousness; some look to connections with fertility rites; while many local guides will tell you the lewd images deter the Goddess of Lightning, a chaste, virginal creature who wouldn't dare strike such an obscene structure with her bolts from the heavens.

In Kathmandu some of the finest erotic carvings can be seen on the struts of **Basantapur tower** of the Hanuman Dhoka palace in Durbar square. Close by the entrance to the palace is **Jagannath temple**, where you will find more erotic carvings. And in the center of Durbar square, the **Shiva temple** is also adorned with some interesting erotica.

Kathmandu's neighboring city of Patan does not have a great deal of erotic carving, though the struts on **Charanarayan temple** in Durbar square will reveal some imaginative group contortions for those who take the time to look.

But overall it's hard to beat Bhaktapur's **Café Nyatapola**, a restaurant that started out as a place of worship. Nowadays you can sit and watch the crowds in the square, sip a drink, and occasionally, if you are that way inclined, look to the ceiling and enjoy your erotica at leisure.

Erotic carving ABOVE on an ancient Kathmandu valley temple. OPPOSITE: Crowds ambling through Patan's Durbar square in the late afternoon.

Cycle into the Hills

YOU DON'T NEED TO BE TOUR DE
FRANCE *FIT TO CYCLE INTO THE* HIMALAYAS,
but a little exercise in the weeks leading
up to your Nepal trip won't go astray.
Himalayan Mountain Bikes ((01)
416596 FAX (01) 411055, P.O. Box 2247,
Kathmandu, on the other hand, gamely
claim that they "cater for all levels of
fitness."

Nagarkot has the best views of
the Himalayas in all Kathmandu
valley, and an overnight stay that takes
in both sunset and sunrise is an
obligatory Nepal experience. Of course,
you can take a bus or a taxi up there,
but why not cycle up on a top-of-the-
range mountain bike, guided by an
expert? You're sure to feel you've
earned the views when you get to the
top.

The first day entails a 38-km
(24-mile) ascent to Nagarkot. Now
this may sound like a long way, but
remember you have all day to do it.
Besides, the tour stops half way, in
Bhaktapur, where you have several
hours to look at some of the valley's
best preserved historic buildings and
temples, cool off and have lunch.
The climb to Nagarkot is rewarded
with lodgings at a rustic guesthouse
complete with a breathtaking
panorama of the Himalayas.

The second-day descent to
Kathmandu keeps the Himalayas in
view, following a track past villages
and rice fields to **Changu Narayan**, a
sixth-century temple complex dedicated
to Vishnu. The descent continues to
Bhaktapur, where you have lunch and
then cycle on to Kathmandu with a
stopover in Thimi, a town known
for its pottery.

It's a ride that is guaranteed to
produce some aches and pains if
you're not a regular cyclist, but the
memories linger long after the aches
are gone, and the second day is
downhill anyway… mostly.

Celebrate with a Living Goddess

*NEPAL IS SUCH A FESTIVE COUNTRY THAT
IT'S ALMOST IMPOSSIBLE FOR YOUR VISIT NOT
TO COINCIDE WITH SOME KIND OF ANNUAL
EVENT.* Some of these are small, local
affairs, but the best of them are vast
colorful pageants that involve
the whole country.

Indra Jatra, a September festival, is
one of the big ones. Indeed, it has been
called the quintessential Nepali festival:
all-encompassing and inclusive, a
celebration of the gods, of history
and of the end of the monsoon, it
involves eight days of music, dance
and drama, as well as the towing
of chariots around Kathmandu.

According to local legend, Indra, the
God of Rain, was arrested for stealing
flowers for his mother in Kathmandu
valley. She came down to rescue him,
and Indra's jailers, realizing they had a
god on their hands, released him and
carried Indra and his mother through
the streets in celebration. The
celebrations continue to this day.

Not that this is all there is to
celebrate: also remembered is the
1768 conquest of Kathmandu valley
by Prithvi Narayan. Bhairav, that
ferocious manifestation of Shiva, also
gets a look in — his horrific visage,
concealed from view the rest of the
year, is displayed on Kathmandu's
Durbar square and at Indra Chowk
in the old city of Kathmandu.

On the third day of the celebrations,
Kumari Jatra — the inner core of the
bigger festival — begins. Golden temple
chariots are assembled outside the home
of the Kumari, Kathmandu's living
diminutive goddess. Hidden from
public view for most of the year, she is
carried out accompanied by attendants:
two boys in the roles of Bhairav and
Ganesh, who will accompany the
Kumari in chariots of their own.
The Kumari's chariot is greeted from
Hanuman Dhoka by the king, and

then the procession makes its way towards the image of Bhairav, from whose mouth beer pours. Men compete for the honor of getting a gulp of the beer, and for the good luck it brings.

The living goddess's chariot continues its course around Kathmandu for the next few days, accompanied wherever it stops by performances of music and dance and costumed drama. The festival culminates with the Kumari anointing the king's forehead with a holy *tika* — that third-eye splash of red — thus confirming his right to rule for another year.

Only in Nepal, you find yourself thinking, does beer flow from the mouth of a demon and a living goddess confirm the right of a king to rule.

Festive crowds are watched over by the all-seeing eyes of the Buddha.

The Great Outdoors

NEPAL IS TOPOGRAPHICALLY THE MOST
DRAMATIC COUNTRY IN THE WORLD. STARTING
IN THE LOWLAND TERAI, a mere 60 m (200 ft)
above sea level, Nepal climbs all the way
to the highest point on earth: the top of
Everest (8,848 m or 29,028 ft). With trails
crisscrossing the foothills and mountain
passes, Nepal is a walker's paradise.

Not that anyone talks about
"walking", or even "hiking" in Nepal.
Trekking — from Afrikaans — is what
outdoors enthusiasts come to Nepal for.
A trek may be as short as one day (there
are several one-day treks around
Kathmandu and Pokhara), but is
more likely to last from three or
four days to as long as a month.

Before setting out on a trek, there
are a couple of local organizations that
are worth referring to for up-to-date
information. The Himalayan Rescue
Association (HRA) has a Trekkers'
Information Center in the Hotel
Tilicho ((01) 418755, Kathmandu.
The Kathmandu Environment Education
Project (KEEP) ((01) 410303, is in the
Potala Tourist Home, Kathmandu.

The chief drawing card of a trek in
Nepal is the incomparable mountain
scenery. Where else can you wake in the
first light of dawn with the snow-
capped peaks of the Himalayas towering
overhead? But the wonder of trekking in
Nepal is not just the peaks: as you head
towards the mountains, you pass through
lowland villages, wayside temples, past
checkerboard rice paddies. At higher
altitudes there are alpine meadows,
awash with flowers in the spring, and
evergreen forests. Add to this a constant
stream of Nepali villagers who share the
trails with trekkers, the Sherpa plodding
along unflinchingly under heavy loads,
the trader urging along a pack of loaded
yaks, and you have an irresistible brew.

There are different treks for different
folks, each offering its own delights: long
and arduous does not necessarily

OPPOSITE: Trekking in Nepal is not just mountain
ridges, but also lowland paddy fields, meadows and
even eerie moss-covered forests such as this one in
the Everest region. ABOVE: Wild flowers bloom in
the spring, usually March, in a beautiful profusion
of pinks, reds and whites.

mean better. If you've never trekked in the mountains before and are not sure whether you are up to it, try one of the shorter treks, such as the four-day **Royal trek** — so named because Prince Charles and a small party of 90 once walked it — out of Pokhara. An even shorter warm-up exercise is **Baglung** to **Tatopani**, which takes just two days. Slightly more ambitious is the Jhomsum trek, a nine-day walk that reaches a maximum elevation of 3,800 m (12,500 ft) and has good hotels and food all the way.

Of course there's also no shortage of hardship for those who fancy pitting themselves against the elements and testing their mettle. The 18-day trek around **Annapurna** reaches an elevation of 5,400 m (17,700 ft) and involves some hard climbs, but at least offers the compensation of mostly decent places to stay. The 20-day slog to Makalu base camp, on the other hand, has no accommodation en route and has a steep climb up to 5000 m (16,400 ft).

Almost at the other extreme to trekking in the Himalayas is a safari in Nepal's lowland Terai. The most popular safari destination is **Royal Chitwan National Park**, one of the few places in the world where you can see a Bengal tiger in the wild. In all honesty your chances of seeing a tiger are remote, but you will undoubtedly feast your eyes on some of the park's one-horned Indian rhinoceroses, deer, wild boars, sloth bears, monkeys and over 450 species of birds.

Getting around the Royal Chitwan National Park is half the fun. The official mode of transport is by elephant, which is reckoned to be the safest way to view a herd of rhinos. If, after a few hours on the back of an elephant — an exercise that will leave you aching the next day — you've had enough, rest assured that you can also get around the park in a vehicle, in canoes or even on foot.

The Royal Bardia National Park is a more remote and less touristed alternative to Chitwan. And, more importantly, nowhere else in Nepal do you have a better chance of laying your eyes on the elusive Bengal tiger.

Rhinoceroses are present in much smaller number than at Chitwan, but there are a host of other mammals — including the barking deer, blue cow and leopard — present in the park. Like Chitwan, local transport is on the back of an elephant.

Sporting Spree

NEPAL'S SPORTING OPPORTUNITIES ARE ASSOCIATED WITH ITS GREAT OUTDOORS, with its mountains, its crashing rivers and its mountain trails.

MOUNTAIN BIKING
Mountain biking is still in its infancy in Nepal, but it's catching on rapidly. The

Kathmandu valley in particular is crisscrossed by trails and minor roads, many of which wind up to spectacular viewpoints where bikers can rest before enjoying the adrenaline rush of a near free-fall descent.

Unless you're an experienced biker and can manage your own repairs (and have your own spares), it's a good idea to book a mountain-bike tour. **Himalayan Mountain Bikes** ((01) 416596 FAX (01) 411055 E-MAIL info@hmb.wlink.com.np, P.O. Box 2247, Kathmandu, are the experts. They have the bikes, the mechanics, the spares, have researched dozens of routes, and can even provide vehicular backup for the more demanding tours.

Serious mountain bikers can even throw themselves at the Himalayas in a competitive spirit. Himalayan Mountain Bikes and the newly formed Nepal Mountain Bikes Association sponsor the annual Himalayan Mountain-Bike Championships, which is held in March. The 27-km (17-mile) course follows the razor-sharp ridges that ring the Kathmandu valley, a grueling but spectacular and exhilarating run.

For the less experienced, Himalayan Mountain Bikes offers some fabulous introductory rides. A good taster is the

Few places are able to offer such exhilarating white-water rafting as Nepal, where the water runs down from the highest places in the world.

two-day ride from Kathmandu to Nagarkot and Sanku, which takes you past farms and villages, the Narayan forest and provides views of the Himalayas at Nagarkot. The uphill section follows the asphalt road to Nagarkot via Bhaktapur and Thimi. The switchback ascent to Nagarkot at 2,000 m (6,600 ft) is a serious workout. The downhill section plunges 900 m (3000 ft) into the Sali Nadi valley and the village of Sanku on a rutted jeep track. From Sanku a metaled road returns to Kathmandu.

Other popular rides include the four-day 125-km (78-mile) ride from Kathmandu to Dhulikhel and Namobuddha, a tour that takes you into the stunning ravines of the Sun Khosi and its tributaries; and the five-day "Goat Tracks" tour, which as the name suggests is mostly off-road.

WHITE WATER

Nepal is considered by many experts to rate among the best places in the world for kayaking and white-water rafting. And with some highly professional rafting and kayaking agencies operating out of Kathmandu, it's worth taking the plunge and shooting the rapids for a few days.

Among the white-water specialists in Kathmandu, the following are highly recommended: **Ultimate Descents** ((01) 419295 FAX (01) 411933 E-MAIL rivers @ultimate.wlink. com.np, P.O. Box 6720, Northfield Café, Thamel. Other agencies include **Equator Expeditions** ((01) 416596 FAX (01) 411933, P.O. Box 8404, Thamel; **Himalayan Encounters** ((01) 417426 FAX (01) 417133, P.O. Box 2769, Thamel; and **Himalayan River Expeditions** ((01) 420322 FAX (01) 414075, P.O. Box 242, Durbar Marg.

Although it's possible to try rafting or kayaking somewhere in Nepal at any time of the year, the best times are from March to early June and from September to early December. From December to

early March, many of Nepal's rivers are icy cold, requiring wetsuits; from June through September, the monsoon runoff turns the rivers into dangerous, raging torrents.

The most frequently rafted river in Nepal is the **Trisuli river**. Its easy access from the Kathmandu-Pokhara highway, means that many budget operators take tours down the river. If you are short of time or just want to dip your toes into the white-water rafting experience, this is probably where you will end up. The remoter rivers of Nepal offer a very different experience, however.

The **Sun Kosi river**, for example, is not just a collection of rapids but a river journey. Starting up near the Tibetan border, you travel 270 km (167 miles) over a nine- to 10-day period, ending up at Chatara on the Gangetic plain. The rapids on the early days of the trip are light, allowing inexperienced rafters to learn as they go along. The combination of foaming rapids, gorgeous mountain and rural scenery, followed by a quiet evening camped by a river, provides an unforgettable experience.

The **Karnali river** is Nepal's longest. It is also one of the most remote: access involves a flight to Nepalganj, a five-hour bus journey to Surkhet and then a two-day trek to Sauli. From here you experience seven exhilarating days on the river, traveling 180 km (112 miles) through some of the remotest parts of Nepal before finishing at Chisophani, close to the Royal Bardia National Park.

AT THE SAME TIME...

Fitness freaks and thrill seekers who are not content to settle on either rafting or mountain biking have the option of taking a tour that incorporates both. Himalayan Mountain Bikes and Ultimate Descents (see above for contact details) have joined together to make a tour that involves two days of rafting on the Bhoti Khosi river and two days of mostly off-road mountain biking out of Dhulikhel. It's a combination that is guaranteed to cure you of the office blues and get the cricks out of your neck.

Breakfast on the rooftop of one of Pokhara's many inexpensive lodges.

The Open Road

UNLESS YOU BRING YOUR OWN VEHICLE, ONE THING YOU WON'T BE DOING IN NEPAL IS DRIVING. While car-hire is available, self-drive rental is not. This is not as great a loss as you might imagine. Nepal's road network is in a poor state of repair and local driving habits range from aggressive to suicidal — overtaking on blind corners and the crests of hills are both accepted road behavior. The highways are littered with the wrecks of vehicles.

Nepal's road infrastructure is expanding at least. Many of the popular trekking routes now have road access to the trailheads, saving days of walking. Bear in mind, however, that in Nepal "road access" is an elastic concept — a rutted trail on which speeds of 20 kph (12 mph) are a bone-jarring nightmare are not uncommon.

It's an unfortunate fact of life that, despite the incomparable views, the open road in Nepal is usually an uncomfortable, aggravatingly slow and dangerous experience. Some old-hands and tour operators recommend flying, even on such popular road routes as Kathmandu to Pokhara.

Backpacking

NEPAL HAS LONG BEEN A MECCA FOR BACKPACKERS. Back in the heady "flower power" era, the very word Kathmandu was the stuff of dreams, and the city's **"Freak Street"** was a magnet to the lost in space generation. Times change. Freak Street's glory days are long gone and today's "freaks" likely as not have a credit card in their money pouch. But for all that, Nepal remains the perfect destination for a backpacking holiday.

ABOVE: Some of Kathmandu's tourist products may incline towards kitsch, but no one can accuse them of being unimaginative. OPPOSITE: A typical Thamel street scene, where the street signs scream food! exports! trekking! and the touts sidle up hopefully and mutter, "Something?"

After all, Nepal is a great bargain. Keeping costs down doesn't mean scrimping and saving, sleeping in a tent and eating out of cans. There's no need for dormitory-style hostel accommodation either. Hotels and guesthouses, even in Kathmandu, cost as little as US$5 a night for a room with an attached bathroom. And, unless you take one of the less-trodden treks, beds are available in tea houses strategically situated three to four hours walk from each other on most of the popular trekking routes. Many young budget travelers take to the high mountain paths to enjoy some of the most spectacular scenery in the world on less than US$10 per day.

If accommodation charges make backpacking a breeze, so too do meals. The restaurants of Kathmandu and Pokhara have a near legendary status among backpackers on the Asian trail. Pokhara's **Lakeside district** and Kathmandu's **Thamel district** are wall-to-wall with restaurants whose menus read like introductory samplers to the cuisines of the world. Hungry diners frequently find themselves forced to choose between dishes as diverse as chicken korma, Mexican burrito, vegetarian lasagna, sizzling steak, moussaka, Tibetan momos and Chinese stir-fry.

Perhaps the ambitious inclusiveness of these assaults on international cuisine leads to a certain lack of authenticity, but there are few who'll deny that the results are tasty. And cheap… . In most such restaurants it's possible to sit down to an enormous sizzling steak and a bottle of beer and, when you've finished, be presented with a bill for no more than US$4.

This remarkable good value extends into the restaurants that offer genuine quality dining, so that it's perfectly possible to splurge on, say, some of the best Indian cuisine the world can offer and spend only US$15 to US$20. It's near impossible to spend more than US$25 per head on a meal anywhere in Nepal.

Nepal's great asset as a backpacking destination is that it is one of the few places in the world where economizing

doesn't mean missing out. With the exception of the Mountain Flight and ballooning, there are almost no activities or sights in Nepal that do not have a budget option. Even the jungle safaris of **Royal Chitwan National Park**, where the well-heeled may spend upwards of US$200 per day on the full safari experience, can be done on a budget of US$20 per day if you stay in the village of Sauraha and organize your own safari — on elephant back, by jeep, by canoe or even on foot.

As for the mountains, independent trekking has long been a popular activity in Nepal. Essentially, you organize your permit and set off into the hills. If you're reasonably fit, the **Annapurna** and **Everest** treks can be done without guides and porters at a cost of US$10 per day for accommodation and food, plus US$5 per week for the permit. The easiest and most popular treks to do independently at these rates are the Everest trek, the Langtang trek, the Helambu trek, the Jhomsum trek, and the Annapurna circuit trek.

One more thing you won't have to resort to in Nepal is hitchhiking. Most budget travelers get around on Nepal's long-haul buses. The driving is erratic, there's never enough legroom and speeds rarely get above a tortured trot, but you do eventually get to your destination. The bus journey from Kathmandu to Pokhara, for example, takes around eight hours and costs US$4. And for the hardy budget traveler the US$60 saved in that eight hours of not flying is equal to six days trekking in the Himalayas.

Living It Up

THE KINGDOM OF NEPAL MAY NOT BE MONTE CARLO, BUT IT STILL OFFERS FIVE-STAR HOTELS, WORLD-CLASS DINING, as well as trekking and adventure tour operators who are in a league of their own when it comes to providing for the needs of their guests.

EXCEPTIONAL HOTELS
Nepal's best hotels are all in Kathmandu. They cannot compare in opulence with the top hotels in Bangkok or Delhi, but they put on a good show given their limited resources. See WHERE TO STAY in the section on Kathmandu for information on hotels such as the Hotel Yak and Yeti, the Everest Hotel and the Hotel Shangri-la.

Elsewhere in Nepal, the best hotels are usually mid-range in standard. The new Shangri-la Village in Pokhara is an exception. Pokhara's Fish Tail Lodge is also an excellent hotel by local standards, but its popularity is due more to its splendidly isolated position overlooking the Phewa Lake than anything else.

The Tiger Tops Jungle Lodge may not offer five-star comforts, but there are few places in the world where you can rough it in such style. Built in the style of a traditional Tharu longhouse with traditional wall paintings and locally woven rugs and bedspreads, the lodge

is the perfect base from which to set out into the Terai on the back of an elephant.

EXCEPTIONAL RESTAURANTS
When it comes to dining out, the high life in Nepal is something just about any traveler can splurge on — it's very difficult to spend more than US$20 per head on a meal even in Kathmandu's finest restaurants. Indian cuisine is what Nepal does best, and restaurants such as Ghar-e-Kabab in Kathmandu can be compared with the best anywhere. See the Kathmandu part in the WHERE TO EAT section for recommendations of top-notch restaurants in the capital.

NIGHTLIFE

By 10 PM, Kathmandu is mostly tucked in to bed and nodding off to sleep. Elsewhere around the kingdom the day might have ended even earlier.

If it's drinking and carousing you are looking for, your options will be decidedly low key. There are several bars in the Thamel area, the best of them being the New Orleans and the Blue Note — small, intimate places with good jazz offerings. Both of them close at 10 PM.

The only discos are in the international hotels such as the Soaltee Oberoi, Yak and Yeti, and Everest Sheraton hotels.

Kathmandu has four casinos: the Casino Nepal ℂ (01) 270244, Soaltee Oberoi Hotel; Casino Anna ℂ (01) 223479, Hotel de l'Annapurna; Casino Everest ℂ (01) 220567, Everest Hotel; and the Casino Royale ℂ (01) 228481, Yak and Yeti Hotel. The patrons are mostly Indian visitors, who stake small fortunes on the turn of a card at baccarat, chemin de fer, and the turn of the roulette wheel. The chips are valued in Indian rupees or other foreign currencies. The casinos are off-limits to Nepali citizens.

Soaring high over the valleys of Nepal, the Himalaya are never far from view.

Family Fun

THERE'S NO POINT PRETENDING THAT NEPAL IS THE PERFECT HOLIDAY DESTINATION FOR THE KIDS. For a start, there's little in the way of children's amusements in Nepal; but even more importantly, there are some health matters to consider. Be sure that your children have had all their vaccinations and any additional immunizations that your doctor recommends for Nepal. Many diseases that have been eradicated or are very rare in developed countries are still present and a threat to the health of children in Nepal.

The narrow, crowded streets of the cities are also a concern. If you have very small children, a stroller is next to useless in such conditions. Bring a baby carrier that straps onto your back or chest. The risk for bigger children is of getting lost. Keep a close eye on them, and as an extra precaution ensure that they carry a photocopy of their passport with them at all times.

Now for the good news: Many people who have traveled with their children in Nepal come back with glowing reports. For a start the Nepalis, like all Asians, are wonderfully tolerant of children, and in the budget and mid-range hotels they'll find playing companions in the adult staff. Most hotels and guesthouses, like many of the restaurants, have garden areas, which are perfect for kids to play in.

There are no theme parks or fun parks and no beaches to keep children amused in Nepal, and it's a rare child who can find as much interest in the architectural and artistic delights of the Kathmandu valley as his or her parents can. What Nepal does have in abundance, however, is mountains. Taking one of the easier treks with good views of the mountainous skyline can be great fun for kids — they'll sleep like logs at night.

Trekking companies can provide advice and make arrangements that will make a trek with children easier. As a bare minimum, it is a good idea to hire porters to carry your luggage and, in the case of small children, the kids themselves in case they become tired or sick.

Cultural Kicks

MENTION NEPAL AND MOST PEOPLE THINK MOUNTAINS. But while it's impossible to visit Nepal without at least catching a glimpse of the towering Himalayas, many visitors are content to admire these peaks from afar and restrict their sightseeing to the cultural attractions of Kathmandu valley.

Early European visitors to Kathmandu valley came away with tales of a land in which every second building was a temple. This is an exaggeration, of course; but to refer to the valley as a "treasure trove" — of art and architecture is to do no more than state the obvious.

THE ARCHITECTURAL LEGACY
For most of the last millennium the compact valley of Kathmandu has been home to three kingdoms: Kathmandu,

Bhaktapur and Patan or, as they were known in the Malla era, Kantipur, Bhadgaon and Lalitpur. The rivalry between the three, no more than a day's march from each other, has bestowed the valley with a remarkable architectural legacy.

To fully appreciate the dizzying scale and painstaking details of the Durbar squares of Kathmandu, Bhaktapur and Patan, you will have to spend at least a day in each. The design of the Newar palaces is based on the same principles as Newar home design, the thick mud walls enclosing a central courtyard. But in the case of the palaces, the architectural design pales in comparison with the carvings that decorate them.

Scattered through the streets and squares of the Newar cities are a multitude of Hindu pagoda temples, and it is arguably here that local artistic expression is at its most eloquent. The pagoda, like the mandala, is a three-dimensional representation of the universe and, like the crowded mandala thangkas you see for sale in around the squares, the surfaces of the pagoda are a mass of carved detail of deities and demons, sometimes erotica. See the **Nyatapola pagoda** in Bhaktapur, one of the valley's few five-storied pagodas (most are three-storied), for the happy convergence of all that is best in Newar architectural design.

MUSEUMS

It is frequently remarked that Kathmandu valley is one big museum. There's no denying this. You might easily spend months scouring the streets of Kathmandu alone and still come up with fascinating daily discoveries: a roadside shrine, a particularly beautifully carved window frame.

Items that have been collected into museums tend to be moveable art pieces that might otherwise be sold or stolen. The National Museum ((01) 271504, Chhauni, for example, has a fascinating collection of religious art, including sculptures, wood carvings and best of all an impressive display of metalwork —

most of it Buddhist in inspiration and created by Patan artisans in the fourteenth century. Look for the life-sized Lokeshvara mandala.

The National Art Gallery ((01) 610004, Durbar square, Bhaktapur, is another essential stop for anyone interested in Nepal's cultural legacy. Displayed inside is a collection of Buddhist thangkas, sculptures and murals from Bhaktapur's Palace of 55 Windows. Bhaktapur also has the National Woodcarving Museum and the Bronze and Brass Museum.

PERFORMANCES

The best cultural performances are held in Kathmandu, where all the major hotels provide cultural entertainment of one kind or another in the evenings. It is also worth checking the noticeboards in Thamel for announcements of performances. Some of the better restaurants in Thamel have live traditional music.

OPPOSITE: Garuda perches on high, hands in prayer. ABOVE: A holy man pores over religious texts in a quiet corner. OVERLEAF: King Yoganendra Malla presides serenely over Patan's Durbar square.

The Everest Cultural Society performs folk dances daily from 7 PM at the Hotel de l'Annapurna. The New Himalchuli Cultural Group stages classical and folk dances together with songs and music at the Hotel Shankar's Cultural Hall daily from 6:30 to 7:30 PM (November to February), and 7 to 8 PM (March to October).

Less touristy performances are held at the Hotel Vajra ((01) 272719, P.O. Box 1084, Bijeswori, Kathmandu. You will need to check for times. Performances vary from folk dances to modern productions, but a trip out to this hotel near Swayambhunath temple is always worth the effort.

Try the Ghar-e-Kabab restaurant, Annapurna Hotel, Durbar Marg, for the best in Indian classical music.

Shop Till You Drop

NEPAL IS NOT HONG KONG OR SINGAPORE — BUSTLING, MODERN PARADIGMS OF THE ASIAN SUCCESS STORY — where tourists depart reeling under the weight of the latest consumer electronics. Rather, the Nepal traveler leaves with bags straining from unexpected purchases of Nepali, Indian and Tibetan arts and crafts.

It's difficult to imagine anywhere in the world in which so many fascinating artistic traditions converge in such tempting profusion. In Kathmandu and Pokhara, entire days can be frittered away browsing through mandalas, textiles, Tibetan carpets, handmade paper, terracotta pottery and ritual artifacts from Tibet and the high mountain valleys of the Himalayas.

There is such a dazzling array of fascinating bric-a-brac, fabrics and clothes that it is easy to rush into purchases. The sensible shopper spends some time exploring Kathmandu, checking prices and comparing quality. Beware: antiques may be no more than a few days old; and anything older than 100 years cannot be taken out of the country.

BARGAINING

For many visitors prices seem so reasonable in Nepal that it seems difficult to believe that prices might be cheaper still with a little bargaining — in some cases the "real" price may be as little as half the asking price.

It takes time to learn successful bargaining, but for starters if you're interested in something (never ask the price or begin to bargain for something you don't want to buy) try a smile and a counter-offer somewhere between a third and a half of the price quoted. If you remain relaxed and lighthearted about the negotiation, you'll probably find that a couple more offers and counter-offers will result in a price that is significantly cheaper than you might have paid.

TIBETAN CARPETS

The Tibetan refugee carpet industry sprang into existence in 1961, when a Swiss foreign aid program started carpet production at the Tibetan refugee camp of Jawalkhel in Patan. Today, Tibetan carpets are Nepal's biggest industry, accounting for around half of the country's foreign exchange. Jawalkhel is still a good place to buy carpets. And not only can you buy the carpets here, you can also watch them being made.

Tibetan carpets are designed to be sat upon, slept upon, but never walked upon: if they seem small, this is the reason. The weave is far less fine than Persian carpets, usually around 40 to 60 knots per square inch (a good Persian carpet may have many times more). The experienced buyer notes the weave, but even more important is the intensity and harmony of the colors. The dyes used are mostly chemical, and have been ever since chemical dyes were first introduced into Tibet in the nineteenth century.

If you want to take a look at some genuinely valuable Tibetan carpets before heading out to see new ones being produced in Jawalkhel, a visit to the **Karma Lama Ritual Gallery (** (01) 226409, Durbar Marg, is recommended.

ART

Almost all Nepali and Tibetan art is religious. *Thangka* is a Tibetan word signifying an illuminated Buddhist scroll

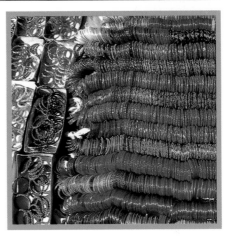

mounted on silk. Every multitudinous detail in such paintings is symbolic — a Bodhisattva might be pictured seated in the center of a geometric *mandala*, concentration on which is used as a meditation aid. When judging prices, take a close look at the quality of execution of the detail and at the quantity of gold leaf, which is used as a highlight in good quality thangka. You will see them for sale in shops all over Kathmandu, and in areas with large numbers of Tibetans.

At one time the metalwork of Nepalese artisans was among the best in the world. Figurines and statues depicting Hindu and Buddhist deities were — and still are — created by the lost-wax method, whereby an image is modeled in wax, coated in clay and then baked to melt away the wax leaving a clay mold into which molten metal may be poured. You can see this process and shop for metalwork at the **Patan Industrial Estate** in Patan.

MODERN ART

Nepal is so steeped in history, that many visitors do not realize that a new breed of

No place in Asia sports a more tempting profusion of traditional souvenirs than Nepal. OPPOSITE: Metalwork masks glitter on the sidewalk (left) while a shop just off Kathmandu's Durbar square (right) displays its colorful wares. LEFT: Tibetan carpets are hung out to tempt passersby on a Kathmandu sidestreet. Bangles ABOVE much beloved by Nepali women, sparkle and dazzle.

young artists are at work, looking for ways to express the modern Nepali experience. The **Indigo Gallery** ((01) 424303, Naxal, is in the same building as Mike's Breakfast, providing a good opportunity to enjoy a splendid meal in soothing surroundings while taking a look at the latest exhibition. The **October Gallery** ((01) 271545, Swayambhu, is another space that exhibits the work of contemporary Nepali artists.

CLOTHES

It's difficult to resist Nepal's silk-embroidered T-shirts. Designs range from unique and fetching to plain off-the-wall, but there is something for nearly everyone. You can have your clothes custom embroidered if you like — at bargain prices.

Elsewhere, clothes in Nepal are a mixed bag. Much of the clothing on sale in Thamel is poor quality and likely to be considered eccentric outside Nepal: conservative dressers are unlikely to find much they like. Items such as the inexpensive cotton drawstring trousers and skirts are fine for in and around Kathmandu, but you are unlikely to wear them out when you get home. The sweaters widely on sale around Thamel look great, but they rarely make it through a winter without starting to fall apart. The claims by shopkeepers that the sweaters are made of yak wool are simply a sales pitch.

Local clothing can make good souvenirs. Saris and lungi are widely available. Look, too, for *topi*, the jaunty caps that are as essential an adjunct to Nepalese formal wear as the tie is to ours.

For local clothing that is a cut above the average, look for **Durga Design** ((01) 610048, Thamel, across from the Potala Guesthouse.

JEWELRY

Traditionally the women of Nepal and Tibet display their wealth in their jewelry. Family savings in many poor villages may go into women's jewelry, which becomes an heirloom passed down through the generations. Such

jewelry — differing in design from village to village — is almost impossible to buy; but the importance of such traditions has bestowed Nepal with fine gold and silver smiths who produce some superb ready-made jewelry and who can also produce high-quality work according to your own design.

For Tibetan jewelry, Bodhnath is the best area to look, though you will see the characteristic silver and turquoise colors of Tibetan jewelry all through the Kathmandu and Pokhara valleys. Patan is commonly agreed to have the best gold and silver smiths.

MISCELLANEOUS CRAFTS

Nepali woodcarving belongs to a long and noble tradition. A few moments gazing at the wood carvings on the struts of temple roofs, the frames of windows in the Durbar squares of Kathmandu, Patan or Bhaktapur is enough to make you realize that the Newar artisans who produced them were in a league of their own.

Nowadays you can buy miniatures of such work — no match for the originals they are modeled on perhaps, but still a popular souvenir. The best place to shop for wood carvings in Bhaktapur, particularly in Dattatreya Square, where you will also find the **National Woodcarving Museum.**

In Kathmandu's Durbar square and in tourist areas such as Thamel, itinerant peddlers carrying "flute trees" are a common sight. For those who seek a greater musical challenge, the *saranghi* is a bowed fiddle-like instrument.

Puppets and masks make good gifts for adults and children alike. Thimi is a particularly good place to look for papier maché masks. The masks are usually depictions of Ganesh, Kumari or Bhairav, and are used in festive masked dances. When buying puppets, check that the heads are made of papier maché rather than clay — the latter are liable to break in transit. Bhaktapur is a good hunting ground for puppets, particularly the woodcarving shops of Durbar square. Bhaktapur is also the place to seek out block-printed handmade paper — perfect for wrapping an unusual gift.

BOOKS

Few travelers go to Nepal expecting to buy books; few leave without an armful of them. If you have interest is in Oriental religions, in the Indian Sub-Continent, in Tibet, or if you simply wish to find some literature with a local setting, the bookshops of Kathmandu are among the best-stocked in the world. Thamel shops are the place for second-hand books — some of them fabulously well stocked with titles in English (mostly), French, German, Dutch, Swedish and Japanese.

For some of the best browsing in town, go to Pilgrim's ((01) 231040, Thamel, next door to the Kathmandu Guesthouse. It's a warren of heaving bookshelves — the kind of shop you pop into for five minutes and emerge two hours later with half-a-dozen books you simply had to buy.

Short Breaks

MOST OF NEPAL'S BEST ATTRACTIONS ARE WITHIN EASY STRIKING DISTANCE OF KATHMANDU. With little time needed to get around, you can pack a lot into a short stay in Nepal.

Kathmandu makes a perfect base. You might spend two or three days exploring the city's attractions, wandering the maze-like alleys of the old city, marveling at the temples and palaces of Durbar square and striking out to the nearby Buddhist stupas of Swayambhunath and Bodhnath. Just as simple is to spend the mornings in Kathmandu and the afternoons in the ancient Buddhist city of **Patan**, half an hour distant by taxi, or in the predominantly Hindu city of **Bhaktapur**, about one hour away, where city and international efforts have

OPPOSITE: A typical rickety suspension bridge on an Everest region trek. Watch out for yaks coming the other way! ABOVE: Gokyo Peak in the Everest region, with views of the lake and glacier of the same name.

achieved a time-warping preservation job on the local architecture.

An excursion out of Kathmandu you will never forget involves an overnight stay at either **Nagarkot** or **Dhulikhel**. Both towns are on ridges that offer panoramic views of the Himalayas. Nagarkot has the best views, but Dhulikhel has better access and is quicker to get to (around two hours by bus). You can arrive in the late afternoon, check into one of the many hotels or guesthouses — there's something to suit all budgets and tastes — and then settle down somewhere comfortable — perhaps the verandah of your hotel room or the rooftop of your guesthouse — to watch shifting colors play over the Himalayas as the sun goes down. The next morning you should be up early to watch a repeat performance (though no two are ever the same) in the light of the rising sun.

A short holiday in Nepal would seem to make a trek out of the question. But this is not entirely true. There are some magical day-walks you can do that serve as the perfect trekking sampler, leaving you fulfilled but hankering for the day you can come back and do something longer.

One of the best day-walks in Kathmandu is the **Namobuddha trek** out of Dhulikhel (see above). The beauty of this six-hour circuit hike is not only that it provides stunning views of the Himalayas, but that it takes you through villages with tea houses, through pine forests, to a stupa, and past water mills just as the longer treks do.

If wildlife is your main interest, even a safari on elephant back at **Royal Chitwan National Park** need not be out of the question on a short trip. Chitwan is just five hours away from Kathmandu by taxi or bus; providing you arrive in Kathmandu by mid-afternoon, you can be in Chitwan Park by the evening, ready to mount your elephant the next morning. And if time is of the essence, don't worry: two days on the back of an elephant is more than enough for most people.

Festive Flings

HARDLY A WEEK PASSES IN NEPAL WITHOUT A FESTIVAL. They fall into three categories: Hindu or Buddhist festivals; historical festivals commemorating the royal family or an epic event from the past (perhaps the mythological past); and seasonal festivals, where offerings are made for good harvests.

Most festivals are local affairs, but there are some large national ones too. All dates are based on Nepal's lunar calendar, and are approximate only.

SPRING

One of the earliest spring festivals is **Ghode Jatra,** which is held in Tundikhel, Kathmandu in March. Held to appease Demon Gurumapa, the King of Nepal is the chief guest. The principal attractions are horse races, acrobatic shows, and a procession of chariots of the goddesses.

Ramavami (March to April) commemorates the epic victory of Rama, hero of the Ramayana, over his arch-rival Ravana. Elephants, ox-carts and horses

OPPOSITE: A Vishnu statue in Bhaktapur glistens with oil and pollen anointed by passing worshippers. ABOVE: All Kathmandu valley turns out to join the eight-day Indra Jatra Festival, the annual celebration of the monsoon rains and the conquest of the area by the ruling dynasty in the eighteenth century. OVERLEAF: Flour fills the air as Buddhist monks at Kathmandu valley's famed Bodhnath stupa celebrate yet another religious festival.

lead thousands of devotees through Janakpur in a milling throng. Other Ramavami celebrations are held in Kathmandu and elsewhere for those unable to travel to Janakpur.

Chaitra Dasain (March) is one of Kathmandu's most colorful festivals. It is often referred to as "little Dasain," a reference to Dasain in October, the greatest celebration of the year. The towering chariot of White Matsyendranath is pulled through the city for three days, and sacrifices are offered to Durga, Shiva's consort, in one of her most terrifying aspects.

Nepali New Year falls in March or April and is celebrated most enthusiastically in Bhaktapur, where it's known as **Bisket Jatra.**

The highlight of the festival is the parade of chariots: one houses Bhairav; the other the goddess Bhadrakali. The chariots lumber through the streets, pause for a tug of war between the east and west parts of town, before descending to a field beside the river, where a 25-m (82-ft) wooden lingam is erected and then sent crashing down. The New Year officially begins with the fall of the lingam. The pennants that flutter from the top of the lingam represent two snakes that were vanquished from a princess of Bhaktapur by a visiting prince who was a manifestation of Bhairav.

The next day, in nearby Thimi, is **Bal Kumari Jatra**, a festival where teams of men from all over Thimi and surrounding districts carry palanquins — known as *khat* — with neighborhood deities on board. Proceedings reach fever pitch with the arrival of a khat bearing Ganesh.

The **Rato Matsyendranath Jatra** festival is held in the first month of the

New Year (April to May), but the actual date is decided on the basis of propitious signs by Hindu priests. Matsyendranath is patron of the rains, and with the monsoon imminent he is drawn through every neighborhood of Patan, on a meandering route that may take a month or more to complete.

Buddha Jayanti celebrates the birth of Buddha with an all night vigil of butter lamps and electric lights in late April or early May at the Swayambhunath stupa in Kathmandu valley.

Overshadowing hundreds of smaller images, a massive gilded figure of Buddha is carried in a colorful procession down the many steps to a cloister where religious rites continue throughout the day before the Buddha is returned to its hilltop shrine.

At the Bodhnath stupa, on the other side of the valley, an image of Buddha is mounted on the back of an elephant and paraded around the dome. Ribbons of colorful flags stretch from the gilt-copper pyramid that surmounts the stupa, as the monks below blow their long copper horns. In the crescendo of the climax everyone hurls fistfuls of ground wheat into the air.

The centerpiece of the festivities is the large portrait of the Dalai Lama held head high and shielded under a large canopy.

SUMMER

Gunla (July to August) is a month-long celebration marked by massive pilgrimages to the Buddhist shrine at Swayambhunath.

Snakes and snake gods — *naga* — are associated with the monsoon rains. At **Nagpanchami,** which usually falls in July, Hindus paste pictures of naga on their front doors and make offerings of milk and boiled rice.

Ghantakama, held in Kathmandu in July, is one of the most riotous Newar celebrations. It celebrates the slaying of Ghantakama, a demon whose name means "bell ears," a reference to the bells he wore on his ears to drown out the name of Vishnu. On the last day

OPPOSITE: Folk dance (top) of a remote Tamang community in Langtang valley's remote Gharku village. A flower seller (bottom) parades his blooms through the streets of ancient Patan during the annual Matsyendranath Jatra festival. ABOVE: Carved stone image of Ganesh (left), the elephant-head god, Kathmandu. Stone carving (right) of Shiva in his incarnation as Bhairav.

before the new moon, worshippers place tripods of fresh reed stalks at crossroads and indulge in cheerful obscenities. At twilight, amid much good humored banter and jostling, an effigy of the demon, is symbolically drowned and evil is banished.

Janai Purnima is the full moon Hindu celebration of the renewal of the sacred thread — *janai* — worn looped over the shoulders of high-caste Brahmins.

as they walk around the city. In Bhaktapur, celebrations are rowdier, with singing, stamping, joking, shouting and much drinking.

Krishna Jantra, in August, celebrates the birth of Krishna, a manifestation of Vishnu in the aspect of Love. Processions bear pictures detailing Krishna's exploits and at night women gather at the Krishna temple in Patan to sing praise.

Celebrations center around the Khumbheshwar temple in Patan. Pilgrims mark the occasion by making a pilgrimage to Gosainkund, the sacred lake at the head of Trisuli valley, 4,300 m (14,100 ft) above sea level, and which is said to have a subterranean connection with the lake at Khumbheshwar temple.

Gai Jatra, which falls in July, is Kathmandu valley's "cow festival." Cows, it is believed by Hindus, lead the way into the other world after death. This festival is held in memory of those who have died in the past year. Cows, cow effigies and children dressed as cows are paraded through the streets. It is also a day for merry-making and fancy dress — in Patan the crowds impersonate cows, holy men, *sadhus*, or madmen

AUTUMN

A favorite with photographers, **Teej Brata**, which falls in August or September, is the colorful Festival of Women. Hundreds of thousands of Nepali women, all dressed in striking dresses of various hues of red, gather on the banks of the Bagmati at Pashupatinah.

Married women wear their scarlet and gold wedding saris, and the unmarried sing and dance in their brightest clothes to pray to Shiva and his consort Parvati for a long and happy marriage. They bathe in the Bagmati in honor of their husbands or husbands-to-be. Throughout Kathmandu valley, there is feasting on the first day and fasting on the second and third.

September in Kathmandu is the time for one of the year's most important festivals: **Indra Jatra** is eight days of noise and color, celebrating the release of Indra, the King of Gods, who, disguised as an ordinary mortal, was arrested for stealing flowers in Kathmandu. When his mother came down to earth to find him, the people, overcome with remorse, fell down before them and then carried them in triumph through the streets in a week-long festival.

Before the event starts, King Birendra consults the Bal Kumari for assurance that all augurs well. The Kumari anoints the King on the forehead with the Hindu's sacred red mark, the *tika*, and he presses his forehead on her feet. Then, watched by foreign and Nepali dignitaries, the Kumari is carried from her temple to a large chariot, for her feet must not touch the ground.

King Birendra and his queen watch from the balcony of their Durbar square palace as the Kumari's chariot, accompanied by images of Ganesh and Bhairav, is drawn through the square and the streets of Kathmandu. Sheep or goats are laid in the path of the juggernaut's wheels, sacrifices to save those who may stumble or fall before the giant vehicle.

Ashwin, which falls in September or October, is the Ganesh Festival, held in honor of the pot-bellied elephant god without whose blessings no journey or religious ceremony, be it private or public, is ever begun. Nepalis believe that even Surya, the Sun God, offers puja to Ganesh before he journeys across the heavens.

October is the month of the biggest of Nepal's national festivals: **Dasain**. Starting at the new moon and lasting for 10 days, this is a time for family and home, a time for gifts and feasts. The "nine nights" — *navaratri* — of Dasain are marked by masked dances, and on the eighth night, the "black night," sacrifices are performed by all who can afford one — preferably on a black goat. Another Dasain activity is the erection of swings and primitive ferris wheels at entrances to villages around the country.

November sees the arrival of India's biggest Hindu festival, **Tihar Dipawali**, known in English as the Festival of Lights. In Nepal Tihar is second only to Dasain. The five days of rituals held in honor of Yama, the God of Death, are probably the most splendid of Nepal's national festivals. On the third day — **Lakshmi Puja** — Kathmandu valley fills with spluttering oil lamps, which are lit to welcome Lakshmi, the Goddess of

Wealth. The fifth and final day is Bhai Tika, when sisters offer gifts to their brothers along with the blessing: "I plant a thorn at the door of death; may my brother be immortal."

WINTER

Bibaha Panchami, which falls in November or December, is a week-long festival held in Janakpur commemorating Rama and Sita's wedding. On the first day, everybody joins the great procession from Rama's

Clad in rich scarlets, reds and golds, women OPPOSITE purify themselves in the waters of a sacred river at Kathmandu's Pashupatinah temple during the Teej festival in a ritual of bathing and ABOVE feasting as they pray for the continuing love and devotion of their husbands.

temple. Rama's idol, dressed as a bridegroom, is placed in a gaily-decorated sedan chair that rides on the back of an elephant — just as elegantly bedecked in brocades and silks — and led to Sita's temple, Naulakha Mandir. Next day, Sita's idol is carried with great fanfare to the side of Rama in a symbolic re-enactment of their marriage.

Maghesnan is a Hindu purification ceremony in which thousands swarm along the banks of the Bagmati river in Kathmandu and elsewhere at the full moon of the 10th month of the Nepali year (January to February).

The new moon in February is Tibetan New Year, or **Losar**. Like Dasain for the Nepalis, Losar for the Tibetans is a family celebration. Go to Bodhnath temple just outside Kathmandu to see lamas parading around the stupa bearing portraits of the Dalai Lama.

The beginning of spring in January or February is marked by **Sri Panchami**, also known as Basant Panchami. Celebrations begin on the fifth day of the new moon during the 10th month of the Nepali year, honoring Saraswati, Brahma's consort and the Goddess of Learning, and Manjushri, legendary Buddhist patriarch of Kathmandu valley, regarded as the God of Learning. It is a festival with special significance for students and scholars. At Kathmandu's Hanuman Dhoka palace, the King is anointed with a tika and slices of coconut while a 31-gun salute is fired and poems and songs are performed in honor of spring.

Temples are decorated with flowers, and schoolchildren parade in the streets, carrying their text and exercise books for blessing by Saraswati. The next day new primary students start their lessons. Older students go to Swayambhunath or Chabahil to ask Saraswati for success in their examinations.

One of the year's most bizarre festivals is **Maha Shivatri**, held in February or March and honoring the birth of Shiva. Hindu devotees make their way from all over Nepal to Pashupatinah temple, but the main attraction (for foreign witnesses) is the huge numbers of Indian sadhus who have covered vast distances on foot to reach the temple.

Also known as the Festival of Colors, **Holi–Phagu**, which falls in March, heralds the coming of the monsoon with a nationwide water festival. The colors are powdered dyes added to buckets of water everybody hurls at each other. If you're out and about this day, be sure to wear the sort of clothes you don't mind getting stained with a kaleidoscope of colors.

Galloping Gourmets

OUTSIDE KATHMANDU AND POKHARA, THERE IS LITTLE SUSTENANCE FOR GOURMETS. The basic fare is dhal bhat, and on some of the tea house treks this is the only food available. *Dhal bhat* is as humble a dish as you can imagine — lentils and rice. How good it tastes depends on what it is flavored with — some spicy fried vegetables if you are lucky. If you are on an overnight or day trip from Kathmandu, you can at least bring the makings of a picnic.

The Nepali diet is largely vegetarian, though for most Nepalis this is by economic necessity rather than choice. As cows are sacred, beef is not eaten; water buffalo is the popular alternative. Nowadays, in the international restaurants of Kathmandu, frozen steaks are flown in from India and farther afield.

Tibetan cuisine has had an influence on Nepal, and in some trekking regions the diet is distinctly Tibetan. As anyone who has traveled extensively in Tibet will tell you, this is not the most fortunate of influences. The Tibetan diet is bland: *thukpa*, is a vegetable noodle soup; while *momos* are small meat-filled dumplings, fried or steamed. Together they encompass the extremes of a modest cuisine. Tibetan yak-butter tea is only for the brave or foolhardy.

Momos are not, perhaps, a great contribution to international cuisine, but on a cold night a steaming bowl of them are a treat.

Without a doubt the best that Nepal has to offer it owes to its vast southern neighbor: India. The top Indian restaurants in Kathmandu rate with the best anywhere in the world. If you are not familiar with Indian cuisine or have only eaten take-outs, you should treat yourself to a modest splurge in one of the Indian restaurants while you are in Kathmandu.

DRINKS

Soft drinks and mineral water are widely available. Always drink bottled or boiled water. Tea, *chiyaa*, is served sweet and milky, and is safe to drink. You should try Indian yogurt, *lassi*, either salted or sweet.

Nepal doesn't produce its own wines. *Chhang* is the Tibetan equivalent of beer, and is made from fermented barley, maize, rye, or millet. *Arak* (potato alcohol), and *rakshi* (wheat or rice alcohol), also have their adherents. The local brewers also produce strong spirits — whisky, rum, and gin.

Nepal's Star and Golden Eagle lager beers are excellent. Imported beers, spirits, and wines are available in most major tourist centers — at a price.

HEALTH

Few travelers make it through a Nepal trip without getting some kind of gastrointestinal upset. For most people this is simply a minor inconvenience, slowing them down for a day or two. But it still pays to be careful.

The number one health rule is never to drink water that has not been boiled and filtered. This is especially true during the wet season, when water supplies frequently become contaminated. Uncooked food such as sandwiches and especially salads are also risky. In Kathmandu, many restaurants claim their salads are washed in water treated with iodine solution; if true, such salads are probably safe. Salads washed in untreated water are most definitely not safe.

The meringue pies and cheesecakes of Thamel should be avoided. Chocolate cakes are safe.

Special Interests

BIRDWATCHING

KATHMANDU IS JUST FIVE HOURS BY BUS OR TAXI FROM ROYAL CHITWAN NATIONAL PARK, which is a birdwatcher's paradise: with over 450 species of birds, there are few destinations in the world that compare. In the more remote Royal Bardia National Park, some 250 species of birds have been counted.

It's unlikely that you will be able to find guides with a particular expertise in birdwatching, but you can at least try to track down a copy of the indispensable *Birds of Nepal* by R.L. Fleming *et al* (Kathmandu: Avalok 1979). A good alternative is the *Collins Handguide to the Birds of the Indian Sub-Continent* by Martin Woodcock (Collins 1990).

TREKKING PEAKS

Most people, when they think of mountaineering, think of huge, lavishly funded caravans snaking their way through the foothills of the Himalayas to a base camp, from where a meticulously planned assault of the mountain is undertaken. While expeditions of this type are still common, not all climbing in Nepal is done on such a massive scale.

In 1978 the Nepal Mountaineering Association (NMA) opened 18 peaks, ranging from 5,500 m (18,040 ft) to 6,584 m (21,596 ft), to trekkers. These so-called "trekking peaks" provide an opportunity to avid climbers — who lack the resources to undertake a major expedition — to tackle a Himalayan mountain.

Application procedures are straightforward and involve a fee of US$200 for peaks under 6,100 m (20,000 ft), US$300 for those over. You are required, however, to have a liaison in Kathmandu, and for most trekkers this means a trekking company. See TRAVELERS' TIPS , TRAVEL AGENCIES for some reliable trekking companies in Kathmandu. Look, too, for the highly recommended *Trekking Peaks of Nepal* by Bill O'Connor (England: Crowood Press 1989).

SPIRITUAL MATTERS

Yoga and Buddhist (the Tibetan variety) meditation are alternatives to trekking and white-water rafting for some Nepal travelers. In addition to the recommendations here, the noticeboards of Thamel in Kathmandu are rarely short of inspirational advertisements aimed at the spiritually inclined.

For meditation, the main center catering to Westerners is **Kopan monastery** ((01) 226717, P.O. Box 817,

OPPOSITE: Drifting in search of wildlife in the Royal Chitwan National Park. ABOVE: Annapurna rears its head above the clouds.

Bodha, near Bodhnath temple. Short courses are available year-round, but month-long courses are available on a periodic basis, and attract students from around the world. Prices for the month course, with full board in the monastery, are very reasonable.

Affiliated with Kopan monastery is the **Himalayan Yogic Institute and Buddhist Meditation Center** ((01) 413094 FAX (01) 410992, which also has short courses on Buddhism and meditation.

Yoga Studio ((01) 417900, P.O. Box 5098, Kathmandu, is a popular school for would-be yogis.

LANGUAGE COURSES

Nepali may not be one of the most widely spoken languages in the world, but those who take the time to learn some — and in comparison to other Asian languages it is not particularly difficult — find that trekking and touring rural Nepal become an altogether more enjoyable experience. It's surprising how quickly a repertoire of useful phrases can be learned.

Two schools in Kathmandu that provide classes and individual lessons are the **School of International Languages** ((01) 211713, and **Insight Nepal** ((01) 418963.

Taking a Tour

NEPAL TOURS USUALLY MEAN TREKKING AND/OR SAFARI TOURS. If you are planning to be in Nepal for a short period and want to restrict your sightseeing to the cultural attractions of Kathmandu valley, you will probably find it easier to book accommodation from home and then sign up for tours of the valley when you arrive.

Tours of the Kathmandu valley are reasonably priced, and you have the option of either joining a group of other tourists in a minibus or of hiring your own driver and guide. Naturally, it is cheaper to join a group tour — around US$5 per half day — than have a personal tour — between US$20 to US$30 per half day.

For group tours, Gray Line ((01) 412899, is the best bet. Their tours take in a large number of destinations around the valley, including Bhaktapur, Patan, Swayambhunath, Bodhnath and Pashupatinah, among others. For personalized tours with a driver and guide of your own, Natraj Tours and Travel ((01) 220001, Durbar Marg, and Adventure Travel Nepal ((01) 223328, Durbar Marg, are the two best options.

Adventure tours that involve trekking, mountain biking and white-water rafting can be booked either in Nepal or at home. If your time is limited, it is best to organize the tour at home. For information on white-water rafting and mountain biking, see the SPORTING SPREE, page 28. For information on local trekking companies, see the TRAVELERS' TIPS, TRAVEL AGENCIES.

Australian travelers can book adventure tours of Nepal from the following agencies: Peregrine Adventures ((03) 9663 8611 FAX (03) 9663 8618, 258 Lonsdale Street, Melbourne, Victoria 3000; and World Expeditions ((02) 9264 3366, 3rd Floor, 441 Kent Street, Sydney, New South Wales 2000.

UK travelers can book adventure tours of Nepal at: Encounter Overland Expeditions ((0171) 370 6845 FAX (0171) 244 9737, 267 Old Brompton Road, London SW5 9JA ; and Exodus Expeditions ((0181) 673 0859, 9 Weir Road, London, SW12 OLT.

Travelers from the USA can book adventure tours of Nepal at: Adventure Center TOLL-FREE (800) 227 8747 FAX (510) 654 4200, 1311 63rd Street, Suite 200, Emeryville, CA 94608; and Himalayan Travel TOLL-FREE (800) 225 2380 FAX (203) 622 0084, 112 Prospect Street, Stamford, CT 06901.

A lowland scene in the Annapurna region, where wooded hills give way to snow-dusted peaks.

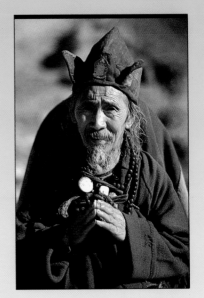

Vertical Perspectives

IMAGINE a land where the only sound is the wind flowing through the mountain passes far above, a river crashing through a canyon far below, a rice mill clicking rhythmically on a verdant hillside, goats or roosters calling from the next valley. Imagine a panorama of green steep hills rising to rolling crests of glissading stone, soaring peaks of sheer white ice towering overhead: These peaks are the Himalayas, the Roof of the World; the land at their feet is Nepal.

From the medieval push and shove of Kathmandu to the precipitous trails that link far-flung villages, from the lowland forests of the Terai to the wind-swept vistas of the high Himalayas, from the Hindi-speaking people of the plains to the proud and kindly Sherpas and Tibetans of the mountain passes, Nepal is fascinating, complex, compelling and unforgettable. Not many people visit Nepal just once: to go to Nepal is to promise to return.

How could it be otherwise? Nepal casts a spell on those who journey there. The peaks seem to leap skywards. Flowers bloom in dazzling profusion, littering the terracotta earth in a kaleidoscope of color. Elsewhere are dappled forest greenery and verdant paddies, granite gray cliffs and glacial ice. Meanwhile the carved façades, gilded temples and sparring rooftops of Kathmandu conjure up visions of centuries past.

Indeed, there are times when the entire Nepal experience seems to belong to a forgotten time — hardly surprising when you consider that until the 1950s the country was the "hermit kingdom." Today, amenities we take for granted elsewhere — roads, vehicles, telephones, television — are in short supply in Nepal. But then some might say that the most magnificent mountain scenery in the world is best appreciated in the absence of such things.

It is the mountains that draw most travelers to Nepal. Eight of the world's ten highest peaks, all of them above 8,000 m (26,250 ft), can be found in Nepal. Not that the country is particularly big — somewhat larger than the state of Florida, or England and Wales combined. But

wedged between the world's two most populous countries, India and China, this small area of 141,414 sq km (53,737 sq miles) packs in more cultural and topographical contrasts than countries many times its size.

Nepal's sub-tropical location and staggering altitude range — from 60 to 8,848 m (200 to 29,028 ft) above sea level — provide conditions under which most types of vegetation can grow, producing a wondrous variety of mammals, birds, reptiles, insects and plants. And although

population growth and increasing competition for scarce natural resources has exterminated many species and reduced others, for those who are prepared to take to the hills on foot, Nepal can still call to mind the Shangri-La of *Lost Horizons*, a place so exotic, so serene and so far away that its very existence comes as a surprise.

PREVIOUS PAGES: Prayer flags (left) flutter in the breeze in the Everest region. Holy man (right) on a high mountain pass. OPPOSITE: The divine fishtail peaks of Nepal's most sacred mountain, Machhapuchhare, which rises 6,993 m (22,940 ft) northwest of Pokhara. ABOVE: An ice-melt stream in the Langtang region.

The Country and its People

THE HIMALAYAS, which curve like a scimitar more than 3,000 km (1,860 miles) across the subcontinent from northern Pakistan in the west to Burma in the east, form the backbone of Nepal. The average elevation of northern Nepal is well above 6,000 m (19,686 ft), yet all this was once a sea. The peak of Everest, Sagarmatha (goddess of the universe), at 8,848 m (29,028 ft), is composed of marine rock from the Cretaceous age. Eighty to 60 million years ago, it formed the bed of the Tethys Sea, separating Asia and India. Then, at the end of the Mesozoic era, the Asian continent collided with the island of India. The tremendous pressure forced up the bed of the Tethys Sea, forming the Tibetan Marginal range on the Nepal-Tibet border.

Later, in the Miocene era, some 10 to 15 million years ago, the movement of the earth's tectonic plates again forced the Indian subcontinent against Asia, folding the Himalayas into existence. These peaks formed buttresses against moist sea winds approaching from oceans to the south, causing increased precipitation on their steep southern slopes. Torrential rivers came into being, cutting through the mountains almost as quickly as they were raised.

It was not until the Pleistocene period, 600,000 years ago, that a final continental collision brought the Himalayas to their current heights. The Mahabharat range and Siwalik hills in southern Nepal also formed at this time, damming rivers and creating a large prehistoric lake in the Kathmandu valley. The lake dried up approximately 200,000 years ago.

The Himalayas run along Nepal's entire 885-km (549-mile) northern border with Tibet. The youngest mountain range in the world, they are still engaged in their slow assault on the heavens. From the air, they present a panorama that stretches farther than the human eye can see; it seems impossible that anyone, or anything, can live within their frozen embrace. Yet locked in

PREVIOUS PAGES: Festive bathing (left) in the waters of the lowland Terai. A minority girl (right) smiles a greeting. RIGHT: Distant view of the highest point on earth, 8,848 m (29,028 ft) Everest, surrounded by its cohorts, Nuptse and Lhotse.

thousands of secret valleys are Nepal's mountain towns and villages, accessible only by narrow footpaths carved or worn into the rock.

All length and little breadth, Nepal measures only 240 km (149 miles) at its widest point, and 150 km (93 miles) at its narrowest. From the narrow strip of flat, fertile, checkerboard plain that lies 67 m (220 ft) above sea level along the Indian border, it climbs to more than 8,848 m (29,028 ft).

Within a span of 12 hours you can fly with the rising sun along the daunting barrier of the Himalayas, from Annapurna to Kanchenjunga and back to Kathmandu then drive along a road cut into the side of a deep Himalayan river gorge and down the precipitous flanks of the Mahabharat range to the emerald plains of the Terai, and there ride an elephant among a herd of rhino as the sun sets. Similarly, the south-north land journey by car from the sea-level border to the mountains is a swift and stunning transformation of environment. You can leave the Indian border in early morning, reach the Tibetan border by late afternoon and be back in Kathmandu by nightfall. The east-west traverse, however, takes many weeks and is only possible on foot. It is one of the world's toughest, most difficult treks.

No more than 160 km (99 miles) separates Mount Everest from the tropical plains where its melting snows swell the floodwaters of some of the major tributaries of the sacred Ganges. Nepal's rivers begin as a trickle of ice melt and become raging waters as they are joined and swollen by countless tributaries. Over millennia these waterways have cut some of the deepest gorges in the world, plunging from 5,180 m (17,000 ft) to just above sea level. At full flood, these waters take just 12 hours to complete a journey from Arctic ice to tropical jungle.

Among Nepal's plains, mountains and rivers is a tapestry of vivid cultural contrasts; there are 35 ethnic groups including those of the Gurkha and the Sherpa. But with an average per capita income of less than $160 a year, Nepal's people live, many of them, on the edge of or in the midst of poverty. The majority of farmers scratch a frugal living from their rice paddies and grain fields in the hills, mountains or the overcrowded Terai plains of the south. In the towns and cities there is also much poverty, particularly among the Tibetan refugees chased out of their own mountain kingdom by the conquering, ravaging Chinese armies in recent years.

Yet whatever faith the people of Nepal follow, be it Hinduism, Buddhism, animism or cheery paganism, they tend to celebrate each other's feasts notwithstanding, and within a poverty of means commemorate life and faith year round with festivals saluting incarnate and reincarnate deities alike.

Kathmandu, the capital and seat of the royal family, lies at the center of the country, 1,331 m (4,368 ft) above sea level, on roughly the same latitude as Florida. Neither too hot in summer months nor too cold in the winter season, Kathmandu, like most of midland Nepal, is favored with one of the world's more agreeable climates. Summer temperatures reach around 30° C (86° F) and the mean winter temperature is 10° C (50° F). The Nepalis attribute the pleasant climate to the generosity of the gods, and justifiably celebrate their divine fortune by reaping at least three harvests a year.

THE MISTY PAST

Some archaeologists believe that even before the Himalaya mountain range reached its present grandeur, *Orepithecus*, one of our early ancestors, inhabited the region's valleys and plains. Primitive humans had formed hill tribes and were making and using primitive tools as long as one million years ago. Little is known about these early inhabitants; however, both Hindu and Buddhist legends confirm that humans resided here during the time a lake filled the Kathmandu valley, and that there were relatively developed societies with oral traditions and an animistic religion.

THE KIRANTI INVADERS AND THE BIRTH OF BUDDHA

Somewhere around 700 BC Kiranti invaders arrived from India. Their military exploits are described in ancient Indian texts such as the Mahabharata and Ramayana, but their influence probably only extended over a portion of the Terai and the midlands, where they established Patan as their stronghold. They assimilated the pre-existing cultures, and, for at least seven centuries, controlled north-south trade and travel.

mingled with existing populations to become the people commonly referred to as Newaris. In the hills and mountains tribal societies and kingdoms also expanded and diversified.

After the Kiranti, the valley was ruled by the Somavashis, who also originally came from India. Under the Somavashis, the Hindu religion flourished and a four-caste system was introduced. They renovated the holy shrine, Pashupatinah, and in the first century AD constructed a temple on the site. It was also during their

It was during this epoch that Buddha was born — in 540 BC at Lumbini. Buddha himself preached in the Kathmandu valley as well as northern India, and his teachings spread throughout Asia. In 250 BC the Indian Emperor Ashoka, recently converted to Buddhism, journeyed to Nepal, where he erected a memorial to Buddha in Lumbini and founded a disputed number of *stupas* in Patan. Nepal then, as now, enjoyed a happy coexistence of both Buddhism and Hinduism.

Over the next two centuries, until perhaps 50 BC, Kiranti influence waned in the valley. Other groups migrated here and

rule that the roofs of the temples in Patan were gilded.

THE GOLDEN AGE

Eventually the Somavashis were conquered by the Licchavi, who ruled the valley from the fifth through seventh centuries. These Hindu rulers also came from India and are credited with bringing an age of enlightenment with them. They fostered the study of Sanskrit and the production of carvings, many with elaborate inscriptions and dedications.

Buddha's 540 BC birthplace at Lumbini on the Terai plains which border India.

One notable Licchavi ruler, Manadeva, built the Changu Narayan temple in 388 Saka Sambat (AD 467), so its inscriptions tell us. A stele there praises Manadeva's victories over the Malla tribes and the subjugation of the Thakuris.

Two centuries later the last Licchavi ruler, Shevadeva, gave his daughter in marriage to one of his strongest Thakuri vassals, Amsuvarman, who was well-educated and had written a Sanskrit grammar. As Shevadeva preferred the monastic life to his royal duties, Amsuvarman assumed many of his father-in-law's duties during the latter's lifetime.

On the death of Shevadeva in AD 605, Amsuvarman appointed himself king. He expanded his influence beyond the valley by marrying his daughter Bhrikuti to the Tibetan King Sron Tsan Gampo. Bhrikuti is credited with converting the Tibetan king and his other wife, a Chinese princess, to Buddhism, thus beginning the eventual transmission of the religion to Tibet and China. The two brides have been canonized in the Buddhist tradition and are worshipped as the goddesses of compassion, Green Tara (Bhrikuti) and White Tara (Wencheng, the Chinese princess).

In AD 643 and 647 the Chinese sent their first diplomatic missions to the Kathmandu valley. The records of Wang Huen Tse, the leader of the second mission, show that he had mixed feeling about Ni-Po-Lo and its inhabitants: "The kingdom of Ni-Po-Lo… is situated in the middle of snowy mountains and indeed presents an uninterrupted series of hills and valleys. Its soil is suited to the cultivation of grain and abounds in flora and fruits…. Coins of red copper are used for exchange. The climate is very cold. The national character is stamped with falseness and perfidy; the inhabitants are all of a hard and savage nature: to them neither good faith nor justice nor literature appear, but they are gifted with considerable skill in the art. Their bodies are ugly and their faces are mean. Among them are both true believers [Buddhists] and heretics [Hindus]. Buddhist's convents and the temples of the Hindu gods touch each other. It is reckoned that there are about two thousand religious who study both the Greater and Lesser Vehicle. The number of Brahmans and the nonconformists has never been ascertained exactly."

Other members of the missions were more impressed with the Nepali culture and art. Years later, Nepali architects were invited to China to build the first pagodas there.

This golden age of Nepal was followed by a dark age during which tribes were at constant war with one and other. Gone was art, learning and religious tolerance; few records or relics remain from this period. Some historians believe that during this era in the reign of a Thakuri king, Guakanadeva, around 950, the city of Kathmandu, then known as Kantipur, became the regional capital, and the towns of Bhdgaon and Kirtipur were established. Commerce with India and Tibet increased and Tantric rites and ideals were introduced and integrated into the religions.

THE MALLA DYNASTY

In the eleventh century Muslims took power in India. Under Muhammed Ghauri, they extended their empire into the northern kingdoms, causing both Hindus and Buddhists to flee north to Nepal and Tibet. The Malla dynasty arose from these refugees, and it dominated the valley until the eighteenth century.

According to popular legend, the name of the dynasty came about when a son was presented to Arideva, one of the earliest Malla rulers, about the year 1200. Arideva was wrestling at the time, and he gave the child the title Malla, meaning "wrestler" in Sanskrit.

There were peaceful periods under the Mallas, but these were interrupted by Muslim invasions from India. During a fourteenth century attack, the Muslims sacked many temples and shrines in the valley. Nonetheless arts, architecture and learning advanced; there were three universities in the valley; religious tolerance was so complete that Buddhists and Hindus worshipped in the same temples and celebrated each other's religious festivals.

During the Malla rule, Christian monks came to the valley and were allowed to preach their religion. For many years there was a Catholic church near Kathmandu. But in their religious fervor, these Christian missionaries supposedly burned more than 3,000 pagan books and manuscripts as works of the devil. For this they were expelled, taking only a handful of native converts with them.

Under the reign of Jaya Sthiti Malla, which began in 1382, a caste system was reintroduced after a Brahman priest convinced the king that the gods look with disfavor upon casteless societies. The Brahman priests placed themselves at the top of the caste, with 64 professional groups below and shoemakers, butchers, blacksmiths and sweepers at the bottom, the untouchables. The second caste was the warriors, to which the royal families belonged. This caste was again subdivided into sub-castes, which led to suspicion and dissent among rulers and contributed substantially to the civil strife of the time.

The most aggressive of the Malla rulers, Jaksha Malla, extended the boundaries of his kingdom to include much of what is now modern Nepal. His territory extended north to Tibet and south to the Ganges river. He oversaw the construction of canals and water supply systems.

Unfortunately, shortly before his death he divided the valley amongst his children: Bhadgaon (also known as Bhaktapur), Banepa and Kathmandu went to his three sons, Patan to his daughter. The heirs, not content with their inheritances, were soon warring with each other. Banepa became part of Bhadgaon and Patan eventually lost its independence to Kathmandu.

The valley remained divided during the next 200 years, but there were several rulers of note in Kathmandu, Patan and Bhadgaon. Pratap Malla, king of Kathmandu from 1640 to 1674, was a man of letters, and demonstrated his knowledge of fifteen languages on a plaque in the Royal palace. He also erected the statue of Hanuman, the monkey god, at the entry to the palace, which since then has been known as Hanuman Dhoka. He was also responsible for the construction of the steps and gold thunderbolt at Swayambhunath.

Under King Siddhi Narasimba Malla (1618–1661), Patan grew considerably. Siddhi Narasimba oversaw a major construction effort that included 2,400 individual houses. He was a religious man, and one day left on a pilgrimage from which he never returned.

The life of King Bhupatendra Malla of Bhadgaon reads much like a fairy tale. The wicked witch was his father's second wife, who wanted her own son to inherit the throne. Bhupatendra was the son of the first wife and therefore first in line. The second

wife decided to have the young prince killed. Her conspirators took the boy from the palace into the forest to murder him. However, they did not have the courage to carry out the stepmother's wish, and abandoned the child instead. The prince was found by a carpenter who raised him as his own son.

Years later, the carpenter took his son with him to work in the Royal palace. The king, the boy's real father, recognized him and welcomed him back as the rightful heir.

Sculptures of Buddhist and Hindu deities encircle an ornamental pool where Patan's eighteenth-century royal families bathed. The pool is surrounded by a protective symbol, a large stone snake known as Nagbandh. OVERLEAF: Elegant medieval architecture in Kathmandu.

Bhupatendra became king in 1696 when his father died, and his reign was marked by incessant construction. The best remaining structures from this period are the Palace of 55 Windows and the temple of Nayatapola. This was one of the most prosperous eras in the city.

THE UNIFICATION OF NEPAL

In spite of, or perhaps because of, the relative prosperity of the many divided kingdoms in the valley, they were at constant

war with each other. Outside the valley, meanwhile, other principalities were flourishing. Little is documented about life in these outlying kingdoms, but from one, Gorkha, came the leader of modern Nepal, Prithvi Narayan Shah.

The following story is told of him as a young boy in the land of the Gurkhas and fortified towns: One day when he was six years old, Prithvi Narayan went to the temple where he met an unhappy old man. "I am hungry. Can you give me some curd?" begged the old man. Prithvi Narayan fetched some curd. The old man ate his fill but kept a little in his mouth.

"Hold out your hand!" ordered the old man. The boy obeyed and the old man spit

what was left in his mouth into it. "Eat!" he commanded. Prithvi Narayan was not inclined to follow this order and dropped the curdled milk to the ground.

"If you had eaten my spittle from your hand, the old man said, you would have been able to conquer all the countries of your dreams. Since you have thrown it away, you will only be able to conquer those kingdoms into which you can walk." And the ancient one suddenly disappeared.

After becoming king of Gorkha in 1742, Prithvi Narayan spent 25 years expanding his territory and unifying a large part of Nepal. He was a great conqueror, but, as prophesied, he never did realize all his dreams.

Prithvi Narayan began his assault on the valley with careful planning and sound tactics. He first took over the fortifications of Nawakot in the Trisuli valley, through which passed much of the commerce with Tibet. The Malla kings united to send troops against Nawakot but were unsuccessful in breaking Prithvi Narayan's commercial blockage. Prithvi Narayan moved on to isolate the valley by cutting off the remaining trade routes and sent Brahman priests into the valley to stir up unrest.

The intrigues in the valley kingdoms helped advance Prithvi Narayan's plans. In Kathmandu, King Jaya Prakash had been exiled by his wife, whom he eventually killed. Jaya's brother, the King of Patan, was deposed by the Pradhans, a rival family, who spared his life but blinded him. Jaya came to his brother's aid, suppressed the Pradhan coup, forced them to beg in the streets and paraded their wives as witches.

Prithvi Narayan's economic blockage was not as successful as he had anticipated. Apparently only Patan offered allegiance in return for the right of passage. Prithvi Narayan sent his brother to rule Patan, but he was deposed and killed after a short time. Changing his tactics, Prithvi Narayan decided to lay siege to the valley, and chose Kirtipur as the first point of attack. He offered amnesty in return for surrender and was flatly refused. He swore to raze the city to the ground and mark every inhabitant for life.

After a two-year siege, the starving city surrendered. Prithvi Narayan forced the men to tear down their own temples and palaces, after which they were led one by one to the executioner who cut off their noses and lips. Only those who played wind instruments were exempt. One account of the episode claims Prithvi Narayan weighed this flesh bounty at 86 pounds in all. For generations the Kirtipur was hence known as Naskatipur, The City of the Noseless Ones.

Neither Patan nor Kathmandu offered much resistance to Prithvi Narayan and his

because he died four years later, leaving his two-year-old son, Rana Bahadur Shah, on the throne. Administration of the kingdom fell to a regent who also followed in the footsteps of Prithvi Narayan. He sent armies to Kashmir, Sikkim and Tibet. The Gurkha invasion of Tibet in 1790 and sacking of the Grand Lama's palace at Tashi-Lhumpo brought China into the conflict. Afraid of being overrun, Nepal requested military aid from the British East India Company. British troops, however, did not arrive until after a treaty had been signed

Gurkha armies. He easily took Kathmandu on September 1768 during the festival of Indra Jatra, when most of the population was celebrating. Jaya Prakash took refuge in Bhadgaon, but within a year the Gurkhas had taken it also. With control of the valley, Prithvi Narayan now held everything from Lamjung to Everest. He made Kathmandu his capital and maintained a policy of exclusion of Europeans, particularly missionaries. "First the Bible, then trading stations, then the cannon," he said. He planned a campaign to conquer Tibet, but died in 1774 without realizing his goal.

Prithvi Narayan was succeeded by his son, Pratap Singh Shah, who made little progress on his father's grand empire

in 1792 at Nawakot. Under the Nawakot treaty, Nepal agreed to honor the Tibetan boundaries and to pay an annual tribute to the Chinese emperor. A British representative remained in Nepal in a semiofficial capacity.

In 1795, at the age of 19, Rana Bahadur Shah assumed leadership of his country and had his regent imprisoned and killed. Bahadur Shah was an erratic if not insane ruler; his wife Tripura Sundavi and chief counselor Bhim Sen Thapa held the reigns of the kingdom. After Bahadur Shah was

OPPOSITE: Young sentinel of the famed Gurkha force of soldiers. ABOVE: Gurkha unit of the Nepali Army on parade in Kathmandu.

stabbed to death by his brother, Bhim Sen assumed the title of Prime Minister while serving as regent for the infant heir, Rajendra Bikram Shah. Bhim Sen directed Nepal for the next 30 years. He oversaw the army during a two-year border conflict (1814–1816) with the British East Indian Company. Against the well-equipped British and Indian armies, he led 12,000 men, some of whom were armed with bows and arrows. For heavier weapons they had only a few leather Tibetan cannons, made from yak hides tightly rolled together.

THE RANA RULE

Rajendra Bikram Shah's wife was a scheming, ambitious and unfaithful queen. When one of her lovers was murdered, she decided to revenge herself, and enlisted the help of one Jang Bahadur Rana, an equally ambitious officer in the Royal Guard. Convinced that a member of the Royal Council was responsible, she asked Jang Bahadur to call a meeting of the Council at the Kot, in the center of Durbar square. Closing the

The Treaty of Segauly, signed in 1816, was a compromise, not a victory for either side. The Prime Minister ceded some territories along his southern border, agreed to the stationing of a permanent British Resident in Kathmandu, and permitted the enrollment of three Gurkha regiments into the British Army.

When Rajendra Bikram Shah came of age, he progressively reduced Bhim Sen's power and eventually removed him as Prime Minister. Later Bhim Sen was imprisoned and in 1839 committed suicide. Another short period of relative chaos and royal intrigue followed out of which came the Rana prime ministers who ruled Nepal until after World War II.

gates to the courtyard, she demanded of the more than 500 noblemen that the person responsible for her lover's death be identified and punished accordingly. One pointed to Jang Bahadur as the murderer; in the ensuing mayhem, all the leading nobles were massacred by three regiments under Jang Bahadur's command. The identity of the assassin is not certain. Some accounts of the Kot massacre claim that Rajendra Bikram Shah himself was responsible for his wife's lover's death.

Nonetheless Jang Bahadur Rana installed himself as "His Highness the Maharaja" and Prime Minister. He then forced Rajendra Bikram Shah to abdicate in favor of his son, and exiled the king and queen to India. He gave the crown to the young prince, Sirendra Bikram Shah, and his eventual heirs, as it was believed that the spirit of Vishnu lived in the royal Shah line. However, Sirendra and his successors were in essence little but royal captives of Jang Bahadur and the other Ranas. Thereafter, only once a year did the Ranas permit the king to show himself before the general public which believed, as some Nepalis still do today, that they would receive forgiveness for all their sins merely by looking at him.

Thus the Prime Minister came to hold supreme command in Nepal; Jang Bahadur Rana decreed the position hereditary, passing from brother to younger brother, or brother to cousin. This first Rana Prime Minister was an adept statesman and politician. He sought the friendship of Europe but kept his country isolated from foreign influences. In 1850 he accepted an invitation from Queen Victoria and Napoleon III to visit Europe. He was royally received in London and Paris, as though he were the king.

His year long journey firmed international friendships but angered the local Brahmans who believed that anyone crossing the "black waters" of the ocean would return an untouchable. On his return, Jang Bahadur Rana purified himself in the Ganges and visited most of the major Hindu shrines in India and Nepal to prove he had not been contaminated by his trip.

The following Rana reign was notable for oppressive policies and favoritism based on its own set of castes within the family. There were A-, B- and C-Ranas, a breakdown that greatly contributed to the demise of the dynasty. The top government position went to A-Ranas, who were the pure Ranas in the direct line descending from Jang Bahadur. The A-Ranas had the right to live in palaces of more than 100 rooms. B-Ranas, descendants of Rana men who had married below them, received important civilian and military posts but could not have more than 70 rooms in their palaces. C-Ranas, offspring of harem girls, had large villas and high army posts, but could never rise to the rank of general.

Autocratic though they were, the Ranas

did bring about some positive advances in the country. Slavery and *sati* (suttee), the practice of the wife throwing herself on the burning body of her dead husband, were abolished; a university was founded, and a railroad, short though it was, constructed. Still, unrest and dissatisfaction with the Ranas was growing.

Nepal had sent 50,000 Gurkha soldiers to the First World War and continued to fill its three regiments in the British Army thereafter. In addition many served as mercenaries in the India Army. These returning

soldiers were Nepal's major contact with the outside world, and came to form a core of resistance to the Rana rule.

In 1940 the Prime Minister arrested 100 men and executed four of their leaders for the crime of communicating with the king. Many of the royal supporters remained in prison for extended periods of time; others took refuge in India. Martyrs' Memorial in Kathmandu commemorates these independence fighters. Although there was not a revolution in the sense of widespread open

OPPOSITE: Members of Nepal's royal family, including King and Queen, acknowledge the salute of the crowds from the balcony of a Kathmandu palace. ABOVE: Sherpa porter climbs a high pass in the Everest region.

warfare, during the last years of Rana domination persecution of the educated non-Rana Nepalis was commonplace, with little or no interference from the British. As Danish journalist Karl Eskerlund wrote, but for the alliance between the British and the Ranas, the country would not have stagnated so long. The British left Nepal alone because they wanted a buffer between India and Tibet. It was in their interest to keep Nepal as primitive as possible.

After World War II, the liberal Prime Minister Padma Shamsher realized that the days of autocracy were numbered. He moved to create a city council for which there were open elections and a new constitution. As far as the other A-Ranas were concerned, however, the Prime Minister took his reforms too far when he proposed an independent judiciary system. In 1948 Padma Shamsher was forced to resign in favor of Mohan Shamsher, a conservative.

Meanwhile, a liberation army of political exiles had formed in India, as well as several underground opposition movements in Kathmandu. On November 6, 1950 King Tribhuvan Shah and his family succeeded in escaping from Rana custody by detouring into the Indian embassy on the way to a picnic. They then flew to New Delhi and joined their supporters in exile. To insure survival of the royal line in the event that the escape failed, Tribhuvan left his four-year-old grandson, whom Mohan Shamsher immediately placed on the throne.

For the next three months, Mohan Shamsher sought international recognition for the new child-king, while from his exile in India King Tribhuvan organized support for himself within Nepal. In February, 1951, liberation forces entered the Terai; there were demonstrations in Kathmandu demanding a new constitution; and a group of C-Rana army officers announced they would no longer support a government which excluded them from the right of succession. The power of the Ranas was broken.

TOWARDS DEMOCRACY

On February 15, 1951, King Tribhuvan returned to Nepal and brought the Shah family back to power after 104 years. Mohan

Shamsher remained as Prime Minister; half the cabinet positions went to revolutionary leaders. Mohan resigned soon after, and went into exile in India. Nepal had finally emerged from isolation to take its place among the nations of the world.

King Tribhuvan ruled for four more years with several different cabinets, and died March 1955 while undergoing medical treatment in Zurich. His son, Mahendra Bir Shah, ascended to the throne and saw the new nation through the establishment of a constitution and its admission to the United Nations.

King Mahendra's coronation marked the first time in history that Nepal opened its borders to foreign heads of state and the international press. It was a gala affair organized and catered by a flamboyant retired Russian ballet star, Boris Lissanevitch, and his Scandinavian wife, who had started the only western-style hotel in Nepal at the request of Mahendra's father.

The King instituted a constitution that established a parliament and allowed political parties. Elections were held from February to April, 1959. The two-month time for voting was essential in this young nation where no internal communications existed except footpaths. The elections were publicized and carried out by *gaines*, wandering chanters. B.P. Koirala, leader of the liberation movement and supporter of the King's father, became Prime Minister.

The first parliament, however, was not long-lived. Locked in continual conflicts with his Prime Minister, the King dissolved Parliament, outlawed political parties, and imprisoned Koirala and several other ministers on December 15, 1960. Mahendra ruled the country until 1962, when he inaugurated a new constitution based on a system of *panchayats,* a pyramidal system that started in village communities and culminated in the king.

In 1963 King Mahendra passed a new social code guaranteeing equality to all citizens, freedom of speech and religion and the right of assembly. Castes were abolished, polygamy forbidden and the mar-

Tethering yaks (top) at Nar Valley. Phortse village clings to a barren mountainside (bottom) near Solu Khumbu.

riage of minors prohibited. Mahendra opened Nepal's doors to foreign visitors, aid and investment, and fostered nationalism in this country where previously many citizens did not even understand the concept of a nation or the meaning of Nepal.

When Mahendra died on January 31, 1972, he was succeeded by his son, Birendra Bir Bikran Shah. By 1990 pro-democracy protests had put pressure on King Birendra to agree to multiparty democratic elections. Nepal's first democratic elections in 32 years were duly held in May 1991, and the country became a constitutional monarchy.

GEOGRAPHY FROM BOTTOM TO TOP

Nepal is divided into five geographical regions: the Terai, Siwalik, Mahabharat, midlands or Pahar, and Himalaya. The government separates the country into 14 administrative zones subdivided into 75 development districts of varying importance.

The Terai, part of the great Ganges Plain, accounts for just over 20 percent of Nepal's land area, extending north from the southern border with India to the first foothills. Never wider than 35 km (22 miles), it is hot and humid most of the year. Until recently it was covered by dense forests filled with wildlife, from rare butterflies to Bengal tigers, but in the last two or three decades these forests have been widely encroached on, the forests cut and the wildlife exterminated. A large influx of settlers means that the Terai is where the majority of the Nepalis live nowadays.

This human settlement has ravaged the Terai. Where British hunter and explorer Jim Corbett in the 1930s stalked man-eating tigers and fished for huge fighting bream in the shade of ancient forests, there are now only eroded river valleys up to a mile wide and a patchwork of forest and cultivated areas. For much of the year river beds are dry; during the summer they are flooded from bank to bank with silted torrents changing course from year to year. Many houses stand on stilts. Like so many places on the planet, the Terai has become proof of the instantaneous and irreversible damage of population growth.

The Siwalik zone, with the Churia range, rises from the Terai to 1,200 m (4,000 ft). Its steep slopes and dry climate have left it relatively uninhabited. To the north are wide valleys, such as Rapti Dun, which in places separate the Siwalik from the Mahabharat.

The Mahabharat forms a barrier between the plains and the fertile midlands. It too is sparsely populated, but covered with terraced slopes. Most of Nepal's water passes through this region, which until very recently had lush deciduous forests that have nearly all been cut for fuelwood. Somewhat off the beaten track, it has mountain passes as low as 210 m (700 ft) and peaks over 2,700 m (9,000 ft).

More than 40 percent of the population occupies the temperate valleys of Kathmandu and Pokhara that dominate the Pahar zone or midlands. Here the soil is largely alluvial and fertile; crops of nearly every kind can be grown at altitudes between 600 and 2,100 m (2,000 and 7,000 ft).

Higher in the Himalayas, human habitation is isolated in remote valleys or sheltered where possible on the elevated plateaus. Here people live much as they did a thousand years ago, some still rooted in the Stone Age. Most of the high country is above treeline, for much of the year its rocky slopes covered by snow.

Nepal has one of the world's highest birthrates, with its population growing so fast the country may soon find itself hard-pressed for food. Over-cultivation of the precipitous valley slopes above the river gorges has already turned the landscape into a textbook case of deforestation and soil erosion. With its steep farmlands unprotected by the deep root systems and sheltering foliage of perennial vegetation, the fierce monsoon rains wash away the fragile topsoil and can bring thousands of tons of mountainside landsliding down the slopes. Yet the beauty of Nepal's landscape remains virtually indestructible. The sheer scale and form, even of the eroded walls of the valleys, are still magnificent enough to take the breath away.

It is these same mountain walls that have kept Nepal remote from the world until this century.

MONSOON CLIMATE

Nepal's climate is dominated by the monsoons of southern Asia. The rains usually come in late April or early May and continue with steady persistence until October. Drought conditions prevail generally for the remainder of the year, with only occasional thunderstorms or snows in the mountains.

October and November are probably the best months to visit Nepal, as the countryside is still lush from the monsoon rains and

Although the monsoon cycle is relatively predictable, remember that the weather, like the hiking trails, can offer surprises. The following note appears on many trekking maps and should be kept in mind:

"In Nepal all paths and bridges are liable to disappear or change at no notice due to monsoons, acts of gods, etc."

FAITH AND SUPERSTITION

In Nepal two of the world's great religions — Buddhism and Hinduism — coexist

neither too hot in the lowlands nor too cold in the mountains. December can be too cold to enjoy trekking in the mountains, and from January to March heavy snowdrifts close the mountain passes. In March and April the countryside is generally very dry, but the rhododendrons are in bloom on the hillsides, and multicolored butterflies and summer birds are omnipresent. May is a fickle month — some years it is dry and pleasant, other wet and gray.

In contrast to the hot-cold extremes of the Terai and the Himalaya, Kathmandu's temperate climate is near perfect. The Kathmandu valley does, however, become dusty in March and April, and can often be shrouded in haze.

peacefully, and it seems that everywhere you look there is a shrine or temple commemorating a god or deity. Indeed, *himalaya* is a Sanskrit word meaning "abode of the gods": The north summit of sacred Gaurisankar, 7,144 m (23,438 ft), represents Shiva; the south Parvati, his consort. Scores of other gods and goddesses make their home among the Himalayas: Sagarmatha atop Everest, and Annapurna, "Goddess of Plenty," atop the 8,091-m (26,545-ft)-high peak of Annapurna I; while Ganesh, the elephant-headed god, resides on top of 7,406-m

Giant statue of reclining Vishnu at Buddhanilkantha in the Kathmandu valley, which measures 4.6 m (15 ft), undergoes daily cleaning by a priest or temple acolyte.

(24,298-ft)-high Ganesh Himal I. All are living deities to most Nepalis.

BUDDHA'S BIRTHPLACE

Lumbini, in the Terai of southern Nepal, is the birthplace of Siddhartha Gautama Buddha. It is as sacred to the world's 300 million Buddhists as Mecca to the Muslims and Jerusalem to the Judeo-Christian faiths. The Buddha was born in 540 BC in a garden under a grove of leafy trees. His mother, Maya Devi, had been on her way to her mother's home in Devadaha when she went into labor and sought sanctuary in the garden. It was hot and humid and the grove of trees provided welcome shade.

Son of King Suddhodhan, the Buddha wanted for nothing as he grew up at his palace home at Tilaurokot, about 27 km (17 miles) from Lumbini. When he played in the garden within the palace walls his eyes often turned northward to the distant Himalayan peaks, then already an inspiration for the founder of what would become one of the world's major religious forces.

At the time of his birth, there was great poverty and hardship among the people, but Siddhartha Gautama, sheltered by royal privilege, knew nothing of this.

He was 29 before he set foot outside the palace, persuading his charioteer to drive him around the nearby countryside. So overwrought was the prince by what he saw that he quit the palace and his family and became an ascetic, wandering the countryside, exploring the religions of the day. Finally, he abandoned his search and became a recluse. He spent his days meditating on life until, under a pipal tree at Gaya near Benares, India, he evolved the philosophy that would sustain millions through the next 2,500 years. Out of this came his name, Enlightened One — the Buddha.

He reasoned that the way to enjoy life to the full was to reject extremes of pleasure or pain and follow an "Eightfold Path" based on "Four Noble Truths." Mankind suffered, pronounced the Buddha, because of its attachment to people and possessions in a world where nothing is permanent. Desire and suffering could be banished by an attachment to rightfulness.

The individual, he theorized, was simply an illusion created by the chain of cause and effect, karma, and trapped in the cycle of incarnation and reincarnation. Nirvana, the highest point of pure thought, could only be attained by the extinction of self — and the abolition of karma.

In the centuries that have followed the Buddha's death sectarian differences have caused schisms in Buddhism so that, broadly, in India there is the Mayahana school of Buddhism and in Southeast Asia and Sri Lanka the Hinayana school. The latter more closely follows the Buddha's original teachings.

The Buddhism of Nepal belongs to the Mayahana school. This school emphasizes less the individual pursuit of nirvana than compassion and self-sacrifice on behalf of all sentient creatures treading the wheel of life. An enlightened being who postpones personal salvation in order to help others on the path to enlightenment is known as a *bodhisattva*. Tibetan Buddhism, the predominant local influence, features a vast pantheon of bodhisattvas — these can be seen featured in the intricate mandalas of the Kathmandu markets.

At his coronation, on February 24, 1975, King Birendra declared Nepal an international zone of peace in keeping with the first tenet of the Buddhist religion — and 10 years later this zone had been endorsed by 75 of the world's nations.

Both the motif and the heart of this international zone is Lumbini garden, which was visited in 1967 by U Thant, the Secretary General of the United Nations. Many Buddhist nations have constructed their own commemorative shrines to the Enlightened One in Lumbini.

A GARRISON OF GODS

To the outsider Hinduism is a bewildering religion, a remarkable convergence of miraculous gods, moral codes and minutely graded social castes. The codes of Hinduism are set forth in ancient texts such as the

One of Nepal's treasured five-storied temples— Nyatapola in the ancient city of Bhaktapur. When it was dedicated more than two centuries ago its doors were locked, never to be opened again.

Vedas, Ramayana, Upanishads and Bhagavad Gita. But the religion finds popular expression mostly in the worship of seemingly countless gods.

The three gods you cannot help hearing about as you explore the countless temples and shrines of Nepal are Brahma the Creator, Vishnu the Preserver and Shiva the Transformer and Destroyer. Each of these gods has many manifestations or avatars, depending on the attribute they represent: Bhairav the Destroyer of Evil, for example, is an avatar of Shiva and comes in 64 forms. Add to this

but by no means exclusively so. The Hindu pantheon jostles with deities who must be propitiated and entertained with a daily round of offerings and oblations *(puja)*.

Sacred to all Hindus is the domestic cow, also Nepal's national animal. It plays a significant role in the country's religious rites. It is used to exorcise evil spirits and to turn an unlucky horoscope into one of good augury. Devout Hindus often touch a cow's tail in the belief that it will help them across the river Vaitarani on their way to paradise.

the fact that the gods all have their consort and deified "vehicle" on which they travel (Garuda, for example, is Vishnu's mount) and already you have a small host of gods. Other supernumerary deities, such as Ganesh the Elephant-headed, bring the number in the full constellation into the thousands — one source claims 33,000.

Hinduism divides into sects. Most Nepalis are Shaivites (followers of Shiva), Vaishnites (followers of Vishnu), Shaktas (followers of Shakti) or Ganpatyas (followers of Ganesh) — there are many others —

As in India, these bovids are left to wander freely in both town and country. The Hindu religious epic, the Mahabharata, avers that those who kill, eat or allow any cow to be slaughtered are condemned to hell.

When someone dies, families give a cow to one of the Brahmans in the belief that the cow will reach their dead kin in heaven. These days the animal has been replaced by a token gift of one or two rupees to the presiding priest at the funeral.

SHAMANISM

ABOVE: Buddhist prayer stones, *mani* (left), on the trail to Everest, at Solu Khumbu. Buddhist stupa (right) at the village of Chaunrikharka on the approach to Everest.

More ancient than either Hinduism or Buddhism, is a belief in a spirit world that is mediated by the *jhankri*, or shaman. In the isolated communities of the Nepal Himalayas all illnesses are believed to hail from the spirit world and must be banished by means of exorcisms, sacrifices and herbal medicines.

Thus spirits with names like "Warrior King of the Black Crag" and "Great Lord of the Soil God" and "Fierce Red Spirit" are invoked from the shadows of eternity. These take hold of the shaman and then exorcise evil and sickness from the patient.

Convulsive shaking during a ceremony known as *puja* is the key sign of possession.

date on which King Vikramaditya of India defeated Saka in 57 BC. That was when the Nepali calendar, Vikram Samvat, began.

Under the Vikram Samvat, the country is now more than half a century ahead of the rest of the world. Thus, Nepal and its citizens celebrated the dawn of the twenty-first century in splendid isolation. This auspicious event took place in April 1943 at a time when the country's borders were still sealed, and the rest of the world — including some brave Gurkhas — was at war.

If the shaman cannot find the lost soul of the patient then the victim will die.

Minor illnesses, however, are less traumatic, for both patient and witchdoctor. The jhankri invokes a magic formula called *phukne*, and caresses away the pain of the affliction with a broom while reciting sacred prayers, *mantras*.

There are four other New Year days — one based on the solar calendar, two on the lunar calendar and one on the Christian Gregorian calendar.

The Vikram Samvat, the official calendar used for administration and followed by all Nepalis, is based on a lunar-solar system of reckoning.

The second most popular of Nepal's calendars — no doubt because it is widely used by many professional astrologers — is the Shakya Samvat, which also follows a

THE NEPALI CALENDAR — AHEAD OF THE TIMES

Just like the rest of the world, except Ethiopia, Nepal has 365 days and 12 months in each year. But the length of the months differs — from 29 to 32 days. Nepal's first century began at the start of the Vikram era, the

ABOVE: Buddhist *mani* stones (left), adorned with prayer flags, in the high country of the Himalaya. A Buddhist stupa (right) at Thangboche monastery, Khumbu, which stands at 4,267 m (14,000 ft) on the slopes of Mount Everest.

lunar-solar system of calculation. But, it can be confusing. This calendar dates back to the accession of an ancient king, Salivahan. Under this scheme, Nepal has only just begun the second decade of the twentieth century.

What might be called Kathmandu's calendar, the Newar Samvat introduced by the Malla dynasty, is roughly 900 to 1,000 years behind the other two.

Perhaps the most confusing of all is the Tibetan calendar. Based on the cycle of Jupiter, which works in spans of 12 and 60

day), *Budhabar*; Jupiter Day (Thursday) or Day of the Lord, *Brihaspatibar*; Venus Day (Friday), *Sukrabar*; and Saturn Day (Saturday), *Shanisharbar*.

BUDDHIST AND HINDU ART FORMS

Nepal is perhaps the world's greatest treasury of Buddhist and Hindu art — most art in Nepal is of a religious nature. More than 2,500 years of the Hindu and Buddhist faith have given Nepal an unrivaled collection of

years, it was established in Western Nepal about 1,400 years ago. It does not begin with any given year nor is there any certainty about its dates. But it's easily the most colorful, each year bearing the name of one of 12 animals: rat, bull, tiger, hare, dragon, serpent, horse, sheep, monkey, rooster, jackal and pig.

Most Nepalis therefore have a choice of three or four New Year days to celebrate but the universal choice, based on the official calendar, falls somewhere in the middle of April.

The seven days of the Nepal week are named after the planets — Sun Day, *Aityabar*; Moon Day, *Somabar*; Mars Day (Tuesday), *Mangalbar*; Mercury Day (Wednes-

religious architecture and art, from the simple Buddhist stupas to the ornate Hindu pagoda temples.

The Indian Emperor Ashoka was one of the earliest known contributors to Nepal's artistic heritage. Not only did he construct stupas in Patan and Lumbini, and numerous monasteries or gompas elsewhere, but he also established trade, cultural and religious ties between the two areas. Ashoka's priests probably originally brought their own Indian artists (wood and stone cutters, carvers, architects and painters); eventually a professional artist class developed in Nepal with its own style.

The development of a wholly Nepali form of artistic expression seems to have begun between the fourth and seventh centuries AD. Five centuries later, Tibetan influences began to appear in the native art forms: Tantric and Lamaistic themes filled with sinister and demoniac images such as Bhairav, the Destroyer of Evil.

In the thirteenth century Chinese influences became apparent, but the admiration for each other's art proved to be mutual. The Nepali architect Araniko was so venerated for his style that the mandarins of China invited him to Beijing to work for them.

The richest periods of Nepali expression were during the early Licchavi dynasty, between the fourth and ninth centuries, and in the Malla epoch, from the thirteenth to eighteenth centuries. These royal houses were great patrons of the arts, as is the ruling house of Nepal today. Many of the art treasures from these periods were destroyed, not only in the recurrent earthquakes, but also by the Muslim marauder Shamsu-din-Ilyas of Bengal, who swept with his armies through the valley in the fourteenth century, and desecrated virtually every temple and piece of religious art he could find in Patan, Kathmandu and Bhaktapur. But those that have survived are considered so priceless that in 1970 West

Germany undertook to finance their renovation and preservation, and also to make an inventory of the major works, especially the temples.

It is said there are more temples in Kathmandu than houses, but the same seems to hold true outside the valley. And although much of this heritage from the Malla dynasty and that of other eras was destroyed in the great earthquakes of 1833, 1934 and 1988, an incomprehensible amount remains. Students of religion, art or architecture need many months to absorb the wonders of Nepal.

THE PAGODA

Of the many architectural styles in Nepal, one of the most striking is the pagoda. The pagoda temple originated here and is said to have derived from the practice of animal sacrifice. One theory on the evolution of the pagoda argues that worshipers found it necessary to have an altar that was sheltered to keep the rain from extinguishing the fire. It was also necessary, however, to cut a hole in the roof in order to let out the smoke. To keep the rain from entering the hole a second roof was added atop the first.

Most pagodas stand on a square base, or plinth, of brick or wood and have two to five roofs, each smaller than the one below. The uppermost roof is usually made of metal and gilded, as are frequently the lower ones. The buildings are richly adorned with carved pillars, struts, doors and other woodwork. Most decorative carvings are of various deities of all sizes and shapes, such as gods with many arms or deified, humanized animals, often in erotic poses.

The deity to whom the temple is dedicated is normally housed on the ground floor; the upper levels are more decorative than functional. Some art historians believe that the receding upper tiers are intended to represent the umbrellas that protect the deity from the elements. Above the main

OPPOSITE: Ornately carved windows testify to the skills of the famed Newari craftsmen of Kathmandu valley. ABOVE: Intricately made door to Buddhist temple in Patan.

entrance is a semi-circular tympanum or to-rana usually with the enshrined deity as the central figure.

The Nyatapola temple in Bhaktapur is considered the most impressive pagoda in the country.

THE *SHIKARA*

Although the *shikara* is of northern Indian rather than Nepali origin, many of Nepal's temples follow its architectural form: a simple square tower of bricks or stones and mortar, with a small room at the base that houses the god or goddess. Variations on the shikara have pillars, balconies and sur-rounding interconnected towers, which may also house deities.

The Krishna Mandir in Patan is an excel-lent example of a stone shikara, but the most interesting shikara in Nepal is the Mahabuddha, temple of One Thousand Buddhas, also in Patan. This shikara is built with bricks, each containing an image of Buddha.

THE *GOMPA* AND THE HINDU MONASTERY

Another form of architecture indigenous to Nepal and neighboring Tibet is the *gompa*, the Buddhist monastery of the high-moun-tain regions. Although they follow a fairly simple floor plan, all gompas are finely adorned and embellished and many date back to the time of Ashoka. The most strik-ing example of this architecture in Nepal is the Thangboche monastery at Khumbu, near Mount Everest. There are about 400 Buddhist monasteries in Kathmandu valley; those near the stupa at Bodhnath are open to visitors.

Of a more intricate style are the Hindu monasteries, thirty of which are located in the Kathmandu valley. These serve as centers of Hindu study and learning. The most beautiful is probably the Pujahari Math in Bhadgaon.

THE STUPA

The Buddhist stupa is the oldest and sim-plest of the Nepali art forms. On its base, most often a stepped pyramidal platform,

is a solid hemispherical mound in white adorned by a spire. The mound represents the universe and the pairs of eyes on the four sides of the spire symbolize the four elements of earth, fire, air and water. The 13 steps between the dome and the spire rep-resent the 13 degrees of knowledge needed to attain nirvana; the canopy that sur-mounts the top of the spire represents nir-vana. Each stupa is usually ringed by prayer wheels, each of which is given a twirl by devotees as they circle the shrine clockwise.

The oldest known stupas in Nepal are those erected by Ashoka in Patan, but the most famous are those of Swayambhunath and Bodhnath.

DELICATE WORKMANSHIP

Most Nepali art is worked in stone, metal, wood or terracotta. Compared to other art forms, there is very little painting in the history of the country's art, but the fine, filigree detail of Nepali sculptures, in these four materials, is as delicate as any brushstroke.

The earliest expression is Buddhist, dat-ing from about the third century BC. Its sur-viving examples are four stupas in Patan, Kathmandu and the Ashoka pillar at Lum-bini.

Nepali art reached a zenith in the Lic-chavi dynasty. Working in stone, local art-ists learned all that they could from India's Gupta, Deccan and Pala schools of art. These they refined and presented in indig-enous creations with distinctive Nepali fea-tures.

They also began to work in a variety of metals, producing incredibly wrought bronzes of mythical and religious figures. Some of their 1,500-year-old works, exquis-ite in their detail and imagery, still survive in Kathmandu valley.

The metallic sculptures of Tara, Vajra-pani, Maitreya, Umamaheshwara and the Buddha are among the most illustrious, both for their style and their antiquity.

Cairn of *mani* mark the entrance to the Thangboche monastery which guards the approach to Mount Everest, Sagarmatha, revered as "The Mother of the Universe."

More recent examples of Nepali metal work exist in the hollow cast statues of kings and queens, in the gilded sculpted doors and in other artifacts of the ancient art cities of Patan, Bhaktapur and Kathmandu.

Tibetan bronzes are notable for the holes set in them for paper prayers, mantras, votive offerings of grain and precious stones, or for religious icons.

Dating some of these masterpieces defies the art historian. Inscribed with the images of a pantheon of gods, both Bud-

dhist and Hindu, most are believed to be from the Pala or an earlier era.

Even more detailed and expressive than stone and metal are the wood and ivory carvings which grace the buildings of Nepal, on struts, pillars, beams, doors, windows, cornices, brackets and lintels inside and outside temples and private homes. The ivory windows of the Royal palace in Kathmandu's Durbar square are a well-known example of this art form, but countless others can be found in varying stages of repair and disrepair on the once-elegant Rana palaces and villas in Kathmandu. On a walk through the back streets of Kathmandu's Old Town, you can find windows peeking through the tail of a peacock, others grotesquely circled by skulls and a variety of suggestive and erotic motifs.

Developed from the twelfth century as an integral part of Nepali traditional architecture, wood art has always been the specialty of the Newaris.

The Newaris established a large vocabulary including every component part and

exact detail of traditional carving. These medieval texts have been passed down through the generations and still serve as the instructional handbooks for today's wood carvers.

The skill of the Newar craftsman is seen in the absence of either nails or glue in his works. And the erotica that adorn the temples throughout the country leave no doubt about the vividness of their artistic imaginations. Given the Hindu philosophy that worships Shiva's lingam, the religious of old considered the sexual nature of such art and temple decoration profoundly significant.

Nepal's history of terracotta craft stretches back to the third century BC, but in Kathmandu it reached its glory during the sixteenth and eighteenth centuries. Outstanding examples of friezes and moldings decorate the buildings from this era in the Kathmandu valley and can also be found in the region's museums. Of particular note are the long bands of male and female figures, *nagbhands*, that stretch around some temples, depicting Hindu narratives and epics. The main gateway of the Taleju temple in Hanuman Dhoka, Bhaktapur and Patan's Mahabuddha and Maya Devi temples are outstanding examples of this art form.

Pottery-making has been practiced for over one thousand years in Nepal and some fine examples survive. The pottery center of Kathmandu valley is Thimi, where potters turn out outstanding figurines, smoking pipes, lamp stands and flower pots.

RELIGIOUS PAINTINGS

Most Nepali painting is of a religious nature and has existed since the ascendancy of the Lichhavi dynasty in the fourth century. The earliest surviving specimens, however, in the form of illustrated manuscripts, date back only to the eleventh century. These manuscripts were produced in Buddhist monasteries and,

ABOVE: Children gaze from the window of an old Newar house on the sidestreets of Bhaktapur. OPPOSITE: Colorfully attired and bedecked in beads, this wizened old man seems to personify the spirit of Nepal's tribespeople.

together with *thangkas* — a form of painting that features favorite gods and lesser deities and are inevitably subdued in form and color — represent the major form of painting in Nepal.

In recent years the government has asked donor nations and UNESCO to help in the restoration and preservation of Nepal's art works.

It has been estimated that at least half of Kathmandu's most priceless works from the last 2,000 years have been lost in the 40 years since Nepal opened its borders to the

rest of the world, much of it spirited away in a vacuum of control by ruthless middlemen and art dealers acting on behalf of wealthy art collectors and museums in the West, thus robbing Nepal of its artistic treasures.

Out of the country's 200 most valuable paintings — all more than one thousand years old — only three still remain in Nepal.

ETIQUETTE

The idea that foreigners are wealthy is deeply ingrained in Nepali minds. Palms extended, children in the streets chant — "Rupee! Paisa!" Ignore them and they usually smile and run away. And if they persist,

adults normally send them away, for the idea of begging is abhorrent to the Nepali people.

The people are immensely friendly and travelers, even lone women, can move almost everywhere with complete confidence. But bear in mind that the Nepalis have different values and standards from our own. For reasons that may be obscure to you, they may ask you not to enter a certain precinct or photograph a certain shrine. The fact is that they regard any foreigner as ritually polluted.

Superstition and religion are indivisible and are deep-rooted, in Nepali society. Never step over someone's feet or body when you can walk around them and never offer "polluted" food — food that you have tasted or bitten into.

In Nepali custom, the left hand is tainted and it is impolite to pass things or offer something with the left hand. It is just as impolite to receive anything with the left hand. Always use the right hand — or both hands together. This will signify that you honor the offering and the recipient or donor. Most Nepalis take off their shoes before they enter a house or a room, so avoid entering any house unless you wish to spend some time in there — for instance, to eat or to drink tea. The cooking and eating areas must be especially respected. Never enter these when wearing shoes — and remember that the fireplace in any home is regarded as sacred. Most Nepalis squat cross-legged on the ground to eat, so take care not to stand in front of them because your feet will point directly at their food.

RACIAL GROUPS

The two main racial groups are Indo-Aryan and Mongoloid. The southern communities, Brahmins and Chhetris, are of Aryan stock. The Sherpas and Tamangs of the north are pure Mongoloid. In between come such groups as the Newars of Kathmandu, the Kirantis of the midlands, the Gurungs and the Magars, who are a mixture of both.

The main ethnic groups of the midlands are the Kirantis (Rais and Limbus), Tamangs, Gurungs, Thakalis and the Newar. Those of the Himalayan mountains are the Sherpas, Lopas and the Dolpos of remote northwest Nepal who number just a few hundred people. On the lowlands, the main groups are the Tharus, Satars, Dhangars, Rajbansis, Danwars, Majhis and Darais. Among the minorities is a Muslim population that numbers around two percent of the population and about 6,000 Tibetan refugees who have settled in Nepal and obtained citizenship.

Nepal's many diverse cultures have been shaped over thousands of years by the weather and the environment and there is a direct living link between groups still in the Stone Age and the metropolitan elite of Kathmandu who have entered the Jet Age. The country's Stone Age groups, where people still make fire with flint and iron and use stone axes, are found in Bajhang and the high, hidden valleys of the west.

THE GURKHAS

Perhaps the best known of all these communities are the Gurkhas and the Sherpas. In fact, the Gurkhas are not an ethnic but a warrior grouping, with more than 300 years of tradition in the armies of Nepal and as mercenaries in the pay of the Indian and British armies. After tourism, military service in foreign armies is the country's second-largest single source of foreign exchange. Salaries, pensions and related services bring between US$15 and $20 million a year.

The bravery of the Gurkha soldier who forms the elite force of the Royal Nepali Army, is legendary. Short and stocky hillsmen, they have fought and distinguished themselves in some of the greatest battles in military history. During the last two centuries, their daring feats have earned them endless awards, notably 13 Victoria Crosses, considered to be Britain's highest award for valor. Most recently, in the 1982 Falklands War between Argentina and Britain, their bravery was acknowledged yet again.

The name Gurkha denotes their status as the bravest of the brave. It originated from the Gorkhali community of central Nepal, which raised the first two Gurkha battalions in 1763 to serve the founder of the present royal dynasty. Calling themselves the Sri Nath and the Purano Gorakh, these battalions first saw action against the British in 1768. They also took part in separate campaigns against Tibet.

By 1814 this force, made up mainly of Thakuri, Magar and Gurung tribesmen, had slashed their way through the central Himalayas with the *kukhuri* — the fearsome, long, curved blade that by the end of

the nineteenth century had become the most celebrated weapon in the arsenal of hand-to-hand combat.

Their derring-do during the two-year Anglo-Nepal War (1814–1816) impressed Western observers and the British East India Company began recruiting Gurkhas on an informal basis. These informal arrangements continued for another 70 years. When the Gurkhas were formally acknowledged as a fighting force, eight units were already in continuous service in India. Most units were made up of Magar and Gurung tribesmen, but officers had already begun

Women of the Tamang community OPPOSITE and ABOVE, one of the major ethnic groups of the Nepal midlands region.

The Country and Its People

to draw other recruits from the Rais, Limbu and Sunwar tribes of the east and from the Khasas in the west. During the 1857 Indian Mutiny, they demonstrated not only tenacity and bravery but also loyalty that would become equally as legendary. As Bishop Stortford, in a 1930 introduction to Ralph Lilley Turner's Nepali Dictionary, remembered:

...my thoughts return to you... my comrades... Once more I hear the laughter with which you greeted hardship... I see you in your bivouacs... on forced marches

or in the trenches, now shivering with wet and cold, now scorched by a pitiless and burning sun. Uncomplaining you endure hunger and thirst and wounds; and at last your unwavering lines disappear into the smoke and wrath of battle. Bravest of the brave, most generous of the generous, never had country more faithful friends than you.

In the last half of the nineteenth century, these warriors fought all across south Asia, from Malaya to Afghanistan — even in Africa, in Somaliland — displaying remarkable endurance as well as courage.

Several Gurkhas have also distinguished themselves as mountain climbers. In 1894, Amar Singh Thapa and Karbir

Burathoki climbed 21 major peaks and walked over 39 passes in the European Alps in an epic 86-day trek during which they covered more than 1,600 km (990 miles). Thirteen years later, Karbir Burathoki, with Englishman Tom Longstaff, completed the first major ascent of any Himalayan peak, 7,119-m (23,357-ft)-high Trisul. (Between 1921 and 1937, Gurkha porters helped to mount five attempts on the then unclimbed Everest.)

By the end of World War I, more than 300,000 Gurkhas had seen service across Europe, Africa and in the Indian Army. In a battle in Flanders in 1915, Kulbir Thapa won the first of the 13 Victoria Crosses; Karna Bahadur Rana won the second in Palestine in 1918. Certainly, without these doughty stalwarts, Britain would have been even more hard pressed to defend itself and its colonies in World War II. Expanded to 45 battalions, Gurkha troops distinguished themselves in action across the Middle East, the Mediterranean and in Burma, Malaya and Indonesia. Two battalions were formed into crack paratroops. By war's end, the Gurkhas had accumulated another 10 Victoria Crosses.

In 1947, Britain began to dismantle its empire and the Gurkha regiments were divided. Six became the Indian Gurkha Rifles and four the British Brigade of Gurkhas. Subsequently, the Gurkha regiments of the Indian Army fought against China in 1962 and in successive conflicts with Pakistan in 1965 and 1971. The British sector served with distinction in Malaya, Indonesia, Brunei and Cyprus and, in 1965, in action in Sarawak, Lance Corporal Rambahadur Limbu won the Gurkhas their 13th Victoria Cross, for "heroism in the face of overwhelming odds".

Today, the descendants of these brave men sign up for service in faraway British outposts — Hong Kong, Singapore, Brunei and Belize in Central America. It was from there that the Gurkhas were rushed into action when war broke out in 1982 between Argentina and Britain. Described by the Argentinean press as a cross between

ABOVE: Grizzled face of a veteran Sherpa mountain porter. OPPOSITE: Young Sherpa boy at Lukla, the community's high country capital.

The Country and Its People

dwarfs and mountain goats, they presented such a ferocious mien as they advanced on the Argentinean positions that the Latin Americans dropped their weapons and fled — not wishing to discover the Gurkhas' legendary skill at disemboweling the enemy with their wicked-looking *kukhuri* blades.

The Kiranti hillsmen from eastern Nepal are now among the principal recruits to the Gurkha regiments. Of Mongoloid and Tibetan stock, they are said to have won the myth-shrouded battle of

Mahabharat. Their religion is a blend of Animism, Buddhism and Hindu Shivaism.

Numbering more than half a million, they speak a language that derives from Tibet.

Most Kirantis, military mercenaries or farmers, carry the Gurkha kukhuri tucked beneath the folds of their robes. Tradition says that once this is drawn it cannot be put back in its scabbard until it has drawn blood.

Until recently, Kiranti honor could only be satisfied by the slaughter of a chicken or duck. Now they settle for yet another compromise. It is cheaper by far simply to nick a finger and spill their own blood to satisfy this centuries-old tradition.

THE SHERPAS

The Sherpas are a Nepali ethnic group that have earned fame as the world's most skillful high-altitude mountain porters and climbers. Of Mongoloid stock and numbering between 25,000 and 30,000 they migrated centuries ago over the Himalayas from Minyak in eastern Tibet. It was Sherpa Norgay Tenzing who, with Sir Edmund Hillary, conquered Everest; and it is the Sherpas who accompany every

major mountain-climbing expedition. For endurance few are known to equal them. They are Buddhists and they earn their living by trading, farming and herding yaks.

It was A.M. Kellas who first brought Sherpas on a mountain ascent in 1907 in the Indian state of Sikkim. But renown came with the opening of the Nepal Himalayas in the 1950s; so courageous and skillful were they on the perilous slopes that the Alpine Club gave them the title, Tigers of the Snow.

Sherpa Tenzing earned immortality from his ascent with Hillary, but he died penniless in exile in Delhi, India, in 1986. Others of his kin have since followed him to the top of the world. One, Pertemba Sherpa, has been there twice.

The high altitude of the Sherpas' environment has prepared them physically and mentally for the challenges of climbing 8,800 m (29,000 ft) into the sky.

Since the Mongol invasions 700 or 800 years ago, they have maintained much of their nomadic lifestyle; in summer they move up to the sparse pastures above 5,800 m (19,000 ft). In the past, they migrated to Tibet in summer, returning in winter to the Khumbu region. Slowly, they

Yaks provide butter for the lamps that burn in the monasteries and private homes and for the rancid Tibetan tea served in these parts. Arts and handicrafts are limited but images, scrolls, murals and rock carving provide lucrative rewards for those Sherpa priests, or lamas, who have become skilled artisans. The Sherpas belong to the oldest Buddhist sect in Tibet, still largely unreformed.

The priests borrow freely from the arts of sorcery and witchcraft to sustain their authority and sacrifice is a ritual tool to

settled in more permanent communities, tilling the fields and growing vegetables and root crops.

Made up of 18 clans, each speaking its own dialect, Sherpas follow tribal laws that prohibit intermarriage not only among members of the same clan but also between members of specific clans. Gifts of the Sherpa home-brewed beer, *chhang*, are exchanged between heads of families when their offspring become engaged. Weddings are elaborate and lavish affairs with great feasting and drinking.

Traders and money-lenders are prominent in Sherpa society. Usury is widespread, loans at 30 percent interest not uncommon.

deal with the mythological demons and gods who inhabit every peak and recess of the high-mountain region and whose presence is confirmed in the Buddhist scriptures.

THARUS

The Tharus are the indigenous inhabitants of the most fertile part of Nepal, the southern corn and rice belt of the Terai. They number close to a million. Over the cen-

Nepal is a diverse mix of ethnic groups. OPPOSITE: Tamang man (left) at Namche Bazaar on the slopes of Mount Everest. Newari man (right) and two Newari girls ABOVE from the Kathmandu valley, represent the country's oldest community.

turies they have been joined by many migrants from the midland valleys and the mountain highlands. The Terai is also host to the majority of Nepal's 300,000 Muslims — lured to the plains by the climate and fertile soil.

The Tharus, especially those of high-caste birth, are much more conservative and rigid in their values than the rest of their countrymen. In the south they live, together with non-caste communities such as the Danuwar, Majhi and Darai, along the Terai's northern edge, and in the west with the Rajbansi, Satar, Dhimal and Bodo people; they can also be found in the east and Morang.

The Tharus have lived there longest, building up a resistance to malaria and living in cool, spacious, airy houses with lattice-work brick walls to allow in any breeze. Besides farming, they hunt, breed livestock and fish.

Their bejeweled women are noted for their stern demeanor. They marry early, but if the groom cannot afford the dowry he must work for the bride's family — up to five years — to be eligible.

They worship tigers, crocodiles and scorpions, in a form of Hinduism tinged with animism.

NEWARS

In Kathmandu valley, the oldest community is that of the Newars. Descended from the Mongols, they practice a form of the Hindu caste system, ranking hereditary occupations such as carpentry, sculpture, stonework, goldsmith and others according to ritual purity. Their crafts adorn almost every corner of the Kathmandu valley and its cities.

To the Newars, every day is a celebration of life and death. Together with their extended families, they observe a constant round of rituals, worshipping and placating the many deities whose blessings rule their daily lives.

Once a year they honor one of the family cows, usually a calf, which personifies Lakshmi, the goddess of wealth, treating it to grain and fruit. Windows are lit throughout the night to please the divinity who circles the earth at midnight and to bring her blessings on cash boxes and grain stores.

Each stage of a Newar's life is marked by colorful ceremonies. In a land where few people live more than 50 years, the old are venerated. When a man reaches the golden age of 77 years, seven months and seven days, there's a re-enactment of the rice-feeding ceremony, *pasni*, which marks the seventh month of every male child. The elder is hoisted on a caparisoned palanquin and paraded through the town, his wife following behind on a second palanquin. He's given a symbolic gold earring that marks him out as a wise one for the rest of his life.

Death is marked by cremation at any one of the many burning places near the holy Hindu bathing sites, or *ghats*, which in Kathmandu, in particular, line the banks of the Bagmati river.

Mourners walk around the body three times before setting the funeral pyre alight, while relatives shave their heads and ritually purify themselves with the slimy algae-laden waters of the river. After this, the ashes are scattered in the Bagmati and the wind-borne smoke carries the soul to the abode of Yama, the god of death, where it will merge with the divine.

Young Newar girls are symbolically wedded to Vishnu. Thus, married for life, they escape any stigma if widowed or divorced from their earthly husband.

These little sisters also pay homage to their brothers — often their only source of support in old age — during the Tihar Bhaitika festival. The boys, seated behind decorative symbols of the universe, *mandalas,* receive the mark of the *tika* and the blessing, "I plant a thorn at the door of death; may my brother be immortal".

OTHER COMMUNITIES

In the Dhaulagiri region, slashes of brilliant orange or white mark the farms of the Brahmins, Chhetris, Gurungs and Magars. Their gardens are filled with the colors of poinsettias, marigolds and other flowers,

In a small village in the Everest region an infant in a topi peers around a corner.

and shady banyan trees. Barley, wheat, millet, rice and maize are grown in the valleys that lie between the mountains.

The people of the Manang valley, however, are famous for their trading. Tibetan in culture, they travel to many parts of the Orient — Singapore, Hong Kong and Bangkok — to do business.

Another trading community is that of the Thakali people, whose colorful trade caravans of mules, loaded with sugar, kerosene and rice, travel through the low-lying Kali Gandaki gorge, the deepest in the world and, for centuries, one of the most important trade routes linking Tibet with Nepal and India. Like the Manang community, their settlements are distinguished by the flat roofs of their houses.

Of Nepal's diverse communities perhaps the smallest is that of the Dolpos, a few hundred people who herd their yaks and goats in the sterile stony moors of Nepal's western Himalayas. They also grow wheat, barley and potatoes. Lamaist Buddhists speaking a Tibetan dialect, they are mainly traders who use pack beasts to move their goods in caravans from Tibet to the more populous areas of Nepal. They ride tough highland ponies and are adept horsemen.

NATIONAL EMBLEMS

Nepal's national bird is a rare, brilliantly colored pheasant, of the species *Galliformes*, found between the 2,400- and 4,500-meter (7,800- and 15,000-ft) contours of the Himalayas. It belongs to the same family as the peacock.

The ubiquitous rhododendron — of which there are about 32 species, most with red and pink flowers, rarely white — is the national flower. Crimson-red, *simrik*, is Nepal's national color. Regarded as both sacred and auspicious it is considered a symbol of progress, prosperity and action and is visible at all national and sacred occasions. Shiva is supposed to draw power from this dark red hue.

During Nepal's many Hindu festivals, red flowers are presented as votive offerings to the different gods and goddesses. Crimson is also the color that symbolizes married bliss and virtually every Nepali

woman wears crimson during festivals and other sacred occasions.

Red is usually the color of the country's national dress, *labeda suruwal*, which is made of homespun cotton. On some occasions the color of this dress is gray or light brown. It consists of a seamed, double-breasted tunic that extends almost to the knees, fastened by two ribbons; and trousers that are baggy around the thighs but tight at the ankles, similar to the *shalwa qamiz* of India.

For some occasions sophisticated Nepali women wear the Indian sari.

Nepal's national flag comprises two adjoining red triangles — symbolizing morality, virtue and unity — bordered by blue. The top triangle contains a crescent moon emitting eight rays, the lower one, a sun emitting 12 rays. These are symbols of the many legendary solar and lunar dynasties to which the royal family belongs.

The family's coat of arms is decorated with leaf-shaped pieces symbolizing the title of Sri Panch five times glorified. For the crest, the heraldic device uses the plume of a bird of paradise which is believed to have been introduced to Nepal by a former premier, Mathbar Singh Thapa. Below this are the footprints of Paduka, the guardian god of Gorkha, ancestral home of the ruling dynasty. Crossed kukhuris represent the national weapon, the traditional, curved sword of the famed Gurkha battalions. On either side are the sun and the moon, symbol of enlightenment and eternity.

The shield depicts Nepal, from the Himalaya to the Terai and at the center, hands clasped, sits Pashupatinah, creator as well as destroyer of the Universe.

The Sanskrit motto avers that love of mother and motherland is superior even to love of heaven. The soldier recruit and veteran are also represented by a prayer exhorting them to defend their country, so long as the universe shall exist.

Nepal's national anthem wishes for the continued prosperity of the "excellent, illustrious, five times glorified King" and a fivefold increase in the number of his subjects.

Tamang woman at Lukla. Highland people like the Sherpas and the close-knit Tamang are descended from Tibeto-Mongoloid stock. They number about one million and are mainly Buddhist.

The Cities of Kathmandu Valley

KATHMANDU VALLEY

The Kathmandu valley, seat of the Malla kings and repository of Nepali art and culture, is the heart of Nepal. A fertile oasis in the foothills of the Himalayas, Kathmandu valley measures just 25 km (15 miles) east to west and 20 km (12 miles) north to south. But within the compass of that small area, the valley packs in the attractions of three ancient cities and a treasure trove of endowments from antiquity.

Not that Kathmandu valley's attractions are all cultural: Set 1,350 m (4,425 ft) above sea level, the valley is ringed by gentle, evergreen hills touching about 2,370 m (7,800 ft), slate-blue in the misty haze of spring and summer. The eternal backdrop is the Himalayas. From the top of 2,200-m (7,175-ft)-high Nagarkot, you can see the Annapurna massif, Dhaulagiri in the west and Everest in the east.

BACKGROUND

Eons ago the Kathmandu valley was a lake; it was probably drained by one of the cataclysmic earthquakes that occasionally shake the region. Legend has it that the sage Manjushri used his sword to slash a gorge — now spanned by a Scottish-built suspension bridge — at Chobar about eight kilometers (five miles) southwest of the modern capital where the Bagmati, one of Kathmandu valley's major rivers, begins its plunge to the Ganges. There's a temple, of course, right by the gorge — Jal Binayak — that pays homage to the myth. Whatever the cause, the waters left behind a loam so rich that Kathmandu farmers can count themselves blessed. Abundant rains and sunshine combine with the loam to ensure that no land goes fallow.

The ox-plow keeps dominion still over the grain and paddy fields and, outside the metropolitan area, most of Kathmandu's 300,000 people seem to have a small patch of ground to till. Indeed, from a distance, this richly fertile basin must look much the same as it did when it was first farmed. Before then, the only communities lived near the shrines and pilgrimage sites that lay on the slopes of the encircling hills. The earliest settlements in the valley go back well beyond 2,500 years, their beginnings shrouded in ancient myths and legends.

Those that remain, such as the Buddhist stupas, evoke eras long before Kathmandu itself came into existence. The Kathmandu valley is peppered with such stupas — the two most visible are Swayambhunath and Bodhnath

KATHMANDU

Kathmandu is one of the world's most intriguing cities. First impressions can be disappointing — the boulevards and thoroughfares are often choked with traffic and air pollution is a major problem nowadays. But step into the back streets and you enter another world — a medieval maze of narrow alleys lined with old world shops, ornately carved windows overhead. Crowds throng these alleys, a sturdy porter trots past under what looks to be a cargo-hold of goods tucked into a vast sack, a woman stoops to leave an offering of flowers and uncooked rice at a centuries old shrine, the plangent strains of unfamiliar music sing out, curious smells assail the nostrils.

Naturally, Kathmandu, like every other city in the region, is on a collision course with the twenty-first century. As everyone knows — Pico Iyer made it the title of a book — in the tourist district the restaurants show videos; fax and e-mail services are abundant; rush-hour traffic jams are a regular occurrence. But for all this Kathmandu manages to retain its charm.

GENERAL INFORMATION

For a country that generates so much income from tourism, the Department of Tourism is surprisingly listless about the task of supplying information to visitors. Kathmandu has three offices: ((01) 470537, at the international terminal of the airport; ((01) 220818, at Basantapur on Ganga

PREVIOUS PAGES: Gilded conical canopy of the Swayambhunath stupa west of Kathmandu (left), known as the monkey temple and (right) an eighth or ninth-century mask depicting Shiva as an incarnation of Bhairav. OPPOSITE: Beautiful Kathmandu valley.

Path; and ((01) 233581, at Babar Mahal. Free fold-out maps of Kathmandu should be available.

The following contacts may be of assistance:

Tribhuvan International Airport ((01) 470537.

Bus bookings can be made by any of the hundreds of travel agents operating in Kathmandu with a minimum of fuss.

Car Rental: Avis is represented by American Express Yeti Tours ((01) 221234.

Health emergencies: Patan Hospital ((01) 521333, is staffed by Western doctors and is the best of Nepal's hospitals. CIWEC Clinic ((01) 410983, is also recommended.

WHAT TO SEE

Kathmandu divides into the Old City in the west and the New City in the east. The dividing line is Kanti Path, or King's Way, which runs from north to south, skirting the Royal palace and cutting across the diplomatic precinct of Lazimpat and north to the reclining Vishnu of Buddhanilkanth.

Kathmandu's main attractions are in the Old City, with most of the highlights clustered in and around Durbar square and on the far-flung edges of town, notably Swayambhunath, Bodhnath and Pashupatinah. Good views of the city can be had from Swayambhunath and Bodhnath. Unfortunately Kathmandu's most visible landmark, **Bhimsen tower**, Dharahara, a 70-m (200-ft)-high edifice, was damaged in the 1934 earthquake that shook the valley, and is now closed to the public — thus denying what was once a popular and spectacular 360-degree view of the city.

Durbar Square

You might consider pausing and taking a deep breath before entering **Durbar square**. You are about to enter a living museum, a miraculous clutter of pagodas, temples, carved windows and timbered gables, statues of man and beast and gods and goddesses, in a happy collision of styles. The result is an organic devotional growth that is quite unlike anything else in the world. Perhaps its only equals are those a few kilometers away in Patan and Bhaktapur.

It's worth bearing in mind as you explore the square that there is much dispute among scholars about the historical details of the structures and statues you're looking at; but such quibbles are best left to professionals.

Entering from **Basantapur square**, immediately ahead and slightly to the right is a **Narayan temple** with a raised seventeenth-century gray stone statue of Vishnu's personal mount, Garuda, in a kneeling position outside. What's inside nobody's quite sure since the inner sanctum has long been closed.

Facing it is the **Gaddi Baithak**, an ornate annex of the old **Royal palace** built early in the twentieth century by a Rana premier, Chandra Shamsher, during the reign of King Tribhuvan Bir Bikram Shah Dev. It's here that Nepal's top brass gather with the royal family to celebrate Indra Jatra and other festivals and state occasions. There's a throne for King Birendra in the main room, which is lined with portraits of his ancestors.

On the other side of the square, behind the Narayan temple, is a temple dedicated to **Kamdeva**, god of love and lust, built by King Bhupatendra's queen, Riddhi Laxmi and adorned with an immaculate sculpture of Vishnu and Lakshmi. Close by, on a flank of **Vishnumati Bridge**, is the fourteenth-century wooden **Kasthamandap** built from the wood of a single tree, from which it derives its Sanskrit name: *kastha*, wood and *mandap*, pavilion. Renovated in the seventeenth century, it's from this structure also that Kathmandu derives its name. Built in

Beckoning customers, tinsel glitters in the afternoon sun in a Kathmandu bazaar.

the pagoda style, with balconies and raised platforms, it was for many years a place for Tantric worship but is now a shrine with an image of Gorakhnath, a deified yoga disciple of Shiva, as its centerpiece.

On the corner of **Chikan Mugal**, opposite this inspiring fountainhead of the capital, is the lion house, **Singha Satal** — built from the surplus timber left over from the Kasthamandap — with a second-story balcony and several small shops on the ground floor. Standing in the shadows of the Laxmi Narayan is a nineteenth-century temple,

built by King Surendra Bir Bikram Shah Dev and dedicated to **Ganesh**, the elephant-headed god, where the kings of Nepal worship before their coronation. Near the temple to the god of love and lust is an eighteenth-century temple, dedicated to **Shiva** and **Parvati**, **Nava Yogini**, guarded by lion statues. Opposite this is another dedicated to the goddess Bhagvati.

Move along past the Big Bell and a stone temple dedicated to Vishnu and you'll come to a **Krishna temple**. Diagonally opposite is the entrance of Durbar square's inner treasury, the **Hanuman Dhoka** palace, which derives its name from a large statue of Hanuman the monkey-god and the Nepali word for gate, *dhoka*.

All this is something of a royal mall. For three centuries or more, the kings of Nepal have been enthroned here. The most noticeable feature is the house on the corner overlooking Durbar square, which has three distinctive carved windows on one side where the Malla kings used to watch processions and festivals. Two of them are carved from ivory, a discovery made in 1975 during preparations for King Birendra's coronation.

Next door you'll find another large, latticed window with a gargoyle face — a grinning mask in white of Bhairav. Carved in the eighteenth century by Rana Bahadur Shah to ward off evil, it's still there offering benedictions. Each Indra Jatra festival thousands clamor to siphon off sanctified rice beer, *jand*, as it pours from Bhairav's mouth. They'll be particularly blessed, it's believed, if cursed with a hangover next day.

The old **Royal palace** — parts of it have survived six centuries — stands next door and is difficult to miss not only for its scale and form but also because of its massive golden door guarded by stone lions. Elaborately decorated with intricate motifs and emblems, it's a fitting entrance for kings-to-be. In the courtyard inside, on February 24, 1975, Birendra Bir Bikran Shah was crowned King of Nepal. At each corner of the palace stands a colored tower representing one of Kathmandu's four cities — the fourth is Kirtipur.

The Hanuman statue stands at the gate and just by its right-hand side a low fence guards an inscribed seventeenth-century dedication to the goddess Kalika on a plaque set into the wall. The inscription in at least 15 different languages — among them English, French, Persian, Arabic, Hindi, Kashmiri and, of course, Nepali — was written by King Pratap Malla, a gifted linguist and poet. Facing the Hanuman Dhoka there's the sixteenth-century **Jagannath temple**, outstanding for the erotic carvings on its struts.

ABOVE: On Kathmandu's Durbar square colorful foreigners are as much a part of the spectacle as locals and their historical heritage. OPPOSITE: The *chowks* — intersections — of Kathmandu bustle with bazaars. A vegetable vendor (top) weighs his products the old-fashioned way. Two women (bottom) pause to chat at a fabric store.

None of these, however, compare to the **Taleju temple** that rises from a mound to the right of the palace, considered the most beautiful in Kathmandu. Dedicated to Taleju Bhavani, the tutelary goddess of the Malla dynasty who was a consort of Shiva, the three-storied temple reaches about 36 m (120 ft) high and each of the three pagoda roofs is gilded with copper and embellished with hanging bells. The temple is only open to the public once a year, and nobody but members of the royal family are allowed to enter the main sanctum.

that support the second story. Nearby is the small **Hari Shankar temple**, dedicated to Shiva. Walk on to a crossroads where the struts of the three-storied, seventeenth-century Shiva temple, **Jaisi Dewal**, on top of a seven-stepped pyramid, has very finely carved erotica. Set in a yoni behind it is a massive, free-shaped lingam. It's thought the lingam may date back to the Lichhavi era.

Not far away is more classic erotica, on the struts of the **Ram Chandra Mandir** — delicate, but explicitly detailed carvings. Next you come to a stupa ruined in the four-

Durbar Square Environs

One of Kathmandu's most famous attractions is **"Freak Street"**, just off Basantapur square. Its apple pies and hashish were once celebrated the length of the overland trail, from London to… well, Kathmandu. Nowadays, it's a down at heel version of Thamel and the only reminder of the heady days of the sixties and early seventies are a few T-shirts shops and a couple of poorly patronized restaurants.

Some distance south of Durbar square, faced in ceramic, is the three-storied **Adko Narayan temple**, one of the four main Vishnu temples of Kathmandu, guarded by an image of Garuda and lions and liberally adorned with erotic carvings on the struts

teenth century — the **Takan Bahal**, a round stucco mound mounted by a brick building.

From here you can wander around the narrow streets and alleys of the southern end of the Old City, discovering ancient houses and more ancient religious shrines. One, **Machhendra temple** plays a significant role during the Seto Machhendranath festival, when the deity's chariot must be driven three times around the temple as part of the final ceremony, after which the chariot is dismantled and the image returned in a colorful palanquin to its principal temple near Asan Tole.

Southwest of Durbar square, near the Vishnumati bridge, is a revered shrine dedicated to Bhimsen, the god of traders and artisans, whose shops occupy its ground floor. Another manifestation of Shiva, Bhimsen has been worshipped in the valley since the seventeenth century. In the days when Nepal's main commercial trade was with Tibet, every 12 years this shrine was carried to Lhasa on the Silk Road. There are some Buddhist stupas next to the temple.

In the opposite direction, to the north of Durbar square, is a popular three-storied temple, the **Nara Devi**, guarded by red and white lions, dedicated to one of the Ashta Matrikas. Inside women prostrate them-

bar square, is approached through the six-meter (20-ft)-wide Makhan Tole, flanked by a many-hued façade with wooden balconies and columns. Six streets radiate out from the Indra Chowk. Various peddlers wander among the cloth and flower sellers, past a dried-fish market into the bead bazaar where the colors of the tawdry bangles and necklaces dazzle the eye. The Chowk is noted for its three temples, of which the most important is a three-storied house to the south, with white, purple and green ceramic tiles, yellow windows and two

selves surrounded by dazzling ceramic tiles and paintings. Nearby is the three-tiered **Narsingha temple** with its image of Vishnu with a lion's head. Along the same road is an open courtyard with a Swayambhunath-like stupa, **Yaksha Bahal**, with four sensual fourteenth-century carvings of the female form. It faces a painted metal door with two figures, one with four eyes, while above, an attractive woman's face appears out of a carved window frame, entrance to the house of the deity, Kanga Ajima.

Indra Chowk

The Indra Chowk, an area praised for its silk bazaar with many fine blankets and textiles, including woolen shawls, northeast of Dur-

balconies, from one of which hang four gilded griffins. The temple holds a highly revered shrine to Akash Bhairav. During the Indra Jatra festival a large image of Bhairav is displayed in the square when a huge lingam pole is raised in the center. Other important shrines and buildings in the Chowk include a highly venerated shrine to **Ganesh** and the Shiva Mandir, a simpler version of Patan's Krishna temple. This solid stone building is set above a four-stepped plinth where carpet sellers lay out their wares.

OPPOSITE: Old men while away an afternoon in the sunshine on Patan's Durbar square. ABOVE: Religious icon in front of Kathmandu's Jagannath temple.

Beyond Indra Chowk is the open space of **Kel Tole** — a fast and furious Nepali bazaar area, a never-ending hubbub of shoppers, peddlers, sightseers, beeping scooter rickshaws and even automobiles, forging through the narrow street watched by families from the balconies of their houses.

Seto Machhendranath

At the other end of the Chowk, to the east, past a small shrine smeared with blood, is one of Nepal's most revered temples: Seto

Machhendranath is at the center of a monastic courtyard, with its entrance guarded by two splendid brass lions. Each evening, beneath the porch that leads to the courtyard, groups of musicians gather and chant sacred verses, gazing at the temple as it rises behind a foreground of steles, *chaityas* (smaller stupas) and carved pillars, with its gilt-copper roof glowing in the evening sun.

The shrine guards the image of Kathmandu valley's most compassionate deity, Padmapani Avalokiteshwara, also known as Jammadyo or Machhendra. Once a year, around March and April, the image is taken from the temple for chariot processions through the city during the Seto Mach-

hendra festival. Built at an unknown date, the temple was restored in the early seventeenth century. Around the inside courtyard are many shops selling a variety of goods — wool, paper prints, cloth, string, ribbons, beads, curios, Nepali caps and pottery. Near the temple, on a street corner, is a small, Tantric temple, the three-storied **Lunchun Lunbun Ajima**, which carries, between portraits of the king and queen, erotic carvings.

Asan Tole

Northeast from here is Asan Tole, the capital's rice bazaar, where mountain porters gather seeking employment. It's a large open space with three temples, including the three-storied **Annapurna temple**, notable for the upturned corners of its gilded roofs. Many come to worship at its shrine, which contains nothing more than a pot. There's a mini-Narayan shrine near the center of the square and a smaller Ganesh temple.

Kanti Path

Leaving Asan Tole to wander through the fascinating narrow alleys and byways of the ancient Old Town you eventually come to **Kanti Path**, one of the city's main thoroughfares, with a notable ghat on one side of it, the **Rani Pokhari**. In the sixteenth century the wife of the Malla King Pratap built a temple in the center to honor her young son after his death, but it later collapsed. Since then a new shrine has been built. Beside the lake stands **Trichandra College**, built by the Ranas, with its clock tower and the wide expanse of the Tundikhel and the landmark column of the **Bhimsen tower**.

If you head northwest from Asan Tole through the city's vegetable and fruit market, the street becomes narrower and narrower until you reach a door that opens into the **Haku Bahal courtyard**. This has a notable carved window balcony, supported by small carved struts and an exquisitely carved door frame, all dating from the seventeenth century. Nearby is

ABOVE: Every byway in the Kathmandu valley turns up religious icons like this one. OPPOSITE: Bhaktapur's Jamuna goddess, mounted on a turtle.

the three-storied **Ugratara temple**, dedicated to the relief of eye infections and ailments. The temple wall is adorned with reading spectacles that have been donated to whatever Hindu deity presides over the gift of sight.

Continue on now until you see the two-storied **Ikha Narayan temple**, with its magnificent four-armed Sridhara Vishnu, dating from the tenth to eleventh century, flanked by Lakshmi and Garuda. There's another monument to a healing deity, Viasha Dev, the toothache god, opposite this shrine. The idea is that you hammer a nail into this large piece of wood and thus nail down the evil spirits causing the pain. If this fails, there's a street of friendly, neighborhood dentists, complete with off-the-peg molars of all shapes and sizes, in the nearby lane.

If you walk futher north, past a sixteenth-century Narayan temple, you'll find one of the capital's oldest and most remarkable antiquities — a carved black stone **fifth-century image of Buddha**; and beyond that a bas-relief **Shiva-Parvati** as Uma Maheshwar set in a brick case. Continue on now to a passage guarded by lions that leads into a monastery courtyard containing the shrine of Srigha Chaitya, a miniature likeness of the Swayambhunath stupa. It's believed that those too old or sick to climb the hill to Swayambhunath can earn the same merit by making a pilgrimage here.

Swayambhunath

The stupa of Swayambhunath looks down from the top of a 100-m (350-ft)-high hill in the west of the city, the rays of the rising sun setting fire to its burnished copper spire as it floats above the sea of early morning mist that fills the valley. Buddha's all-seeing eyes, in vivid hues, adorn all four sides of the base of the spire, keeping constant vigil over Kathmandu. Many believe this sacred ground protects the divine light of Swayambhunath, the Self Existent One who, when the waters drained from the valley, emerged as a flame from a lotus blossom atop this hill.

In the Kathmandu valley, temples and dwellings merge into one another in what must be one of the world's most bewitching urban landscapes.

The Cities of Kathmandu Valley

The site of Swayambhunath was holy ground long before the advent of Buddhism, perhaps at a projecting stone that now forms the central core of the stupa. Here, it is said, Manjushri discovered the Kathmandu lotus that floated in its ancient lake.

The stupa's earliest known work was carried out in the fifth century by King Manadeva — confirmed by an inscription dated AD 460, some 600 years after emperor Ashoka is reputed to have paid homage at the site. Destroyed by Bengali troops in the

mid-fourteenth century, it was rebuilt by the seventeenth-century Malla monarch, King Pratap, who added a long stairway leading to it, two adjoining temples and a symbolic thunderbolt at the top.

The stupa is shaped like a lotus flower and in the last two thousand years saints, monks, kings and others have built monasteries, idols, temples and statues there; they now encircle the original stupa and the entire hilltop. Today pilgrims and the curious climb laboriously up King Pratap's 365 flagstone steps. Even if you have no sense of religion or history, you'll find the antics of the monkeys, which inhabit the temples and the shops, fascinating — they use the handrails of the steps as a slide — and the

views over Kathmandu as breathtaking as the stiff climb. Nepali legend says the monkeys are descended from the lice in Manjushri's hair which, as they dropped to the ground as he had his hair cut, sprang up as monkeys. It is also said that each strand of his hair which fell also sprang up again — as a tree.

On the stupa, the Buddha's all-seeing eyes gaze out in the four cardinal directions. Beneath the eyes, where you would expect a nose, is the symbol for the Nepali numeral "one", a representation of the one path to enlightenment. Above the eyes is the third eye, which represents the omniscience and wisdom of Buddha.

Mounted on a brass pedestal before the stupa is the thunderbolt, or *vajra* — all powerful — representing the divine strength of Lord Indra, King of the Heavens, in contrast to Buddha's all-pervading knowledge. Beneath the pedestal stand the 12 animals of the Tibetan zodiac: rat, bull, tiger, hare, dragon, serpent, horse, sheep, monkey, rooster, jackal and pig.

There's a daily service in the monastery, or *gompa*, facing the stupa — a rowdy and, to western ears, discordant clanking of instruments, blaring horns and a mêlée of saffron-robed worshippers. The eternal flame, Goddesses Ganga and Jamuna, is enshrined in a cage behind the stupa where a priest makes regular offerings.

Opposite, on a neighboring hill, the serene image of Saraswati, goddess of learning, gazes on the often frantic throng around Swayambhunath in benign astonishment.

Bodhnath

For all its size, Swayambhunath takes second place to a stupa northeast of the capital. Dedicated to Bodhnath, the god of wisdom, it's the largest stupa in Nepal — an immense mound surrounded by a self-contained Tibetan township and ringed by the inevitable prayer wheels, each given a twirl as devotees circle the shrine clockwise.

Basic fare in Kathmandu is flavored with seasonings such as chilies ABOVE laid out to dry in a Kathmandu street. OPPOSITE: Kathmandu skyline (top). A jumble of handcrafts and souvenirs (bottom) beckons in a Kathmandu bazaar.

Most worshippers here are from Tibet. The Bodhnath lama is said to be a reincarnation of the original Dalai Lama, for the stupa's obscure origins are tenuously linked to Lhasa, ancestral home of the now exiled spiritual leader.

Legend says the stupa was constructed by the daughter of a swineherd, a woman named Kangma. She asked the king of Nepal for as much land as the hide of a buffalo would cover on which to build the stupa. When the king agreed, Kangma sliced the hide into thin ribbons, which

ambiance. There are a number of new monasteries in the Bodhnath region, and one, in the form of a castle, on the forestd slopes beside Gorakhnath cave. This monastery guards the footprints of a fourteenth-century sage who lived in the cave as a hermit.

Not far from this cave, the Tibetans have built another monastery — commemorating the memory of Guru Padma Rimpoche Sambhava, a saint who rode down to Kathmandu from Tibet to conquer a horde of demons.

were joined into one and laid out to form the square in which the stupa stands. Legend says that a relic of the Buddha lies within the solid dome, which symbolizes water and is reached by 13 steps, again symbolizing the 13 stages of enlightenment from which the monument derives its name, *bodh* meaning enlightenment and *nath*, meaning god.

Saffron and magenta-robed Tibetan monks celebrate their colorful rituals with worshippers chanting prayer verse, mantras and clapping their hands as travelers, especially those heading for the high Himalayas, seek blessings for their journey.

With about 5,000 exiles living in the valley, Kathmandu has a distinctly Tibetan

Godavari Royal Botanical Gardens
Nepal's flora enchanted early European visitors, who exported it lock, stock and root to their own climes. In the words of Nobel laureate Rudyard Kipling:

Still the world is wondrous large —
seven seas from marge to marge —
And it holds a vast of various kinds of man;
And the wildest dreams of Kew
are the facts of Kathmandu

Perhaps the easiest place to see many examples of Nepal's unique flora is Godavari Royal Botanical Gardens, located at the foot of the valley's highest point, 2,750-m (9,000-ft)-high Pulchoki hill, where the sacred waters of the Godavari spring from a natural cave.

Godavari has some 66 different species of fern, 115 orchids, 77 cacti and succulents and about 200 trees and shrubs as well as many ornamentals — though this represents only a small proportion of the country's 6,500 botanical species. It also features orchid and cacti houses, as well as fern, Japanese, and water gardens. Throughout, by lily ponds and on grassy slopes, the visitor finds rest and shade in thatched shelters.

Every 12 years, thousands of pilgrims journey from all over Nepal and India to bathe in the divine and healing waters of the Godavari spring.

Changu Narayan temple

On another hilltop stands Kathmandu's most ancient temple, Changu Narayan, glorious in its almost derelict splendor; its struts and surroundings are decorated with hundreds of delicately-carved erotic depictions. Founded around the fourth century AD, it represents the very best in Nepali art and architecture. It's difficult indeed to imagine a more stunning example of what Kathmandu valley is all about. Woodwork, metalwork and stonework come together in dazzling harmony nowhere to greater effect than in the sculptures of Bhupatendra, the seventeenth-century Malla king and his queen. There's also a human-sized figure of Garuda, with a coiled snake around his neck, close to the country's oldest stone inscription which records the military feats of King Mana Deva who ruled from AD 464 to 491. Although fire and earthquake have often damaged Changu Narayan and its environs over the centuries, this link with the ancient past is still evident in the image of a lion-faced Vishnu ripping the entrails out of his enemy.

Life's daily rhythms here in the cobblestone square are unchanged, too, with its pilgrim's platforms and lodges, *dharmsalas,* surrounding the square and the central temple. Cows, chickens, pye-dogs and runny-nosed urchins wander around while women hang their saris out to dry in the warm evening sunlight, which like some pastoral idyll of old, bathes the red brick in glowing orange.

The Cities of Kathmandu Valley

Pashupatinah

Pashupatinah is the holiest and most famous of all Nepal's Hindu shrines. Perched on the banks of the Bagmati, at **Deopatan**, Pashupatinah is reserved exclusively for Hindu worshippers. A series of terraces on the opposite bank — thickly populated with hundreds of rhesus monkeys, regarded by Hindu believers as kin of the gods, sun and stars — provides the best view of the pagoda's gilded copper roof, sadly surrounded by tatty, corroded tin roofs and higgledy-piggledy power lines.

There was a temple here as early as the first century AD; a settlement here in the third century BC may well have been the valley's first.

In the age of mythology Lord Shiva and his consort lived here by this tributary of the holy Ganges, making it, by the reckoning of some, a more sacred place of pilgrimage even than Varanasi on the Ganges. The Hindu holy men, *sadhus,* dressed in loin cloths and marked with cinder ash, looking immensely wise — but still wanting cash for picture sessions — sit cross-legged everywhere meditating, surrounded by the

Novice monks OPPOSITE at a Kathmandu monastery and ABOVE Buddhist monks at Bodhnath stupa in Kathmandu valley.

temple's delicate gold and silver filigree work.

For the visitor, the most astonishing thing about almost any Hindu shrine is its shabbiness. It's best to bear in mind that after centuries of use these are not historic monuments or museums but living places of worship, in many cases sadly in need of immediate renovation to preserve their glories. Pashupatinah is no exception. Much of the exterior is close to collapse, stained with the patina of centuries and with litter lying everywhere. Pashupatinah's most precious

treasure is its carved Shivalings or Shiva's phallus, stepped in a representation of the female sex organ, or yoni, of Parvati, Shiva's consort.

Gokarna Safari Park

Pashupatinah is not far from the forested slopes of Gokarna, close to the open glades and myriad birds of a Royal Game Sanctuary that's now open to the public as a safari park. For those who hanker after a touch of Maharajah-style travel, elephant rides are available between 9:30 AM and 4:30 PM across a nine-hole golf course among herds of grazing chital, rare black buck and other deer, rabbits, monkeys and pheasants.

New City

New road (Juddha Sadak) connects the Old City and the New City. Built over the devastation caused by the 1934 earthquake, it runs east from Basantapur and Durbar square to **Tundikhel**, the vast swathe of land that serves as Kathmandu's parade ground. The royal pavilion is used by the king to review parades on state occasions. It is decorated with statues of the six Gurkha heroes of the two world wars and around the park are equestrian statues. The park, according to local lore, was the home of a mythical giant, Gurumapa and each year, during the Ghode Jatra festival, a buffalo and mounds of rice are laid out in supplication to Gurumapa, to keep the peace.

As for New road itself, it is a commercial hub, harboring everything from the latest electronic appliances, cosmetics, expensive imported food and drugs, to jewels and priceless antiques. Halfway along the road is a small square shaded by a pipal tree, where intellectuals meet to philosophize and debate. Facing the Crystal Hotel at the end of New road is a supermarket close to a small, isolated shrine. There's also a statue of Juddha Shamsher Rana, prime minister from 1932 to 1945, who masterminded the building of New road.

Running off New road are a network of paved alleys, each with squares and corner patis, central chaityas and occasional temples, between traditional terraced houses. The medieval ambiance creates an authentic time warp, save for the gossiping crowds and the persistent whine of transistor radios. Westward is **Basantapur**, a large open space where the royal elephants were once kept — it takes its name from a large tower looming over the massive Hanuman Dhoka palace.

When New road was completed, the square turned into a marketplace, to be replaced by a brick platform built for King Birendra's coronation celebrations in 1975. Touts sell an assortment of cheap bric-a-brac — local trinkets, bracelets, bangles, religious images, swords and knives — throughout the square.

The two architectural triumphs of the

New City are the imposing **Narainhiti Royal palace**, built during the reign of King Rana Bahadur Shah and extended in 1970 to commemorate the wedding of Crown Prince Birendra, who is now the king; and Kathmandu's most impressive architectural work, the **Singh Durbar**. With the restoration of royalty in 1951, the Singh Durbar's 1,000 rooms, in the middle of a 31-hectare (77-acre) compound, were put to use as government offices. Unfortunately, much of it burned down in 1973. Its most impressive feature, the mirrored Durbar hall furnished

Auto-Rickshaw

Kathmandu's auto-rickshaws or "public scooters" follow fixed routes. Sensibly, very few foreigners use them. Black-and-yellow metered scooters are more popular. Although metered, fares are negotiated and should cost about half that of the taxis.

Rickshaw

Kathmandu's gaudy, honking rickshaws form part of the capital's vibrant street canvas. These large tricycles accommodate

with a throne, statues, portraits of dead rulers and a line of stuffed tigers, still survives. Today the Nepali Parliament, the Rastriya Panchayat, meets in the Singh Durbar, which also serves as the headquarters of the national broadcasting system (the first television transmissions didn't begin until May 1986).

GETTING AROUND

Trolley Bus

A fleet of quiet, pollution-free trolley buses, provided by China, ply the 18 km (11 miles) between the traffic circle beside the National Stadium and Bhaktapur; they cost next to nothing.

two passengers under cover in the back. Be sure that you agree on the fare before you set off and that the driver knows your destination. They should not cost more than taxis.

Taxi

Taxis, with white on black registration plates, travel throughout the Kathmandu valley. Fares are negotiated before setting off — the meter is purely decorative. Special half- and full-day rates may be negotiated.

OPPOSITE: A woman prostrates herself in prayer at the ancient Buddhist Swayambhunath temple, Kathmandu. ABOVE: Giant Buddha statue at Swayambhunath .

Bicycle

Cycling is one of the most popular means of exploring the capital and the valley. These days, mountain bikes can be hired from many shops in the Old City and near the main hotels, though standards vary enormously — check that the bell, brakes and lights work. If there are no lights carry a flashlight as it is required by law — and enforced. For a few rupees children will take care of the bicycle when you visit a popular tourist spot. Elsewhere, it is safe to leave it unattended (but locked) while you go sightseeing.

Motorbike

Motorbike hire is popular among young travelers. An international license is essential. Rates are economical for Indian-made 100 cc Hondas motorbikes, but more substantial motorcycles are also available for hire.

Bus

Kathmandu's severely overcrowded local buses are not recommended. For long-distance buses, the main bus station is on the Ring road, northwest of town, though most foreign travelers make their bus journeys on tourist buses which leave from the Thamel end of Kanti Path.

WHERE TO STAY

Kathmandu provides travelers with a wide range of accommodation options — from the lap of luxury to basic guesthouse bed and washroom standards — and everything in-between. There is truly something for everyone.

LUXURY

The best all-around choice if you're looking for five-star standards combined with some local color is the **Hotel Yak and Yeti** ((01) 248999 or (01) 240520 FAX (01) 227782, P.O. Box 1016, Durbar Marg, Kathmandu. Located in the city center and built around the wing of an old Rana palace, with 270 rooms, 19 suites, swimming pool, tennis courts, gymnasium, jogging trail, casino, shopping plaza and all the other services you might expect, the Yak and Yeti also maintains a much cherished historical association with Boris Lissanevitch's Royal Hotel: the copper chimneyed fire place from Boris's legendary Yak and Yeti bar (once the only expatriate haunt in all Kathmandu) can now be found in the Yak and Yeti's Chimney Room Restaurant (see WHERE TO EAT, below). The rooms with garden views are particularly sought after.

One of the great attractions of the **Hotel Shangri-la** ((01) 412999 FAX (01) 414184, P.O. Box 655, Lazimpat, Kathmandu, is its back garden, much favored as a sunny

retreat to while away an afternoon with a book — the unusual swimming pool is constructed along the lines of a traditional bathing ghat. The Shangri-la has the full complement of services and restaurants, the latter including Tien Shan, probably the best Chinese dining in all Nepal. As is the case at the Hotel Yak and Yeti, request a room with a garden view.

Less conveniently located but also boasting impeccable standards is the **Everest Hotel** ((01) 220567 FAX (01) 224421, P.O. Box 569, New Banesworth, Kath-

OPPOSITE: A treasury of ornate medieval architecture (top and bottom) adorns the cities of Kathmandu valley. ABOVE: The delicate filigree on Bhaktapur's Golden Gate.

mandu. First impressions in the lobby, which brims with fascinating displays and bric-a-brac, are unlikely to be dashed elsewhere in the hotel — the room furniture is tasteful, if slightly worn in some rooms. The hotel has a swimming pool, tennis court, shopping arcade, restaurants, a rooftop bar and restaurant (at eight floors, the Everest is Kathmandu's tallest hotel) a casino and one of the few discos in Kathmandu.

MID-RANGE

Without a doubt the most unique hotel in Kathmandu is **Dwarika's Kathmandu Village Hotel** ((01) 470770 FAX (01) 471379, P.O. Box 459, Battisputali, Kathmandu. A winner of the Heritage Award from the Pacific Asia Tourist Association (PATA), Dwarika's is a hotel that comes close to being a museum. Many of the fittings in the hotel have been rescued from buildings slated for demolition or on the verge of collapse and faithfully restored by a team of craftspeople employed by the hotel. The rooms combine modern comforts with tasteful antique fittings and there's a wonderful sense, if you stay here, of having made a small contribution to the maintenance of Nepal's rich but threatened artistic heritage.

Coming in at the expensive end of the mid-range is the **Hotel Shanker** ((01) 410151 FAX (01) 412691, P.O. Box 350, Lazimpat, Kathmandu. This is one instance, however, where that little extra makes all the difference. The majestic old building — in the style of a European palace — makes staying here is a grand experience. The one catch is that room standards and sizes vary considerably, and some of the rooms are disappointing.

There's a lot to be said for the convenience of a Thamel location — great shopping and almost unlimited opportunities for dining out. One place that provides this along with standards above the average Thamel guesthouse is the **Hotel Manang** ((01) 410933 FAX (01) 415821, P.O. Box 5608, Thamel, Kathmandu. Rooms are air-conditioned, sport mini-bars and satellite television and on the upper floors offer good views.

INEXPENSIVE

Most of Kathmandu's best deals are in the tourist enclave of Thamel, an area in which sizzling steak restaurants rub shoulders with handicraft stalls, providers of e-mail services and trekking agencies. Of near legendary status is the **Kathmandu Guest House** ((01) 413632 or 418733 FAX (01) 417133, P.O. Box 2769, Thamel, Kathmandu. The rooms are simple, ranging from back-to-basics to lower mid-range comfort, but praise is reserved mostly for the garden area, which in Kathmandu's perennially sunny weather is usually littered with basking travelers recuperating from the rigors of the last trek or reading up on the next one. Services are basic — laundry, travel bookings and so on — but the building is a delightful warren and it's in the heart of Thamel.

A relative newcomer to the crowded Thamel accommodation scene is the Tibetan-managed **Utse Hotel** ((01) 226946 FAX (01) 226945, Jyatha, Thamel, Kathmandu. The spotless, carpeted rooms with television and private bath are a good value, but it is the rooftop garden that wins most guests' hearts. Downstairs, off the lobby, is a popular Tibetan restaurant.

For inexpensive lodgings outside the busy Thamel area, the embassy district of Lazimpat has the appropriately named **Hotel Ambassador** ((01) 410432 FAX (01) 413641, P.O. Box 2769, Lazimpat, Kathmandu. Given that you're still only a 10-minute walk from Thamel, the Ambassador provides the best of both worlds — peace from the touts and bustle and easy access to the restaurants and attractions of Kathmandu. The hotel has a good range of well-maintained rooms; downstairs are a sunny coffee shop and Indian restaurant.

WHERE TO EAT

For weary world travelers, Kathmandu has a reputation as the gourmet capital of the sub-continent. Whether you feel this sobriquet is deserved will probably depend on where you have arrived from. It has to be said that most of the restaurants in Thamel,

A Thamel souvenir stand displaying gleaming metalwork.

which offer a vast range of continental, Mexican, Tibetan, Chinese and even Thai cuisine, are doing a good job under the pressure of limited resources; but few Thamel restaurants bear up to repeat visits.

Most of Kathmandu's best restaurants are outside Thamel, on Durbar Marg, or in the major hotels around town. Prices here are very reasonable: even scaling Kathmandu's culinary heights, you'll be hard pressed to spend more than US$20 per person. Naturally it is Nepali and Indian food that locals do best, but there are also one or

Al'Fresco Restaurant, Soaltee Oberoi ((01) 272550/6, may be indoors but it does at least offer pleasant views of the hotel gardens, not to mention the best Italian dining in Kathmandu. It's popular with the "expat" community — who like to forget they are in Kathmandu from time to time. Open daily. Reservations are recommended.

The **Chimney Room**, Hotel Yak and Yeti ((01) 413999, owes its reputation at least in part to a nostalgic connection with Boris Lissanevitch, the Russian ballet dancer,

two good Chinese, Japanese and Italian restaurants for those seeking a break from the spices.

EXPENSIVE

Universally lauded as Kathmandu's premiere Indian restaurant, **Ghar-e-Kabab**, Hotel de l'Annapurna ((01) 221711, is the perfect spot for a memorable evening out. The tandoori here is as good as you'll find anywhere. You can watch the chefs at work, and in the evenings listen to the exotic sounds of live classical Indian music. Open daily. Reservations are recommended.

A rickshaw operator ABOVE waits for customers while a sidewalk vendor OPPOSITE sells garlic and shallots in a Kathmandu street.

world traveler and chef who is remembered as having established Kathmandu's first hotel. The name is taken from the copper fireplace that came from Boris's Royal Hotel. The Russian–continental menu features some of Boris's specialties, such as his celebrated borscht and chicken Kiev. Open daily. Reservations recommended.

Providing you are prepared to forego sushi and sashimi, you can have a surprisingly good Japanese meal at **Fuji Restaurant** ((01) 225272, Kanti Path. The setting — French windows giving out onto a pond and summer alfresco dining — is as much a treat as the food. Regular diners wax enthusiastic about the *obento*, set meals — for both lunch and dinner.

Closed Mondays. Reservations recommended.

Probably the best Chinese food in town is the Sichuan and Cantonese fare at **Tien Shan** ((01) 412999, Shangri-la Hotel. Try the Sichuan dishes — the chef, from Chengdu, knows what he is doing.

INEXPENSIVE

Thamel is teeming with inexpensive restaurants, but if you want to take a look at where the locals eat and drink, wander down to **Nanglo** ((01) 222636, Durbar

to the original Mike's, which of course does it better. Open daily.

The **Old Vienna Inn** ((01) 419183, Thamel, is one of the few Thamel restaurants that deserve a special mention. It's another long-runner, with a small army of aficionados. The menu features Austrian and German favorites. The chocolate cake is legendary. Open daily.

Another excellent Thamel restaurant is the **Third Eye** ((01) 227478, Thamel. It has two major selling points: the best tandoori in Thamel; and an intimate, sit-on-the-floor

Marg. There's a rough and ready bar and Chinese restaurant downstairs, but out the back and on the roof is a beer garden with tasty barbecue dishes and some average generic Western cuisine. In the winter months, local "expats" gather downstairs, knock back the beers and munch on Tibetan momos. Open daily.

Mike's Breakfast, Naxal, is an institution. As the name suggests, breakfasts are the specialty, but lunch and dinner are excellent too. Meals are served in a delightful garden. There's an art gallery upstairs featuring local artists and occasional exhibitions by foreign photographers and painters. The **Northfield Café** in Thamel is run by the same management, but this is no excuse to skip a trip out

room at the back. This is one of the few Thamel restaurants where a reservation is a good idea. Open daily.

It's impossible to leave Thamel without mentioning two more restaurants: **Le Bistro** ((01) 411170, Thamel, and **KC's** ((01) 416911, Thamel. It is the upstairs views over one of Thamel's busiest intersections, the faint strains of blues and jazz coming from the Blue Note café next door, that make Le Bistro an essential stop on the Thamel restaurant circuit — the food is average. KC's, on the other hand, is remembered as one of the Thamel pioneers: many of the Thamel standards — such as sizzling steak — had their start here. The sizzling steaks and vegetarian lasagna are still good.

NIGHTLIFE

Kathmandu is not a place for late night carousing. Everything closes at 10 PM. For a quiet drink before an early night, try **Blue Note**, an upstairs Thamel bar with candlelit tables and a wide selection of jazz and blues.

Kathmandu's casinos are an exception to the early-to-bed rule. There are four of them these days, catering largely to an Indian clientele — Nepalis are denied entry. Kathmandu's casinos are: **Casino Anna**

((01) 223479, Hotel de l'Annapurna; **Casino Everest** ((01) 220567, Everest Hotel; **Casino Royale** ((01) 228481, Hotel Yak and Yeti; and **Casino Nepal** ((01) 270244, Hotel Soaltee Oberoi.

HOW TO GET THERE

For details of air and bus services to Kathmandu see GETTING AROUND and GETTING THERE sections of TRAVELERS' TIPS.

The easiest way into town from the airport is by taxi. There is an official taxi stand just outside the exit to the Departure Lounge at Tribhuvan International Airport. Avoid touts offering free taxi rides into town. The major hotels all offer airport connections.

PATAN

Patan, around five kilometers (three miles) south of Kathmandu, over the Bagmati River, is less a distinct city than a district of Kathmandu these days. But in medieval times, until the Gurkha conquest of the valley in 1768, it was the largest of the three Kathmandu valley kingdoms. As Kathmandu rose to prominence, Patan became a quiet backwater.

It is this that makes Patan such a charming retreat from Kathmandu. The city is resolutely Newari; there's an old-world ambiance to the tangled skein of alleys, where domestic animals wander freely and locals still have time to pass the time of day with each other. When you need a break from Kathmandu but you're still not ready for the hills, Patan is the perfect getaway.

WHAT TO SEE

Durbar square

At the entrance to Patan's Durbar square, another royal mall, is an octagonal **Krishna temple**. Nearby is an immense copper bell cast in the eighteenth century by Vishnu Malla and his queen, Chandra Lakshmi. Traditionally, its deep sonorous clanging summoned worshippers, but it was also used as an early warning system in the event of emergencies: fires, earthquakes and raiding armies. How the people of Patan distinguished between the call to divine duty and the warning to take cover remains unexplained.

Set next to the Krishna temple is a three-storied **Vishnu temple** notable for its tympanums, the ornate triangular recesses set between the cornices of its low gables.

One of Patan's oldest temples, **Charana-rayan,** is believed to have been built around 1566 by King Purendra, although now architectural historians suspect it belongs to the seventeenth century. The struts of this two-storied pagoda building, embellished with lively erotica — either inspiring or inspired by the *Kama Sutra* — will impress gymnastics enthusiasts.

The centrally placed **Krishna temple** is unmistakable. One of the most beautiful

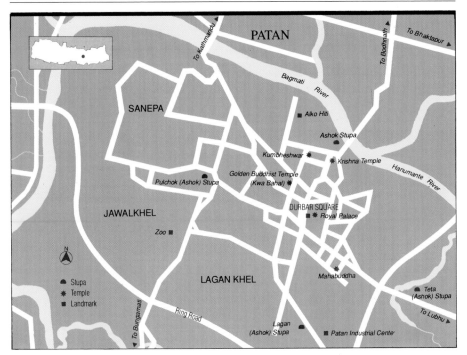

temples in the country, generally regarded as a masterpiece of Nepali architecture, it's built entirely of limestone, a legacy of King Siddhi Narsimha Malla, who reigned for 41 years in the seventeenth century. The annual focus of thousands of devotees celebrating Krishna's birthday around August to September is the narrative carving on the frieze, depicting the stories of the epic Mahabharata and Ramayana. It was the king's son, Shri Nivasa Malla, who in 1682 restored the undated Bhimsen temple after it was damaged by fire. Since then, following the 1934 earthquake, it's been restored once more. The gods make Patan tremble frequently.

Not only the gods wreak havoc in Patan. When King Prithvi Narayan Shah swept into the valley in 1768 to oust the Mallas, Patan's fourteenth-century Royal palace was badly damaged, but its ornate gates, delicately-carved struts, statues, open courtyards and many rooms — conference halls, sleeping chambers, kitchens and so forth — remain to recall the glory of Malla architectural splendor. One of these many splendors is the eighteenth-century **Taleju temple,** built as an additional story to the palace itself and tragically destroyed in

1934. Now rebuilt, it's open only 10 days each year, during the September to October Chaitra Dasain festival. This temple, **Taleju Bhavani,** though smaller and less impressive than the original, is held more sacred.

Of all of its statuary, Patan's most imposing monument is the sculpture of **King Yoganarendra Malla** seated on a lotus atop a six-meter (20-ft)-high pillar in front of the **Degatule Taleju temple.** He ruled at the beginning of the seventeenth century and is the subject of a still popular belief among Patan folk that one day he will return to take up his rule again. For this reason, one door and one window in the palace always remain open to welcome him.

Patan's treasures are not confined to the immediate precincts of its Durbar square. Five minutes walk away there's a **Golden Buddhist temple** and another Buddha shrine, Mahabuddha, two kilometers (1.2 miles) distant. There's also **Kumbheshwar,** one of two five-storied temples in Kathmandu valley where Shiva is believed to winter for six months before leaving to spend his summer with Parvati on the crest of Gaurisankar.

A Kathmandu vegetable market.

SHOPPING

Be sure to shop around before committing yourself to any purchases: prices — and quality — vary considerably.

The best **Tibetan carpets,** old and new, are found at Jawalkhel, near Patan, in the **Tibetan Refugee Center** and many shops.

The **Cheez Beez Bhandar, (Nepali Handicraft Center)** near Jawalkhel, sells **handicrafts** from all parts of Nepal.

Excellent quality **antiques and rare art objects** are on display at the **Tibet Ritual Art Gallery,** Durbar Marg, above the Sun Kosi restaurant; it's run by two experts in the subject.

Woodcarvings, metalwork and thang-kas can be seen at **Patan Industrial Estate**. Bear in mind that it is forbidden to export thangkas and bronzes if they are more than 100 years old.

WHERE TO STAY

Patan has few hotels. Most travelers stay in Kathmandu, which is just twenty minutes away by taxi.

LUXURY

The top hotel in Patan is the **Hotel Hima-laya** ((01) 523900 FAX (01) 523909, P.O. Box 2141, Sahid Sukra Marg, Lalitpur, Kath-mandu. Although it does not match the standards of the best hotels in Kathmandu, the Himalaya can justly boast of its views of the mountains for which it is named. Ask for a room with a view.

MID-RANGE

The **Hotel Narayani** ((01) 525015 FAX (01) 525017, Pulchowk, Patan, was once Patan's best. These days, competition from the newer Himalaya has forced it to bring its prices down. The expansive garden and large swimming pool are winning features of this hotel, but otherwise it is undistinguished.

For many repeat visitors, the **Summit Hotel** ((01) 521894 FAX (01) 523737, Kupondole Height, Patan, is in a class of its own. It may be slightly inaccessible, but this contributes to the hideaway character of the hotel. There's a pleasant garden and swimming pool; but best of all are the views of Kathmandu and the Himalayas from the rooms.

Patan's Durbar square holds matchless treasures of medieval architecture and art.

INEXPENSIVE

The **Aloha Inn** ((01) 522796 FAX (01) 524571, Jawalkhel, Patan, is a good escape if you're fed up with big impersonal hotels. It has a family guesthouse atmosphere, with a small well-tended garden, while maintaining higher standards than the average guesthouse.

Lastly, for a room with a view, the **Third World Guesthouse** ((01) 522187, overlooks Patan's Durbar square. Wake up here in the first glimmerings of dawn and it's easy to feel that you've been spirited into an ancient Oriental citadel.

WHERE TO EAT

Nobody goes to Patan for the dining. The most popular restaurants are more notable for their views of Durbar square than for the dishes they turn out. **Café de Pagode** is typical. It overlooks the square and serves an eclectic range of local and international dishes. If you stop here for lunch, stick to what they do best: the Indian and Nepali dishes. Other, similar, restaurants around the square include the **Café de Patan** and the **Café de Temple**. None of these has a phone or will take a reservation — they are simple, informal places that are perfect for watching life go by.

The **Chalet Restaurant** ((01) 523900, Hotel Himalaya, does good quality Indian, continental and even Japanese food. The ambiance can't compare with the cafés on the square, however.

HOW TO GET THERE

Getting to Patan from Kathmandu is easy — you could walk if the traffic wasn't so disagreeable. Taxis make the 15-minute run from Thamel for less than US$2. The public buses are best avoided.

AROUND PATAN

At the southwestern edge of Patan is **Jawalkhel,** site of the valley's largest Tibetan refugee camp. This area is a center for **Tibetan handicrafts.** In two large buildings, 200 men and women are always busy carding wool and weaving carpets. In the first building, five rows of women in traditional costume sit on the floor, one to three on a carpet, weaving traditional patterns, chatting and singing. In the next building, old men and women comb the wool and spin it into threads. Shops display these handicrafts for sale. Portraits of the King and Queen of Nepal and the Dalai Lama look down from the walls on a maze of carpets, blankets, woven bags and small coats.

Jawalkhel Zoo, near the craft shops in the industrial area, has a selection of exotic

south-Asian animals, especially Himalayan species. Open daily.

South of Patan, various vehicle and walking tracks line settlements and sacred sites of the one-time capital. West of the Bagmati river are **Kirtipur** and its satellite hamlets, **Panga** and **Nagaon.** The twin settlements of **Bungamati** and **Khokana** lie on either side of the sacred Karma Binayak site. There is a road leading to the **Lele valley** and a trail to **Godavari** and **Phulchoki,** passing through **Harisiddhi, Thaibo** and **Bandegaon.** An eastern lane takes travelers to **Sanagaon** and **Lubhu.** All these villages have close links to Patan.

BHAKTAPUR

About 16 km (10 miles) from Kathmandu is Bhaktapur, eastern gateway of the valley. In its present form the city dates back to the

OPPOSITE: Carved stone sentinels guard the secrets locked inside the temple of Nyatapola in Bhaktapur. ABOVE: Bhaktapur after rain shower.

ninth century — King Anand Malla made it his seat in AD 889.

Central Bhaktapur, particularly its Durbar square is something of a showcase. Of the three historic cities in Kathmandu valley, Bhaktapur best retains the medieval flavor of the Malla era. This is no accident. Since the 1970s the German-funded Bhaktapur Development Project has set out to ensure that Bhaktapur's development takes place along lines that best suit the heritage and character of the old city.

good hour can be spent sipping the piquant local tea and studying the erotica on the tea room struts.

Nyatapola is one of two five-storied temples in the valley. (Kumbheshwar is the other; see page 127). From as far back as you can stand it looks like a fretted pyramid climbing up to the clouds, reaching a height of more than 30 m (100 ft). Its inspiration is said to have been appeasement to the terrifying menace of Bhairav, who stands in another temple. There seems to be more than just fancy to this tale. Now more than

Bhaktapur is not just the historically best preserved of the three valley cities, it is also the most thoroughly Hindu and Newar. Even though Kathmandu is just a day's walk away, the Newar people of Bhaktapur speak a different dialect.

WHAT TO SEE

Nyatapola Pagoda

Durbar square is dominated by Nyatapola Pagoda. Tourists stand before it overwhelmed not only by the dimensions of the temple but also by the nonstop hurly-burly of hawkers, pedestrians and children who overrun the place. You can find sanctuary in the Café Nyatapola, opposite, where a

200 years old, its doors were sealed and bolted when the builders finished their job, and have never been opened since. What's inside is anyone's guess. Certainly, no menace terrifies the hordes who swarm over its plinth and up its steps. After all, they are guarded at the bottom by legendary sentinels, Jaya Mal and Patta, two wrestlers said to have the strength of 10 men; next, two huge elephants, each 10 times stronger than the wrestlers; then, two lions, each as strong as 10 elephants; now, two griffins each as strong as 10 lions; and finally, on the uppermost plinth, two demi-goddesses — Baghini in the form of a tigress and Singhini, as a lioness — each 10 times stronger than a griffin. It's a pattern of sentinels

found nowhere else in Nepali temple architecture and considered significant evidence of the measure of appeasement required to placate Bhairav.

Durbar Square

You'll need time to digest all this ambiance, both exotic and enthralling, before walking on to Durbar square to feast on its treasures which begin at its very gate, built of lime-plastered brick in the eighteenth century by Bhupatendra. Its arch is a depiction of the face of glory, Kirtimukha,

gate, alas, is only bronze, but when it catches the sun's rays it glitters and sparkles like the precious metal itself. Ranjit Malla commissioned it in 1754 to adorn the outer entrance to the Taleju temple within the Royal palace, a one-storied shrine with many struts. During the Vijaya Dashami festival the goddess is believed to take up residence in the south wing of the building. It's a superlative example of the artwork of Kathmandu valley, regarded by many as its finest. One of the carved windows is believed to be the personal handicraft of Bhupatendra, whose

guarded on either side by two wooden carvings: one of Bhairav, the other of Hanuman. The gate looks out on three remarkable temples of different styles, whose divine proportions are concealed by all being huddled together: one, the single-storied Jagannath, housing an image of Harishankara; the second, a two-storied Krishna temple standing in front of it and housing images of Krishna, Radha and Rukmani; and the third, the Shiva Mandir, built in the shikara style with four porticoes each with a niche above them for plated images of gods.

Both evening and morning, the sun falls on the north-facing **Golden Gate,** the entrance to the **Palace of 55 Windows.** The

bronze statue — sitting, hands folded reverently before Taleju — faces the Golden Gate. Each of the corners has images of Hindu goddesses Devashri and Lakshmi and in the temple area there's a large bell cast out of copper and iron. The temple opens its doors only once a year — between September and October — during the Dasain festival celebrations, when Taleju's golden statue is placed on the back of the horse that is stabled in the courtyard and led around town in a procession.

After a day craning their necks at the beautiful roofs of Newar temples OPPOSITE, travelers can relax and while away the evening in one of the Thamel district's countless rooftop restaurants such as the Brezel Bakery ABOVE.

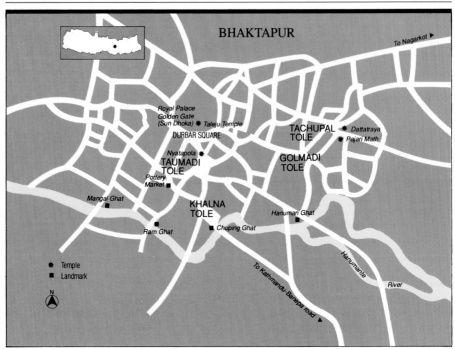

The adjacent palace is renowned mainly for its 55-windowed Hall of Audience, an elaborately carved balcony and its collection of priceless wood carvings, some damaged in the 1934 earthquake but still considered invaluable. Originally built in the fifteenth century, the palace was remodeled by Bhupatendra. Again, this Durbar square also boasts a large bell that was used both to summon worshippers and to give alarms, particularly if there was a night curfew, when it was rung to send citizens scurrying home. There are many more temples in Bhaktapur's Durbar square: to **Kumari, Vatsala, Durga, Narayan, Shiva,** and **Pashupatinah.** The last is the oldest in the city, built around the end of the fifteenth century by the widow and sons of King Yaksha Malla to honor his memory, though some argue it was built much later in 1682 by Jita Malla, father of Bhupatendra.

Bhaktapur legend avers that Lord Pashupatinah appeared before him in a dream and ordered him to build the temple. Another legend has it that the king wanted to visit the temple at Deopatan but was unable to cross the Bagmati since it was in full flood and so ordered another temple to Pashupatinah to be built in Bhaktapur.

The western end of the palace, previously known as Malati Chowk, has been converted into the **National Art Gallery** ((01) 610004. Highlights include wall murals from the Palace of 55 Windows, a large collection of thangkas and some superb sculpture — both Buddhist and Hindu. It's open from 10:30 AM to 4 PM. Closed Tuesdays and national holidays.

Tachupal Tole

It's just a 10-minute walk along the fascinating Main Bazaar from Nyatapola Pagoda to Tachupal Tole, the original center of the old city. Some architectural historians maintain this part of the city may date back to the eighth century. The heart of this district is Dattatreya square, named after **Dattatreya temple**. The temple is very old indeed; it was built in 1427, though alterations were made half a century later. Look for Jaya Mal and Patta flanking the entrance — the same two wrestlers you saw at Nyatapola Pagoda.

Behind Dattatreya temple is the **Bronze and Brass Museum** ((01)   610488, which has a collection of metalwork from around the valley — both ritual and domestic in function. Most visitors find the **National Woodcarving Museum** ((01) 610005, opposite, more interesting. The collection of both architectural carvings and free-standing sculptures is not extensive but quite captivating. Both museums are open from 10 AM to 5 PM (3 PM on Fridays). Closed Tuesdays.

WHERE TO STAY

Bhaktapur is a day-tripper's city. Your ac-

commodation choices are more limited than even Patan. Most of the accommodation is of the extreme budget variety.

INEXPENSIVE

The Golden Gate Guesthouse ((01) 610534, Durbar square, Bhaktapur, may be somewhat spartan, but it's just a hop away from the gate from which it takes its name. The roof offers great views.

If you're looking for a little more comfort, try the **Bhadgaon Guesthouse** ((01) 610488 FAX (01) 610481, Durbar square, Bhaktapur. The rooms are simple but comfortable with basic bathrooms. Again, the rooftop views are picture postcard material.

WHERE TO EAT

Though not a true restaurant city, Bhaktapur, at least provides you with the rare opportunity to dine in a converted pagoda. The **Café Nyatapola**, opposite Nyatapola temple, started life in the eighteenth century as a place of worship; nowadays it does palatable pizzas and tasty samosa, along with all the other international fare you've come to expect of Nepali tourist restaurants.

The **Café Peacock** is on Dattatreya square and possesses what many find to be one of the most charming prospects in the whole Kathmandu valley. The international menu is both cheaper and better than that of the Café Nyatapola.

THIMI

Just three kilometers (1.9 miles) west of Bhaktapur is Thimi — Kathmandu valley's fourth-largest settlement. Founded by the Malla dynasty, Thimi takes its name from the Nepali word *chhemi*, which means "ca-

Potters shape their vessels in traditional fashion at the village of Thimi, near Bhaktapur in the Kathmandu valley.

pable". It's an honor bestowed upon Thimi's residents by the Bhaktapur monarchs for their skill in fighting the forces of the rival kingdoms in the valley.

Thimi is a town of potters where families, taught skills handed down from generation to generation, turn out handsome stoneware fashioned from the red clay of the valley — vessels for domestic use and art works such as peacock flower vases and elephant representations. The colorful sixteenth-century **Balkumari temple** is the town's main shrine and nearby in a much smaller dome-shaped shrine is a brass likeness Bhairav.

Thimi is most renowned as the location, along with two other adjacent villages — **Nade** and **Bode** — of the most riotous of Nepal's New Year (Bisket Jatra) celebrations. Nade is noted for its multicolored, three-storied Ganesh temple, while on the other side of the many dikes that meander through the rice paddies, Bode boasts a famous two-storied seventeenth-century **Mahalakshmi temple**. It stands on the site of an early temple built, according to local lore, in 1512, after Mahalakshmi appeared in a dream to the king of Bhaktapur.

Every year on New Year's Day, the square around the Balkumari temple in Thimi witnesses a spectacular gathering of 32 deities carried in elaborate multi-roofed palanquins under the shade of ceremonial umbrellas after which the Nade idol of Ganesh arrives. Later the crowds move across the field to Bode to witness another extraordinary New Year's ritual (see also YOUR CHOICE, FESTIVE FLINGS, pages 45–53).

LAND OF THE NEWARS

KIRTIPUR

About five kilometers (three miles) southwest of Kathmandu, perched on a twin hillock, twelfth-century Kirtipur was to become an independent kingdom and ultimately the last stronghold of the Mallas when Prithvi Narayan Shah rode into Kathmandu to conquer the valley in 1769–70.

Bhaktapur woman preparing traditional Nepali bread, *roti.*

The city withstood a prolonged siege, during which the Malla army taunted Pritthvi's Gorkha forces as they hurled them back down the fortress-like hill.

It was a mistake. When Kirtipur finally fell, the vengeful Gorkha ruler ordered his men to amputate the nose and lips of all Kirtipur's male inhabitants — the only exception being those musicians who played wind instruments.

Now only the ruined walls remain to remind Kirtipur's 8,000 residents of this epic battle. These days Kirtipur is a place of

trade and cloistered learning. Part of nearby Tribhuvan University's campus now sprawls across the former farmlands.

The traditional occupations, apart from farming, are spinning and weaving. At Kirtipur's **Cottage Industry Center,** 900 handlooms spin fine cloth for sale in Kathmandu.

Though it has withstood the savage earthquakes that have caused so much damage elsewhere in the valley, Kirtipur has been unable to withstand the ravages of time: there's a decayed and neglected air to the city. Still, a walk beneath the exquisitely-carved windows of its multi-storied houses — laid out on terraces linked by ramps and sloping paths — is a worth-

while excursion and there are some fine temples to command your interest.

Kirtipur lies on the saddle between two hills, beside a small lake. The main approach is via a long flight of stairs. Atop the hill to the south there's a huge stupa, the **Chilanchu Vihar,** encircled by eight shrines decorated at their cardinal points by stone images. There are many Buddhist monasteries around the stupa also. On the hill to the north, which is higher, Hindus have settled around a restored temple dedicated to **Uma Maheshwar.**

The three-storied **Bagh Bhairav temple** stands at the high point of the saddle between the two hills, a place of worship for both Hindus and Buddhists. It's decorated with swords and shields taken from its Newar troops after Prithvi Narayan Shah's eighteenth-century victory. It contains an image of Bhairav, manifested as a tiger and the *torana* above the main sanctum shows Vishnu riding Garuda and Bhairav attended on either side by Ganesh and Kumar. From the temple there are striking views of the valley and the brightly colored patchwork of farm fields below, with the villages of **Panga** and **Nagaon** in the southeast.

You can take a path through the rice fields from Kirtipur to Panga, which was established by the Mallas as a fortress town to stall invaders from the north. None of its six or so temples dates prior to the nineteenth century. The path continues from Panga to Nagaon, a name that means "new village".

The sixteenth-century Malla who ruled Kathmandu from Patan, concerned that his subjects might move too far from the city to serve its defense, established the twin settlements of **Bungamati** and **Khokana,** near the Karma Binayak Shrine, amid fertile fields. During a major drought, the king sought the blessings of the rain god, Machhendra, at a temple in India, inviting the deity to come and settle in the valley. He built a shrine at Bungamati where, in the last decade of the sixteenth century, it became the custom to keep the image of the Rato Machhendra during winter, moving it back to Patan by palanquin in summer.

Guardian elephant outside a temple at Kirtipur village in Kathmandu valley.

KATHMANDU VALLEY

Many small votive chaityas line the processional way from Patan to Bungamati, which nestles against a hillside, surrounded by terraced rice paddies and small copses of trees. The village is noted for its strongly-stated, shikhari-style **Rato Machhendranath temple**. The adjacent Lokeshwar shrine contains an image of Bhairav's massive head in full, demoniac fury.

There's another shrine, **Karma Binayak,** on a tree-clad hill and beyond that, a 10-minute walk away, is a brick-paved village famous for the manufacture of mustard oil, **Khokana.** It has a temple dedicated to the nature goddess Shukla Mai, or Rudrayani. Rebuilt after the 1934 quake, its main street is noticeably wider than in similar villages.

THROUGH KATHMANDU VALLEY

TO THE WEST

Many interesting rural communities, with fascinating temples and shrines, are close to Kathmandu. In the west, on the old "Silk Road" to Tibet, stand the villages of **Satungal, Balambu, Kisipidi** and **Thankot.** The first three cluster together within walking distance, no more than six kilometers (3.7 miles) from the capital city.

Satungal, Balambu, Kisipidi

The first, **Satungal,** was built in the sixteenth century as a fortress to thwart invaders from the north. Many of its 1,000 residents work in Kathmandu. Its **main square** is notable for the two-meter (6.5-ft) stone image of a seated Buddha on a free-standing platform. Nearby, to the north of the square, steps lead through an embellished gate to a **Vishnu Devi temple.**

Several inscriptions testify to the antiquity of the second village, **Balambu,** built more than a thousand years ago when the Lichhavi dynasty ruled Kathmandu valley, but fortified later. Its main feature is the two-storied **Mahalakshmi temple,** in the central square along with some smaller temples. Among the three-storied houses that line the square is one dedicated as the god house of Ajima Devi.

The third village, **Kisipidi,** with its lush green trees and small, stone-walled gardens, is renowned for the two-storied **Kalika Mai temple** in its center.

Thankot

Travel on along the main highway, the Raj Path and after two kilometers (1.2 miles) you come to the fourth village, **Thankot,** built by the Mallas and later made a fortress by Prithvi Narayan Shah — its name, in fact, means "military base". On a hill above the village stands an impressive two-storied

Mahalakshmi temple, much admired for its patterned tympanum and columns, erotic carvings, open shrine and images of kneeling devotees.

Four kilometers (2.5 miles) to the southwest of Thankot stands the 2,423-m (7,950-ft) peak of **Chandragadhi,** "The Mountain of the Moon", reached by a trail through a dense forest of bamboo, pine and sal trees. At the crest there's a small Buddhist chaitya and splendid views of Kathmandu valley.

Back on the Raj Path look for the **monument to King Tribhuvan,** built to com-

OPPOSITE : Typical village sights in Kathmandu valley: Serene bathing ghat (top) in Bhaktapur. A market stall (bottom) in Nala village. ABOVE: Ancient, yet elegant house in Patan.

memorate the re-establishment of royalty after the Rana regime. It has a raised hand. There's another monument along the road that honors the men who built it between 1953 and 1956 — Indian engineers and Nepali laborers. Before then, goods were moved laboriously from India to the Nepal border by railway, then transferred from the Terai to Daman via overhead cables, and finally carried by porters to Kathmandu.

The Lele Valley Road

Two of the valley's most ancient villages, **Chapagaon** and **Lele,** date back to Lichhavi times. The road to them cuts through a green and yellow quilt of mustard fields and rice paddies stretched out beneath the hazy gray-blue foothills of the mighty Himalayas.

Sixteenth-century **Sunaguthi,** standing on a high plateau at the edge of another valley, has a **shrine to Bringareshwar Manadeva**, which houses one of the most sacred lingams in the Kathmandu valley. Next to the shrine is a two-storied **Jagannath temple.** Now the path climbs gently upward through the emerald, terraced fields to **Thecho** with its brightly decorated **Balkumari temple.** There's another one, to **Brahmayani,** in the north of the village guarded by the deity's vehicle — a duck, of all things — atop a column, with the usual lion on the steps of this two-storied temple.

About two kilometers (1.2 miles) beyond Thecho, guarded by a metal Ganesh shrine and a statue of Brahma beside a huge yoni, the road enters **Chapagaon** where, says a famous valley legend, one of the Malla kings sent his son into exile for founding a caste of his own. The central square contains two temples, both two-storied, dedicated to **Narayan** and **Krishna.** The struts carry incredibly-detailed erotic carvings. Close by, in a single-storied building, is an image of **Bhairav,** the village's major deity. South of Chapagaon are the two small hamlets of **Bulu** and **Pyangaon.**

villages in the east of Kathmandu valley, but of these, three predated him: Banepa, Nala and Dhulikhel. The four that he did build are Panauti, Khadpu, Chaukot and Sanga, though not all lie within the valley. Nonetheless, King Anand Malla's vision gave Banepa and Dhulikhel, situated, as they were, on the main Silk Road from Kathmandu to Tibet, status and a greater strategic value.

SANGA AND THE ARANIKO HIGHWAY

The road climbs out of the valley over a pass, five kilometers (three miles) east of Bhaktapur, where it cuts through **Sanga.** There's a small lane to the north, off the Araniko highway, that takes you into

TO THE EAST

King Anand Malla, founder of the Bhaktapur dynasty, is said to have built seven new

Sanga, where a vantage point offers an incredible panorama of the entire valley. Despite its antiquity, the only object of historical merit is a small **Bhimsen shrine** to commemorate a Kathmandu legend that, when the valley was a lake, Bhimsen crossed it by boat, rowing from Tankhot in the west to Sanga.

From Sanga, the Araniko highway zigzags steeply down into the lush **Banepa valley** and the village from which it takes its name. Standing at the foot of a forested hill, much of the village was razed by fire in the early 1960s, but it remains the main center of commerce for the surrounding hill areas. Banepa's **Chandeshwari shrine** overlooks the valley from the top of a hill to the northeast of the town. Northwest, there's a rough trail to **Nala**, seat of a Buddhist meditation site and **Lokeshwar,** about 100 m (330 yards) west of Nala, by the old Bhaktapur road. Pilgrim shelters surround the temple, which has a water tank in front of it. A steep alley in the village center takes you to the four-storied **Bhagvati temple** in the center of a square — the locale for many colorful processions during the village's annual festivals.

DHULIKHEL

Back on the highway at Banepa, you can drive on to Dhulikhel, which is popular as

Annapurna's majestic beauty dominates the landscape of Nepal's midlands and provides an awe-inspiring backdrop for its many small villages.

a place to stop and contemplate the Himalayas. Not that the views are the only reason to linger. Dhulikhel's main square contains a **Narayan shrine** and a **Harisiddhi temple**. The village houses are renowned for their beautiful, carved woodwork. On a northern hill above the village stands the magnificent three-storied **Bhagvati temple**, which is famous for its ceramic-tiled façade.

Dhulikhel remains one of the trade gateways between Kathmandu valley, eastern Nepal and Tibet.

mountain-facing rooms are a good value — there can be few more exhilarating feelings than to open your eyes in the morning to a view of the world's highest peaks. The hotel has a good restaurant.

INEXPENSIVE

The **Dhulikhel Lodge** ((011) 61152, P.O. Box 6020, Kathmandu, has long been a favorite with budget travelers. Though it's a convivial place, expect only the bare minimum of creature comforts. The lodge's guestbooks make for fascinating reading.

WHERE TO STAY

MID-RANGE

The **Dhulikhel Mountain Resort** ((011) 61466 FAX (01) 226827, P.O. Box 3202, Kathmandu, is something of a luxury trekking lodge. The resort's 43 rooms are thatch-roofed chalets in a garden with Himalayan views. The Mountain Resort has a good restaurant and even a bar. If you want a few days away from it all contemplating the mountains, there are few places in which you can do it in such comfort.

The **Himalayan Horizon Sun-N-Snow Hotel** ((011) 61296 FAX (011) 61476, P.O. Box 1583, Kathmandu, is a step down in comfort and price from the Mountain Resort, but its

PANAUTI

One of the most fascinating Newar towns in this area, Panauti stands at the confluence of two rivers south of Banepa in a small valley surrounded by mountains. There used to be a king's palace in the square and the town is noted for two fine examples of Malla temple architecture. Both the three-storied sixteenth-century **Indreshwar Mahadev temple** and a **Narayan Shrine** have been restored.

Architecturally and historically, the Indreshwar Mahadev temple is one of the most important Newar shrines in Kathmandu valley and is thought to have replaced an earlier one built in the eleventh to twelfth centuries. The carving on its struts conveys the profound serenity of Shiva, in his many incarnations. Two shrines guard the courtyard; one is to Bhairav, another to a primeval nature goddess, represented by a simple stone. There's another **Krishna temple** on a peninsula at the confluence of the two rivers, with several Shiva lingams nearby and a sacred cremation ghat. On the other side of the Bungamati river is a famous seventeenth-century temple, also restored, where a chariot festival is held each year. It's dedicated to **Brahmayani,** chief goddess of Panauti after Indreshwar Mahadev.

THE ROAD TO NAGARKOT

The village of Nagarkot is, like Dhulikhel, a popular Himalayan viewpoint on the eastern rim of the Kathmandu valley. It's north of Dhulikhel and is approached by a rough road via Bhaktapur and Thimi. Unlike Dhulikhel there is little in the way of village life in Nagarkot; but the views are indisputably better.

WHERE TO STAY

MID-RANGE

The most desirable of Nagarkot's hotels is the **Club Himalaya Resort** ((012) 90883 FAX (012) 417133, Nagarkot, which is run by

the same management as the Kathmandu Guesthouse in Thamel. The rooms all have balconies with views of the Himalayas and the resort also has an indoor swimming pool — it gets cold up here in the winter months.

The Fort ((012) 90896 FAX (012) 228066, Nagarkot, strives hard for ambiance, decking out its rooms with Tibetan rugs and thangkas. The effect is quite traditional, with an unobtrusive overlay of modern comforts and amenities. The rooms all have good views.

INEXPENSIVE

The **View Point Hotel** ((01) 417424, Nagarkot, is an agreeable compromise between the rock-bottom budget hotels and the more expensive and mid-range places. It's a cozy affair, with views, rooms with attached bathrooms and even some cottages for a more private retreat. The restaurant at the View Point is also good; while you eat, a glowing fireplace keeps the cold at bay.

OPPOSITE: Verdant rice paddies of the Suikhet valley near Pokhara. Women harvest grain ABOVE at Pokhara. OVERLEAF: Above the rice fields north of Pokhara rise (left) Machhapuchhare and (right) 7,525-m (24,688-ft) Annapurna IV and 7,937-m (26,041-ft) Annapurna II.

THE ROAD TO TIBET

KODARI

Kodari's setting is remarkable enough — no more than 50 km (31 miles) from the crest of 8,013-m (26,291-ft)-high Shisha Pangma, or Gosainthan in the west and much the same distance from 8,848-m (29,028-ft)-high Everest, in the east. Just 100 km (62 miles) from Kathmandu, Kodari also marks the official border crossing with Tibet.

Chinese. Although fairly new, it is already badly damaged by the frequent landslides and washouts that send whole sections of road — and sometimes the vehicles on them — plunging to the swollen torrents below.

Though it winds through the foothills of the greatest mountain range in the world, these hills themselves are so high and sheer that views of the snow-capped peaks are rare. **Dhulikhel,** which offers a stunning vista of the Himalayas, including Everest, is an exception.

Kodari itself is of little interest — a cluster of wooden shacks straggling along the roadway that links Nepal and China. But the journey to Kodari presents a picturesque panorama of raging rivers, valley towns and green, forested slopes. Visas for China are difficult to obtain for non-group tourists in Kathmandu. If you organize your visa before you get to Nepal, however, you are free to walk across the border at Kodari and travel all the way to Lhasa and beyond.

ARANIKO HIGHWAY (RAJMARG)

Like most roads in midland Nepal, the Araniko highway was constructed by the

A few kilometers after Dhulikhel, at **Dolalghat**, a long low bridge crosses the wide bed of the Sun Kosi, just below its confluence with the Indrawati river. Almost half a kilometer (1500 ft) long, the bridge was built in 1966. Not long after Dolalghat, on the Sun Kosi, is one of the country's first hydroelectric schemes, built in 1972 with Chinese aid.

The power station lies less than 900 m (3,000 ft) above sea level between Lamosangu and Barabise. Continuing north from bustling Barabise the road begins to climb upwards. All along the road the sparse winter and spring waters are tapped for irrigation and domestic use through ancient but well-maintained aqueducts, models of traditional engineering. Dug out above the sides of the stream and lined with stone, the aqueducts move the fast-flowing water off the main body which soon descends below.

Many visitors stop at **Tatopani,** where hot springs from the raging cauldron beneath the Himalayas have been tapped, pouring forth day and night an everlasting supply of hot water.

At occasional intervals there's the inevitable temple — and at **Khokun,** only seven kilometers (four miles) from the Tibetan

Business here is still slow; but a trickle of Tibet-bound tourists arrive daily and the occasional day-trippers descend from their coach to be photographed with the Tibetan town of **Khasa,** 600 m (2,000 ft) higher up the gorge and the brilliant snows of 6,000-m (19,550-ft)-high Choba-Bahamare in the background. To the east, directly in line with Kodari, mighty Gaurisankar, only 35 km (22 miles) distant, remains invisible beyond the rise of the gorge wall.

A yellow line across the middle of the bridge marks the border between China's

border, a temple occupies a rock in the middle of the gorge — with no indication of how worshippers climb up its sheer rock faces. A magnificent waterfall leaps and jumps like scintillating diamonds hundreds of meters down the sheer lush green wall of the mountain.

The perpendicular rock walls of the gorge press inexorably closer and closer. They seem to lean over the narrow ribbon of road that clings so precariously to the hillside. The road cuts beneath a cliff and you can almost reach out and touch either side of the gorge. Round one more bend and there's the immigration post and beyond the police post. Finally you reach the border spanned by the **Friendship Bridge.**

The Cities of Kathmandu Valley

Tibet and Nepal. Nepalis can cross unhindered. Foreigners must have a visa. (See FORMALITIES, page 231.) The best hotel in the Tibetan border town of Khasa is the grim Zhangmu Hotel, run by a depressed crew of Han Chinese who can rarely summon the energy to turn on the hot water in the rooms.

Where the border actually crosses — which side of the hill is Tibet or Nepal — is anyone's guess. On the other side the road winds back into what, hypothetically anyway, must be Nepal. The waters of the Bhote Kosi rage down the intervening gorge with a thunderous roar even though it's

OPPOSITE: Every afternoon clouds roll into the vertiginous valleys surrounding Gokyo peak.
ABOVE: Evening settles on Phewa lake, Pokara.

the dry season. It's an awesome thought, the Bhote in flood during the monsoons and thaw. Thick, strong walls that buttress the bridge foundations suggest the power they are designed to withstand.

THE ROAD TO POKHARA AND THE WEST

PRITHVI–TRIBHUVAN HIGHWAY

Southwest of Kathmandu, the Trisuli gorge meets that of the Mahesh Khola

river. From the capital to the confluence of the two rivers you take another of Nepal's major roads, the **Prithvi–Tribhuvan highway,** as scenic as it is dramatic. A memorial to those who died building both highways stands at the top of the pass close to a Hindu shrine.

PRITHVI HIGHWAY

The pass out of the valley leads down the almost sheer escarpment in a series of tortuous and terrifying hairpin bends to the Prithvi highway, which starts at the town of **Naubise,** leaving the older Tribhuvan highway and heading southward to Hetauda. The building of the Prithvi highway — in 1973 with Chinese aid — is marked at Naubise by a stone tablet set in the side of the rock wall.

Hamlets and villages — the main highway being their one street — abound along the road. On the level sections on either side are emerald-green rice paddies. Cultivating rice is a family affair — the men bullying the

oxen teams with the plows, the women and children planting young green shoots with astonishing speed and dexterity. Paddies cling to the mountain hundreds of meters above, protected from sliding away only by a fragile buttress of precious topsoil. Fields end abruptly at the edge of a gully or cliff. Many disappear in the monsoons, leaving only a void where once stood half an acre of sustenance.

Charoudi, the most popular "put-in" place for shooting the Trisuli's rapids, is a small one-street hamlet after which the road drops quickly to **Mugling,** veering westward over the elegant suspension bridge. Not long after Mugling there's a northward turn off the highway that leads to **Gorkha,** ancestral seat of the Shah dynasty, rulers of Nepal since the eighteenth century. King Prithvi Narayan Shah's old palace still stands on a mountain ridge overlooking this ancient capital from which the Gurkha soldiers derive their name. There are some famous and distinctive temples in the town, including the pagoda-style **Manakamana** dedicated to a Hindu deity with the power to make dreams come true.

Between October and March there are stunning views from Gorkha of Annapurna and its sister mountains, but nothing beats the panorama that awaits you in the trekking and climbing capital of Pokhara, where the mirror reflection of sacred Machhapuchhare shimmers in the still, crystal waters of **Phewa lake.** Just 50 km (31 miles) from the village street at 900 m (3,000 ft) above sea level, Annapurna and its surrounding peaks rise up another 7,176 m (23,545 ft).

POKHARA VALLEY

Like the valley of Kathmandu, Pokhara valley is blessed with fertile soil. Add to this an average of more than 420 mm (155 inches) of rain a year and it is no surprise that the land burgeons with lush vegetation: cacti, bananas, rice, citrus trees, mustard fields, hedges of thorny spurge spiked with red blossoms, walls studded with ficus. The patchwork terraces are cut through by gorges channeled by the Seti river and scattered with lakes that glitter like diamonds in the spring sunshine. The ochre mud-and-thatch homes of the Hindu migrants from the Terai contrast with the white-walled, slate-roofed homes of the native Lamaistic tribes from the flanks of the mountain.

POKHARA AND PHEWA LAKE

Thirty years ago, Pokhara was an insignificant, little-known town. The first motor vehicle, a Jeep, arrived in 1958 — by airplane. Progress since then has been swift, encouraged by tourists and climbers, the advent of hydroelectric power in 1967 and the completion of the Prithvi highway in 1973. Within a decade Pokhara's population doubled to 50,000. There's even a movie house.

Local legend says Phewa lake covers an ancient city engulfed during a cataclysmic earthquake millennia ago. Today local fishermen ply their *donga* (long dug-out canoes, fashioned from tree trunks) on the placid waters, ferrying pilgrims to the **shrine of Vahari,** a golden temple nestled on an island. There's also a **Royal Winter Palace** for winters on the lake shore.

WHAT TO SEE

Unlike the Kathmandu valley, which is teeming with cultural attractions, Pokhara's sights are mostly natural. Try and find the time to hike out of town and gaze at the mountains; alternatively, hire a bicycle, pony or a donga.

Bicycle rental rates are next to nothing (always check the brakes and tires before setting out). Pony hire is more expensive — around US$30 per day with a guide. **Pokhara Pony Trek ℂ** (061) 20339 is a long-established operator. Those who want to cruise the lake can hire dongas for around Rs 50 per hour — a bit more if one of the boat-boys does the paddling. Modern boats are also available.

Swimming in **Phewa lake** is probably not advisable given that it's used as a dumping ground by many villagers. You can take a boat out to the small pagoda-style temple situated on the lake's tiny island, however. This temple is dedicated to goddess Barahi and is one of the most famous places of pilgrimage in the region.

There are three natural sites of interest in the area. **Devlin's falls** is located southwest from the airport along the Siddhartha highway. This dramatic but seasonal waterfall, known locally as Patle Chhango, is created when a small stream flows out of the lake and suddenly collapses and surges down the rocks into a steep gorge. **Seti gorge** is equally fascinating. To get there, drive to the middle of the first bridge along the Kathmandu highway. Look down below and you will see the four-and-a-half-meter (15-ft)-wide gorge carved more than

14-m (36-ft)-deep by the flow of the Seti river. The third interesting natural site is at **Mahendra cave,** north of Shining Hospital and the university campus near **Batule-chaur** village. It is one of the few stalagmite and stalactite caves in Nepal, known locally as a holy place. Carry a flashlight.

SHOPPING FOR CRAFTS

Near the Himalayan Tibet Hotel and the airport is **Pokhara Craft,** a shop specializing in local handicrafts and featuring nettle fabric (made from the stinging hill nettle)

OPPOSITE: Decorated house in central Nepal.
ABOVE: Village craftsman weaving rush baskets.

and woodcrafts. You can see local craftsmen at work there during the day.

The entire Lakeside area of Pokhara is one big art and crafts fair. Shops here sell everything from second-hand books and hiking gear to Tibetan thangkas.

WHERE TO STAY

Pokhara has three main accommodation areas: Lakeside, Damside and the airport. The airport area has a couple of Pokhara's better hotels but it has little going for it as

a base. Lakeside is the busy part of town — a colorful, bustling enclave of shops, restaurants and guesthouses. Few of the hotels or guesthouses have views of the lake, however. Damside, in the south of Pokhara, is a quieter version of Lakeside.

Accommodations in Pokhara are not as sophisticated as in Kathmandu. Generally you'll find that the luxury and inexpensive categories of accommodation provide the best value for money. Most of the true mid-range hotels are disappointing.

LUXURY

The latest arrival on the Pokhara accommodation scene is the **Pokhara Shangri-la Village** ((061) 22122 FAX (061) 21995, Pok-

hara, south of the airport. This luxury development has 61 rooms and is run by the Shangri-la group — bookings can be made at the Shangri-la Hotel ((01) 412999 in Kathmandu.

Despite the emergence of competition, for many Pokhara visitors the **Fish Tail Lodge** ((061) 20071 FAX (061) 20072, Lakeside, Pokhara, is still the only place to stay. Accessible only by a pontoon raft, it stands on a rocky promontory at the eastern end of the Phewa lake. The views are spectacular and the glass-walled restaurant overlooking the lake and the Annapurna massif is one of the best places to dine in all Pokhara. In Kathmandu reservations can be made at the Hotel de l'Annapurna ((01) 221711.

MID-RANGE

The **New Hotel Crystal,** Nadhunga ((061) 20035 FAX (061) 20234, Pokhara, has the look of a hotel that was constructed with the tour group market in mind. Although many mid-range travelers put up here, it's worth bearing in mind that there are rooms at half the price in Lakeside that come close to the same standards provided here.

The **Hotel Tragopan** ((061) 21708 FAX (061) 20474, Damside, has just one drawback: its location on a busy intersection. Otherwise, it's a good mid-range hotel, with a restaurant, pub, garden and shops.

The **Base Camp Resort** ((061) 21226 FAX (061) 20990, Lakeside, is a good alternative to the mainstream mid-range accommodations. It's an informal affair, with two-storied bungalows grouped around a pleasant leafy garden, and offers all the amenities you would expect of a good hotel — air conditioning, international phone service and satellite television — at affordable prices.

FAX (061) 21670, Lakeside, you'll find another new hotel with a charming ambiance. All rooms have attached bathroom with 24-hour hot water, satellite television and international direct-dial telephones. Located in the same lane are two excellent lodge-style accommodations with rates starting around US$10. The **Tranquility Lodge** ((061) 21030, Lakeside, as its name suggests, is a restful spot set in an expansive garden. Close by is the **Butterfly Lodge** ((061) 22892, Lakeside, a similar operation.

INEXPENSIVE

The best advice for finding inexpensive accommodation is to hire a taxi to Lakeside or Damside and take a look around at the hotels. There's no shortage of very comfortable rooms, with attached bathrooms and balconies from US$10 to US$20 per night.

The **Hotel Meera** ((061) 21031 FAX (061) 20335, Lakeside, is one of the new breed of budget hotels. It's right in the heart of Lakeside and the comfortable rooms are fitted with large windows to make the most of the lake views. The downstairs restaurant serves good Nepali and Indian cuisine.

At the **Hotel Khukuri** ((061) 21540

WHERE TO EAT

Lakeside is the area for dining, but frankly, there's little to distinguish the dozens of restaurants in this area from one another. Some have better views, some better service, but mostly they all serve up the same eclectic mix of dishes from around world and play the same music over their sound systems.

The **Fish Tail Restaurant** (Fish Tail Lodge) ((061) 20071, is an exception and

OPPOSITE: A team of yaks plods through the barren high-altitude landscape on the road to Muktinath. ABOVE: Wooden aqueducts (left) irrigate fields in the Annapurna region. A tumble-down stone wall (right) snakes across the barren earth.

highly recommended. If you go for an evening meal, try to be there in time to see the sun set — whether in the garden or in the restaurant itself, the Fish Tail is a wonderful spot to see out the day. The menu is the usual mix of European, Nepali and Indian dishes, but done to higher standards than at most other places around Pokhara. There's live Nepali music and dance every evening.

For Lakeside dining, the **Fewa Park Restaurant** is a tranquil spot. It's better for breakfast or an afternoon snack than for dinner or

lunch. Next door is **Beam Beam**, another Lakeside restaurant with views. The food is better here, but the alfresco dining area is cluttered and the live music performed in the bar area can sometimes be too loud.

Over in Pokhara's Damside area, **KC's** ((061) 21560, is a branch of the successful Kathmandu chain and is generally packed with diners. Vegetable lasagna and sizzling steaks are popular orders. As is the case elsewhere in Pokhara, the European dishes rarely approach authenticity but they are often tasty just the same.

AROUND POKHARA

Ram Bazaar
East of Pokhara, Ram Bazaar is a small but picturesque village with shops, a school and artisans.

Tibetan Villages
The most interesting of the Tibetan settlements, situated just to the north of Pokhara in Lower Hyangja, is **Tashi Phalkhel**. South-

west of the airport, and beyond Devlin's falls, is another settlement, **Tashiling**.

Batulechaur
A few miles north of town, Batulechaur is famous for its *gaine* singers who tell of the rich history of Nepal in their rhapsodic songs. They accompany their voices with a small four-stringed, violin-like instrument, *saranghi*, played with a horse-hair bow.

Sarangkot
At the peak of the 1,600-m (5,250-ft) Sarangkot, are the remains of a fortress used by King Prithvi Narayan Shah the Great during the eighteenth century. Going west of Pokhara, past Kaskidanda ridge to Gyarajati village, you climb to the summit.

Muktinah
One of many places of pilgrimage in these hills that line the Kali Gandaki basin, is **Muktinah**. Set at 3,800 m (12,460 ft), its eternal flame draws Hindu and Buddhist worshippers alike. Black ammonite fossils, thought of as the embodiment of the god Vishnu, are found in profusion and pilgrims travel long distances over rugged trails to collect these.

Kali Gandaki Gorge
The deepest gorge in the world, Kali Gandaki, is flanked on one side by the daunting massif of Annapurna and on the other side, only 35 km (22 miles) away, by 8,167-m (26,795-ft)-high Dhaulagiri I. In between, almost eight kilometers (five miles) below, at only 1,188 m (3,900 ft), sits the village of **Tatopani**. (See also page 149).

With Dhaulagiri and Annapurna you are at the frontier of the highest land in the world. The peaks of Annapurna and its cohorts form the world's greatest natural amphitheater. Its only equal — in scale, form and drama — is directly opposite, across the Kali Gandaki valley, where Dhaulagiri's six peaks and those around them, form another breathtaking panorama.

MAJESTIC MOUNTAINS

On Nepal's western border, the Himalayas curve southward enfolding the country and dividing it physically from the northern-most reaches of India. The highest of these western peaks is **Api.** Though small by comparison with its sister peaks in central and eastern Nepal, few mountains in the world outside Asia rise as high as Api's 7,131 m (23,396 ft), forming a formidable massif in the far west. Peak to peak, directly in line with Api, only 60 km (37 miles) away is its easterly neighbor, **Saipal,** just 97 m (318 ft) lower. The actual Nepal–India border is marked by the Kali river, which flows at the foot of lonely Api.

through tough country — winds between these two massifs, cresting a saddle more than 5,500 m (18,000 ft) high between Nampa and Firnkopf West, before entering Tibet over the Urai pass.

Eastward of the remote western regions the Himalayas climb steadily higher. In the little-known **Kanjiroba Himal**, a cluster of mountains that takes its name from the highest peak, 11 crests rise above 6,000 m (20,000 ft), including 7,409-m (22,583-ft)-high Kanjiroba Himal. The mountains encircle the ancient **kingdom of Dolpo** and

Api dominates a range of magnificent but rarely seen and little-known peaks including **Jetibohurani**, 6,848 m (22,468 ft); **Bobaye**, 6,807 m (22,333 ft); **Nampa**, 6,755 m (22,163 ft); and **Rokapi**, 6,466 m (21,214 ft). Not far from Saipal stands the jagged peak of **Firnkopf West** at 6,683 m (21,926 ft); to the north is the lonely **Takpu Himal** gazing down on the lovely Humla valley and its remote capital of **Simikotat** from 6,634 m (21,766 ft).

Minnows compared to the peaks of central and eastern Nepal, these mountains remain relatively untouched by climbers. Japanese teams conquered Api in 1960, Saipal in 1963 and Nampa in 1972. A major trade route from the plains — a long trek

the sacred **Crystal Mountain** (see DOLPO, page 179–180), forming the natural boundaries of the 3,540-sq-km (1,345-sq-mile) **Shey-Phoksondo National Park.** Dolpo came into the kingdom in the eighteenth century as a result of King Bahadur Shah's conquests.

Eastward, across the fortress of Langtang Himal's peaks, lies the **Rolwaling Himal,** that little-known and overshadowed annex of the great Everest massif. Accessible only from the west, it is considered as beautiful as Langtang.

Main street of Chapagaon village OPPOSITE in Kathmandu valley where legend says a famous Malla king exiled his son for founding a caste of his own. ABOVE: Traditional scene in Chame village en route to Annapurna.

The Cities of Kathmandu Valley

At the far end of the Bhote Kosi gorge, 7,180-m (23,557-ft)-high **Menlungtse** and the slightly lower 7,144-m (23,438-ft)-high mass of **Gaurisankar** stand sentinel, as do Lhotse and Nuptse, for Sagarmatha — Everest — hiding her massive pyramid from prying and curious eyes.

The twin citadels of Gaurisankar and Menlungtse are the westernmost bastions of the Everest massif. Peak to peak, a distance of about 70 km (43 miles) separates Shiva's abode from that of Sagarmatha, Goddess of the Universe. In between, around and about, are literally dozens of lesser ramparts extending to the central pinnacle, most rising above 6,100 m (20,000 ft). Thirty kilometers (18 miles) from Everest, 8,153-m (26,750-ft)-high **Cho Oyu** guards the northwest approach while, less than eight kilometers (five miles) from the pinnacle of the world, 8,511-m (27,923-ft)-high **Lhotse** guards the eastern flank and 7,879-m (25,850-ft)-high **Nuptse** the southwestern flank. Sixteen kilometers (10 miles) beyond Lhotse, 8,481-m (27,825-ft)-high **Makalu** and its four other peaks barricade the approach from the southeast. Well-guarded, from the ground or the air, Everest hides herself, demurely, behind her cluster of courtier peaks.

The first major attempt to scale Everest took place in 1924 when George Mallory and Andrew Irvine disappeared on the mountain close to the summit. Their bodies still lie somewhere beneath Sagarmatha's eternal snows. They took a route along the northeast ridge from Tibet. It was only when Nepal opened its borders that the south face, the line taken by Hillary and Tenzing, was approachable.

Leaving behind the shadows of the brave and foolish who still lie on Sagarmatha's slopes, (including an English religious zealot without any mountain experience who fell to his death in the 1930s, leaving in his diary this epitaph: "Off again. Gorgeous day.") It's 125 km (78 miles) eastward from Everest as the crow flies to the top of 8,598-m (28,208-ft)-high **Kanchenjunga** astride Nepal's border with India's Sikkim state. Here too is a massif of giant peaks — 15 of them are above 7,000 m (23,000 ft).

A remote chorten in the Everest region.

The Terai

WILDLIFE AND RICE PADDIES

Along Nepal's southern border with India lies a narrow band of fertile plains, the Terai. Flat and never wider than 35 km (22 miles), it covers 24,000 sq km (9,120 sq miles). In addition to providing a dramatic contrast to the rest of the terrain of the world's most mountainous nation, the Terai has a charm all its own.

During monsoon season, tributaries of the Ganges flood the Terai's fields and pad-

countryside is a lush hub of activity. The recently completed Mahendra or East-West highway links the major towns of the region; footpaths connect everywhere else. Buses travel the main route and can get you to the birthplaces of Buddha and Sita and the jungle wildlife parks and reserves, but your feet or a bicycle are the only ways to get off the beaten track.

BIRATNAGAR

On the eastern reaches of the Terai lies

dies, depositing soil eroded from the Himalayas. Often rivers and streams change course, uprooting stilted huts and villages, washing out roads and destroying communication links. In the following months, crops are planted — rice, wheat, cane, jute, tobacco, beans and lentils — and harvested before the scorching desert winds arrive, preceding the next year's monsoons. Home for more than half Nepal's population and most of the kingdom's industries, this one fifth of Nepal's land area produces more than 50 percent of the gross domestic product and provides habitat for the country's remaining Bengal tigers and horned rhinoceros. In October and November, the ideal months for visiting this part of Nepal, the

Biratnagar, Nepal's second largest city with over 100,000 people. A major industrial center with sugar, textile and jute mills, small- and medium-scale factories for timber products and rice mills, in itself it is a town to pass by rather than through, but nearby attractions make it a worthwhile stopover.

WHERE TO STAY

Reservations for hotels in Biratnagar can be made in Kathmandu travel agencies before setting out. One of the better places to stay in town is the **Hotel Himalaya Kingdom** ((021) 27172 FAX (021) 24141, Mahendra Chowk, Biratnagar. Rooms are inexpensive and come with attached bathroom.

AROUND BIRATNAGAR

To the west of Biratnagar lie the principal natural resources of the area: green rice paddies, jute fields, floodplains and marshes. On the Indian border, the massive Kosi dam impounds the Sun Kosi river, which is fed by the Tamar river from the slopes of Mount Kanchenjunga and the Arun river from the snows of Makalu. Built by India, the Kosi dam is one of Nepal's major hydroelectric projects. Besides con-

to have been the ancient capital of Maithili and birthplace of Sita, consort of Rama (one of Vishnu's incarnations and hero of the epic Ramayana). It is a major pilgrimage center for Hindus from all over the subcontinent.

An eight-kilometer (five-mile) brick-paved road encircles the city and its many sacred Hindu shrines and ponds, of which **Gangasagar** and **Dhanushsagar** are the most outstanding. Pilgrims to its two famous festivals, commemorating Rama and Sita's wedding and Rama's epic vic-

trolling unpredictable floods and generating much of the country's energy, the dam has created new wetlands that now form the **Kosi Tappu Wildlife Reserve**. Here you can see one of the few remaining herds of wild buffaloes and thousands of migratory birds. The only accommodation in the reserve is at the **Tappu Wildlife Camp (** (01) 226130 FAX (01) 224237, P.O. Box 536, Kamaladi, Kathmandu.

JANAKPUR

Of more historical interest is Janakpur, 120 km (74 miles) west of Biratnagar, on the Indian border. With 40,000 Maithili-speaking inhabitants, Janakpur is reputed

tory over evil, immerse themselves in these sacred waters and flock to **Janaki temple** to pay homage to Rama and Sita. Built by a queen of Tikamgarh (in Madhya Pradesh, northern India) in 1900, its delicately-carved marble traceries were inspired by seventeenth-century Mughal architecture. The delicate exquisitely-shaped filigrees are seen at their best on the elaborate cupolas, ceilings and tiles. Nearby is the **Vivah Mandap** where legend holds that Rama and Sita were wed.

PREVIOUS PAGES: Stone-walled rice paddies of the Midlands region (left) and Tharu youngster (right) of the Terai plains. Farm workers tend the fertile fields of the Terai using the ubiquitous oxen for ploughing OPPOSITE and ABOVE transportation.

The Terai

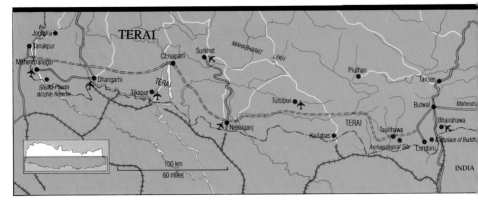

The town is also famous as the main stop on one of the worlds shortest railways — the 52 km (32 mile) narrow-gauge **Nepal Railway** that links Nepal with Jayanagar, India. The line is a colorful anachronism that delights inveterate travelers, a time-serving echo of the old British Raj.

WHERE TO STAY

Most hotel accommodation in Janakpur is primitive. The **Hotel Rama (** (041) 20059, is the only place in town that comes close to deserving a recommendation. The air-conditioned rooms are best and cost about US$15.

BIRGANJ

Eighty kilometers (50 miles) west of Janakpur, the Mahendra highway links up with the Tribhuvan Rajpath, for many years the country's main trans-Asia link. To the south is the border town of Birganj; to the north, through Amlekhganj and across the Mahabharat Lekh hills, is Kathmandu valley. Along the route is a dramatic view at Daman.

Birganj has seen better days. In the sixties and seventies, western hippies and mystics queued for clearance into Nepal on the Indian side at Raxaul and spent the night in one of Birganj's many cheap lodging houses before taking the high road to Kathmandu.

It is, however, still a bustling industrial area with timber yards, a sugar mill, match factory and a raucous bus depot where itinerants jostle each other in their eagerness to catch the next, often over-crowded,

coach to Kathmandu. It is also a jump-off point for visitors to Royal Chitwan National Park and Parsa Wildlife Reserve.

ROYAL CHITWAN NATIONAL PARK AND PARSA WILDLIFE RESERVE

The highlight for most visitors to the Terai is a visit to Royal Chitwan National Park and Parsa Wildlife Reserve, wilderness retreats recreated out of the once fertile rice and wheat fields that swiftly covered the Rapti valley after the fall of the Rana dynasty in the 1950s.

Royal Chitwan, spread over 932 sq km (354 sq miles), was the first of Nepal's extensive network of wildlife sanctuaries that now protect over seven percent of the nation's territory. The valley in which the park lies forms the flood plains of the Narayani river, joined here by the waters of the Rapti and other streams and feeders to become the second largest tributary of the sacred Ganges that flows approximately 200 km (124 miles) to the south.

Before the park's creation in 1973, Nepal's population explosion had pushed migrants down from the hills, forcing the indigenous Tharu tribes into this area formerly reserved as royal hunting grounds. Using slash-and-burn techniques, they opened up the forests and planted rice and grain.

Concerned with the destruction of its traditional hunting grounds, the Nepali royal family planned new strategies for the protection of its wildlife and in 1973 King Mahendra established Chitwan. The grasslands were rehabilitated, along with the sal (*Shorea robusta*) forests and slowly

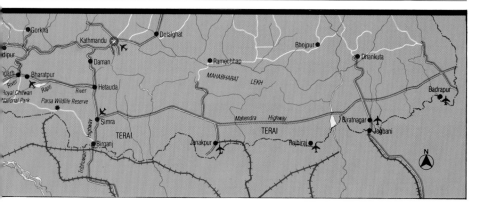

the game began to creep back from the uncertain havens it had found outside. An exemplary model of wildlife management, Royal Chitwan and its denizens have continued to prosper. Subsequent extensions, Parsa Wildlife Reserve, have given it a much larger area, embracing smaller forests of khani (*Acacia catechu*), sisso (*Dalbergia sisso*) and simal (*Bombax malabaricum*) — all valuable indigenous woods.

Monsoon fluctuations in the course of the rivers have created new ponds and lakes in a park–reserve that now covers an area of 1,200 sq km (456 sq miles) of subtropical lowland, bounded by the Rapti river in the north, the Reu river and the Churia or Siwalik range in the south and the Narayani river in the west.

Several animal observation blinds have been constructed next to water holes where patient visitors might see leopards and tigers and most will sight rhinoceros, wild boar, deer, monkeys and a multitude of birds. Throughout the park, small fenced enclosures contain varieties of grasses from which agronomists and conservationists hope to determine the ideal pastures for Chitwan's wild animals.

On clear winter days this jungle has one of the most dramatic backdrops in the world: the stunning ice slopes of Ganesh Himal, Annapurna and Himal Chuli stand out on the horizon in magnificent detail. Travel in the park is difficult during the monsoon season (May to September) and the best animal-viewing is from February to April. Any stay shorter than two days is probably not worth the effort as the key to enjoying the wild animal park is patience. Accommo-

dations should be arranged before leaving Kathmandu or from Birganj, if you are entering Nepal from India.

Riding an elephant is the best form of transport in the park. The Royal Nepali Army, which polices the park and enforces conservation laws, makes its patrols by elephant and park workers move about in similar fashion. It is not uncommon to see a small work crew resting in the shade of a clump of bombax trees around midday, the elephants' trunks relentlessly foraging; their *pahits*, handlers, perhaps sleeping on their backs with umbrellas raised as protection against the sun.

Elephants can usually be rented at the park offices or at one of the lodges listed below. Each beast has its own handler and individual gait. For most, these game rides are the memories that will last longest. The pahit, astride the elephant's neck, brushes the lianas and giant ferns aside with his steel goad and the seemingly ungainly three-ton steed steps nimbly over fallen logs.

In the dark shadows of a thicket, a sudden flash of fawn reveals the flight of a startled sambar deer. Giant butterflies flit from leaf to leaf and beyond the wall of leaves shadows move — perhaps a tiger or a leopard. However briefly, you can be the last of the maharajahs. Out on the plains the great Asiatic one-horned rhinos are moving with steadfast purpose, cropping the grass as a herd of *chital* — timid, fawn-like deer, edge nervously away from the young elephant. Back in the forest, a jungle fowl suddenly struts across the trail and from a low-lying branch a wild peacock takes off in a brilliant cascade of feathers.

It is also possible to travel part of the way down the Rapti river and its streams by canoe, to view crocodiles basking in the sun, as well as a variety of riparian flora and fauna. Arrangements for a canoe trip are best made at the Sauhara park office, four miles south of Tadi Bazaar (on the Mahendra highway between Marayangarh and Hetauda).

Hiking is allowed in the Chitwan jungle, but an experienced guide is necessary as trails are not marked and the wildlife can be dangerous. Rather than being an encumbrance, a guide is an asset who can find and identify animals and many can reel off with computer-like accuracy the names of the sanctuary's prolific yet rare bird species.

WHERE TO STAY

Most visitors to Chitwan arrive on a package tour from Kathmandu that includes guides, accommodation and meals. Advance bookings are essential. Accommodation standards vary surprisingly little. Budget travelers organizing their own Chitwan trip stay in the nearby village of Sauhara.

A more remote wildlife jungle can be experienced in far west Nepal, five hours drive from Nepalgunj, in the Royal Bardia National Park (see page 169).

LUXURY

Luxury here reflects prices rather than five-star comfort. If it's pampered treatment you want, then you should probably avoid Chitwan. Even the resorts run by Tiger Tops, where you might shell out upwards of US$1,000 for a two-night, three-day package, comprise accommodation made from local materials and lacking amenities such as electricity.

Tiger Tops ((01) 420322 FAX (01) 414075, P.O. Box 242, Durbar Marg, Kathmandu, is the original and still the most prestigious of the resorts in Chitwan. There are three Tiger Tops resorts in total: the **Jungle Lodge**, the **Tented Camp** and the **Tharu Village Safari Resort**. In all three you can expect high standards of guide services, solar heated water and a beautiful rustic environment. The Jungle Lodge is home to the famous

tree-house accommodation; as the name suggests, in the Tented Camp you stay in safari-style tents fitted with twin beds and stools; the Tharu Village Safari Resort is the most luxurious of the three, even having a swimming pool and holding Tharu dances in the evenings.

The **Chitwan Jungle Lodge** ((01) 228918 FAX (01) 228349, P.O. Box 1281, Durbar Marg, Kathmandu, is an operation in which rooms are provided in traditional mud-wall Tharu huts — all with private bathrooms and hot water. The lodge is deep in the

jungle and when traditional dances are held in the rustic restaurant in the evenings it's easy to imagine yourself on safari in another era.

The **Island Jungle Resort** ((01) 225615 FAX (01) 223814, P.O. Box 2154, Durbar Marg, Kathmandu, has a beautiful location on an island in the middle of the Narayani river — crocodiles are frequently seen in the river and if you are lucky you might even see Gangetic dolphin. Accommodation is available in both cottages and safari tents.

BHARATPUR AND NARAYANGHAT

The twin towns of Bharatpur and Narayanghat are the nearest urban centers to Chitwan.

OPPOSITE: Sunrise travelers take an early morning wildlife safari abroad an elephant in Royal Chitwan National Park (top) where park workers (bottom) rest in shade during the midday heat. Wild monkey ABOVE at Chitwan.

Bharatpur's role in the lowland infrastructure is as an airfield for what the domestic air carrier rashly promises are daily flights to Kathmandu. Renowned for the reliability of its international schedules, Royal Nepal Airlines has an equal reputation for the erratic time-keeping of its internal flights: understandable in mountain regions where weather suddenly closes in but perplexing to passengers waiting in the balmy and reliable climes of the Terai.

Narayanghat —lying on the banks of one of Nepal's three largest rivers, the

Narayani, and known as the "Gateway to Chitwan"— is in fact the major junction on the Mahendra highway with a spur climbing up through the hills along the east bank of the Narayani to the town of **Mugling**, the main junction between Kathmandu and Pokhara on the Prithvi highway. It is also a vital administrative and commercial center of the Terai region and indeed the economic capital of the indigenous people of this region, the Tharus.

Bustling Narayanghat, with sizable industries and flourishing markets, is also something of a pilgrimage spot. Each year, in January, a major fair attracts tens of thousands to the nearby village of **Deoghat**, where they immerse in the waters at the

confluence of the Kali Gandaki andTrisuli-Marsyangdi rivers.

Travelers continue their westward journey from Narayanghat over the modern bridge that spans the river, veering southwest along the Narayani's flood plains and over the shallow crest of a spur of the Siwalik hills to join the **Siddhartha highway** — a direct India–Pokhara link — at **Butwal,** on the banks of the river Tinau. This market town, with 25,000 to 30,000 inhabitants, is famous for its produce gardens and fruit orchards.

TANSEN

Northward of Butwal, a small eastward spur of the Siddhartha highway doubles back on itself as it climbs, in just a few miles, to **Tansen** — a town of 15,000 souls, famed for the erotic carvings decorating its **Narayan temple.** Tansen is also justly renowned as a landscape artist's *El Dorado*. Craft industries and the traditional Newar houses also make the town a worthwhile stopover. Its **Bhairavnath temple,** legend says, was carried — lock, stock and timber beams — all the way from the Kathmandu valley by King Mani Kumarananda Senior: one of history's biggest removal jobs. For anglers, Tansen's leaping streams provide fine sport.

BHAIRAWA

Hugging the Indian border, 40 km (25 miles) south of Tansen, Bhairawa is the Terai's second largest industrial center and a major producer of liquor. There's another British military base, five kilometers (three miles) outside the town, which signs up more of the stout Gurkha military stock.

WHERE TO STAY

The only reason to stay in Bhairawa if you're not leaving for or arriving from India is to visit Lumbini. Bear in mind that there is also some accommodation in Lumbini itself, notably the Japanese-managed Hokke Hotel.

ABOVE: Stone carving of Buddha in Patan.
OPPOSITE: Terraces are cut into the hillsides to enable the cultivation of grains here in the Everest region and elsewhere in Nepal.

MID-RANGE

Bhairawa's best accommodation is the **Hotel Yeti** ((071) 20551 FAX (071) 20719. It has clean, air-conditioned rooms with attached bathrooms and a reasonable restaurant.

The **Hotel Himalayan Inn** ((071) 20347, offers basic mid-range to budget accommodation in an uninspiring setting.

LUMBINI

Nineteen kilometers (12 miles) southwest of Bhairawa is Lumbini, the birthplace of Sid-

one was born here," had been split in two, probably by lighting.

Later excavation has revealed a brick temple, Maya Devi — said to mark the exact spot where the Buddha was born.

WHERE TO STAY

If your finances stretch to a worthwhile splurge, the **Lumbini Hokke Hotel** ((071) 20236, is that most surprising of things: a Japanese-managed hotel in the Terai. Its raison d'être is the large number of Japanese

dhartha Gautama Buddha in 540 BC. Since 1958 Lumbini has been in the hands of an international committee established by the Fourth World Buddhist Conference and initially funded by a substantial contribution from King Mahendra.

At the turn of the century, German archaeologist, Dr. Feuhrer, began excavating the ruins of the area, including the Lumbini palace and gardens, several shrines and a monastery. He discovered a sandstone sculpture depicting Buddha's nativity (now in the National Museum) and a soaring obelisk erected to honor Buddha by Mauryan emperor Ashoka when he visited the Lumbini gardens in 249 BC. The pillar, inscribed in Brahmin, "Buddha Sakyamuni, the blessed

pilgrims who come to Lumbini in homage to Buddha. The Japanese-style rooms complete with *tatami, shoji* and deep baths will be a nostalgic treat for anyone who has ever traveled in Japan.

TILAUROKOT

When Buddha was born, his father King Suddhodhan had as his capital Tilaurokot, 27 km (17 miles) west of Lumbini. Although the stupas, monasteries and palaces that Chinese travelers wrote about over two centuries ago no longer exist, the Nepalis have preserved it as a heritage site. Unfortunately very little distinguishes this site from the rest of the present-day Terai.

NEPALGUNJ

The western-most city in Nepal and capital of its region, Nepalgunj is an industrial center on the Indian border. It has a population of 40,000 and little to recommend it to tourists.

ROYAL BARDIA AND SHUKLA PHANTA RESERVES

The Royal Bardia National Park and the Shukla Phanta Wildlife Reserve have been

growing in popularity since the construction of the Mahendra highway linking the east and west of Nepal.

The Royal Bardia National Park is the Terai's largest wilderness area and offers the best opportunities in all Nepal to see a tiger in the wild. The park is home to over 30 species of mammal and hundreds of species of birds. **Karnali,** part of Royal Bardia, located on the eastern bank of the Karnali river, is a sanctuary for the endangered swamp deer. Accommodation in the park is still developing.

Shukla Phanta, in Kanchanpur district in the westernmost reaches of Nepal, is one of the few places in the country where the endangered black buck are found.

Like Bardia, you have a good chance here of seeing tigers and rhinos. Tourist facilities are virtually non-existent, however.

WHERE TO STAY

As at Chitwan, **Tiger Tops** resorts ((01) 420322 FAX (01) 414075, P.O. Box 242, Durbar Marg, Kathmandu, provide superb accommodation. There are two resorts: **Tiger Tops Karnali Lodge** and **Karnali Tented Camp**. The lodge is at the park boundary, the camp — as comfortable a

camp as you'll ever come across — is inside the park. Rates are around US$165 per night all inclusive. Some budget accommodation is also starting to spring up: a good option is the **Forest Hideaway Cottages,** where you can make reservations by calling ((01) 41768, in Kathmandu.

There is no accommodation at Shukla Phanta, but **Silent Safari** ((099) 21230 FAX (099) 22220, P.O. Box 1, Mahendranagar, runs tours into the reserve.

OPPOSITE: A forest skyline overlooks the Rapti river in the Royal Chitwan National Park. ABOVE: Threatened survivor of the greatest of the world's cats, the royal Bengal tiger (left), pads through Chitwan's lush grasslands. One of Nepal's two species of crocodiles, the gurial (right) basks in the muddy shallows of a river.

The
Eastern
Midlands

ILAM AND THE ILAM VALLEY

In the narrow neck of land that connects northeast India with the rest of that vast country — and also divides Nepal from Bhutan, another tiny Himalayan kingdom — are West Bengal and Sikkim. From **Siliguri** the road crosses the **Mechi river,** a tributary of the Ganges, to **Kakar Bhitta** in Nepal. You can also take an alternative hill road from **Darjeeling** through the **Mane pass** and down to the rolling tea fields of Ilam.

Set at around 1,300 m (4,000 ft), the tea fields are particularly lovely, rolling away from either side of the road in every direction, a carpet of vivid green laid out at the feet of Nepal's northeastern mountains with dramatic views of mighty Kanchenjunga, the world's third-highest mountain, astride the Sikkim–Nepal border.

With its weathered brick houses, **Ilam** is a gracious town, by Nepali standards, of about 12,000 people. Its principal industry is tea and you can visit the factory where the leaf is cured before it is shipped to Kathmandu and to the rest of Nepal. Villagers also run cottage industries turning out a wide and attractive range of handmade cloth, blankets, sweaters and carpets.

Access is by bus from **Biratnagar** or **Dhahran** to **Birtamodh** and another bus from **Birtamodh** to **Ilam.** Ilam is also one hour by bus from **Bhadrapur (Chandragadhi).**

DHANKUTA REGION

DHARAN BAZAAR

Focal point of this region, lying at the base of the ever-green Vijaypur hills, is Dharan Bazaar. An unusual feature of town life is the Union Jack that flies over one of the squat single-storied buildings. This is one of the British Army Gurkha recruiting centers. Wiry teenagers from the hills continue a long and noble tradition, enlisting — usually for life — while older generations, now retired, make the long trek each month from the same hills to pick up their pensions.

The orchards of the Vijaypur hills are rich and productive and surplus fruit is preserved in a recently established canning factory. Access is by bus from Biratnagar.

DHANKUTA

Dhankuta stands on a ridge in the hills above Dhahran, pleasantly cool at an elevation of 1,200 m (4,000 ft) and famous for its ancient orange groves and its leafy scenery punctuated by many mountain streams, their crystal clear waters dancing between grassy banks flanked by pine and oak forests. Its streets are lined with myriad tea houses, the market town itself serving as a commercial, banking and government center. One modern wonder for townsfolk has been the arrival of electric power. Its gabled black-and-white houses and dreamy ways are strikingly reminiscent of an Alpine village. A modern motor road winds its way from Dhahran to Dhankuta. By foot

PREVIOUS PAGES: In spring and summer, ice-melt streams (left) pour in torrents from the mountains down into the lush valleys and lowlands.
A fisherman (right) poses with his triangular net.
ABOVE: An old Tibetan woman sells turquoise jewelry and metalwork in Namche Bazaar.
OPPOSITE: Worn brick façades (top) provide a pleasant backdrop to village life. A weaver (bottom) works a handloom.

it takes about five hours to climb the 32 km (20 miles), via Bijaipur to this ancient Newar town.

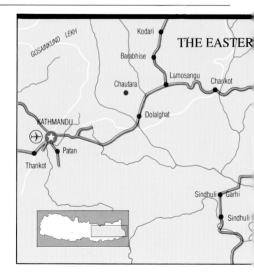

TUMLINGTAR AND THE ARUN VALLEY

Close to Dhankuta lies one of Nepal's most remote and beautiful regions. Nowhere are the country's stunning scenic contrasts more sharply defined than in the **Arun valley,** lying in the shadows of the Khumbu Harkna Himal, below Makalu's daunting 8,481-m (27,825-ft)-high peak with the wide and lazy Arun river meandering along the valley floor.

The river bestows a mantle of verdant green and nourishes the cool leafy trees, which provide shade all along this enchanted valley and its many companion valleys, equally as lovely. Its villages have remained unchanged for centuries.

Flights touch down in the meadow at **Tumlingtar,** the Arun valley's main settlement, on scheduled runs from Kathmandu or the Terai. There is access by road from Biratnagar.

Though only a short distance northward above the tree-clad hills rise the world's mightiest mountains, at its lowest levels the valley could be part of Africa.

The red bare earth is dotted with stunted sparse semi-arid savanna grassland. Groves of succulents and stands of banana trees repeat the African image. The heat of the sun's rays, funneled into the valley by the rising hills, is merciless. Brickmakers use the heat to bake their product for the thatched Tudor-like cottages of the hamlets that dot the valley and perch on the hillsides.

In the north, the valley is bounded by the snow-covered 4,100-m (13,500-ft)-high Shipton pass — beyond which lie the mountain ranges surrounding the three great peaks of Everest, Makalu and Lhotse.

Anglers delight in the **Ishwa valley,** its slopes thick with rhododendrons and magnolias and its mountain streams alive with fish.

Barun, another valley, its walls a tangled jungle of undergrowth, with rushing streams and plunging waterfalls, forms an amphitheater with distant Makalu center-stage.

It was in one of the rivers in this area — at a height of almost 5,000 m (17,000 ft) — that a wildlife expert discovered what may well be the only high-altitude salamander in the world.

RUMJATAR

A stiff two- to three-day trek over the western ridge takes the fit and the active out of the Arun valley and down into **Rumjatar,** at 1,300 m (4,500 ft) in the valley of the **Dudh Kosi river.**

OKHALDUNGA REGION

Some kilometers away, **Okhaldunga,** a pleasant unspoiled village with an old fortress, has given its name to this lyrical essay of hill and valley, river and lake.

Many of the birds, which give Nepal one of the most richly varied collections of avifauna in the world, are found on the forest-clad 3,000-m (10,000-ft)-high crests of the **Neche Dahuda hills,** overlooking the valley floors. Flocks of them, some vividly colored, flit from tree to tree — their dawn chorus in springtime a hosanna to life reborn.

Okhaldunga lies directly at the foot of Everest but few attempt the exhausting trek through these foothills to the roof of the world.

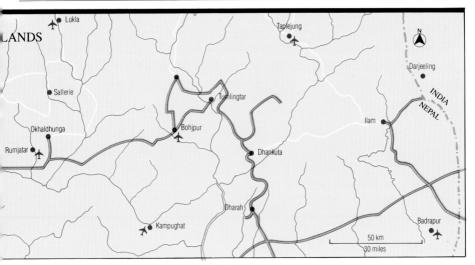

CHARIKOT AND THE ROLWALING VALLEY

West by northwest from Okhaldunga as the Himalayan crow flies, **Rolwaling valley** (*rolwaling* is a Sherpa word that means "the furrow") lies in the shadows between the Everest region of Khumbu Himal and Langtang Himal.

Long has this valley — shaped by the floodwaters that burst out of a nine-meter (30-ft)-wide opening in a sheer rock wall on the east bank of the Bhote Kosi river — fascinated those who visit it. Many pilgrims believe that this is the spot where Shiva thrust his trident into the mountainside to let the waters cascade down to the holy Ganges. It's in the upper reaches of the Rolwaling valley that members of the Sherpa and Tamang communities talk about the *yeti* — that elusive Abominable Snowman that has been seen so often by the Sherpa guides who live in the valley.

Perched at around 2,000 m (6,500 ft), just a few hours drive from Kathmandu, the small pleasant village of **Charikot,** with hotels and shops, is gateway to this region. But progress through Rolwaling valley from thereon is solely by foot (see SOME CLASSIC TREKS, ROLWALING HIMAL, page 199).

Three dining chairs stand outside the tea house in the tiny 10-house hamlet of **Piguti,** its quietness broken only by the scurry of pye-dogs chasing a lone trekker through its one street.

Here too trekkers are few, leaving Rolwaling's many splendors — including the magnificent amphitheater of Gaurisankar — to delight only the rare visitor.

Higher up, one-, two- and three-storied houses cling to the edge of the precipitous rice paddies, now brown, awaiting the monsoons, as cotton wool clouds dab the little knolls and grassy shoulders with a cool balm to ease the sting of the sun.

The paths that climb up the mountain slopes veer left and right, across perilous-looking rope or steel-hawsered suspension bridges. Many require a toll.

Slowly the trail winds through the forests to the highest settlement — a small close-knit Sherpa community. The 200 families of **Beding** live in small but striking stone houses with elegantly painted and carved exteriors.

There's also a monastery. Among the many holy places of the Himalayas, Beding is remembered as the refuge of Guru Padma Sambhava, the mystic Tantric recluse who chose the small cave in the cliff, about 150 m (500 ft) above the monastery, as his place of meditation 1,200 years ago.

Soon after this the trail passes beyond the tree line to the land of the yeti...

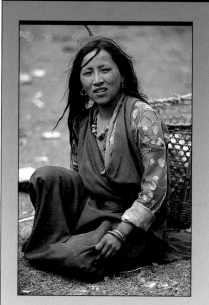

Off the Beaten Track

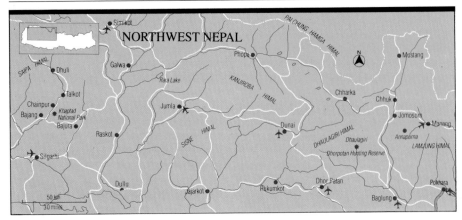

NORTHWEST NEPAL

JUMLA AND LAKE RARA

Southwest of Pokhara lies **Baglung** — approachable only on foot or by dubious road from the Terai — gateway to the **Royal Dhorpotan Hunting Reserve.** Handmade paper, used for packing and bamboo crafts, is its most famous product. It's the home of the Thakalis, a small group of no more than 20,000 people of Tibetan–Mongoloid stock, speaking a Tibetan–Burmese vernacular, whose faith is a mixture of Buddhism, Hinduism and Bonpo.

Baglung also earns praise, from the impotent and those on the wane, for the power of the local aphrodisiac, *silajit.* Locals travel far north to exploit deposits of this tar-like substance that oozes from rocks and fetches high prices in India. Tastefully produced crafts include woolen vests, blankets, rugs and other sewn or woven handicrafts.

After Baglung you're deep into Nepal's mystical west: closed, barred and still little known. Yet it once nurtured a great kingdom of the Mallas that reached its height in the fourteenth century. The capital of this ancient kingdom, **Jumla,** set almost 2,400 m (8,000 ft) above sea level, and only reachable by plane — unless you're an untiring trekker prepared to walk for weeks. There are few visitors to this region.

Ringed by magnificent peaks, Jumla is truly a natural paradise, a quaint rural town with a bazaar, lined by the flat-roofed houses of the region and boasting no more than 50 shops, a bank, police station and the inevitable tea houses.

The Mallas kept a winter capital at Dullu, in the south of the Mahabharat Lekh range of hills and maintained a territory that stretched from the humid Terai to the Taklahar in western Tibet — connected by trails that even today few tackle. Yet the Mallas left a magnificent legacy in Jumla: sculptured temples, stone pillars and the still-living folk songs of the region. This beauty is well-guarded; few disturb its tranquillity and population is sparse. The **Karnali** — one of 14 Nepali zones — has a total population of around 300,000: no more than 12 people to every square kilometer.

There's an old highway along the Tila Nadi valley where you measure your pace by the distance between the ancient milestones placed here as long ago as the fifteenth century. Two days hard slog bring reward — a refreshing dip in the hot springs at **Seraduska.** Walk east for three days and you'll reach **Gothichaur,** an alpine valley set more than 2,900 m (9,500 ft) above sea level. In the valley's pine forests a stone shrine and a water spout are a reminder of the Malla dynasty. The area offers marvelous views of two little-known peaks, Chyakure Lekh and Patrasi Himal. Jumla is also the stepping off point for a long, hard trek to the Shangri-la valley of **Humla.**

Best of all, make a four-day trek over high passes like **Padmara, Bumra,** and the 3,456-m (11,341-ft)-high **Ghurchi pass** and finally **Pina,** to **Lake Rara,** Nepal's most en-

PREVIOUS PAGES: Porters (left) toil over high mountain passes. A young Sherpa woman (right) pauses to rest from her labors. OPPOSITE: A yak on the banks of Gokyo Lake.

chanting national park. The lake is the kingdom's largest body of water, covering 10 sq km (four square miles) almost 3,000 m (10,000 ft) above sea level. Snow lingers here as late as May and June but its crystal-blue waters are haven to a treasury of hardy avian visitors, particularly mallards, pochards, grebes, teals and other species from the north. The park itself covers 104 sq km (40 sq miles). Alpine meadows line the lake shores and fields of millet and wheat are flanked by pine forests.

There are apple orchards and the lake waters are rich with fish. Several villages stand on Rara's shores, their houses, terraced like the land, backed on to steep hillsides. Wildlife includes hordes of impertinent monkeys who raid farms and grain stores with seeming impunity. Set like a sapphire in its Himalayan brooch, Lake Rara is both a botanical and zoological treasure.

Another national park, **Khaptad** — several days distant, southwest of Rara — stands at much the same elevation, covering 187 sq km (71 sq miles): a floral repository of high-altitude conifers, oak and rhododendron groves, its open meadows reserved for royalty.

To the west lie more little-known valleys reachable only on foot. Southwards the trade caravans — even goats and sheep are used as pack animals — must travel daunting distances over forbidding terrain before reaching the temperate and fertile lands of the Mahabharat and the tropical fields of the Terai.

HOW TO GET THERE

Permits are needed for travel to these areas. If you obtain one, you next face the obstacle of getting on a flight. Guides can be difficult to find in this part of Nepal, as can be food.

DOLPO

Northeast of Jumla, so remote from the nearest road it takes three weeks of tough walking to reach, Dolpo and its monasteries straggle up a pitch of long, tortuous ridges, above an expanse of rumpled, brown and barren mountains. The creed of

the shaman — spirit-possessed holy man — still rules here, as it has done for 15 centuries. In the rarefied air of these 3,000- to 5,000-m (10,000-to 16,000 ft-)-heights, perceptions and sensations are acute. Sitting atop a mountain ridge in the dark night in a yak-hair tent, wind howling, rain lashing down, watching the Shaman as he is taken hold of by "Fierce Red Spirit with the gift of the life force of seven black wolves" is enough to convince even the most cynical witness from western civilization of the power of the supernatural.

The population of a few hundred in Dolpo has been swollen by Tibetan refugees. All make votive offerings, some of tablets made from a compound of clay and funeral ash and delicately carved with a pantheon of Buddhist deities. At a height of more than 4,000 m (13,000 ft), Dolpo's grain fields are among the highest cultivated land in the world. The paths and trails that lead through this tiny principality of old are often no more than fragile, crumbling shale strata sticking out of sheer cliff faces. With a precipitous drop a step away on one side, as you stoop low beneath an overhang, you'll agree it's a climb only for the agile.

This is a land of holy peaks of which the most revered is the valley's sacred Crystal Mountain. According to local legend, a thousand years ago a Tibetan ascetic, Drutob Senge Yeshe, flew to the top of the harsh slab of rock, a massif that rises out of the shale around it, aboard a magic snow lion and challenged the god who lived there. When he defeated the deity, the rock turned to crystal. Now Dolpo people circle the

16 km (10 mile) circumference of the mountain's base in an annual pilgrimage, or *kora*. Its many strata — layers of rock — also draw pilgrims of a different faith: geologists hunting fossils.

HOW TO GET THERE

The only way to get into the Dolpo area is to trek. A special permit is required, as are experienced guides. It takes at least 14 days from Pokhara to hike into the region.

MUSTANG

Dolpo's neighboring kingdom, Mustang, is reached by a long trek through the Kali Gandaki gorge and over the one, desperately high, southeast facing pass into Dolpo. The native name for this lunar land of canyons and ridges is Lo. In the capital, **Mantang,** dominated by fortress walls, the central feature is the massive white-walled **Royal palace** in which lives the world's least-known monarch. Schools are bringing change. But while the youngsters come home filled with stories of space flights, which they've heard on the classroom wireless, their grandparents still believe the world is flat and shaped like a half moon.

Lo Mantang, in fact, is the full name of the 2,000-sq-km (760-sq-mile) kingdom of His Highness King Jigme Parwal Bista, founded in the fourteenth century by the Tibetan warlord Ama Pal. It lies on a barren valley floor at around 4,800 m (15,000 ft), snug against the Tibetan border on three sides and guarded by formidable 7,300-m (24,000-ft)-high mountains, pierced only by narrow passes. On the Nepal side, massive Dhaulagiri I, at 8,167 m (26,795 ft) the world's seventh-highest mountain, provides the defense that has sealed Lo from the outside world through the centuries.

Fabled Mustang, as it's now known on the maps, is only an "honorary" kingdom these days but each night King Jigme, the 25th monarch since the 1480s, orders the only gate of the mud-walled capital shut and barred to keep out invaders. Twelve dukes, 60 monks, 152 families and eight witches occupy the capital. King Jigme still owns serfs who plow his stony fields for grain crops. But Lo's treasures are many and priceless: a wealth of Tibetan art, monasteries and forts set in its 23 villages and two other towns. Many of Mustang's monasteries — the name derives from the Tibetan phrase meaning "plain of prayer", *mon thang* — are carved into cliff faces. You climb a ladder to reach them. Other wealth lies in the rocky hills: turquoise and rich deposits of alluvial gold on the beds of the rivers that course through the land. But Lo's citizens consider the task of panning for this metal beneath their dignity.

The King's subjects — Lopas, who are Lamaist Buddhists — number around 8,000 and speak a dialect of the Tibetan language. The women practice polyandry — often marrying two or three brothers. The king

keeps his authority as a ruler by virtue of a 160-year-old treaty with King Birendra Shah's dynasty and annual payment to Nepal of 886 rupees and one horse. In return King Jigme holds the rank of colonel in the Nepali Army.

So archaic is the kingdom, matches were unknown until a few years ago and superstitious fears are rampant. The whole land goes to bed in terror of Lo's 416 demons of land, sky, fire and water and life is dedicated to warding off the evil spirits that cause Lo's 1,080 known diseases as well as five forms of violent death. Thus, for three days each year, King Jigme's subjects celebrate New Year by "chasing the demons": with the noise of cymbals, drums and notes made by playing on human skulls, filling the air.

Not a single tree grows in this arid and withered land. To supplement their monotonous diet of yak milk and sour cheese, the Lopas nurture fragile gardens. For trade, they deal in salt from Tibet. The trail they follow winds for 240 km (149 miles) along the Kali Gandaki gorge between Dhaulagiri and Annapurna.

HOW TO GET THERE

Closed for many years, Mustang can now be reached on foot from Pokhara with guides and porters. Permits for the region cost US$700 for 10 days.

Valley in the shadows of Tibet's Cho Oyu, one of the world's highest mountains.

High Altitude Trekking and Treks

THE HIGH MOUNTAIN VALLEYS AND PASSES

For many visitors, the reason for coming to Nepal is the prospect of a high-altitude trek. The best time to trek is late September and early October when the mountain views are superb (and can continue to be so throughout crisp winter). The first quarter of the year provides perfect trekking conditions, with the one drawback that views of the peaks are often obscured by hazy conditions. Summer

from Pokhara with dozens of high-altitude walks to choose from, including the Royal trek that follows in the footsteps of the Prince of Wales and gives you three to five days in Gurung and Gurkha country, east of the Pokhara valley. Highlights of the six- to 10-day Ghandrung to Ghorapani trek are outstanding panoramas of Machhapuchhare, Annapurna and Dhaulagiri. The 17- to 19-day Kali Gandaki to Muktinah route is in excellent condition in the winter, although you might encounter some snow at Ghorapani.

is usually condemned as sticky and the trails are infested with leaches; but those who have trekked in the summer say that the leaches are found only in fairly low altitudes and summer treks are gloriously free of crowds.

There are literally hundreds of treks to choose from in the eight major trekking regions of Nepal. Your choice will depend upon the time you have and the season.

The major trekking regions are: **Annapurna Himal, Dhaulagiri Himal, Manaslu, Langtang Himal-Jugal-Himal Ganesh Himal, Khumbu Himal, Kanchenjunga, Makalu,** and **Rolwaling Himal.**

The most popular trekking areas are **Annapurna Himal** and **Dhaulagiri Himal**

Treks in **Dhaulagiri** take you through a veritable wonderland of meadows, forest and villages and among some of the happiest and most generous people in the world, allowing you to savor the simple lifestyles — and delightful scenery — to the full. The contrast between the stark, ice-white peaks set against the conifer and rhododendron forests, the azure sky above, verdant spring and summer fields below, can steal your breath as much as climbing these heights.

Villages straggle down the hillsides in a series of terraces, just like the paddies and grain fields and there's always time and reason enough to rest in one of the many tea houses, simple little cafés where the refreshments help beat the debilitating dehydration brought about by high altitudes and exercise.

In contrast to the dozens of trekking options around Dhaulagiri and Annapurna, there are few around **Manaslu.** This is all the more delightful because these tracks take you to the feet of such giants as 8,158-m (26,766-ft)-high Manaslu and its sister peaks, including sacred 7,406-m (24,298-ft)-high Ganesh Himal I with its seven lesser peaks and forbidding 7,893-m (25,895-ft)-high Himal Chuli.

lakes up to a height of more than 4,500 m (15,000 ft).

Close to the border is **Somdu,** Nepal's most remote permanent settlement, a village of 200 souls — about 40 families — whose fields and paddies are covered with snow until late in the year. Nearby, there are also the twin villages of **Li** and **Lo.** All along the way the trails are lined with the inevitable prayer stones, *mani,* of the staunch Buddhists who inhabit the region.

Retracing your footsteps to **Trisuli Bazaar,** turn northeast and climb the trail that

Take the Trisuli valley through Trisuli Bazaar around the north face of Himal Chuli and Manaslu and you'll walk through hills clad with evergreen forests, thundering waterfalls and alpine flora: oaks, alders, firs and rhododendrons. Village houses are sturdy gabled, two-storied brick and thatch affairs. Among the many large and striking monasteries are some which are surprisingly small — one, with a pagoda-style roof and a circular top, is like a cross between a lighthouse and a Suffolk grain store.

A 14-day trek leaves **Ganesh Himal** in the east and takes you around the north face of **Himal Chuli** and **Manaslu** — almost into China's backyard, through bleak and windswept passes, skirting glaciers and frozen

winds along the east bank of the Trisuli River to enter one of Nepal's most enchanted regions and another classic trekking region — fabled **Langtang Himal** with its monasteries, stupas, prayer walls and places made sacred by the Hindu scriptures.

When Nepal opened its doors to foreigners in 1950, the first to venture into its hidden mountain sanctuaries were British climbers Eric Shipton and H.W. Tilman who "discovered" Langtang Himal's many

PREVIOUS PAGES: Trekking along a precipitous trail in the high country of the Himalayas (left). A mountain woman (right) enjoys the fine weather. OPPOSITE: The Sherpa village of Namche Bazaar, main gateway to Everest, glows at night. ABOVE: Namche Bazaar, by day, nestles in neat rows beneath icecapped Khumde.

High-Altitude Trekking and Treks

marvels — just 75 km (47 miles) north of Kathmandu — unknown then to many Nepalis. No city in the world can claim a more incredible backdrop. Tilman's comment that it is "one of the most beautiful valleys in the world" is still considered an understatement by some.

Outside the rustic tea houses that refresh the traveler, ancient bo trees, their gnarled limbs like rheumy fingers, spread a thick canopy of shade over Langtang's version of the patio, old stone terraces with seats stepped into the stonework.

Dominating the valley at its north end is Nepal's 7,245-m (23,769-ft)-high Langtang Lirung, a few kilometers beyond which, on the Tibetan border, rises its sister peak, 7,238-m (23,748-ft)-high Langtang Ri; both overshadowed by Shisha Pangma — sacred 8,013-m (26,291-ft)-high Gosainthan of Hindu mythology — one of the legendary abodes of Shiva. You get sudden and unexpected views of some of these peaks as you take the trail hacked out of the gorge above Trisuli Bazaar. On the more level areas, it cuts through stands of juniper and rhododendron, blue pine and cushion plants.

Shops and boarding rooms ABOVE in Namche Bazaar, at Solu Khumbu. OPPOSITE: Sherpa porters on market day at Namche Bazaar.

For centuries this trail has been a trade route between Kathmandu and Rasuwa Garhi across the border in Tibet. During July and August this rocky track becomes a mass of humanity as devout Hindu pilgrims, worshippers of Shiva, head for Langtang's **Gosainkund** lakeland. These half-a-dozen small lakes sparkle like jewels in the midday sunshine and are said to have been formed when Shiva thrust his trident into the mountainside. From Gosainkund it's possible to continue over the pass into the remote but eternally beautiful reaches of upper **Helambu**, best in springtime when the rhododendrons bloom. Here, too, the headwaters of Nepal's major river, the **Sun Kosi**, mingle together from scores of tumbling waterfalls, roaring rivers and laughing streams.

Swiss explorer, geologist, adventurer Tony Hagen shared Tilman's passion for Langtang Himal and ignited the same feelings in another Swiss — a UN farm advisor — who built a Swiss cheese factory close to Kyangjin monastery at around 3,840 m (12,500 ft) and which, whatever the quality of the cheese, provides some of the most spectacular mountain views found anywhere.

Langtang's principal purpose is as a wildlife and botanical sanctuary — **Langtang National Park**, a haven for the endangered snow leopard, leopard, Himalayan black bear, red panda and wild dog. Outside the 20 or so alpine villages roam 30 different species of wildlife, while more than 150 different kinds of birds have nested among the region's 1,000 botanical species. It is the most popular of all Nepal's wilderness areas — a wonderland of hardy mountain people, animals, birds, forests and mountains — much of it preserved within the nation's second largest national park spread across 1,243 sq km (472 sq miles).

Khumbu Himal is for the serious, hardy trekker — a 25- to 30-day walk interspersed with Sherpa villages. Though the scenery is sensational, it's extremely cold. If you are flying in and out, expect some delays. **Lukla** flights are inextricably tied to the weather — and if you miss your flight the staff drop you back to the bottom of the list which, on one occasion, meant an extended

stay of some three weeks for one unlucky person.

By plane it is only forty minutes from Kathmandu to Lukla, more than 2,700 m (9,000 ft) above sea level. Its landing strip is on an uphill gradient, one side of which drops precipitously thousands of meters to the floor of the Dudh Kosi valley.

Namche Bazaar is well above Lukla. There is also a 4,000-m (13,000-ft)-high airfield nearby — at **Syangboche** where guests of the Everest View Hotel alight. Each bedroom in this hotel is equipped with oxygen.

Almost everybody who visits Nepal dreams of standing at the foot of the world's greatest mountain, but it's a realistic goal only for the fittest. Most of the trail takes you above 4,000 m (13,000 ft) in thin, freezing, raw air — chest pounding, lungs gasping — to the 6,000-m (20,000-ft)-high Everest base camp, higher than any point in Africa or Europe.

Yet it's not just the mountain and its huddle of neighboring peaks, three of the world's seven highest, which is the sole attraction, for this is also a land of fable and monastery, remote meadows, wildlife and the home of the hardy Sherpas and their colorful culture.

The trail from Lukla climbs up the Dudh Kosi canyon zigzagging from side to side through stone-walled fields, rustic villages and hardy forests. The Buddhist prayer — *Om mani padme hum,* Hail to the jewel in the lotus — is carved everywhere, on the huge boulders that look like enormous tables standing by the side of the trail and on top of long stone walls.

These carvings are built to pacify local demons, deities or the spirit of some dead person and should be circled clockwise, because the earth and the universe revolve in that direction. If you are walking straight on, keep them on the left as a mark of respect. These are prayers and supplications artistically inscribed with great devotion. Don't take them as souvenirs — it's sacrilege, much as defiling a Christian church or Muslim mosque would be.

Elsewhere, scraps of colored cloth flutter in the breeze, or a bamboo framework is covered with colored threads woven into an

intricate design; sometimes you may find dyed wheat-flour dumplings lying on the ground — offerings to malignant demons or deities and not to be touched or disturbed by strangers. These prayer flags may look old and ragged but to the Nepalis, especially the Sherpas, they never fade — their prayers of supplication and gratitude are always carried on the breeze to Buddha, the Compassionate One.

Before Namche Bazaar, at the village of Josare, lies the headquarters of **Sagarmatha National Park** where rangers and wardens, used to high-altitude living, relax at 4,000 m (13,000 ft) with volleyball games. More than 5,000 trekkers a year climb this trail to enter the national park's 1,243 sq km (472 sq miles) of mountain wilderness; the rumpled

brown-green buttresses of Everest ascending ever higher as you climb.

The town, capital of the Sherpa community, is set on a small plateau at the foot of sacred 5,760-m (18,901-ft)-high Khumbila which stanches the long run of the Ngojumba glacier as it slides down from the base of Cho Oyu. It is the focal point of everything that occurs in the Everest region. Every Saturday morning there's a colorful market when hundreds trek in from the surrounding villages and towns to haggle and argue, buying and selling. Namche's streets step up the barren, rocky slopes of Khumbila lined with pleasant white-washed two-story homes with shingle and tin roofs.

Sherpa monasteries, reflecting their Tibetan heritage, are the most striking in

Nepal. You'll find them in the towns of **Khumjung** and **Kunde**, which stand above Namche Bazaar on the slopes of Khumbila. They are well worth visiting if you can make the climb. West of Namche, at the foot of the Bhote Kosi valley, which is fed by the Jasamba glacier, there's a particularly impressive monastery in the village of **Thami.**

You can use Namche to approach **Cho Oyu,** either west up the Bhote Kosi valley or north of Khumbila up the Dudh Kosi valley. The westward route takes you up the Renjo pass, coming down to **Dudh Pokhari,** a beautiful glacial lake in the Ngojumba glacier. There's a passable chance en route

Buddhist prayer stones, *mani,* mark the trails to many sacred mountains in the high Himalayas.

of seeing some of Sagarmatha National Park's wildlife: wolf, bear, musk deer, feral goat species, even the brilliantly colored crimson-horned or Impeyan pheasants of this region.

A hard four-hour slog, or a full day's strenuous effort from Namche on the trail to Everest, you'll come to Khumbu and the most famous of its monasteries, **Thangboche,** known the world over for its stupendous views of Everest, Lhotse, with the unmistakable 6,855-m (22,491-ft)-high obelisk of Ama Dablam, in the background.

After his successful ascent of Everest, on May 29, 1953, Sir Edmund Hillary became New Zealand's Ambassador to India and Nepal and devoted much of his diplomatic career and personal life to improving the lot of the Sherpa community that he has come to love. He is a frequent visitor to the monastery and its presiding lama. It was his initiative that led to the establishment of Sagarmatha National Park in 1975. The park was run by New Zealand experts until 1981 when Nepal took over its management. Hillary has been back frequently, helping to build schools and community centers.

Civilizing forces, not all for the better, have come apace to the once-isolated Sherpas whose festivals add color and fantasy to life in this otherwise barren but beautiful region. There's also a much more relaxed trek — for those who don't wish to scale great heights — by foot or pony along the old trade route between Kathmandu and Pokhara. Including a visit to Gorkha, this takes between eight and 10 days.

In the far west, trekking from **Jumla** always poses problems — simply because it's so difficult to reach this remote region. But the spectacular scenery makes the effort worthwhile. The trekking "high season" — between October and December — is the best time for high-altitude climbing when the more popular routes — Khumbu, Pokhara, Ghandrung, Ghorapani and Annapurna — are congested.

SOME CLASSIC TREKS STEP BY STEP

KANCHENJUNGA

Astride the Sikkim border with eastern Nepal, **Kanchenjunga** is the world's third-highest mountain and this 13-day outward journey depends on absolute fitness and acclimatization, as it takes the trekker from the subtropical lowlands to a height of more than 5,000 m (16,000 ft) above sea level — around the base of some magnificent satellite peaks — to Yalung glacier. You need Sherpa guides and first-class equipment including rugged tents, together with adequate rations as food supplies are not easy to obtain in this region.

It should go without saying that a trek of this sort will need to be organized with a reliable trekking agency. Permits are only issued to groups. See the TREKKING AGENCIES section of the TRAVELERS' TIPS chapter for some recommended agencies.

Most agencies will organize a flight to Biratnagar. From here a rented vehicle should be able to get you to the trailhead, Basantpur, on the same day. The alternative is an 11- to 13-hour bus journey from Kathmandu to Dhahran, where you stay overnight before traveling on to Basantpur.

First Day

From Basantpur the path goes to **Dobhan;** it splits into two — one continuing along the ridgeback, the other winding up and down the hillside to the right. Stick to the ridge: it's shorter and the mountain views are spectacular.

An irrigation duct takes water to the nearby fields as the trail climbs a gentle slope through the twin villages of Tsute. Beyond them, through the forest, the path turns right, leaving the ridge to climb through stands of rhododendrons before emerging in a delightful alpine meadow — ideal for camping but without water.

Re-enter the forest, however and climb gently upwards for about another fifteen minutes to the two houses of **Door Pani,** at a height of 2,780 m (9,000 ft), where there's a beautiful meadow in which to camp with plentiful water.

Second Day

From the meadow you now climb through the forest to another ridge where the trail now begins to switchback — up and down — in true Himalayan fashion. Follow this for approximately half an hour before descending steeply to the left for about 200 m (650 ft) to the village of Tinjure Phedi with its tea house.

From here the trail follows a ridgeback through copses of rhododendrons beneath sprawling alpine meadows and is relatively smooth and even, until the hamlet of **Chauki,** with its 11 houses and a tea shop.

There's no cultivation around these parts and the meadows are used for summer pastures. As you walk from Chauki, the magnificent peak of Makalu dominates the horizon, but not long after this you get your first glimpse — and what a glimpse — of Kanchenjunga. Soon after this, the trail arrives at the foot of the Mongol Bharari pass.

Lined with mani stones, it winds gently up to the saddle, through rhododendron forest, cresting the ridge at the hamlet of Ram Pokhari — two lakes and five small houses.

Now the trail winds along the top of a grassy, undulating ridge before descending to **Gupha Pokhari** and its enchanting lake, at a height of 2,985 m (9,790 ft).

Third Day

Take the pass to the right, skirting the ridge directly in front of you, when you leave Gupha Pokhari. You'll get your last glimpse of Makalu and Chamlang before turning northeast into the Kanchenjunga massif.

You enter this range on your right, along a winding switchback trail; after an hour's

walk you come to the crests of a 3,025-m (10,000-ft)-high pass that descends to **Dobhan.** Along the downward trail are many bunkhouses for trekkers and porters where it's possible to spend the night.

After passing the bunkhouses, the trail climbs the second of two small hills before beginning the real descent, through thick forest, to the bottom of the pass and the rice paddies and grain fields of the hamlet of **Gurja Gaon.** From this trail, there are magnificent views of Jannu and Kanchenjunga.

The path continues its descent from Gurja Gaon, rejoining, on the right, the alternate route from Basantpur, to a campsite near **Nesum,** at 1,650 m (5,400 ft).

Fourth Day

Trekking in the Himalayas is not for those who seek to climb ever upward. Trails plunge up and down 3,000 m (10,000 ft) or more and from Nesum the trail continues its descent through a maze of rice paddies to Dobhan and the valley of the **Tamar river.**

Trekkers OPPOSITE rest outside a tea house on the trail to Mount Everest and Sherpa women take to the trail ABOVE near Lukla.

There are many hamlets, villages and tea houses along the way. After about a 90-minute walk you reach **Dobhan**, a picturesque Newar settlement, with a village store and many houses.

It's here that the trail crosses the **Meiwa Khola**, a tributary of the Tamar, on to a level plain with a small hamlet, after which it reaches the **Tamar.** Cross here to the left bank, via the suspension footbridge, where the road divides — one a narrow path to Ghunsa, the other a long, climbing ridgeback trail to **Taplejung.**

From here, the track starts climbing steeply as it zigzags its way to **Deoringe school** before easing back into a more moderate climb through terraced fields and scattered forests, passing by the hamlet of **Taribun.** There are many more houses along this well-traveled route.

Finally, just above a public bathhouse, you reach **Taplejung** at 1,798 m (5,800 ft), the administrative headquarters of this district with a post and telegraph office, hospital, government offices and a military post. Taplejung is a good place to replenish food and other supplies, but fresh meat and vegetables are only available on Saturdays, when the city's markets are open.

Fifth Day

You leave Taplejung and its cobblestone streets, pass the water reservoir, and follow the path to the airfield — a very steep climb.

There's a hotel at the edge of the airfield on a level plateau and there's now a gentle climb through the flower-filled meadowlands to the forest, with the mountains to your right, before descending to **Lali Kharka.**

Across the valley stands **Bhanjyang,** which you reach the next day but for now your descent culminates in the fertile fields around **Tambawa,** at 2,000 m (6,500 ft), where you can camp in the fields or near the school.

Sixth Day

From Tambawa to **Pa Khola** takes around 90 minutes, first to get to a ridgeback trail and then circuitously down the mountain to Pa Khola.

At Pa Khola, the trail cuts through terraced rice paddies, then across a suspension footbridge to **Kunjar.** Before you reach this lovely alpine village, surrounded by thick rain forest, it passes through a few hamlets.

The path carries on gently upward out of Kunjar until you are high above **Tambawa.** Soon it reaches **Bhanjyang** with many tea houses and striking views of Kanchenjunga, framed by South peak, Main peak and Yalung Kang.

The path descends again, to the left, on a pleasantly easy slope to the terraced fields of **Khesewa,** at 2,100 m (6,800 ft), where you can camp in the surrounding fields.

Seventh Day

From Khesewa, the trail descends through forest to the **Nandeva Khola** on the left and, crossing the river, continues down along its banks before entering the forest to the left to begin the climb up the next range of hills to **Loppoding.**

Now the path switchbacks up and down to the rest area, at the delightfully-named hamlet of **Fun Fun.** After this, follow the ridgeback into the hills on the right bank of the **Kabeli Khola,** before a gradual descent through rice paddies and grain fields to the village of **Anpan.**

From Anpan, the trail follows a ridge-back up an easy slope to **Ponpe Dhara,** which sits on its crest. You can pause here to take in the splendid view of distant Jannu before continuing the winding descent through hamlets and farm fields to the Kasshawa Khola, which you cross by suspension bridge. On the other side you make the slow climb to the village of **Mamankhe.**

Eighth Day

This hike starts with an easy climb, skirting a formidable ridge, to the village of Dekadin. After this, the trail follows the right bank of the Kabeli Khola, about 200 to 300 m (600 to 900 ft) above its raging waters, winding around various ridges, cliffs and streams.

On the whole, this three-and-a-half hour walk is an easy up and down trek with constant views of the river below and the little farmsteads and their fields on the hills opposite.

Finally, you descend some stone steps to the river itself and then on to another that takes you on a gradual climb away from the river through villages and fields.

Eventually, after about two hours hard climbing, the trail reaches the remote village of **Yamphudin,** at 2,150 m (7,000 ft). Report to the checkpost.

Camp here in fields or in house compounds. You may prefer to engage new porters for the hazards of cold, snow and altitude ahead, as those from Dhahran are not well-suited to the rugged challenge of the Kanchenjunga range.

Ninth Day

Yamphudin is where the real climbing begins. There are two options for the route to Lamite Bhanjyang. The favorite choice is to cross the river and trek through Dhupi Bhanjyang.

For those who prefer a tougher challenge, the second route requires a climb up a mountain path from **Yamphudin,** on the right bank of **Omje Khola,** that crosses a stream early in its course.

It then plunges down two hours through the fields back to the **Omje Khola,** which you must cross again to reach an extremely steep mountain ridge that, at first, demands

care with every step. But the trail soon enters the forest where there is little or no sense of height. Gradually the severity of the gradient eases into a relaxed climb, still through thick forest, until it emerges on a level open saddle.

Eventually the trail reaches the climbing hut at **Chitre** where you can spend the night. However, in the dry season there's no water and you will have to walk on another 90 minutes to a little tarn beneath **Lamite Bhanjyang.** You can ask at **Yamphudin** before you set off if water is available.

Tenth Day

The ridgeback from Chitre is lined with magnolias and bamboo but when the trail climbs beyond the bamboo belt it reaches **Lamite** and its single shelter — a simple structure consisting of a roof with supporting posts.

The trail then ascends through thick stands of rhododendron, along a ridge to **Lamite Bhanjyang,** at 3,430 m (11,250 ft), with Jannu rising up before you above the ridge in all its magnificence and behind you panoramic views of the foothills around Dhahran.

Climb about 150 m (550 ft) from here on the right before descending, through thick forests of rhododendron, to the **Simbua Khola,** with Kanchenjunga's majestic snowclad peak floating above the trees.

The gentle descent takes the trail almost to the river and then climbs along the left

Sherpa woman and children OPPOSITE outside a high country tea shop on one of Nepal's many popular trekking trails. Sherpa father and son ABOVE at Lukla.

High-Altitude Trekking and Treks

bank for a short distance before crossing over a wooden bridge to the right bank and the campsite at **Torontan**, at 3,080 m (10,100 ft), where you can sleep in one of the caves.

Eleventh Day

Follow the path, past the caves, along the right bank of the **Simbua Khola**. The forested walls of the valley are thick with pine and rhododendron.

Eventually, after about two hours walking, the trail reaches **Whata** with its single hut, where it crosses to the right bank of the stream in front of the hut and continues through the thick forest to the snowline.

You'll see a Sherpa shrine with a huge boulder, shaped like a snake. It's designed to ward off the demons, for the Sherpas believe that if anyone dies beyond this point, evil spirits will fall upon the mountains.

The path leads down to the river bank and up a difficult trail to **Tseram** where you can see your ultimate destination — the terminal moraine of **Yalung glacier.** Behind it are the 7,353-m (24,120-ft)-high Kabru and 7,349 m (24,112 ft) Talung peak. Camp in one of the caves.

Twelfth Day

A steep slope, descending from the left, bars the way out of Tseram and you have to retrace your trail to the bank of the **Simbua Khola,** then around its base, before climbing up through stony, terraced field to **Yalung Bara** where a single stone hut marks the end of the tree line. From here you have to carry enough fuelwood for the rest of the trek.

Just above, past several small stone huts, the path comes to the right bank of the entrance to the **Yalung glacier** and **Lapsang,** with Lapsang La valley at the left.

Now the trail comes to a tiny pond and skirts a protruding cliff face — when you suddenly see before you a stunning panorama: the peaks of 7,317-m (24,005-ft)-high Kabru S., 6,678-m (21,910-ft)-high Rathong and 6,147-m (20,168-ft)-high Kokthan. Follow the flat trail to the **Ramze** at 4,560 m (15,000 ft) where there is a hut in which you can sleep.

Chortens and temples appear unexpectedly in the high places of Nepal.

Thirteenth Day

The magnificent Yalung glacier veers left at Ramze and just around the corner next morning you will get your first close up views of mighty Kanchenjunga.

Now the trail climbs the lateral moraine to a **Buddhist stupa** from which it descends steeply to the glacier floor and a path marked by cairns. Lungs gasp in the rarefied air but eventually, after about four hours of really intense effort, you reach the campsite atop the glacier, at 4,890 m (16,000 ft), with magnificent views of 7,710-m (25,294-ft)-high Jannu.

The vista of the mountains surrounding Yalung glacier opens before you — and at the final camp, **Corner Camp,** at 5,140 m (16,900 ft), on the left bank of the glacier, there is a stupendous mountain panorama — a fitting reward for the effort it takes to reach this point.

Fourteenth to Twenty-Second Day

Depending on how your agency has staged your trek, you will either trek nine days back to Basantpur or six days to Suketar, which has flights to Biratnagar and sometimes direct connections to Kathmandu.

MAKALU

One of Nepal's most splendid — and demanding — treks, takes you from **Tumlingtar** north through the subtropical **Arun valley** and over the 4,000-m (13,000-ft)-high **Shipton pass,** to the slopes of the three great peaks of Makalu, Everest and Lhotse. You must carry all your supplies and Sherpa guides are absolutely essential. Altitude sickness is an ever present threat and, until the monsoons, Shipton pass is buried in snow.

First Day

From **Tumlingtar** airfield, climb the hill and walk through level rice paddies and scattered houses and then across a series of terraced hills. To the right you see the waters of the **Shawa Khola**. In the distance stands

Chamlang. Soon the path becomes a ridgeback with many travelers, tea houses and shaded rest areas.

After passing a bubbling spring the path moves to the right flank of the ridge and, after a short climb, you will see more houses and finally arrive at the checkpost at the entrance to **Khandbari,** with its shop-lined main street and large open bazaar.

Khandbari is the administrative capital of the district with a bank, hospital and school. It's a good place to stock up on food and other essentials. A meadow out-

side the village makes an excellent campsite.

The ridge trail continues to **Mane Bhanjyang,** where it divides — one branch going left to the ridge route; the other straight through the rice paddies. Follow this latter route on the gentle climb to the village of **Panguma.**

There's not too much to see here and the walk is somewhat monotonous as you climb to **Bhote Bash,** set at about 1,720 m (5,600 ft), where you can camp in one of the fields.

Second Day

When you leave Bhote Bash, you also leave the farmlands and turn right onto

A precarious log and stone bridge leads across the swollen floodwaters that interrupt a rough mountain trail.

the left side of the ridge as it climbs to the pass above. The level path passes through scrub and fields to **Gogune** and on into forest.

After a walk of about two hours, the switchback trail exits at the Gurung village of **Chichira,** set on top of a ridge, then continues to Kuwapani. At this point you get impressive but far distant views of Makalu.

From the three-house settlement of **Kuwapani,** the path veers to the right of the ridge, arriving at **Samurati's** lone house, with the fields of **Sedua** visible on the hillside opposite and, beyond, the walls of the Shipton pass.

Not long after this, the trail cuts down the ridge where it veers left, at a single house, to **Runbaun.** Now the trail becomes extremely steep and rough.

Great care must be exercised — and not only on the trail. The suspension bridge over the Arun river, which takes about three-and-a-half hours to reach, is narrow and precarious with missing footboards. One careless step could be fatal.

where there are painted mani stones and a cave in which you can sleep.

Leaving the village, the path divides into two. Take the left fork into the forest through **Fururu** to the rest area in **Daujia Dhara Deorali**, where the path levels out. Down in the forest on the left, across a small stream and over another ridge, there's an unusual combination of painted mani stones.

Eventually, the trail reaches **Mure,** a village at the right of the path, where you can camp in the fields or in one of the house compounds.

Third Day

Leave the village down a slope facing it

After the bridge, the trail climbs steeply along a precarious and crumbling incline on the right bank up to the grain fields and hamlet of **Rumruma.**

The trail leaves the hamlet through terraced fields to **Sedua,** at 1,480 m (4,855 ft), where you can camp at the school near a spring.

Fourth Day

From **Sedua,** the trail leaves the Arun river and enters the watershed of the **Kashuwa Khola.** Climb a mountainside dotted with terraced fields and forests. After about two hours walk a *chorten,* or Buddhist stupa, marks the Sherpa village of **Naba Gaon** with its monastery.

Climb a ridge, lined with mani stones on the right and follow the trail along the right bank of the **Kashuwa Khola** through **Kharshing Kharka,** which has two huts. The path cuts through thick hill forest where fallen trees can make walking difficult. Eventually, it crosses a small stream and leads into the remote village of **Tashi Gaon,** at 2,050 m (6,700 ft), with its attractive timber houses covered with bamboo roofing. You can camp in the fields near the village.

Fifth Day

Leave **Tashi Gaon** through forest up a gentle slope, across a rocky area and stream, to the meadows of **Uteshe.** From the top of the next ridge there are striking mountain panoramas where the path veers right.

The path continues gradually upwards, across a stream into thick bamboo. When it leaves the bamboo, the trail enters a rhododendron forest and becomes markedly steeper; passing Dhara Kharka on the crest of the ridge and then to **Unshisa** on the Ishwa Khola side of the ridge, finally reaching the campsite at **Kauma,** at the top of the ridge, after about five hours walking. Just below the ridge, about 20 m (60 ft) down on the Kashuwa Khola side, there are some caves where you can sleep.

Sixth Day

From Kauma, the trail climbs to the top of a ridge that offers the best mountain landscape of the whole trail — a truly dramatic panorama at the far end of the valley of 7,317-m (24,005-ft)-high Chamlang, 6,739-m (22,110-ft)-high Peak Six, 6,105 m (20,030 ft) Peak Seven and the long-awaited 8,481-m (27,825-ft)-high Makalu, with the outline of the Kanchenjunga range to the east.

The trail now begins to climb **Shipton pass.** In fact, there are two passes — **Keke La** and **Tutu La.** Rugged cliffs bar the way and the trail traverses left to a small pond, then climbs up to **Keke La,** at 4,127 m (13,500 ft), then down into an s-shaped valley, past a small tarn and up to **Tutu La.**

Here the trail descends to a level stretch before veering left, past a waterfall and across a stream and on through forest to **Mumbuk,** set at 3,500 m (11,500 ft) amid pines and rhododendron.

Seventh Day

The trail leaves the campsite, following the course of a winding stream for about 200 m (650 ft) before turning left and down along the side of another stream, turning left yet again, past a cave, to the **Barun Khola.**

The path takes the right bank with views of Peak Six. Beware of the frequent rockfalls. Soon Makalu comes into view and the trail exits onto a terraced hill and the meadows of **Tematan Kharka.**

The trail continues along flat hills to **Yangre Kharka** where there are some caves, and on into rhododendron forest.

Here it leaves the **Barun Khola,** climbing gently up the side of a wide valley and turns right, across a stream, to the single hut of **Nehe Kharka** 2,670 m (8,760 ft).

Eighth Day

Leave the campsite, past a cave and cross to the left bank of the **Barun Khola** over a bridge set on a large boulder in midstream, into rhododendron forest. The path becomes steep as it zigzags up to the meadowlands on the slopes of **Ripock Kharka.**

Here the path leads away from the Barun Khola, on a modest gradient, through **Jark Kharka** to **Ramara** — offering views along the way, one after the other, of 6,830-m (22,409-ft)-high Pyramid Peak, 6,720-m (22,048-ft)-high Peak Four, 6,477-m (21,251-ft)-high Peak Three, 6,404-m (21,101-ft)-high Peak Five, Peak Six and Chamlang.

At Ramara, approaching the Barun Khola, the trail reaches the snout of **Lower Barun glacier** and continues along the glacier's left bank to the headwaters of the **Barun Khola** and **Mere** where there is a cave for camping. There are no more forests and you must carry fuelwood with you from this point.

The trail continues on the right across some rocky, glacial terrain to **Shershon,** at 4,615 m (15,000 ft).

Ninth Day

The majestic crest of Makalu dominates the horizon at Shershon as the trail skirts the base of its southeast ridge in an easy climb onto lateral moraine. Here, glowering down from its massive height, the mountain seems to fill the sky.

Take the trail down to the riverbed, across the stream and up a terraced hill to **Makalu base camp,** set in a pastoral meadow at 4,800 m (15,750 ft), where there's a stone hut without a roof.

Makalu base camp is an ideal place from which to explore the area around the foot of this great mountain, including the Barun glacier.

Tenth to Sixteenth Day
The return trek to **Tumlingtar** takes about seven days.

Turn right in the village square to a steep ridge route that descends to the right bank of the Tamba Kosi and the bridge, which crosses to a trail just above the rushing water.

Eventually, the trail arrives at **Piguti** where it crosses the **Gumbu Khola** to a pleasant meadow where you can camp.

Second Day
Leave camp, past the suspension bridge over the main stream and follow the path along the right bank with views of Gaurisankar rising up at the far end of the valley.

ROLWALING HIMAL

Few tourists or trekkers visit Rolwaling Himal — getting permits for the region is not easy — yet it offers some of the finest mountain trekking anywhere. You need full equipment, including durable tents and Sherpa guides. To reach the trailhead take a bus from Kathmandu to Lamosangu and then a van to **Charikot.**

First Day
From Charikot, Rolwaling Himal is clearly visible in the distance. The trail out of town leads down a wide, gentle gradient through many hamlets to the village of **Dolakha**, with its striking three-storied houses.

Soon the trail reaches **Shigati,** where there is a checkpost and a large tributary of the Bhote Kosi that enters the river from the left.

Once across the suspension bridge over the Shigati Khola, the valley narrows and walls become precipitous cliff faces. The trail leads on to another suspension bridge that takes it back to the left bank and along an undulating path to the village of **Suri Dhoban.**

Leaving this settlement, the trail crosses the **Khare Khola** over another suspension bridge and on through the precipitous

ABOVE: Three generations of Sherpa women.
OVERLEAF: Winter sunset on Lhotse.

Bhote Kosi valley. The trail is reasonably good, but occasional landslides may mean making a detour down to the riverbed or up over the hills.

Eventually, the trail reaches the terraced hills and cultivated fields of **Manthale,** at around 1,070 m (3,200 ft), where you can camp.

Third Day

Leave the village by taking the winding path through the fields and over a bridge to the right bank and a moderately sloping,

undulating, walled path to Congar, at which point the trail crosses a stream.

After some distance, the valley narrows and becomes precipitous and the trail traverses an area of tumbled rock and boulders to a waterfall on the opposite bank.

Here there is a crossroads, where you leave the old Silk Road to Tibet and take the path on the right, down to the bridge and the river below, which then climbs steeply in zigzag fashion through breaks in the valley walls.

At the top the path exits onto terraced fields, where it is lined with many stones and chortens, to **Simgaon,** set at 1,950 m (6,300 ft). No longer visible, but still audible far below, the Bhote Kosi cuts deep through the valley gorge, its waters diverted to the fields spread over the hills on either side.

Fourth Day

Follow the path from the campsite, through terraced fields, to the summit of the next ridge — with splendid views of 7,146-m (23,438-ft)-high Gaurisankar — and into a dense rhododendron forest that zigzags up the mountain to the crest of another ridge.

The trail follows the crest of the ridge through more rhododendron to emerge in the fields and meadows around **Shakpa** and then up the mountains on the Rolwaling side of the valley into more thick forest.

Leaving this, the path climbs steeply down some dangerous and tricky sections to cross a stream. It then skirts a ridge to reach **Cyalche,** at 1,760 m (5,570 ft), where you can camp on the grass.

Fifth Day

From the campsite, the path descends steeply and diagonally to the **Rolwaling Chhu.** It then follows the riverbed, before veering to the left bank and through a narrow valley and over a covered wooden bridge to the right bank.

The path continues across a stream by the bridge and climbing gently, follows an undulating course to **Nyimare,** then **Ramding** and **Gyabrug,** where the roofs of the rock-walled houses are weighted down with stones.

Follow the path across another stream before climbing, briefly, to the last permanent village in this region, **Beding,** set at 3,690 m (12,100 ft), which boasts 32 houses and a monastery. You can camp near the river with panoramas of 7,180-m (23,557-ft)-high Menlungtse, Rolwaling Himal's major peak.

From this base you can make a three-day diversion to **Manlung La** by taking the trail, along the mountain flank on the right bank, just after the village.

The first day, the trail climbs to a 4,900-m (16,000-ft)-high campsite, via Taten Kharka. The second day takes you to Manlung La, set at 5,510 m (18,000 ft) and back. The trail is crevassed and you will need ropes, picks and ice axes.

Sixth Day

Leave the village, past the **Manlung La** diversion on your left, follow the right bank of the Rolwaling Chhu on a gradual climb through the valley to **Na Gaon,** a village with terraced and walled potato fields.

Leaving the village, the trail crosses a wooden bridge and mountains come into view — 6,698-m (21,976-ft)-high Chobutse and 6,269-m (20,569-ft)-high Chugimago — before the snout of the Ripimo Shar and Tram Bau glaciers push in to block the valley.

Seventh to Eleventh Day

It takes five days to return to Charikot from Rolpa Chobu.

MANASLU

An inspiring 14-day outward trek, from **Trisuli Bazaar** to the **Burhi Gandaki,** winding through huge and steep valleys, over snowclad passes and foaming rivers, to the three peaks of Manaslu, known as "the Japanese peaks". Long a restricted area, this trek was only opened to tourists in 1991.

The trail crosses a wooden bridge, shortly thereafter leaving the main path and turning left to **Omai Tsho** up a ridge that offers a spectacular vista of 6,735-m (22,097-ft)-high Kang Nachungo and the mountains surrounding Ripimo glacier.

The path to **Tsho Rolpa** skirts the base of the Ripimo glacier and passes between **Ripimo** and **Tram Bau glaciers** on to the right bank of Tram Bau glacier. It becomes narrower and narrower as the valley becomes shallower.

At the far end of the valley are 6,730-m (22,081-ft)-high Pigphera-Go Shar and 6,666-m (21,871-ft)-high Pigphera-Go Nup.

Soon you arrive at the last camp, **Rolpa Chobu,** at 4,540 m (15,000 ft).

Trekkers must be part of an organized group and be accompanied by a liaison officer. There is an annual quota on the number of people that may take this trek. Excellent equipment and guides are essential and because of its duration, so are adequate food supplies and physical fitness. Build in extra rest days to help you recover during the trek.

Board a bus at **Sorkhuti** on the northern side of Kathmandu for **Trisuli Bazaar.** Reserve your seat in advance. The journey takes four hours.

Dry stone wall OPPOSITE marks the trail into the Himalayan village of Phakdingma. Harvesting potatoes ABOVE in a high country village on the approach to Mount Everest.

High-Altitude Trekking and Treks

First Day

Camp in the meadow in front of the military post, a short climb up from Trisuli Bazaar town. Take the path along the riverbed and up the right-hand plateau to Raxun Bazaar.

It's a wide, smooth pathway that cuts through the rice paddies to **Gote Thati.** The path crosses a suspension bridge over the Somrie Khola, runs along the river's right bank and continues on through the villages of **Ghorakki, Shiraune Bash** and **Kaple Bash.**

Before long, signs of cultivation vanish and the river is dry. Now the path climbs a ridge to **Somrie Bhanjyang,** at 1,290 m (4,200 ft), continuing over a tea house-lined pass to the valley floor and the hamlet of **Kinu Chautara** with its many tea houses.

The path continues through farmland and then crosses to the right bank of the **Thofal Khola,** down a gradual incline to the hamlet of **Jor Chautara.** Soon after this, it reaches **Baran Gurun** where you can camp in the compound of people's homes or in the fields.

Second Day

Leaving camp, the trail crosses a small stream and then up some steep stone steps to **Baran,** through a small hamlet and along a winding mountain path, to the Tamang village of **Tharpu.**

Shortly afterwards, it reaches **Tharpu Bhanjyang,** with its one general store, then climbs down a pass to Boktani. Not long after reaching here it begins to climb a ridge to **Col Bhanjyang,** where it joins the mountain trail along the side of the Thofal Khola.

It's gentle, pastoral countryside — small foothills rolling away to distant horizons, sheltering gentle valleys — and eventually the trail takes you through **Katunche,** which boasts a bank and post office, onto the trail to **Charanki Pauwa** and **Charanki Phedi,** where you can camp in the fields outside the village.

Third Day

Leaving the village, the narrow path crosses a small stream, over Achani Bhanjyang pass and down to the left bank of the Ankhu Khola where it crosses a suspension bridge to **Kale Sundhara Bazaar.**

At this point, the landscape is sweltering and subtropical all the way to **Gaili Chautara** where, just beyond the village, you leave the main path and take the trail to the left, much of it along the side of the river, through **Hansi Bazaar,** with its tea houses and shops and between rice paddies in the riverbed.

Where the Ankhu Khola bends to the left, the path veers to the right on its way to **Arughat Bazaar,** through a small, narrow valley and over a sprawling terraced hill that stands between the Ankhu Khola and Burhi Gandaki.

Reaching the village of **Soliental** and the **Burhi Gandaki,** you can see Arughat Bazaar below. Take the path along the left bank of the Burhi Gandaki for **Arughat Bazaar,** a small, bustling town on either side of the river. Its central shopping area, with bank, is on the right side of the river across a suspension bridge.

You can camp in the grove near the school, just outside town.

Fourth Day

Out of Arughat Bazaar the trail follows the right bank of the Burhi Gandaki to its source, along a path through farm fields and **Mordar.**

When you reach **Simre** the dry season trail follows the riverbed to **Arket.** During the monsoon it climbs over the hills. You cross the Arket Khola at **Arket,** through the village and its tea houses and across more farmland to the **Asma Khola** which you cross to climb up to **Kyoropani.**

From this hamlet, the path is straight and level for a short distance and then descends to the river bank and on through another hamlet to its confluence with the Soti Khola where you can camp in the fields on the right bank.

Fifth Day

Follow the trail along the riverbed for about ten minutes and then take the winding path up the forested hill to **Almara, Riden** and **Riden Gaon.**

Tea house and restaurant (top) in Trisuli Bazaar's main street (bottom).

Soon the Burhi Gandaki valley becomes a precipitous gorge until it reaches another valley that cuts into the opposite bank and opens up. Now the trail crosses farmlands to **Lapbesi** and then down to the white riverbed of the **Burhi Gandaki.**

Another path follows the mountain contours, rejoining the trail from the riverbed near the hamlet of **Kani Gaon.**

Continue along an undulating path above the river to **Machha Khola,** with its tea house, where you can camp in the fields outside the village.

Sixth Day

Leave across the Machha Khola and follow the path along the river bank into a precipitous valley and across the abundant flow of the Tado Khola to **Kholabensi,** a hamlet of eight houses.

The trail now continues along the bank of the **Burhi Gandaki,** between two walls of sheer cliff, to the hot springs of **Tatopani.** Soon after, it crosses a suspension bridge to the left bank into forest and then along a gravel path by the river to **Dobhan** where there is a tea house.

Here the trail crosses the Dobhan Khola and some rocks, to the point where the Burhi Gandaki bends right into raging rapids. It climbs up the hill above the rapids

which suddenly broaden out into a sluggish, meandering stream between white beaches.

Now cross the **Yaru Khola,** climb into the forested hillside to **Lauri** and the suspension bridge to the right bank, where the trail climbs again — along a winding path that dips down once more to the riverbed and an easy walk through the fields to the checkpost at **Jagat,** set at 1,350 m (4,400 ft). This is the last village with a shop. You can camp in the fields outside the village.

Seventh Day

You leave Jagat down some stone steps to the river, crossing the tributary flowing in from the left and then walk along the right bank before climbing a terraced hill to **Saguleri** where you can suddenly see 7,177-m (23,540-ft)-high Sringi Himal rising up at the end of the valley.

Follow the undulating path along the right bank to **Sirdi Bash** and on to the next village, **Gata Khola,** where you cross the suspension bridge to the left bank. This is where the trekking trail to Ganesh diverges to the right. You continue along the river bank to **Seirishon Gaon.**

It is here that the hills surrounding the valley start closing in, trapping the Burhi Gandaki between sheer and precipitous cliffs. A bit further on, you reach the **Chhulung Khola** tributary, flowing in through the opposite bank and you cross the bridge to the right bank.

The trail climbs for about l00 m (328 ft) before turning right, following a winding path through a pine forest above the Shar Khola stream, that flows in from the opposite bank.

The trail follows the river through the center of the valley before crossing over to the left bank. Walk for about another thirty minutes and it returns once more to the right bank.

Soon you come to the junction of the **Nyak trail** that climbs up to the left, the main trail continuing along the river's right bank until you have to climb up to traverse its gorge.

Finally, you cross the **Deng Khola** into the tiny hamlet of **Deng,** with four houses. You can camp in the fields outside.

Eighth Day

Leave the village along the high, winding path that soon takes you down to the river bank where you cross a suspension bridge to the left bank and start the steep ascent to **Lana**. Then begins a more gentle, gradual climb through **Unbae**, with its stone gate and mani stones, before the trail dips down once more to the river, curving past a waterfall on the right.

Now the path climbs up again across a terraced hill, past the village of **Bih** and across the **Bihjam Khola,** on a twisting course lined with mani stones, to a tiny hamlet near the Burhi Gandaki.

The trail soon reaches farm fields and a stone gate — entrance to the Tibetan village of **Ghap,** at 2,095 m (6,800 ft) — where there is a suspension bridge across the Burhi Gandaki. You can camp in the meadow on the left bank, near the entrance to the village.

Ninth Day

Follow the path along the right bank, past a long mani-stone wall, into the forest and then through **Lumachik,** with its one lone house, and across the wooden bridge over the **Burhi Gandaki gorge**. Here the trail climbs upward through forest to a wooden bridge that takes it across to the right bank and on through the forest to the checkpost at **Namru.**

Leave Namru by crossing a stream to a grassy field with a waterfall and stone cliff to the left, over the pastures to **Bengsam** where the trail climbs out of the village through a stone gate and continues on to **Li.**

Here the trail crosses the **Hinan Khola,** streaming down from the Lidanda glacier, to climb up to **Sho,** guarded by its stone gate. Soon afterwards, it rounds a bend to and reveals enchanting views of Naike peak, 7,154-m (23,500-ft)-high Manaslu North and finally, 8,158-m (26,766-ft)-high Manaslu.

Climbing gradually, the path passes between houses, farm fields and a bubbling spring to **Lo,** at 3,150 m (10,300 ft) and its stone-walled fields. Behind you, at the head of the valley below, stands 7,406-m (24,298-ft)-high Ganesh Himal I. You can

camp by the spring at the entrance to the village.

Tenth Day

Cut through the village, lined by a long mani stone wall, down across the **Damonan Khola** and then climb along the river. Ahead, the horizon is dominated by the snowcap of 7,835-m (25,690-ft)-high Peak 29, while the Shara Khola flows in from the right.

After a few minutes the trail comes to a left fork — the main path ascends the ridge to **Sama** — that climbs to **Pungen glacier,**

via **Honsansho Gompa** and despite the effort is a worthwhile diversion simply for the views of Peak 29 and Manaslu.

The narrow path climbs through thick forest to **Honsansho Gompa** and over a gentle ridge and cuts diagonally across a rocky riverbed to another small ridge. Not long after this it reaches seven stone huts at **Kyubun,** then climbs over a small ridge formed by the moraine of Pungen glacier, from which you get a stunning view of the battlements of Peak 29 and graceful Manaslu.

Trekkers OPPOSITE cross the foaming waters of the Dudh Kosi in the Everest region. Porters ABOVE trek high into the great mountain fastness of Nepal.

This moraine leads onto **Ramanan Kharka** but to reach Sama climb down the glacier and, from the small ridge, cut across its snout to the rock-strewn riverbed and a chorten.

From this point it is just a short climb back down to the main path and the potato fields and houses of Sama village, set at 3,500 m (11,500 ft). Just twenty minutes of hiking will bring you to the meadow at **Sama Gompa** where you can spend the night before a panoramic view of Manaslu peak.

climbs above the trickle of the Burhi Gandaki before climbing down to the riverbed.

Cross the river, up a terraced hill on the opposite bank and through a stone gate to the remote village of **Somdu,** where around 40 families share life's alpine travail. There's no more fuelwood after this so take what you will need with you.

The path goes down the mountain from the village, through a stone gate and across the **Gyala Khola,** before climbing gradually upwards. Below you, to the left, you may see the ruins of Larkya Bazaar.

Eleventh Day

Leave the meadows, skirting a ridge of lateral moraine, to the banks of the **Burhi Gandaki** after crossing a stream born in the ice-melt of Manaslu glacier. If you turn left you can make a 60- to 70-minute excursion to a glacial lake.

Meanwhile, the main trail leaves the grasslands, traveling down to the riverbed and onto **Kermo Kharka** with stupendous views of Manaslu. From here it passes a long mani-stone wall, at **Kermo Manan,** where the valley begins to close in and the trail

Larkya glacier soon appears on the opposite side of the valley after the trail crosses two streams and skirts around **Sarka Khola.** Then it climbs to a strong shelter, at 4,450 m (14,600 ft) where you can spend the night.

Twelfth Day

From the shelter, a short climb takes the trekker up to a glacial valley with fine views of Cho Dhanda along the way. As the gradual ascent continues, the unmistakable image of Larkya peak comes into sight opposite a small glacier on the other side of the valley.

Soon the trail leads into a level glacier and gradually upwards until a final short,

Four thousand eight hundred meters (16,000 ft) up in the Himalaya, rough, scattered moraine ABOVE and a smooth, glassy lake OPPOSITE are contrasting elements of a glacial landscape.

steep climb brings you to **Larkya La,** set at 5,135 m (16,850 ft) — and a breathtaking view to the west of 7,126-m (23,380-ft)-high Himlung Himal, Cheo Himal, Gyaji Kang, 7,010-m (23,000-ft)-high Kang Gulu and 7,937-m (26,041-ft)-high Annapurna II.

Climbing down the steep, snow-covered west face of the pass, unlike the east face, is a tricky business, so be careful.

Continue down to **Larcia,** opposite a hill on the other side, called Pangal, that also offers superb mountain views. From Larcia, the trail climbs down some glacial moraine

Now follow the riverbed, cross over the wooden bridge above the headwaters of the Dudh Khola and up a lateral moraine, before descending through a magnificent rhododendron forest to **Hampuk.**

Finally, before reentering the forest, draw breath for your last look at the west face of Manaslu, then continue through the forest along the right bank of the **Dudh Khola** to **Sangure Kharka** and its one hut.

Manaslu North peak and Larkya peak are now behind you as the trail continues

to the roofless stone hut of **Tanbuche,** at around 3,900 m (12,800 ft).

Thirteenth Day

Leaving Tanbuche, as you head for **Bimtang,** you can study the west face of Manaslu and 6,398-m (20,100-ft)-high Phungi. From the ghost town of **Bimtang,** with its mani stones and deserted houses, the trail climbs a lateral moraine and then continues down to a riverbed where it enters the Burdin Khola to **Manaslu base camp.**

If you climb the 4,160-m (13,600-ft)-high ridge hereabouts you'll be rewarded by fine views of the west face of 7,154-m (23,500-ft)-high Manaslu North, Annapurna II and 6,893-m (22,609-ft)-high Lamjung Himal.

down the right bank of the narrow valley, crossing the **Surki Khola** where it enters from the right, to the farm fields of **Karche,** set at 2,785 m (9,130 ft), on the opposite bank.

Fourteenth Day

The trail leads up to the paddy fields on top of the terraced hill and over **Karche La pass,** then down through the fields to **Goa** and along the right bank of the Dudh Khola to **Tilije.**

Here the trail crosses a wooden bridge to continue down along the left bank to the Marsyangdi Khola where it returns, across a wooden bridge, to the right bank and the checkpost at **Thonje.**

High-Altitude Trekking and Treks

From here you will leave the village of Karte and follow the trail on the left bank of the **Marsyangdi Khola,** returning to the right bank across a covered wooden bridge. Now there's a short climb and the trail joins the trekking trail that leads around Annapurna.

Fifteenth to Eighteenth Day
Now the path leads gradually down to the checkpost at **Darapani** and, on to **Bhotehura** and **Dumre,** where you can take a bus to Kathmandu.

ANNAPURNA HIMAL

An 11-day outward trek along the **Marsyangdi Khola,** into the **Manang basin,** over **Thorung pass** and down into the **Kali Gandaki gorge** — the world's deepest — gives the trekker a roundabout tour of the Annapurna massif. It is also one of the most varied and comfortable. There are many hotels and tea houses en route so you do not have to carry camping equipment.

If you are traveling by bus from Kathmandu to Pokhara, you can bypass Pokhara altogether and start this trek from Dumre. Road improvements mean that it is now possible to take a bus from Dumre to Besi Sahar. If you fly in to Pokhara, you will have to take a Kathmandu-bound bus to Dumre.

First Day
The trek begins with a long walk through the bazaar of **Besi Sahar,** before ascending steeply over marble rocks.

Now Manaslu and Peak 29 rear their heads above the far end of the valley as the

trail reaches **Khudi,** at the base of a suspension bridge across the Khudi Khola.

Walk through the village, past a school on the lower right, to the path on the right bank. Just after the school it crosses a stream and then travels through two hamlets, across a suspension bridge to the left bank, to **Bhul Bhule,** which has hotels and tea houses.

The path begins to climb but in the dry season you can follow the riverbed and then up a gradual incline to the Manang village of **Ngatti,** lined with hotels and tea houses.

The trail out of the village crosses a stream to the left bank of Ngatti Khola, a tributary that has its source in the snows of 7,893-m (25,895-ft)-high Himal Chuli and across a long suspension bridge to the right bank.

The trail soon leaves the bank and climbs up to the crest of the ridge that divides the Marsyangdi and Ngatti. By the tea house at the summit is a well-shaded rest area.

From the rest area the path follows the left bank of the **Marsyangdi river,** climbing gradually all the way, through the village of **Ranpata,** to the **Bahundhara pass** set at 1,270 m (4,100 ft) where there is a checkpost. There's a village on the hill overlooking the pass. Here you'll find tea houses, shops and hotels. You can stay overnight in one of the hotels or camp somewhere in the fields around the **Bahundhara** pass.

Approximate walking time: six hours.

Second Day
Follow a small ridge, branching out from the pass, down to flat and fertile farm fields, then through a forest, across a stream and up again to a tea house, on to a stone path that takes about ten minutes to traverse before it crosses the rice paddies and grain fields into Kani Gaon.

Ahead, the Marsyangdi valley narrows into a steep and precipitous gorge, along a winding mountain path. On the opposite bank of the river a waterfall heralds the approach to **Sange,** passes over a suspension bridge to the right bank, past hotels, tea shops and houses and down to the riverbed where the trail almost at once begins to climb upwards, past a single house, to a flat plateau.

Not long after this, the rocky trail dips down some 200 to 300 m (650 to 1,000 ft), past a spring, to the riverbed and then into **Jagat,** at 1,290 m (4,200 ft), where there are hotels and tea houses. You can also camp in the fields near the village.

Approximate walking time: three and a half hours.

Third Day
From Jagat, the path leads down almost to the riverbed and then climbs an extremely precipitous trail opposite a sheer cliff. When

closed by precipitous walls of rock. But the path is level, extremely soothing after the perilous journey that preceded it. It goes down to the river bank and into **Tal,** which has hotels and tea houses.

Soon after this village, the valley narrows and the riverbed becomes much narrower, while the trail cuts through rock walls high above, before descending to **Karte.**

(For a day-and-a-half diversion, take the steps behind Karte, past **Naje,** and climb up to **Kurumche Kharka** with a view of the southwest face of Manaslu.)

the climb ends, the trail levels out all the way to **Chyamche,** which is notable for the splendid waterfall on the opposite bank.

Soon after it dips down to cross a suspension bridge to a hair-raising trail on the left bank — precarious and narrow along the edge of the gorge's sheer wall. One slip could be fatal. It's not for the dizzy.

Now the path undulates until it reaches a tributary that flows in from the other bank. The main river is littered with massive boulders, some as big as office blocks and in the dry season it's hard to see the river water at all.

Not long after this, the trail leaves the river bank and takes a zigzag course to the top of a hill overlooking the Tal river, en-

From Karte, the path continues down to the river bank and across a suspension bridge to the right bank, close to **Darapani** and its checkpost, at 1,860 m (6,000 ft).

You can sleep in one of many hotels or camp in the fields behind the checkpost.

Approximate walking time: five hours, possibly longer if you exercise extreme caution on the dangerous sections.

Fourth Day
Follow the trail through a narrow field when you leave the village and come to the confluence with the **Dudh Khola,** spawned

OPPOSITE: On the trekking trail around the mighty Annapurna massif. ABOVE: Rain sheds its blessings over the terraced paddies of Chame Valley.

in the ice-melt of Manaslu's south face, on the opposite bank.

Below, to the right as you climb the path through, you will be able to make out the roofs and streets of the village of **Thonje.** Now the Marsyangdi bends left and when you see Annapurna II ahead, you are at the entrance to the Bhote village of **Bagarchap,** prayer flags fluttering in the breeze.

The path continues its climb, past the tea houses at **Dhanagyu,** across a stream and by a cascading waterfall on the left, to where the Marsyangdi Khola valley becomes a gorge traversed by steep stone steps.

Look back here for splendid views of Manaslu and Phungi, then continue the lung-sapping climb to a level path through a colorful rhododendron forest and two houses at **Ratamron,** then on up and across a stream to the lone house at **Tanzo Phedi.**

Here the trail cuts through pine forest, over an area of crumbling rocks, to the checkpost of **Kodo,** dominated by the mighty mass of Annapurna II and Peak 29 towering, it seems, almost directly over the hamlet.

The trail cuts through the village and up through more pine forest to **Chame,** at 2,670 m (8,750 ft), with government offices, shops and hotels. It's a good place to replenish your food rations. You can stay in one of the hotels or camp near the school — or by the hot springs across the bridge on the left bank.

Approximate walking time: six hours.

Fifth Day

Cross a wooden bridge as you leave the village to the left bank and, with wonderful views of the shimmering snows of 6,893-m (22,609-ft)-high Lamjung Himal, pass through **Chame.**

As the trail climbs up the valley, past **Kreku,** the mountain is hidden by the foothills and then the trail cuts deep into pine forest and up a winding rocky face. On the other side, the valley wall is a sheer cliff, evidence of the change of terrain.

This valley is extremely steep and the path leaps back and forth across the river, following the easiest route available until it crosses a wooden bridge to the former military fortress at Buradhan on the right bank. Now only ruins remain of the fortifications.

From here, the trail climbs a rocky path to first one wooden bridge and then up again to another timber bridge leading into thick forest on the right bank.

When you leave this forest the valley broadens out into more gentle terrain and the east peak of Annapurna II dominates the horizon as the track leads gradually down, past a mani stone, to a level field with a pond. The trail leads to another timber bridge over the river and through a terraced field with scattered clumps of trees. There are good views of the north face of Annapurna II.

Finally, the trail skirts the lower level of the village of **Upper Pisang** and crosses the Marsyangdi to **Lower Pisang,** set at 3,200 m (10,500 ft). You can stay in one of the village's many hotels or camp in the meadow next to the spring.

Approximate walking time: five hours.

Sixth Day

Take the timber bridge across the **Tseram Tsang Changu,** past a mani stone and some chortens, to the right bank and through a thick forest, climb up to the mountain pass marked by a chorten. From here you can see Manang airfield dead ahead.

The trail descends to a level section, past **Ongre** where the northeast face of Annapurna III is visible, to the airstrip at **Omdu** and then across flat broad plain and across the Sabje Khola. Here the massive peak of 7,525-m (24,688-ft)-high Annapurna IV appears on the horizon.

The trail then traverses another bridge, over the trickle of the newborn Marsyangdi Khola, over to the left bank and the village of **Mungji,** encircled by verdant farm fields. To the right, sheltered beneath a small mountain, stands **Braga** with its magnificent monastery.

Here there are many large chortens and mani stones and before long you arrive at **Manang,** set at 3,520 m (11,500 ft) beneath

---

A narrow footbridge spanning an alpine gorge makes a challenging passage for trekkers and porters on the trail.

a panoramic vista most certainly made in heaven — from a terraced hill above the town spread out before you are Annapurna II, Annapurna IV, Annapurna III, 7,555-m (24,787-ft)-high Gangapurna and, behind, 7,134-m (23,406-ft)-high Tilitso peak.

Manang's streets and houses are lined with many fluttering prayer flags and there are numerous hotels. You can stay the night in one of these or camp on their rooftops.

Total walking time to Manang is about four hours.

Tinke. All along this route you will see Annapurna Himani on the horizon with Peak 29 and Himalchuli in the distance behind it.

Tinke is the last permanent settlement in the Marsyangdi Khola valley but the path continues along up through the summer village of **Kutsuan** and, soon after a deserted village, the trail flattens out and crosses a bridge over the Gundon Khola. Carved out of the mountains ahead you can see the walls of the Thorung pass — your destination.

Seventh Day

Most experienced trekkers recommend having a rest day in Manang to acclimatize to the high altitudes. Manang is a good place to stock up on anything you may have forgotten to bring — medical supplies, warm socks and gloves and so on — and the hotels here are a cut above the average, providing luxuries such as hot showers. Throughout the trekking season, the Himalayan Rescue Association operates an aid post in the village, giving lectures on altitude sickness and providing a doctor's services.

Eighth Day

Now begins the toughest part of the trek, through Manang and up to the village of

The trail now becomes a gentle switchback before crossing a delta with many yak meadows and then across the Kenzan Khola to **Churi Latter** (also spelled Letdar or Lathar), where there are three hotels. You should consider staying here for the night. Some trekkers push on to Thorung Phedi, but in the interests of acclimatizing to the high altitudes, it is far better that you take this leg of the trip at a more leisurely pace. Besides the lower altitudes (4,250 m or 14,000 ft), accommodation and food are better here than at Thorung Phedi, and **Churi Latter i**s less likely to be crowded with other trekkers.

Approximate walking time: three to four hours.

Ninth Day

From here the trail climbs a gradual incline to the snout of a ridge. Then it dips down to cross the bridge over the Marsyangdi Khola and ascending the mountain path on the right bank, then down a rocky section to the riverbed which it follows for 10- to 15-minute walk.

Finally, the path climbs a rocky track to the plateau and **Thorung Phedi,** at 4,500 m (14,750 ft), which has one combined hotel-tea house, serving very basic Tibetan fare. You can bed down on its earth floor or camp

rear, passes out of sight. Now the angle eases as you begin the ascent to Thorung pass at 5,416 m (17,770 ft), its crest marked only by cairns and no shelter from the cruel wind.

This is one of the entrances to the eight-kilometer (five-mile)-deep **Kali Gandaki gorge** and ahead — as you enter an old lateral moraine for the precipitous descent — Dhaulagiri II, III and Tashi Kang, rise up over the valley. The final leg is down an extremely steep cliff. Finally, you arrive at **Chabarbu** and its one hotel.

nearby. When there's snow on the pass, this cramped and not particularly friendly place can be host to up to 100 trekkers.

Approximate walking time: three hours.

Tenth Day

Leave early, prepared for extreme cold and severe gale-force winds as you climb the most testing section of this trek — **Thorung pass.** Climb the zigzag trail up the steep hill in front of the hotel, through a rocky area to the top of the ridge. Here it crosses a frozen stream, then some lateral moraine and continues over a frozen lake to the glacier.

The trail then traverses to the left, between small hill-like ridges above 5,000 m (16,500 ft) and soon Annapurna II, in the

From here on out, the path flattens out through the valley and across the **Khatung Kang** which flows in from the left, to the lunar landscape of the Jhong Khola valley which you descend with magnificent views of 8,167-m (26,795-ft)-high Dhaulagiri I and 6,920-m (22,704-ft)-high Tukuche peak.

Once through the valley, you are approaching the checkpost at **Muktinah,** set at 3,798 m (12,500 ft). There are no hotels, and no camping is allowed in Muktinah itself, but after an easy 10-minute walk down to **Ranipauwa** you'll find a rash of

---

OPPOSITE: A baby goat in a remote highland village. Two youngsters at Dhampus ABOVE in the shadows of mighty Annapurna.

houses, hotels, tea houses and camping sites — apple pies await the foot-weary trekker here.

Approximate walking time: seven to nine hours.

Eleventh Day
With Dhaulagiri I, Tukuche peak and Dhaulagiri II and III still in view, the trail leads down from Muktinah to **Jharkot**, where there are the ruins of an ancient fortress and several hotels.

Now the path passes through two stone walls to a gradual descent down the mountains and leading along a wide level trail to **Khingar,** after which it dips gradually to a crossroads. The right turning leads to Kagbeni, famous for the ruins of its medieval castle.

The path on the left leads you down the mountain flank to the left bank of the Kali Gandaki river and **Akkara Bhatti** and then on to **Jhomsumba** (also spelled Jomsom) in the afternoon.

Jhomsumba has an airfield which offers daily flights to Pokhara — they tend to be heavily booked. It also has a large selection of accommodation, including **Om's Home,** a cut above the average, where rooms have heaters and attached bathrooms.

Twelfth to Nineteenth Day
The trek from Jhomsumba to Pokhara, is the return leg of the Jhomsum trek, sometimes referred to as the "classic tea house trek". There are decent hotels all along the route and it's unlikely that you will ever be short of company: it's probably the most popular trek in Nepal and it's also used heavily by locals. The altitude on the Jhomsum trek never exceeds 3,000 m (9,800 ft) — easy streets after the heights from which you've just come.

DHAULAGIRI

Beginning in **Pokhara,** this trek leads you through some of the most beautiful mountain and pastoral landscapes in Nepal — providing the savor of simple lifestyles in and around the **Myagdi Khola basin.** You need full camping equipment, rations and Sherpa guides.

First Day
Although it is possible to hike directly out of Pokhara in around three days, improvements in road conditions mean that most trekkers take the bus to Maldhunga (three hours), which is directly below the trailhead at **Baglung.**

From Baglung the trail goes to **Pharse,** where there are tea houses and hotels and houses.

Still on the left bank, the path crosses a stream into **Diranbhora,** then up a gentle incline to **Beni,** on the opposite bank of the **Myagdi Khola,** where there is a checkpost.

It's a bustling town and administrative center and you can camp in fields outside the village.

Second Day

The trail from Beni cuts through **Beni Mangalghat**'s single street of shops and into desolate mountain country, past the lone tea house at **Jyanmara** and on a wide, level path to **Singa,** with many shops and tea houses.

Beyond the village of Singa, the trail follows the left bank of the **Myagdi Khola** above the riverbed, past a hot spring to the left below and through the farm fields that herald the approach to **Tatopani** and its **hot springs.**

Soon after leaving this village, the trail crosses a suspension bridge to the right bank, through the hamlet of **Bholamza,** and more fields, before swinging back to the left bank via another suspension bridge, to **Simarchor.** Some distance beyond this village there's a bridge across the Newale Khola which flows in from the right.

The trail continues along the left bank of the **Myagdi Khola,** past the villages of **Shiman** and **Talkot** and then climbs up to the shops and tea houses of **Babichor.** You can camp on the grass next to the village granary.

Third Day

From Babichor, the high, winding trail crosses the mountainside into a broad and fertile valley, across grain fields and through the cobblestone street of **Shahasharadhara,** where you cross the Duk Khola. Continue

---

The peaks of regal Annapurna, crowned with snow.

through the rice paddies to the hamlet of **Ratorunga** where the valley ends.

Now the undulating trail follows the river bank on the left, past **Bodeni** to **Chachare.** The valley narrows at the town of **Darbang,** its main street lined with shops.

Here the trail crosses to the right bank, via a suspension bridge, past the Ritum Khola tributary at left and through the hamlet of **Darbang.**

The trail then skirts a gaunt cliff face to **Phedi,** set at 1,100 m (3,500 ft), where there are some tea houses. It's not a pretty place but it's the only camping site for several miles around.

Fourth Day

When you leave Phedi you face a lengthy climb to **Phalai Gaon** and should make an early start. Not long after leaving the village the trail crosses the **Dang Khola,** where it flows in from the left and climbs a ridge on the opposite bank in a series of hairpins, above the Myagdi Khola.

Soon the gradual climb brings you to **Dharapani** and steeply out again, before descending to the farm fields beyond **Takum.**

After **Sibang,** it cuts through forest, past **Mattim,** to the crest of a ridge which provides a magnificent view of Dhaulagiri Himal, dipping down to the Gatti Khola, to skirt the base of the ridge and enter **Phalai Gaon,** at 1,810 m (6,000 ft). You can camp in the school grounds outside the village.

Fifth Day

Follow the stonewalled path from Phalai Gaon over the terraced fields to the right and cross the suspension bridge over the Dhara Khola river. During the dry season the trail goes down the valley next to the school, across to the opposite bank and up a steep hill.

But the main path from the suspension bridge climbs up the mountain, above the village of Dhara and through a hamlet to an undulating walk that joins up with the shortcut. After skirting a ridge it emerges once more on the right bank of the Myagdi Khola.

Now the path climbs again, in a series of hairpins and then skirts another ridge, to reveal astounding views of Dhaulagiri I and

7,193-m (23,600-ft)-high Gurja Himal. Soon it reaches the Magar village of **Muri** which you leave by walking down a gentle slope, across a rocky stream.

Continue down to the farm fields along the Dhara Khola, cross the river and then climb up the mountain on the right to **Ghorban Dhara pass** with its superb views — including your first glimpse of 6,465-m (21,211-ft)-high Ghustung South.

From the pass, the trail leads down to the right bank of the **Myagdi Khola** and a lone house where you can camp in the surround-

ing fields — beneath the village of **Jugapani,** perched on the mountainside above.

Sixth Day

Leave along the right bank, past **Naura** and climb the mountain for a short while to a path that traverses a steep, grass-covered hill. Where the traverse ends, the Myagdi Khola valley becomes a precipitous gorge. Even though the path along the steep, grassy edge of the gorge is well-constructed with many stone steps, take care.

At the top of the climb, the trail traverses right — take great care to avoid falling into the gorge. Eventually, the trail dips down through forest, across a ridge and some terraced fields to **Boghara,** at 2,080 m (6,800 ft).

You can camp in the compounds of the houses or the terraced fields.

Seventh Day

Leaving Boghara, the trail descends through the fields, crossing a small ridge to the left and on through thin forest to **Jyardan,** the region's most remote village.

From the village the trail is high and winding, then it cuts across a boulder-strewn landscape to a grass-covered traverse, before dropping down some steep stone steps to the river bank.

Here the trail continues through thick forest with occasional glimpses, through breaks between the trees, of the west face of majestic Dhaulagiri I. Some distance beyond, the trail dips down and the Myag-di Khola comes into view. You cross to the left bank by a wooden bridge with a hand-rail.

Once again the path cuts through forest as it climbs the course of the **Pakite Khola,** never too far from the river. The crest of 6,062-m (19,889-ft)-high Jirbang dominates the end of the valley and then you cross a

The path goes upstream some distance, then starts climbing again, crossing a stream beneath a beautiful high waterfall, where it eases into a gradual incline to **Lipshe.**

Now the trail continues its undulating course through the forest-lined walls of the steep **Myagdi Khola gorge** before emerging at a little glade, **Lapche Kharka,** where you camp overnight.

Eighth Day

When you leave camp, the trail continues to climb through forest to a level area at **Dobang**. Soon after this, it crosses a timber bridge over the Konabon Khola, flowing down from the Konabon glacier.

stream, to the plateau at **Chartare,** set at 2,820 m (9,250 ft).

There's a crystal clear stream flowing through the middle of the meadow, making it excellent for camping.

Ninth Day

From Chartare, return to and follow the forest trail until it passes two small caves. Here it leaves the forest, cutting across a rocky mountainside, then crossing a small stream, to the **Choriban Khola** which it

OPPOSITE: The contents of a wooden aqueduct freeze in the frosty winter weather of the high mountains. Woman ABOVE carries firewood up a precipitous stone walkway overlooking lush, terraced hillsides.

skirts for some distance, before finally crossing it to climb the bank on the other side.

Look behind at this point and you will
get a splendid view of the ice-white silhou-
ette of 6,380-m (20,932-ft)-high Manapati.
Soon after climbing the steep hill, the path
narrows into a gentle gradient, through the
forest, to a small grassy clearing at **Puchhar.**

The trail now crosses a small glacier
down to another glacier born on the west
face of Dhaulagiri and then climbs the
opposite wall to another grassy area, **Pakabon,** set at 3,585 m (11,750 ft), where you
can camp.

Ahead stand the massive western ramparts of Dhaulagiri I. To the right is Manapati — and behind, the granite walls of
Tsaurabong peak shadow the sky as if
about to fall over the camp.

Tenth Day
From Pakabon, you will follow a lateral moraine to a rocky ridge which you descend
to the right and into a valley deep in snow
and glacial detritus. Approaching the headwaters of the Myagdi Khola, you are closed
in by daunting and forbidding rock walls.

The precipitous path runs high above
the right bank before descending to the
valley floor and on, by an intermittent foot-
path through the gorge, to the terminal
moraine of **Chhonbarban glacier.** It enters
the glacier area from the right bank, crossing the undulating glacial surface where the
valley bends right through a large gorge.

At this point, 6,837-m (22,432-ft)-high
Tukuche peak West stands brooding over
the far end of the glacier.

Soon the trail levels out into easy walking up the gradual gradient of this section,
then the glacier veers left and the trail
moves onto the right bank.

The trail terminates at **Dhaulagiri base
camp,** at 4,750 m (15,500 ft), with stunning
perspectives of Dhaulagiri I to the north
and, to the west: 7,751-m (25,429-ft)-high
Dhaulagiri II; 7,703-m (25,271-ft)-high
Dhaulagiri III; and 7,660-m (25,133-ft)-high
Dhaulagiri IV — a sheer ice fall streaming
from the northeast col.

Early morning sun lights up a frosty trekkers' camp
at 5,500 m (18,000 ft).

Eleventh Day

By this point, you have a sound risk of getting altitude sickness as the trail climbs out from the camp, up the right bank of the glacier and then ascends another mountainside to where it cuts across the flank and crosses the moraine on the side of 6,611-m (21,690-ft)-high Sita Chuchura, to an easy snow-covered incline on the right that brings you to **French pass,** at 5,360 m (17,600 ft).

From here you can see Sita Chuchura, the mountains of Mukut Himal and the 6,386-m (21,000-ft)-high Tashi Kang. To the

right is Tukuche peak West and to the rear stands Dhaulagiri I.

Twelfth to Twenty-First Day

It takes nine to 10 days to retrace this route to Pokhara.

LANGTANG

Regarded as the most perfect alpine landscape in the world, the **Langtang massif** — visible from Kathmandu — is right on the city's back door and this five- to six-day outward trek allows you to enjoy it in full. With many hotels and eating places it's also one for the casual and not-so-hardy trekker. However, to extend the trek from **Langshisa Kharka** to **Langtang glacier** you must be well-equipped and in excellent physical condition.

ABOVE: A wall, where wood, stone and mortar meet in a delightful combination. OPPOSITE: A distant view of Manang airport, a place so remote that staff often have to chase away grazing yaks for incoming flights.

First Day

From Kathmandu take a bus to **Trisuli Bazaar,** a journey that can take up to six hours. Change there for a bus to **Dunche,** set at 2,040 m (6,700 ft), focal point of the district with hotels, shops and government offices.

Second Day

The road leaves Dunche across some fields, down the forested banks of the **Trisuli Khola,** across a suspension bridge and up a steep hill along a small stream.

After some twenty minutes of walking, the trail leaves the stream and travels up the hillside on the left to a tea house atop a ridge. There's a fork in the trail here — straight on to **Gosainkund,** the sacred Shiva lake and left to Syabru, a rather narrow path past the tea house.

The trail skirts the ridge, with Dunche in view on the opposite bank and carries along the mountainside on the left bank of the Trisuli river to some fields where the path to **Syabrubensi** branches left, near **Bharkhu.**

Leaving Bharkhu, cross the fields and climb the steep mountain pass, an exercise rewarded — to your rear where the path flattens out and leads left through forest — by a view of Ganesh Himal. Then it passes another village, to the left below and through more forest to a rest area at the crest of a ridge.

From here the path dips down gradually to **Syabru,** at 2,230 m (7,300 ft), where you can camp in the monastery grounds or hotel garden.

Approximate walking time: five and a half to six hours.

Third Day

Walk down the ridge, between the houses, turn right past some fields, then through forest, across a stream and a flat mountain trail on the left that leads to a ridge crest.

The other side leads down a steep slope through thick forest to the **Langtang Khola,** then follows the left bank. Soon it crosses a stream and continues to climb the valley to a wooden bridge across the Langtang Khola which takes it to the right bank.

Here the path climbs high, leaving the river far below and then down around the

flank of the mountain, to join the path from Syarpa Gaon.

Not far from this junction the trail veers back to the river bank and later, climbs up to the **Lama Hotel,** surrounded by other tea houses and hotels. When the trail cuts into forest, through breaks in the tree cover you will see majestic Langtang Lirung off in the distance.

The path climbs steadily past **Gumna-chok** and its lone hotel, to a short steep hill where it leaves the river bank and the valley broadens. Not long after this it reaches the checkpost at **Ghora Tabela,** set at 3,010 m (9,900 ft).

Approximate walking time: six hours.

Fourth Day

The trail leaves Ghora Tabela through the farm fields that stud the valley floor and after a short distance crosses over a steep hill. Here the forest ends and the path becomes gentle, running through colorful shrubs and meadows.

Now Langtang appears, against the backdrop of 6,387-m (21,000-ft)-high Ganchempo. The trail climbs gradually up a grassy knoll, above a monastery, to **Langtang,** where gardens are enclosed by stone walls. Some little distance from the village there is a chorten followed by one of the longest mani walls in Nepal.

The trail leads along the top of green and lovely hillsides, past two villages, after which the valley broadens out and the path enters a flat, dry riverbed. Where it crosses the flow from **Lirung glacier,** 6,745-m (21,250-ft)-high Kimshun and 6,543-m (21,467-ft)-high Yansa Tsenji can be seen to the left.

Now the trail crosses a moraine covered with loose stones to **Kyangjin Gompa,** at 3,840 m (12,500 ft) where there's a cheese factory.

To the north of the village, on a 4,000-m (13,000-ft)-high crest there are magnificent views of Langtang Lirung's north face and the surrounding mountains.

You can stay in the town hotel or camp in one of the stonewalled fields. Beyond this point you will need tents and supplies and should be watchful for symptoms of altitude sickness.

Approximate walking time: five to six hours.

Fifth Day

The trail from Kyangjin Gompa crosses a wide alluvial delta, across a stream, to an airstrip with stupendous vistas of Langtang Lirung's full profile.

From the airstrip, the trail follows the river and 6,300-m (20,600-ft)-high Langshisa Ri comes into view at the far end of the narrow valley, with Ganchempo visible on the opposite side.

Up from the river, the trail goes through the rocky hills, to the seven stone huts of **Jatang.** Just beyond, the path descends once more to the dry riverbed, then up some more hills with views of Shalbachum glacier pushing its snout into the valley. Near the glacier is the hamlet of **Nuba-matang,** with five stone huts.

Now the trail cuts across the grassy fields and climbs the glacial moraine with perspectives of the far end of the valley, dominated by 6,830-m (22,400-ft)-high Pemthang Karpo Ri, Triangle and 6,842-m (22,490-ft)-high Pemthang Ri; to the right is Langshisa Ri.

Now the trail descends to **Langshisa Kharka,** at 4,125 m (13,500 ft) for views of 6,078-m (20,000-ft)-high Kanshurum and

6,151-m (20,200-ft)-high Urkinmang at the far end of the Langshisa glacier.

You can camp in the stone huts at **Langshisa Kharka** or in the grassy fields.

Approximate walking time: four hours.

Sixth to Ninth Day

The return to Dunche from this point takes three or four days.

Extension I

To trek from Langshisa Kharka to **Langtang glacier** you have to be exceptionally fit and well equipped.

Extension II

It is possible to visit Langshisa glacier, following the trail upstream from **Langshisa Kharka** for a short distance to a log bridge. (It sometimes gets hurled away by landslides so check before you start if it is there).

Then the trail climbs through scrub before descending to one of the streams running off the glacier which you enter at the snout. It gradually climbs until 6,966-m (22,855-ft)-high Dorje Lakpa comes into view — magnificent from Kathmandu, fabulous when so close.

The trail from Langshisa follows the top of a level hill and down a winding path to the riverbed. Here it begins to climb, past a small stone hut and through thorny scrub, to a second hut. The trail now becomes vague and difficult as the trek is not often used.

Some distance after this a valley leads to the **Morimoto peak base camp** on a wide plain with views of 6,874-m (22,550-ft)-high Gur Karpo Ri and 6,750-m (22,150-ft)-high Morimoto peak.

The trail crosses the plain and enters the valley again. Around the corner, where the valley ends, it begins to climb to the glacier. This is the terminus for most trekkers, with an excellent camp and outstanding views.

The glacier veers right and when you round the corner you get a breathtaking view of 7,083-m (23,240-ft)-high Lenpo Gang, the highest of the Jugal Himal's peaks.

You can camp at a site set at 4,800 m (15,750 ft) often used as a base camp by climbing expeditions.

High-mountain denizens frolic on a wall.

High-Altitude Trekking and Treks

Travelers'
Tips

GETTING TO NEPAL

By Air

Most international visitors — more than 90 percent — fly into Nepal's **Tribhuvan International Airport**, eight kilometers (five miles) from Kathmandu.

If the skies are clear there is no more exciting flight in the world. Passengers in left-hand seats on eastbound flights to Kathmandu will see in succession Gurja Himal, 7,193 m (23,600 ft); Dhaulagiri I, 8,167 m (26,795 ft); the deep gorge of the Kali Gandaki river leading north to Mustang; the six peaks of the Annapurna range; Manaslu, 8,158 m (26,766 ft); and finish their flight with the three humps of Ganesh Himal at 7,406 m (24,298 ft) dominating Kathmandu valley.

Passengers in right-hand seats on westbound flights will see, in succession, Kanchenjunga, 8,598 m (28,208 ft) on the border with Sikkim; Makalu, 8,481 m (27,825 ft); Everest, 8,848 m (29,028 ft); Cho Oyu, 8,153 m (26,750 ft); Gaurisankar, 7,144 m (23,438 ft); Dorje Lhakpa, 6,966 m (22,855 ft); and finish their promenade with Langtang Lirung, 7,245 m (23,769 ft) above Kathmandu valley.

There are few direct flights to Kathmandu from outside Asia. Most travelers will have to change — usually in Bangkok if they're coming from the USA; from Delhi if they're coming from Europe. Royal Nepal Airlines has the greatest number of direct flights, including London, Paris, Frankfurt, Delhi, Calcutta and Bangkok. Lufthansa also operates direct flights through London and a number of flights to the USA via Frankfurt.

All those departing Nepal on international flights pay Rs 700 airport tax as they check-in.

The major international airlines with offices in Kathmandu are (all in the 01 area code):
Aeroflot Soviet Airlines (227399, Kamaladi.
Air India (419649, Hattisar.
Bangladesh Biman (416852, Durbar Marg.
British Airways (222266, Durbar Marg.
Cathay Pacific (411725, Kamaladi.

China Southwest Airlines (411302, Kamaladi.
Dragonair (223162, Durbar Marg.
Druk Air Royal Bhutan Airlines (225166, Durbar Marg.
Indian Airlines (410906, Hattisar.
Lufthansa (223052, Durbar Marg.
Myanmar Airways Corporation (224839, Durbar Marg.
Northwest Airlines (215855, Kanti Path.
Pakistan International (223102, Durbar Marg.
Royal Nepal Airlines (220757, Kanti Path.
Singapore Airlines (220759, Durbar Marg.
Thai International (224917, Durbar Marg.

By Land

Land travelers have a vast choice of routes and means of transport by which to enter Nepal. In addition to Tribhuvan Airport, there are 11 other official entry points: **Kakar Bhitta** (Mechi zone), with connections to Darjeeling and Siliguri, India; **Rani Sikijha** (Kosi zone), just south of Biratnagar; **Jaleshwar** (Janakpur zone); Birganj (Narayani zone), near Raxaul, India, the most common entry point for overland travelers; **Kodari** (Bagmati zone), on the Chinese–Tibetan border; and **Sunauli** (Lumbini zone), near Bhairawa on the road to Pokhara.

The other entry points, which can only be reached on foot, are at **Kakarhawa** (Lumbini zone); **Nepalgunj** (Bheri zone); **Koilabas** (Rapti zone); **Dhangadi** (Seti zone); and **Mahendranagar** (Mahakali zone). These entry points are all unsuitable for motor vehicles.

By Rail

India provides frequent railroad service throughout the country including trains to the Nepal border. But there are only two lines in Nepal. The 47-km (29-mile) line between Raxaul, India and Amlekhganj, built in 1925, is no longer used. The only line still

Royal Nepal Airlines Twin Otter takes off PREVIOUS PAGES from Lukla's clifftop runway (left) at 2,760 m (9,200 ft) as trekkers (right) make their way on foot to Everest base camp. OPPOSITE: Moonrise over the distinctive peak of Ama Dablam on the trail to Everest base camp.

working in Nepal, for freight only, built in 1940, runs a brief 27 km (17 miles) through Janakpur.

By Road and Rail

The combined rail–road route to Nepal from Delhi offers two viable options. The quickest route is via **Gorakhpur,** while the other allows an interesting stopover in **Varanasi.** From either city, buses go to Kathmandu or Pokhara via **Sunauli.** Taking this route allows one to visit **Lumbini,** Buddha's birthplace, close to Sunauli.

Seasoned travelers might consider making their way by train from **Darjeeling** to **Siliguri,** followed by a 60-minute taxi drive to **Kakar Bhitta**. Here you can catch a bus to **Kathmandu.** The advantages to be gained from taking this route are the ride on the miniature Darjeeling railway followed by traveling through almost 400 km (248 miles) of the Terai, including panoramic views of the Siwalik hills.

You will need a special permit to enter Darjeeling (required for all, including British Commonwealth passport holders). And

If traveling on to **Kathmandu,** you can also stop over at **Narayanghat** and visit **Royal Chitwan National Park,** just two hours away by local transport.

Similarly, taking the combined rail–road route to Nepal from **Calcutta, India** offers two interesting alternatives — traveling through **Muzaffapur** or **Patna** — with bus connections to Kathmandu by way of **Birganj.** The land journey takes about 36 hours altogether. Taking a ferry from Muzaffapur, across the Ganges river to Patna, takes approximately 90 minutes. Most other routes to the Nepali border from inside India require a great deal of effort, patience and aggravation and are of little interest to the traveler.

on your return from Nepal remember that you'll need an Indian visa to enter India through a border post. If you intend on traveling more than once between Nepal and India, a multiple-entry Indian visa is useful.

Driving into Nepal

Those who drive to Nepal by private car should allow at least two hours to clear the Indian border and make sure that they carry a *carnet de passage en douanes* (for cars and motorcycles) which gives a three-month exemption from customs duty.

Motor vehicles in Nepal are driven on the left side of the road. Drivers must hold a valid international driver's license.

                                             Travelers' Tips

FORMALITIES

All visitors require a visa and must carry a valid passport. Three kinds of visa are available: 15 days (US$15); 30 days (US$25) and 60 days multiple re-entry (US$60). Visas are available on arrival at Tribhuvan International Airport or at Nepal embassies and consulates. Be warned, the lines for visas at the airport are glacially slow and payment is required in US dollars (bring some with you). You will also need one passport photo.

Visas issued for travel in Nepal are valid only for the Kathmandu and Pokhara valleys, Chitwan National Park and for major roads between these destinations. To leave these areas you will need additional permits.

TREKKING PERMITS

Trekking Permits are available at the Central Immigration Office ((01) 412337, in Maiti Devi, Kathmandu. The office is open 10 AM to 1 PM (closing at noon on Fridays)

Visas can also be extended for up to 150 days, at a rate of US$1 per day. Tourists are not allowed to spend any more than 180 days in Nepal in any calendar year.

Visa extensions (and trekking permits) are issued at the Central Immigration Office ((01) 412337, in Maiti Devi, Kathmandu. Office hours are 10 AM to 1 PM (closes at noon on Fridays) for applications; 3 to 5 PM for picking up passports; closed Saturdays. Bring your passport and two passport-sized photos.

Visitors wishing to cross the border at the Friendship Bridge to the Tibetan town of Khasa need a Chinese visa. It's best to organize one before you arrive in Kathmandu. The Chinese Embassy in Nepal only gives visas to group tourists.

for applications; 3 to 5 PM for picking up passports; closed Saturdays. Bring your passport and two passport-sized photos. If you are part of an organized group, the permit will be arranged for you, saving a great deal of time and effort.

Costs for permits vary according to where you plan to trek. Most areas, such as Annapurna, Everest and Langtang (among others), cost US$5 for the first week and

Young women of Pokhara OPPOSITE reap an additional harvest of small fish from the muddy waters of their rice paddies. ABOVE: Other youngsters (left) use a fish trap in the rushing waters of the Trisuli river to catch their supper while a conical net (right) hauls in a writhing catch for another group fishing the same waters.

US$10 for every additional week. Kanchen-junga and Lower Dolpo cost US$10 for the first week, US$20 for every additional week. Manaslu is US$75 per week in the low season, US$90 in the high season. Permits for Mustang and Upper Dolpo cost US$700 for 10 days, and you must be accompanied by a government liaison officer.

CUSTOMS

Duty Free Travelers are allowed to carry 200 cigarettes, 50 cigars, one bottle of spir-

its and two bottles or 12 cans of beer free of duty. Personal effects exempt from duty include one pair of binoculars, one camera, 15 rolls of film, one video camera, one tape recorder, one transistor radio and one fishing rod and accessories.

Forbidden imports Firearms and ammunition (unless you hold an import license obtained in advance), radio transmitters, walkie-talkies and drugs.

Movie cameras require special permits.

Souvenirs On departure, souvenirs can be exported freely but antiques and art objects need special clearance.

Antiques and art objects need special clearance from the Department of Archaeology, National Archives Building, Ram Shah Path,

Kathmandu, which takes at least two days. Nepal is concerned to preserve its priceless art treasures and forbids the export of any object more than 100 years old. If in doubt, consult the Department of Archaeology.

Forbidden exports Precious stones, gold, silver, weapons, drugs, animal hides, trophies, wild animals.

Pets such as Tibetan dogs, may be exported.

NEPAL EMBASSIES AND CONSULATES ABROAD

AUSTRALIA **Sydney (** (02) 9233 6161, Level 1, 17 Castlereagh Street, NSW 2000, or **Melbourne (** (03) 9379 0666, 72 Lincoln Road, Essendon, Victoria 3040, or **Brisbane (** (07) 3232 0336, Level 21, AMP Place, 10 Eagle Street, Queensland 4066, or **Perth (** (08) 9386 2102, Suite 2, 16 Robinson Street, Nedlands, Western Australia 6009.

BANGLADESH **Dhaka (** 601890, United Nations Road, Road 2, Baridhara Diplomatic Enclave, Baridhara.

BELGIUM **Genese (** (02) 358 5808, 21 Avenue Champel, B-1640 Rhode Street.

CANADA **Toronto (** (416) 226 8722, Royal Bank Plaza, South Tower, Ontario.

CHINA **Beijing** Embassy (010) 532 1795, № 1 Sanlitun Xilujie or **Lhasa** Consulate **(** (0891) 36890, Norbulingka Road 13, Tibet.

DENMARK **Copenhagen (** (01) 3312 4166, 2 Teglgaardstraede, 1452.

FRANCE **Paris (** (01) 46 22 48 67, 45 bis rue des Acacias, 75017, or **Toulouse (** (061) 329 1222, 7 bis allée des Soupirs, 31000.

GERMANY **Bonn (** (0228) 343097, Im-Hag 15, D-5300, Bad Godesberg 2, or **Frankfurt am Main** 60 Z 069-40871, Flinschstrasse 63, D-6000; **Munich** 21 **(** 089-5704406, Landsbergerstrasse 191, D-8000, or **Berlin** 15 **(** (030) 881 4049, Uhlandstrasse 171/2, 1000.

INDIA **New Delhi** Embassy **(** (011) 332 9969, Barakhamba Road, 110001, or **Calcutta (** (033) 711224, 19 Woodlands, Sterndale Road, Alipore, 700027.

ITALY **Rome** Consulate **(** (06) 348176, Piazza Medaglie d'Oro 20, 00136.

JAPAN **Tokyo (** (03) 3705 5558, Tokoroki 7-chome, Setagaya-ku 158.

MYANMAR (BURMA) **Rangoon (** 550633, 16 Natmauk Yeiktha (Park Avenue), P.O. Box 84, Tamwe.

PAKISTAN **Karachi-2 (** 200979, 4th floor Qamar House, 419 MA Jinnah Road.
RUSSIA, FEDERAL REPUBLIC **Moscow (** 2447356, or **(** 2419311, 2nd Neopolimovsky Pere Look 14/7.
SPAIN **Barcelona (** (03) 323 1323, Mallorca 194 Pral 2A, 08036.
SWITZERLAND **Zurich (** (01) 475993, Asrylstrasse 81, 8030.
THAILAND **Bangkok** Embassy **(** 391 7240, 189, Soi 71, Sukhumvit Road, 10110.
UK **London (** (0171) 229-6231, 12A Kensington Palace Gardens, W8 4QU.

India ((01) 410900, Lainchaur.
Israel ((01) 411811, Lazimpat.
Italy ((01) 412743, Baluwatar.
Japan ((01) 231101, Durbar Marg.
Myanmar (Burma) ((01) 521788, Chakupat, Patan City Gate, Patan.
Pakistan ((01) 411421, Pani Pokhari.
Russia, Federal Republic ((01) 412155, Baluwatar.
South Korea ((01) 211172, Tahachal.
Thailand ((01) 213910, Thapathali.
UK ((01) 410583, Lainchaur.
USA ((01) 411179, Pani Pokhari.

USA **Washington, District of Columbia (** (202) 667 4550, 2131 Leroy Place N.W., 20008, or **San Francisco (** (415) 434-1111, Suite 400, 909 Montgomery Street, CA 94133, or **Dallas (** (214) 931-1212; 16250 Dallas Parkway, Suite 110, TX 75248, or **Atlanta (** (404) 892-8152, 15th Street N.E., GA 30309.

EMBASSIES

Australia ((01) 411578, Bhat Bhateni.
Bangladesh ((01) 414943, Naxal.
Canada ((01) 415193, Lazimpat.
China ((01) 411740, Baluwatar.
France ((01) 412332, Lazimpat.
Germany ((01) 412786, Gyaneshwor.

CULTURAL CENTERS

British Council ((01) 223000, Kanti Path.
French Cultural Center ((01) 224326, Bag Bazaar.
Indian Cultural Center and Library ((01) 211497, RNAC Building.
Goethe Institute ((01) 220528, Sundhara.

TOURIST INFORMATION

Nepal's tourist information offices are of limited use to the traveler, though they may have a map or two on hand. The offices are:

Trekkers rest OPPOSITE on the Everest trail while umbrellas guard rickshaw drivers against sun and rain ABOVE in Kathmandu valley's benign climate.

Main office (English-language) ((01) 220818, Ganga Path, Basantapur, (in front of Hanuman Dhoka palace; open 10 AM to 4 PM, Sunday to Friday).
Tribhuvan Airport Exchange ((01) 470537 (other offices in airports at **Pokhara, Bhairawa, Birganj** and **Kaka Bhitta**).
Department of Tourism ((01) 214519.

RELIGION

Minority faiths practice freely in the Hindu kingdom of Nepal. The major places of worship are:

Roman Catholic
Jesuit St. Xavier College ((01) 521050, Jawalkhel.
Annapurna Hotel (Sunday Mass) ((01) 211711.

Protestant
Church of Christ, Nepal, Ram Shah Path. Blue Room, USIS, ((01) 213966, Rabi Bhawan.

Muslim
Main Mosque, Durbar Marg.

Jewish
Israeli Embassy ((01) 211251.

TRAVEL AND TREKKING AGENCIES

There are hundreds of travel and trekking agencies in Nepal — far more than it would be practical to list here. The agencies below are some of the best-known, longest-running and most reliable.
Adventure Nepal Trekking ((01) 412508 FAX (01) 222026, Tridevi Marg .
Annapurna Mountaineering and Trekking ((01) 222999 FAX (01) 226153, Durbar Marg.
Asian Trekking ((01) 413732 FAX (01) 411878, Tridevi Marg.
Equator Expeditions ((01) 425800 FAX (01) 425801 E-MAIL equator@expeds.wlink.com .np, Thamel.
Himalayan Adventures ((01) 411866 FAX (01) 418561, Maharajganj.
Himalayan Encounters ((01) 417426 FAX (01) 417133, Thamel.
Himalayan Expeditions ((01) 226622 FAX (01) 526575, Thamel Chowk.

Lama Excursions ((01) 220186 FAX (01) 227292, Durbar Marg.
Malla Treks ((01) 410089 FAX (01) 423143 E-MAIL trekinfo@mallatrk.mos.com.np, Lainchaur.
Tiger Mountain ((01) 414508 FAX (01) 414075 E-MAIL tiger@mtn.mos.com.np, Lazimpat.
Wayfarers ((01) 212810, Thamel.

CURRENCY AND EXCHANGE

There are 100 *paisa* to one Nepali *rupee*. Banknotes are in denominations of 1,000, 500, 100, 50, 20, 10, five, two and one rupee. Coins are in denominations of one rupee; and 50, 25, 10 and five paisa. The *mohar* is a half rupee (50 paisa); the *sukaa*, 25 paisa.

The official exchange rate is set by the Nepal Rastra Bank and published daily in *The Rising Nepal* newspaper. It is also broadcast by Radio Nepal in the Nepali language. At press date the exchange rate was approximately 56 rupees to the US dollar.

Excess Nepali rupees can be converted back into dollars as long as they do not exceed 15 percent of the total amount changed. Keep your exchange receipts as you will need to show them in order to be able to change rupees back into US dollars.

There is an exchange counter at Tribhuvan Airport open nonstop, daily. The New road gate exchange counter of Rastriya Banijya Bank is open daily from 8 AM to 8 PM. The Nepal Bank on New road is open from 10 AM to 3 PM, Sunday to Thursday, from 10 AM to noon on Fridays.

Official exchange rates fluctuate against all currencies. Dollars are in high demand, but exchanging money unofficially is illegal.

TRAVELING IN NEPAL

INTERNAL FLIGHTS

Flying is the quickest way of getting around Nepal; just bear in mind that flights are subject to cancellations and delays due to weather conditions. Low visibility flying is simply too dangerous to be risked in a mountainous country like Nepal.

A Newar priest dressed in sacred crimson, Kathmandu.

The domestic monopoly enjoyed and operated by national flag carrier, **Royal Nepal Airlines (** (01) 220757 is a thing of the past, though it still has the most extensive network with a fleet of 44-seat Avro 748s, 19-seat Twin Otters and five-seat Pilatus Porters.

Other domestic operators are: Necon Air **(** (01) 473860; Nepal Airways **(** (01) 412388; Everest Air **(** (01) 480431; Asian Airlines **(** (01) 410086; Manakamana Airways **(** (01) 416434; and Gorkha Airlines **(** (01) 423137. The last three operate helicopters.

From **Kathmandu** there are scheduled services to **Dang, Dhangadi, Jumla, Mahendranagar, Nepalgunj, Rukumkot, Safi Bazaar, Siliguri Doti, Surkhet,** in the west; to **Baglung** and **Bhairawa** in the midlands; and to **Bhadrapur, Biratnagar, Janakpur, Lukla, Lamidanda, Rajbiraj, Rumjatar Taplejung, Tumlingtar** in the east.

Book well ahead, especially to destinations only served by the smaller aircraft. If you cancel 24 hours in advance, you pay a 10-percent cancellation fee; 33-percent if less than 24 hours in advance and 100-percent if you fail to show up. If the flight is canceled the fare is refunded.

Charter flights are available.

If you are flying to a restricted area you will need to produce your trekking permit before you depart from Tribhuvan Airport.

AIRPORT TRANSFERS

Royal Nepal and Indian Airlines provide a bus service from Tribhuvan Airport to Kathmandu. Travelers on the other airlines must use a taxi, which accommodates three passengers. Rates are set at Rs 200. The driver often has an "interpreter". Travelers from Kathmandu to the airport can board the bus that leaves the RNAC building, New road.

HIRE CARS

Hire cars are available from most travel agencies, though it is not possible to drive yourself in Nepal. The hire fee is high, but the cars are comfortable and likely to be in good repair. A car holds three or four people; metered taxis usually no more than two.

Yeti Travels, near the Annapurna Hotel, runs the **Avis** agency **(** (01) 227635, and Gorkha Travels, also on Durbar Marg, runs the **Hertz** franchise **(** (01) 224896.

ROADS IN NEPAL

Until the fifties Nepal was virtually roadless. The only links between different communities were village trails and mountain paths. Trading was a laborious affair, conducted over weeks and months. Since then, there has been a major highway con-

struction program supported mainly by Nepal's neighbors, India and China.

There are six main roads: the **Tribhuvan Raj Path**, linking Kathmandu with Raxaul at the Indian border, 200 km (124 miles) away, opened in 1956 and was built with Indian aid.

The **"Chinese road"** or **Araniko highway,** 110-km (68-mile)-long, to the Tibetan border at Kodari, was built by China and opened in the mid-Sixties.

Chinese engineers also helped build the 200-km (124-mile)-long **Prithvi Raj Marg** between Kathmandu and Pokhara, opened in 1973. There have been two extensions: Dumre to Gorkha and Mugling to Narayanghat and in 1970, Indian engineers completed the 188 km (117 mile) extension from Pokhara to Sunauli on the Indian Border, the **Siddhartha Raj Marg**.

Nepal's most ambitious road building project came about as a cooperative effort between the Soviet Union, United States, Britain and India. The 1,000 km (620 mile) east-west **Mahendra Raj Marg** through the southern lowlands is part of the planned Pan-Asian highway, linking the Bosphorus with the Far East.

The new 110-km (68-mile)-long highway, from **Lamosangu** to **Jiri** east of Kathmandu,

routes. Bookings are best made a day ahead with a travel agency.

ON FOOT

Nepal is a land best explored on foot. The most beautiful and the most interesting places can only be reached by walking. True Nepalis don't count distance by kilometers or miles, but by time traveled. And a leisurely promenade through the green terraced rice paddies and mustard fields, through villages and hamlets, up, down

built with Swiss help was opened in September 1985.

During the rainy season, whole portions of existing roads are damaged and must be repaired. It is essential to inquire locally before setting off on a long-distance road trip.

BUS SERVICES

Nepal's bus services remain primitive, no matter what travel agents may say about "tourist buses", "luxury coaches" and "express services". On the road, the buses are invariably slow, cramped and erratically driven. **Minibuses**, less crowded, faster, but more dangerous, operate along the same

and around trails — is certainly the best way to soak up Kathmandu valley and the other regions of the country, the people and their culture.

TREKKING

Every trekker — or traveler for that matter — needs a permit to visit areas outside those included in your Nepali visa. These special permits are issued for one destination at a time on a set route. The charges

Fields under snow OPPOSITE and weathered roofs ABOVE at Nar village. OVERLEAF: Warden's house nestles beneath the high peaks of Sagarmatha National Park.

are based on weekly rates and the permits can be obtained in Kathmandu and Pokhara.

Any reasonably fit person can trek, but the fitter you are, the more you will enjoy it. Do as much walking and exercise as possible to prepare yourself for Nepal's mountain trails.

Health and Precautions on the Trail
Trekkers should have inoculations against tetanus, polio, cholera, typhoid and paratyphoid. A gamma globulin injection pro-

vides some protection against hepatitis, an endemic infection in Nepal.

A risk the trekker shares with climbers is altitude sickness: a combination of nausea, insomnia, headaches and potentially lethal edemas, both cerebral and pulmonary. Sudden ascents to heights of 3,650 m (12,000 ft) and more, without acclimatization, can lead to accumulations of water, either in the lungs or brain. Swift descent for medical treatment is the only answer (see ALTITUDE SICKNESS, following page).

Trekking Gear
Trekking along Nepal's rough, rocky trails demands that you wear strong, comfortable boots with good soles. At low altitude, tennis shoes or running shoes provide adequate cushioning for the feet. But good boots are essential at higher elevations and in the snow; they should be large enough to allow one or two layers of heavy woolen or cotton — never nylon — socks. Wearing light casual shoes or sneakers after the day's hike will help rest your feet.

For women, wrap-around skirts are preferable to slacks or shorts, which offend many mountain communities. Men should wear loose fitting trousers or hiking shorts. For clothing, two light layers are better than a single thick one. If you get too hot, you can peel the top layer off. At extremely high altitudes wear thermal underwear. It's best to carry too many clothes than not enough. Drip-dry fabrics are best.

Your pack should be as small as possible, light and easy to open. The following gear is recommended:

Two pairs of woolen or corduroy trousers or skirts; two warm sweaters; three drip-dry shirts or T-shirts; ski or thermal underwear (especially from November to February); at least half-a-dozen pairs of woolen socks; one pair of walking shoes; an extra pair of sandals; light casual shoes or sneakers; a woolen hat; gloves or mittens; a strong, warm sleeping bag with hood; a thin sheet of foam rubber for a mattress; a padded anorak or parka; a plastic raincoat; sunglasses; toilet gear; some towels; medical kit; water bottle; and a light day pack.

Your medical kit should include pain killers (for high-altitude headaches); mild sleeping pills (for high-altitude sleeplessness); streptomagna (for diarrhea); septram (for bacillary dysentery); tinidozole (for amoebic dysentery); throat lozenges and cough drops; ophthalmic ointment or drops; one broad spectrum antibiotic; alcohol (for massaging feet to prevent blisters); blister pads; bandages; antiseptic solution and cotton; a good sun block; and a transparent lip salve.

In addition to these, you should carry a flashlight, candles, lighter, pocket knife, scissors, spare shoelaces, string, safety pins, toilet paper and plastic bags to protect your food, wrap up wet or dirty clothes, carry your litter, and protect your food, tents and photographic equipment. Much of this can be bought in Kathmandu.

Cooking and eating utensils are normally provided by the trekking agency and carried by the porters.

Always carry your trekking permit in a plastic bag where you can get to it easily. Lock your bag against theft or accidental loss. Make sure you have plenty of small currency for minor expenses along the way.

Carry a good supply of high-energy food like chocolate, dried fruits, nuts and whisky or brandy for a warming nightcap.

Water is contaminated so do not drink from streams no matter how clear or sparkling they look. Chlorine is not effective against amoebic cysts. All water should be well boiled or treated with iodine: four drops per liter (¼ gallon) and left for twenty minutes before drinking.

But note that at high altitude water boils at temperatures below 100°C (212°F) — not hot enough to kill bacteria. A pressure cooker solves the problem and also cooks food quicker.

Normally the day starts with early morning tea at around six o'clock. Trekkers break camp and pack, then breakfast on hot porridge and biscuits. Everyone is ready to begin the day's march by around seven o'clock.

Lunch is taken around noon, the cook having gone ahead to select the site and prepare the meal. By late afternoon, the day's trek comes to an end. Trekkers pitch camp and then sit down to dinner. At these high altitudes, after a long hard day's walking, there's little dallying over the campfire. Though sleep is often fitful and shallow, most are ready to hit the sack by 8 PM.

Speed is not of the essence. Pause frequently to enjoy the beauty of a particular spot, talk to the passing locals, take pictures or sip tea in one of the rustic wayside tea shops.

Walk at your own pace. Drink as much liquid as possible to combat high altitude and heat dehydration. Never wait for blisters to develop but pamper tender feet with an alcohol massage.

ALTITUDE SICKNESS

There are three main types of altitude sickness. Early altitude sickness is the first and acts as a warning. It can develop into pulmonary edema (waterlogged lungs) or cerebral edema (waterlogged brain). The symptoms are headache, nausea, loss of appetite, sleeplessness, fluid retention and swelling of the body.

Altitude sickness develops slowly, manifesting itself two or three days after reaching high altitude. The only cure is to climb no higher until the symptoms have disappeared.

Pulmonary edema is characterized, even when resting, by breathlessness and a persistent cough, accompanied by congestion of the chest. If these symptoms appear, descend at once.

Cerebral edema is less common. The symptoms are extreme tiredness, vomiting, severe headache, staggering when walking,

abnormal speech and behavior, drowsiness, even coma. Victims must return at once to a lower altitude and abandon all thoughts of their trek.

If left untreated altitude sickness can lead to death. It's endemic in the high Himalayas where even experienced mountaineers sometimes forget that the mountains begin where other mountain ranges end. Everest base camp, for instance, is some 1,000 m (more than 3,000 ft) higher than the summit of the Matterhorn. Above 3,000 m (10,000 ft) the air becomes noticeably thinner.

Kathmandu's Freak Street LEFT where the beats and hippies of the 1950s and 1960s found their pot if not their gold. Traditional Nepali dance ABOVE honors Bhairav, Shiva's demoniac incarnation.

Youth, strength and fitness make no difference. Those who climb too high, too quickly, expose themselves to the risk of **acute altitude sickness**. At elevations of 4,300 m (14,108 ft), for example, the body requires three to four liters (three quarts to one gallon) of liquid a day. At lower altitudes try to drink at least one liter (one quart) a day.

You should schedule frequent rest days between the 3,700- and 4,300-m (12,000- and 14,000-ft) contours, sleeping at the same altitude for at least two nights. Climb

higher during the day but always descend to the same level to sleep.

Never pitch camp more than 450 m (1,500 ft) higher in any one day, even if you feel fit enough for a climb twice that height.

If you begin to suffer early altitude sickness, go no higher until the symptoms have disappeared. If more serious symptoms appear, descend immediately to a lower elevation. Mild symptoms should clear within one to two days.

If the victim is unable to walk he should be carried down on a porter's back or by yak. No matter what the reason, never delay, even at night.

Some victims are incapable of making correct decisions and you may have to force them to go down against their will. The victim must be accompanied.

Treatment is no substitute for descent. If a doctor is available, he can treat the victim but the patient must descend.

Because of a lack of radio communications and helicopters, emergency evacuations are difficult to organize. Rescue operations take time and cost a great deal of money.

Some agencies may be able to arrange helicopter rescues for its client trekkers but individual trekkers stand no chance of such aid.

COMMUNICATIONS

Few travelers bother with the government-run post offices and communications centers. In Kathmandu and Pokhara numerous private operators offer postage, international phone calls and faxes and even e-mail.

The Central Post Office in Kathmandu has three sections, each located close to one another at the junction of Kanti Path and Kicha-Pokhara road. The **Foreign Post Office** ((01) 211760, handles parcels sent or received from abroad, but the best strategy is to avoid the need of sending or receiving anything during your stay as it will just cause headaches. If you do want to send a parcel, take advantage of the packaging and parcel service offered by many shopkeepers.

Letters can be received poste restante at the **General Post Office** ((01) 211073, 10 AM to 5 PM, daily except Saturdays and holidays; the closing time is 4 PM between November and February. When mailing letters, check that stamps are franked in front of your eyes. Major hotels and bookshops such as Pilgrim's in Thamel, Kathmandu, will also handle your mail, which is much easier.

The **Telecommunication Office** at Tripureshwar handles telephone calls, cables and telexes. The telex at the Central Telegraph Office works only during government hours. The country code for Nepal is 277. Dialing from abroad, drop the "0". There are no city codes in Nepal.

TIPPING

As a rule, for good and exceptional service, a gratuity of about five percent will be appreciated. For exceptional service by taxis, a tip of 10 percent of the fare is in order. This is also now customary in restaurants that cater to tourists and travelers.

CLIMATE

Nepal enjoys an extreme variety of climates. Altitude and exposure to sun and rain are the most influential factors.

Kathmandu valley has three seasons. The winter — from October to March — is the best time to visit Nepal. Night time temperatures drop close to freezing point, but by day these climb from 10°C to 25°C (50°F to 77°F) and the skies are generally clear.

Mornings and evenings are invigorating. There is often an early-morning mist. October and February are particularly pleasant.

Pokhara valley is much warmer — temperatures rise to 30°C (86°F) at midday in the lower altitudes.

From April to early June the weather becomes hot and stuffy, with occasional evening thunderstorms. The land is frequently shrouded in heat mist.

Temperatures in Kathmandu can range between 11°C and 28°C (52°F and 83°F) in April to between 19°C and 30°C (66°F and 86°F) in June, with maximum temperatures of 36°C (97°F).

Pre-monsoon rains usually start in May and the monsoon, normally at the end of June, lasts three months. For most of this time the Himalayas remain hidden. The torrential downpours cause much flooding but it is still possible to tour Kathmandu valley.

With the rains come the leeches (*jugas*), however — trekking stops and the lowlands are cut off by swollen rivers and landslides.

When the monsoon ends, around mid-September, the skies clear, the nights become cooler and the landscape is a symphony of fall colors, brown and gold.

CLOTHING

Comfortable, casual clothing is recommended unless meetings with businessmen and government officials are planned.

During winter days in the Kathmandu valley you'll be warm enough with light clothing but carry a warm sweater, padded anorak or jacket for the evenings.

Forget fashion. Jeans, cord trousers or long skirts, are fine and casual shoes essential, even if you don't intend to walk much.

During the rainy season you can buy umbrellas locally for protection from both rain and sun.

Trekking gear, in standard sizes, can be bought or rented in Kathmandu and Pokhara together with sweaters, ponchos, caps and other woolen or down clothing.

During the hot season, between April and September, all you will need is light summer clothing, preferably cotton. This is true for most of the year in the Terai except in December and January when you need a sweater or jacket for evening wear.

HEALTH

Travelers are advised to have inoculations and immunization against typhoid, hepatitis, cholera and tetanus.

Never drink unboiled and unfiltered water. Avoid ice cubes and raw vegetables. Always peel fruit and clean your hands often. Never walk barefoot.

Stomach upsets are known locally as the "Kathmandu Quickstep". If trouble persists, it can develop into more serious amoebic or bacillary dysentery or giardiasis, so get a stool test and seek medical help.

OPPOSITE: Happy Sherpa youngsters reflect the spirit of their mountain homeland. ABOVE: Colorful market stall.

Malaria is on the rise, but most of Kathmandu is too high to support the malaria-carrying species of mosquitoes. For visits to the south, however, take a recognized prophylactic two weeks before you arrive in the Terai and continue to take this for six weeks after you leave. Carry mosquito repellent during the warm months.

Pharmacies in Kathmandu, mainly along New road, offer a wide range of Western drugs at low prices and some traditional Indian ayurvedic remedies.

Most international hotels have a doctor

sometimes fluctuates. Outside Kathmandu blackouts are frequent. At least three varieties of power sockets are used: three round pins (small); three round pins (large); and two round pins (large). Plug adapters are available in electronics stores on Kanti Path.

PHOTOGRAPHY

Film stock is only available in Kathmandu and Pokhara. Prices are only slightly higher than you would pay, for example, in Bangkok, though about twice the price of Hong

on call and there are several treatment centers in Kathmandu that have Western doctors and nurses on their staff. In the event of an emergency or a serious illness, however, you will have to either go home or to Bangkok, which has excellent facilities.

The following hospitals and clinics in Kathmandu and Patan are recommended: **Patan Hospital (** (01) 521034 or (01) 522266, Lagankhel, Patan; **CIWEC (** (01) 228531, Durbar Marg, Kathmandu; **Nepal International Clinic (** (01) 412842, Naxal.

POWER

Major towns in Nepal are on the 220-volt alternating current system, though power

Kong or Singapore. Color print film can be processed quickly in Kathmandu and Pokhara, but you should leave slide film to be processed somewhere else no matter what local shop owners tell you.

TIME

Nepal is fifteen minutes ahead of Indian Standard Time and five hours forty-five minutes ahead of Greenwich Mean Time.

Government office hours are from Sunday to Friday between 10 AM and 5 PM. They close one hour earlier during the three winter months. Only embassies and international organizations enjoy a two-day weekend. Shops, some of which remain open on

Saturdays and holidays, seldom open before 10 AM but do not usually close until 7 or 8 PM.

Remember that in this deeply religious country there are many holidays devoted to various deities, mythological events, astrological signs, traditional festivals, in addition to several secular holidays marking phases of Nepal's modern history.

ACCOMMODATION

Travelers to Kathmandu have a wide range of choices — from five-star international hotels to basic board and lodging with shared toilets and bathrooms.

Apart from the five-star game lodges in Royal Chitwan National Park the choice outside Kathmandu valley is more homey and less expensive.

During the high seasons — spring and fall — Kathmandu's international hotels have near 100-percent occupancy, so it's advisable to book well in advance. At the lower end of the price scale there are plenty of comfortable hotels. Most offer a choice of bed and breakfast; half board (breakfast and one other meal); or full board.

There are also a number of basic lodges with minimal amenities. Rates vary depending on facilities. Toilets and showers are generally communal, heating extra. Most are in old Kathmandu, around Durbar square or in Thamel district.

Tariffs are subject to a 12 to 15 percent government tax.

MOUNTAIN LODGES

In the mountains there are many basic lodges, usually near airstrips, as well as the many traditional Nepali tea houses found in every village on the trekking routes. The most comfortable accommodation available in the high Himalayas are at **Lukla** (see page 186) and **Jumla** (see page 178).

NATIONAL PARKS AND WILDLIFE DIRECTORY

CHITWAN NATIONAL PARK: 932 sq km (354 sq miles). Elephants, tigers, leopards, rhinoceros, wild boar, deer, monkeys and a multitude of birds (see pages 16–19 and 162).

GODAVARI ROYAL BOTANICAL GARDENS: 66 different species of fern, 115 orchids, 77 cacti and succulents and about 200 trees and shrubs (see page 116).

KHAPTAD NATIONAL PARK: A floral repository of high-altitude conifers, oak and rhododendron forests (see page 179).

KOSI TAPPU WILDLIFE RESERVE: Wild buffaloes and thousands of migratory birds (see page 161).

LAKE RARA NATIONAL PARK: 187 sq km (71 sq miles). Repository of high-altitude conifers, oak and rhododendron forests (see page 178).

LANTANG NATIONAL PARK: 1,243 sq km (472 sq miles). Haven for the endangered snow leopard, leopard, Himalayan black bear, red panda and wild dog (see page 186).

PARSA WILDLIFE RESERVE: 1,200 sq km (456 sq miles). Elephants, tigers, leopards, rhinoceros, wild boar, deer, monkeys and a multitude of birds (see page 162).

ROYAL BARDIA RESERVE: A sanctuary for the endangered swamp deer (see page 169).

SAGARMATHA NATIONAL PARK. 1,243 sq km (472 sq miles). Wolf, bear, musk deer, feral goat species, and the brilliantly colored crimson-horned or Impeyan pheasants (see page 188).

SHEY-PHOKSONDO NATIONAL PARK: (see page 155).

SHUKLA PHANTA WILDLIFE RESERVE: Endangered black buck (see page 169).

OPPOSITE: The 7,131-m (23,771-ft) Langtang Lirung near the Tibetan border at the head of Trisuli valley. Protected against glaring snow and high-altitude ultraviolet rays, a climber ABOVE reaches 4,500 m (15,000 ft) during an attempt on one of the major peaks of the Himalayas.

JAWALKHEL ZOO, Patan: A selection of exotic south Asian animals, especially Himalayan species (see page 131).

MEDIA

English language news bulletins are broadcast twice daily by Radio Nepal at 8 AM and 8:30 PM, with a special 45-minute "tourist program" at 8 PM. Local television is unlikely to be of much interest to the average visitor, but satellite TV is now available at the international hotels and at many of the mid-range hotels in Kathmandu.

Several English language newspapers are published in Kathmandu, as well as many in Nepali.

The Rising Nepal and *Kathmandu Post* both cover local and international events in a style that puts most foreign readers to sleep. Both devote much of their front page to the activities of the royal family.

The *International Herald Tribune*, one day old, is on sale at newsstands and in hotels, as are *Time, Newsweek, The Far Eastern Economic Review, Asiaweek, The Economist* and *India Today*. Newspapers from Germany, France, Australia and Britain are often available, several days old, in Kathmandu bookshops.

LANGUAGE

Nepali is an atonal and phonetic language. No matter how long the word, the accent is always placed on the first or second syllable. Words are pronounced exactly as they are spelled.

Apart from a few peculiarities, consonants are pronounced as in English:

ch is pronounced *tch* as in bench
chh is pronounced *tch-h* as in **pitch here**
th is pronounced *t-h* as in **hot head**
kh is pronounced *k-h* as in **dark hole**
ph is pronounced *p-h* as in **top hat**
j is pronounced *d-j* as in **Jesus**
dh is pronounced *d-h* as in **adhere**

The *t, d, th and dh*, with a dot beneath them are pronounced by rolling the tongue back and putting it in the center of the roof of the mouth, so that the sound produced is like *"rt"* in "cart" or *"rd"* in **card.**

Pronounce vowels either long or short:
e is always *e (ay)* as in *café*
u is pronounced *oo* as in **moon** (never *yu* as in *mute)*
y is pronounced *yi* as in **yield** (never *ai* as in *my)*
i is pronounced *oh* as in **toe.**

Further Reading

AMIN, WILLETTS, TETLEY. *Journey through Nepal*. London: The Bodley Head.

ANDERSON, MARY. *The Festivals of Nepal*. London: George Allen and Unwin, 1971.

ARMINGTON, STAN. *Trekking in the Nepal Himalaya*. Melbourne: Lonely Planet, 1994.

BERZRUSCHKA, STEPHEN. *A Guide to Trekking in Nepal*. Seattle: The Mountaineers, 1981.

FLEMING, R.L., et al. *Birds of Nepal*. Kathmandu: Avalok, 1979.

GREENWALD, JEFF. *Shopping for Buddhas*. Melbourne: Lonely Planet, Journeys, 1996.

HAGEN, TONI. *Nepal: The Kingdom in the Himalaya*. Berne: Kümmerly and Frey, 1961. (Second edition, 1971).

INDRA. *Joys of Nepali Cooking*. New Delhi: 1982.

IYER, PICO. *Video Night in Kathmandu*. Vintage: 1989.

MATTHIESSEN, PETER. *The Snow Leopard*. London: Chatto and Windus, 1979.

MACDONALD, A.W. AND ANNE VERGATI STAHL. *Newar Art*. New Delhi: Vikas, 1979.

PEISSEL, MICHEL. *Tiger for Breakfast*. London: Hodder, 1966.

O'CONNOR, BILL. *Trekking Peaks of Nepal*. England: Crowood Press, 1989.

PYE-SMITH, CHARLIE. *Travels in Nepal*. Penguin.

SCHALLER, GEORGE B. *Stones of Silence*. London: Andre Deutsch, 1980.

SCOTT, BARBARA J. *The Violet Shyness of Their Eyes: Notes from Nepal*. Calyx, 1993.

SNELLGROVE, DAVID L. *Himalayan Pilgrimage*. Shambala, 1981

SUYIN, HAN. *The Mountain Is Young*. London: Jonathan Cape, 1958.

TILMAN, W. *Nepal Himalaya*. Cambridge: Cambridge University Press, 1952.

UNSWORTH, WALT. *Everest*. London: Allen Lane, 1981.

WOODCOCK, MARTIN. *Collins Handguide to the Birds of the Indian Sub-Continent*. Collins, 1990.

Photo Credits

Quick Reference A–Z Guide
to Places and Topics of Interest with Listed Accomodations, Restaurants and Useful Telephone Numbers